*Fred Zinnemann
and the Cinema of Resistance*

FRED ZINNEMANN
and the Cinema of Resistance

J. E. Smyth

University Press of Mississippi / *Jackson*

www.upress.state.ms.us

The University Press of Mississippi is a member
of the Association of American University Presses.

Copyright © 2014 by University Press of Mississippi
All rights reserved
Manufactured in the United States of America

First printing 2014

∞

Library of Congress Cataloging-in-Publication Data

Smyth, J. E., 1977–
Fred Zinnemann and the cinema of resistance / J.E. Smyth.
    pages cm
Includes bibliographical references and index.
ISBN 978-1-61703-964-5 (cloth : alk. paper) — ISBN 978-1-61703-965-2 (ebook) 1. Zinnemann, Fred, 1907–—Criticism and interpretation. I. Title.
    PN1998.3.Z56S69 2014
    791.43′0233′092—dc23   2013025419

British Library Cataloging-in-Publication Data available

For Robert Sklar

CONTENTS

Acknowledgments [ix]

Introduction [3]

CHAPTER ONE [25]
From Germany to Algeria, and Other Historiographies of Resistance

CHAPTER TWO [57]
Surviving Voices and the Search for Europe

CHAPTER THREE [95]
The Un-American Western

CHAPTER FOUR [123]
American Fascists

CHAPTER FIVE [149]
Breaking the Silence of Women in the Resistance

CHAPTER SIX [175]
Aging Revolutionaries and the Loss of History

CHAPTER SEVEN [201]
Resistant Women in Contested Frames

Notes [239]

Bibliography [283]

Index [305]

ACKNOWLEDGMENTS

When I began this book twelve years ago, my image of Fred Zinnemann was made up of treasured fragments from his films. I had no idea what he looked like. Unlike many of his famous Hollywood colleagues, he didn't wear an eye patch, flourish a swagger stick, or make cute cameo appearances in his films. He was Hollywood's quiet but formidable enigma. But this book would not exist if Fred Zinnemann hadn't saved every photograph, letter, sketch, note, and research notebook from his Hollywood career. And so my first and greatest debt of gratitude is to him. I know the face now—the posed shots beside the camera or with smiling coworkers on the set. And then there are the outtakes, as I like to call them: pictures of him alone, turned away, lost in thought, silent and closed. I have come to know the other Zinnemann, too, in the infinite varieties of his handwriting, the finely etched sketches, comments, and scrawls on everything from studio stationery to Post-it notes and toilet paper. It seems almost an impossible dream to map the artistic practice of a filmmaker so consistently innovative, intellectually engaged, and complex. As with any Zinnemann film, every detail counts—and they're all there in the archive as well as on the screen. It has been my pleasure and privilege to try to see as he saw and feel as he felt.

Tim Zinnemann helped immeasurably with his insights and generosity in sharing personal memories of his father. I am especially grateful to Tim for allowing me to reprint substantial portions of his father's correspondence and to reproduce private photographs and sketches in the collection. And yet, I am haunted by Tim's memory of an exchange between his father and his uncle George. Years ago, Fred Zinnemann told George of the existence of another brother who had died before George's birth. When his younger brother asked him why he hadn't mentioned this before, Fred Zinnemann replied, "Because you never asked me." There are parts of his life that will always remain closed.

I am also indebted to Ned Comstock, Linda Harris Mehr, Barbara Hall, May Haduong, Faye Thompson, Natali Morris, Rachael Keene, Sandra Joy

Lee, Laura La Placa, Jonathon Auxier, Lauren Buisson, Julie Graham, Amy Wong, the staff of the Beinecke Library at Yale University, the staff of the New York Library for the Performing Arts, the staff of the Rare Book and Manuscript Library at Columbia University, and the staff of the Academy of Motion Picture Arts and Sciences Library. I am very grateful to Jenny Romero, who coped with my requests to read and scan more and more of Zinnemann's production records. Alvin Sargent, Walter Murch, Marsha Hunt, Janet Leigh, Paula Friendly, Linda Ayton, Robert Rosenstone, Nahid Massoud, Robin Vaccarino, Donna Vaccarino, Richard Koszarski, Charles Musser, Virginia McKenna, Walter Mirisch, Larry Mirisch, Walter Hill, Suzanne Zada, Tibor Zada, Maria Cooper Janis, A. C. Lyles, Cynthia Lucia, Roy Grundmann, Sam B. Girgus, Tom Schatz, Tom Stempel, David Eldridge, Gwendolyn Audrey Foster, Mark Glancy, Sue Harper, Christine Geraghty, Brian Neve, Leshu Torchin, Michael Lawrence, Alan Marcus, Debra Ramsay, Keith Goldsmith, Rob Meyers, Amy Meyers, and Claudia Mattos offered insight and encouragement. I would also like to thank Gregory Waller, Gwendolyn Audrey Foster, Wheeler Winston Dixon, Constantin Parvelsecu, and Robert Rosenstone for allowing me to reprint substantial portions of chapters 2, 3, and 7, which appeared in *Film History*, *The Quarterly Review of Film and Video*, and the Wiley-Blackwell *Companion to the Historical Film*. I'm delighted to have had the opportunity of working again with Leila Salisbury, a truly supportive, generous, and imaginative editor, and with Valerie Jones, Anne Stascavage, and Peter Tonguette.

The Getty Research Institute generously supported this project in 2011–12, and provided the best kind of geographical and intellectual environment. I am especially indebted to the energetic Raquel Zamora and Jennifer Schmidt, to Michelle Fahmi, Janae Royston, Amy Hood, Ryan Lieu, Alexa Sekyra, Sabine Schlosser, Barry Rosen, and Rebecca Zamora, and to Marsha Hunt, Maria Cooper Janis, Alvin Sargent, Walter and Aggie Murch, Chris Horak, and especially Tim Zinnemann for their roles in the Getty's Zinnemann film series, "A Cinema of Resistance." Special thanks go to colleague and director of the University of Warwick's Humanities Research Center, Tim Lockley, for supporting this project in its final stages.

One Sunday afternoon many years ago I watched my first Fred Zinnemann film, and it set my mind in motion. Now, my children Zachary and Zoe are solid Zinnemann fans at the ages of six and three, something I hope will stay with them throughout their lives.

And finally, there is Robert Sklar, my ideal reader, gentle critic, and dear friend. I knew that I would dedicate this book to him, but hesitated telling him so directly before it was finished. He only read parts of it before his death in July 2011. But the rest is also for him, because it is the best that I can do.

*Fred Zinnemann
and the Cinema of Resistance*

INTRODUCTION
The Cinema of Resistance

"I will resist until I am nothing."
—**Chaim Potok and David Rudkin**, *The Dybbuk* (1984)[1]

"The knowledge of a person is a negative feeling: the positive feeling,
the reality, is the torment of being always a stranger to what one loves."
—**André Malraux**, *Man's Fate*, 1933[2]

Few of Hollywood's legendary directors remain as consistently enigmatic as Fred Zinnemann. Over the years, through interviews, autobiographies, and biographies, striking pictures have emerged of Alfred Hitchcock's menace and charm, of John Ford's grim bad temper, of Orson Welles's buccaneering streak, and of John Huston's wry humor.[3] There are no biographies of Fred Zinnemann to date, and his autobiography, published in 1992, is focused almost entirely upon anecdotes from his film productions. Unlike other European émigré directors William Wyler and Billy Wilder, Zinnemann never really "went Hollywood," or, for that matter, American. His personal life did not make the front page of *Confidential*; he did not attend Hollywood parties or poker games; he was not a baseball fan. He stayed married to the same Englishwoman for sixty years, lived in simple houses on Mayberry Road and Westridge Road in Santa Monica until returning to Europe in the late 1950s, and, when he needed a holiday, went skiing or climbing in Austria or Switzerland. In the 1940s and early 1950s, critics and friends often compared Zinnemann with another cinematic cipher, who, despite his American career, remained "foreign": Charles Chaplin.[4] Though far less in the public eye, Fred Zinnemann shared Chaplin's intense but highly individual political commitments, a

FIG. 1 Fred Zinnemann calling the shots on *The Search*, 1947 (with Emil Berna measuring the focus), AMPAS.

small but loyal circle of friends, and a professionalism that barely concealed deep workaholic drives.

Almost unknown during his first fifteen years in Hollywood, Zinnemann finally achieved critical acclaim in 1948 for his European production, *The Search*. After the release of *High Noon* (1952) and the Academy Award–winning *From Here to Eternity* (1953), he became one of Hollywood's "star" directors, yet Hollywood publicists, unable to do much with his seemingly innocuous private life, merely gushed about his artistry and quiet professionalism.[5] As time passed and film criticism became increasingly motivated by European auteurism and its American variants, semiotics, structuralism, psychoanalysis, and Marxist cultural criticism, Zinnemann constructed and reinforced his own public image, firmly resistant to the emerging agendas of "professional" film criticism that sought to categorize and dismiss his work with a few simple themes. The public Zinnemann persona—elegant, soft-spoken, European—was grave, gently ironic, and supremely professional. Yet behind that image was another less familiar figure, sometimes glimpsed in photographs: slight, alert, intense, his body close against the camera, watching and waiting for every detail, composing and calling the shots (fig. 1). Here was the Zinnemann that seemed to echo the countless production notes and sketches he kept so meticulously, a visual thinker who nonetheless could write endlessly about the contexts and nuances of scripts and rushes, a man who lived and breathed film in the studios, on location, and at home. Here was the Fred Zinnemann who, with single-minded ruthlessness, defended creative control over his films from screenwriters, composers, producers, even friends—the Fred Zinnemann sometimes spoken of by cast and crew members as "the iron hand in the velvet glove."[6]

Hollywood Collaborator or European Loner?

Of all studio-era Hollywood directors, Fred Zinnemann's work has been the most difficult to categorize. Auteurist critic Andrew Sarris famously condemned the filmmaker for not adhering to a set film style and for not "committing" to his subject matter, while other critics and historians, frustrated in their efforts to find a common theme in his work, have labeled him a director of "conscience" pictures.[7] Zinnemann would occasionally toss potential clues to his interviewers by comparing *The Seventh Cross* (1944) with *High Noon* (1952), or Gabrielle van der Mal (*The Nun's Story*, 1959) with Robert E. Lee Prewitt (*From Here to Eternity*, 1953), but he grew impatient when some challenged him for violating conventions of American genre and cinematic heroism—most famously in his series of interventions about *High Noon*. He also dismissed the conceits of auteurism, arguing with *Cinema*'s editor James Silke that while he would appreciate audiences recognizing a "Zinnemann look," he thought it impossible because his visual style and focus shifted to accommodate different subject matter. "I don't feel the need for a trademark in that sense," he observed, recognizing the auteurist brandings as just another simplistic way of marketing films.[8] He emphatically did not want to be the type of director he perceived Howard Hawks to be, a man so obsessed with "professional" heroes that he remade the same film again and again: "I'm not really interested in somebody who knows what he's about. Because it bores me . . . I don't believe that human beings can go through life untouched and knowing all about themselves. And the older I get, the more certain I am. It's not human."[9] Yet many critics of the 1950s and 1960s, bent on interpreting

Hollywood cinema's simple themes and stark contrasts, claimed that Zinnemann's more nuanced narratives betrayed a cold, intellectual vision which "stays aloof from all these questions, looking down on the emotional involvement without becoming itself involved."[10] Treading a path between Europe and Hollywood, objectivity and subjectivity, and individual artistry in a collaborative industry, Zinnemann resisted the polarizing trends of contemporary film criticism as though they were products of a callow studio publicity department.

Yet, despite his antagonism toward postwar auteurist criticism and "auteurs" like Hawks, Zinnemann had one of the most unique and consistent of film styles. What Sarris, Silke, and so many others failed to grasp was that while the mise-en-scène and cinematographic tone of a Fred Zinnemann film would change with the demands of the subject matter and cinematographer, Zinnemann, who was trained as a cameraman in Paris in the 1920s, returned to particular set-ups and structures throughout his career. He was a master of the close-up, often refusing to begin a scene with a medium or establishing shot. People were what interested him, and the establishing space was therefore the face. His work on *The Member of the Wedding* (1952) immediately springs to mind; forced to abandon plans to shoot Carson McCullers's story on location in Georgia, he used the claustrophobia of the stage play, Hollywood sets, and adolescence to focus on a protagonist at odds with her world.[11] His first major A feature, *The Seventh Cross* (1944), begins at night in a concentration camp, and each of the escapees is revealed in a tight, but blurred close-up as he veers in and out of one shot (fig. 2). *High Noon*, one of the most controversial Westerns ever made, turned the conventional form of the genre inside out by replacing long shots with close-ups (fig. 3). Years later, in *The Day of the Jackal* (1973), Zinnemann began the Jackal's (Edward Fox) August 1963 conversation with the gunsmith (Cyril Cusack) in close-ups, refusing to show the wider space until one question ("Will the gentleman be moving?") reveals John F. Kennedy's magazine cover photograph on the coffee table between them, an ominous ghost. Compositionally, Zinnemann preferred to have a face in close-up off-center, with the subsequent shot's most important element centered, but in the background (*The Seventh Cross, Act of Violence*, 1949; *The Nun's Story*). He used long shots, crane shots, and zooms sparingly, but to great effect: one recalls the pivotal crane shots in *High Noon*, as Will Kane (Gary Cooper) faces the empty street; the Jackal's first moments in Paris on his "research trip" to kill de Gaulle; and Julia (Vanessa Redgrave) and Lillian Hellman (Jane Fonda) walking in Oxford as the future of the Holocaust colors Hellman's memories (*Julia*, 1977) [Figs. 4–6]. While other Hollywood filmmakers often crammed smart dialogue and constant action into narratives to cover silences, Zinnemann was famous for slashing dialogue from a script, even one as taut as Carl Foreman's *High Noon*, exploring silences and searching for the internal revelations of performers' close-ups in a way few directors on either side of the Atlantic could match. As Zinnemann later revealed, he preferred to have long, quiet conversations with all of his performers, discussing "what I want, but not how to do it," and sometimes he was so attuned to actors' creative processes that they shot scenes in one take—in rehearsal.[12] And, given his long apprenticeship making short films at MGM on miniscule budgets (not to mention his lifelong stubborn insistence on getting things his way), he camera cut.

FIG. 2 Opening close-ups in *The Seventh Cross*, 1944, MGM.

FIG. 3 One of *High Noon*'s many famous close-ups, 1952, United Artists.

FIG. 4 *High Noon*'s crane shot, United Artists.

FIG. 5 *The Day of the Jackal*'s crane shot, United Artists.

When I began researching this book, I was sensitive to Zinnemann's interpretive warnings about the complexity and mutability of his work, but I also saw in his chameleon responses to film critics the need of an artist to maintain creative control over his films and public legacy. It is true that the settings of Zinnemann's films range over the American West (*High Noon*), sixteenth-century England (*A Man For All Seasons*, 1966), and 1950s New York City (*A Hatful of Rain*, 1957), but most of Zinnemann's films are united by his commitment to visualizing the past and recording the voices of mavericks and social misfits who defy the ideological hypocrisy and dehumanizing powers of social, religious, and political organizations. In looking even

FIG. 6 *Julia's* crane shot, 1977, Twentieth Century-Fox.

closer, Zinnemann, more than any other director, was a maker of historical films about the rise and resistance to fascism, the Spanish Civil War and Second World War, and their postwar impact on Europe and America.

To a certain extent, Zinnemann's own background determined his film focus. Like many European Jewish émigré directors, Zinnemann lost family members in the Holocaust, including his Polish-born parents, Dr. Oskar and Anna Zinnemann. His brother George, who immigrated to America in 1938, would eventually join the military, working for the United States Typhus Commission during the war. Zinnemann tried repeatedly to join the OSS, but was denied service and remained in Hollywood. While George was overseas, he attempted many times to locate missing family members. One V-Mail from George is typical: "Dear Folks, I tried to contact the Russian authorities the other day in order to get in touch with the parents... All the 'Consulate' consisted of was one typewriter, one picture of Stalin, and one guy who spoke even worse French than I do. And all he had to say was that he was sorry but he couldn't do a thing for me and couldn't offer any suggestions either. So all there is left to do is to go to the Red Cross; but I don't have much hope of succeeding there either, after the experiences I had in London."[13] While other family members were located, Fred and George Zinnemann learned that their father was deported to Belzec, Poland, where he was murdered in late 1941. Anna, accompanied by her niece, Dr. Helena Hirschhorn, was deported to Auschwitz where they most likely died in early 1942. According to records Fred Zinnemann left with Yad Vashem years later, Helena volunteered to accompany her aunt. Zinnemann kept his personal feelings about his family members' murders hidden, though he would later admit in a 1978 interview that he had strong feelings of "survivor guilt" that motivated his film work. For four decades he attempted to get Hollywood producers interested in remaking the classic Yiddish film, Ansky's *Dybbuk* (1958–84). He went on: "I am not religious in the sense that I go to the Temple, but there is in my blood a very strong Jewish tradition. I cannot pretend to live up to this religious life, but it gives me strength in all that I do, and has always done so."[14] While Vincent Brook has argued that the "Jewishness" of many major Hollywood *film noir* directors infused the genre with a critical edge and attitude toward mainstream American culture,[15] Zinnemann's resistance to traditional filmmaking techniques, as well as contextual representations of war and anti-fascism, crossed more than one Hollywood genre.

George's letters also reveal his brother's other obsession at this time: becoming a great director. His anxiety about his Zinnemann and Feiwel relatives was at its height when he began making *The Seventh Cross* for MGM in 1943. The film's narrative of a German concentration camp escapee's flight from the Nazis would be the first of many films he would make about the war and its contexts. George knew how important this film was for his brother. As he wrote, "I want to know, and without your usual evasions, how *Seventh Cross* turned out. How badly did they tear your heart? What happened to the film after it was put on the belt and whisked away from you? How many pounds did you lose? And did you come out of it with more confidence, or less? And do you think you'll ever become a good director?" While George loathed Hollywood (his brother had pulled strings to get him a brief job at MGM), he understood his brother's passion and commitment.

Yet, Zinnemann's views of war and resistance were as individual as his visual style. George Heisler was not a US soldier fighting evil Nazis, and his three early postwar films, *The Search* (1948), *Act of Violence* (1949), and *The Men* (1950), are equally idiosyncratic in their approaches to heroism and victory. Marlon Brando's first film, *The Men*, showed him as a tormented paraplegic veteran, and Van Heflin's sunny façade as the town's war hero in *Act of Violence* hides his past as a Nazi collaborator responsible for the deaths of his men. The iconic scenes of December 7th are only the last ten minutes of *From Here to Eternity*'s tough exposé of the Depression-era military establishment. Unlike other Hollywood and European filmmakers, he did not subscribe to a heroic, masculine, and

FIG. 7 *The Day of the Jackal*, 1973, United Artists.

predominantly French view of the Resistance. Instead, Paris was often gently lampooned for its commercialized heroism (as in *Day of the Jackal* and *Julia*), and iconic Resistance heroes like Charles de Gaulle served other cinematic purposes. Take, for example, the final moments of *The Day of the Jackal*. In this film about the assassination of the former Resistance hero-turned-president and—for some—tyrant, Zinnemann focuses almost exclusively on the solitary, secret planning of his dashing would-be killer (Edward Fox). In the final Liberation Day sequences, de Gaulle's tall, stooped figure silently salutes a line of exclusively male Resistance colleagues. In one of the most evocative images in Zinnemann's career, we see the French president through the telescopic site of that anonymous assassin's rifle (fig. 7). With Zinnemann's approval, it became one of the film's key publicity images.

Zinnemann's documentation of the Resistance was completely at odds with de Gaulle's view of an elite, French-dominated, nationwide movement against Nazi oppression born in 1940, and the prevailing conservative historiography. There were no towering French heroes in Zinnemann's histories, but there were Belgians, Austrians, Germans, and Americans who opposed Hitler and National Socialism from the 1920s. From early in his career, Zinnemann was drawn to the possibility of European resistance to fascism rather than to standard nationalist historiographies and traditional heroes. Certainly *The Search* probes the consequences of extreme nationalism while documenting the postwar efforts of UNRRA and the United Nations to rescue Europe's victimized children. Though many after 1945 conveniently forgot that one fascist dictatorship remained in Western Europe, Zinnemann did not. His exploration of anti-fascist resistance to Franco in Spain, *Behold a Pale Horse* (1964), arguably avoids the tendency of most "revisionist" historical studies of the conflict to emphasize the "glamorized" foreign components of the ideological struggle (i.e., the intervention of Americans, Germans, Russians, and Italians) and instead considers the conflict between Spanish resistance and exile.

Zinnemann's concept of resistance, honed by his generation's political experiences in the 1920s and 1930s, also influenced his work on Mexican revolutions (*Redes/The Wave*, 1936; the unproduced *Zapata*, 1941; the unproduced *Carlotta and Maximillian*, 1973),[16] the American West (*High Noon*, 1952; the unproduced *Custer and the Sioux*, 1965), the postwar Soviet Union (the unfilmed *First Circle* and *The Last Secret*, 1978); the Chinese Revolution (the unfilmed *Man's Fate*, 1969), colonial and postcolonial India (the unfilmed *Terrorists* for the UN, 1964–65; the unfilmed *Gandhi*, 1966), and the English Reformation (*A Man For All Seasons*, 1966).[17] He saw resistance to oppression outside of its rarefied, twentieth-century European context. The United States had its own special relationship with fascism in its entrenched xenophobia, its fascination with images of masculinity and the military, and its fierce protection of its national myths, and during the productions of *High Noon* and *From Here to Eternity*, Zinnemann would confront it on several levels.

But Zinnemann was uncomfortable with clear-cut definitions of saintly heroism and tyranny, and, even in his adaptation of Robert Bolt's *A Man For All Seasons*, did his best both to humanize Paul Scofield's iconic performance and to present the king's dilemma over the succession and the church's power in Britain and Europe. It was significant that Scofield was Zinnemann's first choice to play André Malraux's Clappique, the corrupt European expatriate caught up in plans for a communist revolution in China in 1927.[18] Such a role would surely have reinvented Scofield's heroic film image, yet the actor was not as adventurous as his director and Peter Finch (*The Nun's Story*) took the role. Zinnemann's passion for filming Malraux's *Man's Fate* would become his greatest professional disappointment when MGM's new chief, James Aubrey, canceled the production. Although many speculated that the film's sympathetic treatment of communist revolutionaries determined its fate, others have attributed it to the practicalities of capitalism and MGM's long-term financial crisis.[19]

For Zinnemann, *Man's Fate* would remain a touchstone for his career and philosophy. As he commented in an interview, "I had an enormous, enormous need to do *Man's Fate* because that book was a bible to us in my generation. It was one of the great novels of the 1930s and 1940s, and to be asked to make a film of it was one of the greatest events of my life."²⁰ But Malraux's *Man's Fate* has other resonances with histories of Resistance. Malraux, like de Gaulle, was another mythomaniac and Resistance hero, and once claimed that he had written his novel on the barricades in Shanghai and that *Man's Fate* was more historical than fictive. Malraux's image as European revolutionary and anti-fascist crusader in Spain and later France was—like much of popular Resistance history—half invented, half true, and deeply invested in the fallacies of male mythology.²¹ These were questions Zinnemann would explore and interrogate, rather than replicate and eulogize, in his works of Resistance—most particularly, in *Julia*.²² Yet the painful paradox for Malraux, that revolutionaries working for the people against oppressive states isolate themselves from humanity, was something of particular resonance for Zinnemann. As Malraux wrote, "He was not one of them. In spite of the murder, in spite of his presence. If he were to die today, he would die alone. For them, everything was simple: they were going forth to conquer their bread and their dignity. For him . . . he did not even know how to speak to them, except of their pain and of their common battle."²³ Though Zinnemann would be honored with multiple Directors Guild and Academy Awards, toward the end of his life he realized that he had lost his critical and popular audiences.

While his film narratives often explored the contexts and histories of "resistance," Zinnemann's career in Hollywood and its critical legacy followed a similar creative trajectory. It is significant that the director repeatedly credited Robert Flaherty (*Nanook of the North*, 1920) as his greatest professional and personal influence. Flaherty attracted his share of attention as an auteur long before the term was invented and codified in the 1950s. More often the terms used by film reviewers and cultural critics to describe him were "maverick" or "Hollywood outsider." These words, embedded with their resistance to Hollywood's industrial practices and film style, appealed to Zinnemann throughout his life. The two men were trained for different professions before turning to film. Flaherty had worked, like his father, as a surveyor and explorer for large mining companies in Canada before deciding to take a motion picture camera along for one of his treks. Zinnemann had resisted his father's wish that he become a doctor and instead got a law degree, then toyed with the idea of studying music before turning to filmmaking. When they met in 1930, both were Hollywood outsiders. Flaherty was famous but detested Hollywood, and MGM in particular, for the way they used his talents as a documentarian to sell South Sea Island romances like *White Shadows in the South Seas* (codirected with W. S. Van Dyke, 1928) and *Tabu* (cowritten with director F. W. Murnau, 1931). At the time, Zinnemann was unknown in Hollywood, but in years to come, he would have his own titanic battles with MGM, over both *The Search* and his adaptation of *Man's Fate*. When he met Flaherty, he had worked as an assistant cameraman on Robert Siodmak's German documentary *Menschen am Sonntag/People on Sunday* (1929), and appeared as an extra in Universal's antiwar drama *All Quiet on the Western Front* (1930).[24] He also served as director Berthold Viertel's personal assistant and became a frequent guest at Salka Viertel's "Sunday afternoon coffee-klatsches" where everyone from Charles Chaplin to Sergei Eisenstein dropped in.[25] But Viertel's "scintillating gossip" was beginning to pall, and Zinnemann was not temperamentally suited to be a personal assistant. Flaherty recognized a restless, kindred spirit, and Zinnemann found the mentor and friend he needed. In December, Flaherty asked Zinnemann to work with him on a planned documentary of a remote nomadic people inside the Soviet Union. For six months he was with Flaherty in Berlin, negotiating with the Soviet Trade Mission to obtain permission to film the society.[26] It was eventually refused, but while in Berlin, Zinnemann had not only Flaherty's constant company, but also saw Eisenstein and Pudovkin, who were there to pay their respects to Flaherty. Zinnemann also began a lifelong friendship with Flaherty's co-cameraman on *Tabu*, Floyd Crosby, and the two would work together on *High Noon* and the very early stages of *From Here to Eternity*.[27] In the spring of 1931, Flaherty left Berlin to make a film in the UK at the suggestion of John Grierson, and Zinnemann returned to Hollywood as an assistant director and then director of shorts in MGM's famed department under Jack Chertok. The two men would never work together again, but remained close until Flaherty's death in 1951 (fig. 8). Zinnemann would name his only child David, after Flaherty's brother, and no interview was ever complete without a tribute to Robert Flaherty, not only for influencing Zinnemann "technically," but also "his whole spirit of being his own man."[28]

Ironically, Zinnemann achieved lasting critical fame for his European production, *The Search*, when he, like Flaherty before him, broke with the arch-conservative studio, MGM. Zinnemann was the first MGM director to go on suspension, and enjoyed telling the story of walking down the studio's empty corridor like Will Kane in *High Noon*: "Entering it at one end I would see tiny figures of associate producers in the distance, coming toward me, turning around, and disappearing into offices, stairways, or toilets."[29] Eventually, highly placed friends Arthur M. Loew (president of

FIG. 8 With Robert Flaherty, 1931, AMPAS.

Loew's International, the parent company of MGM), and agent Abe Lastfogel (future president of the William Morris Agency) managed to secure his return to Europe to work for the Swiss-based Praesens Films. Together with producer Lazar Wechsler and Swiss screenwriter Richard Schweizer, he created a script and film that confronted the limitations of historicizing the Holocaust and attempted to give an international voice to Europe's past and future. The film, a hybrid fictional narrative-documentary, was the earliest effort to represent child Holocaust survivor testimony by avoiding the pitfalls of re-emergent nationalism. Many of the children participating in the film were deported sons and daughters of resisters.

The Search was in many senses a tribute to the values Zinnemann and Flaherty shared: the passion for documentary locations and research, the need to take time on a project, and invest it with personal risk, and the commitment to the entire film process. Later, when he recalled *The Search*'s impact on his career, he again cited the influence of Robert Flaherty: "When I returned, I found, to my amazement—that the film was well liked, and I received a kind of notoriety in Hollywood for a while. The only problem was that people had forgotten who I was and thought I was a new European director who had just arrived from Switzerland. But the real influence on my point of view was again Bob Flaherty. He was a tremendous individualist in the days when that was unheard of . . . It took great courage to stand up against the system, because you could find yourself out of work, and being branded a troublemaker, you would then just cease to function. People like Flaherty were admirable to me, because they had the guts to stand up to that kind of pressure of easy money and refused to make junk or things they didn't believe in."[30] For all their shared love of the documentary approach, Zinnemann's perspective on nonfiction filmmaking was strikingly different from Flaherty's. However, several critics would criticize the two filmmakers for similar reasons. Iris Barry and others would take Flaherty to task for "fabricating" realism and for remaining aloof from the social and racial contexts of his films' subject matter.[31] Years later, critics would attack Zinnemann for creating "anti-movies" and for "not taking sides," particularly in his story of the aftermath of the Spanish Civil War, *Behold a Pale Horse*.

But while Flaherty was arguably more interested in pictorial composition than in political or social issues, the same could not be said for Fred Zinnemann. Though neither a committed Marxist nor a publicly vocal political filmmaker (he was too pragmatic about his Hollywood career for obvious gestures), Zinnemann was arguably Hollywood's answer to social documentary and the potential intellectual complexity of the commercial fiction film. Early in his career, Zinnemann's documentaries and feature films—most notably *The Seventh Cross*, *The Search*, and his fundraising documentary for the Los Angeles Orthopedic Hospital, *Benjy* (1951), and his unmade UN films about decolonization in Africa and the Muslim-Hindu conflicts in Northern India—explored the transformative power and political impact of cinema that blended history, fiction, and documentary with the lives of non-professional actors and Hollywood stars. Some of his most prominent films involved serious efforts to combat censorship by the US military (*From Here to Eternity*), the Catholic Church (*The Nun's Story*), and fascist governments (*Behold a Pale Horse*). Neutrality was never an option for Zinnemann, yet as time passed, his appreciation for historical issues and contemporary ideological distortion created an aesthetic so complex and nuanced that few critics could do more than appreciate its professional surface.

The final moments of *The Nun's Story* are a case in point. While Zinnemann focuses on Gabrielle's (Audrey Hepburn) struggle in the convent, in the final moments of the film, he chose to silently anchor the camera within the open doorway of the convent.[32] As Gabrielle leaves the cloister to join the Belgian resistance, the camera does not go with her, but merely records her vanishing figure. Zinnemann argued that this positioning represented an effort to let the audience make up its own mind in the final moments.[33] It was a strategy used in several of his films, where after following a protagonist through hours of close-ups, point-of-view shots, motivated cutting, and dialogue, he concluded by creating an additional visual or physical barrier between the screen and the audience, pushing viewers into a self-conscious realization of their own perspective inside and outside the film space. After Will throws his star in the dust and leaves Hadleyville with Amy (Grace Kelly) in the final shots of *High Noon*, the camera and audience do not leave with them, but can only watch them go. When Thomas More kneels at the scaffold, the audience is not at his side, but below in the crowd. With Artigas dead at the end of *Behold a Pale Horse*, Zinnemann's final shot is of the oblivious Spanish crowds going about their daily business. After staging his own closeness to these heroic misfits, Zinnemann created deliberately interrogative endings, in which the real question—"Would *you* have the courage to do this, or do you belong in the convent with the rest of the conformists?"—becomes the final challenge.

Resistance Histories

The uniqueness of Zinnemann's perspective on anti-fascist resistance is more apparent when one looks at the wider historiography and ideology of the Resistance. The focus is overwhelmingly on Western Europe and France.[34] Scholarly interest in American variants of fascism and resistance is relatively recent, though the intervention of American individuals in European crusades against fascism is an enduringly popular subject in literature (Hemingway), history (the Abraham Lincoln Brigade), and cinema (*Casablanca*, 1942). Spain is all but neglected due to the Allies' embarrassing accommodation of the Franco regime during and after the wider European war. In Europe, public commemoration of the victims of Nazi persecution began in 1943–44 with repatriation efforts of the London-based governments of Belgium, Holland, and the Netherlands. Governments had to consider how to manage the population of returning nationals and to determine who were national heroes, resisters, victims, or collaborators. French officials were beset with the mass identification of the communists as the party of the Resistance. By August 1945, almost all prisoners had returned to their home country, yet there were different responses to returning political resisters, forced laborers, willing laborers, and of course Jewish survivors. In Belgium, attempts were made to recognize "the criterion of suffering" which "elevated all victims to the rank of heroes of the Nation," and included Jewish deportees, communists, and Catholic political resisters. Because the Catholic party wanted an equal share of the representation of public heroes, state aid, and the political capital they represented, they rejected this inclusive definition for one which carefully defined "political prisoners" as the great Resistance heroes and ones most entitled to public recognition and pensions. By excluding Jews, prewar anti-fascist Freemasons and atheists, and the high numbers of murdered communist resisters, Catholics now were represented.[35] As Pieter Lagrou concludes, "Forced to concede over the inclusion of the governing communists, the Christian Popular Party settled for the peace offering which the marginalization of Jewish survivors constituted."[36]

One might argue that Zinnemann's body of Resistance histories commemorated not only the powerful role of the communists in the resistance to Hitler (*The Seventh Cross*), but also reinstated Jewish victims via Karel and his displaced, orphaned child peers (*The Search*), as recognized and heroic survivors of Nazi oppression. In effect, he recognized an inclusive "criterion of suffering" to constitute his heroes of the Resistance. While George Heisler's acts of resistance are more conventionally defined (political agitation, internment, escape, continued political work), Karel and his mother survive the murderers' system and live as a family once more. The immediate system of postwar identification and classification of resisters also sidelined the achievements of women, particularly in France. As Margaret Collins Weitz has pointed out, many résistantes deported to camps in Germany had no survivors from their réseaux to back up their stories.[37] Public commemoration of the Resistance focused on armed maquisards where women were often but not always prevented from fighting. And many women, tortured, interned, and deeply scarred by their experiences, preferred to forget. Until fairly recently, Resistance historiography virtually ignored the presence of women, but with the proliferation of women's memoirs, popular histories, and the interest in oral history, by the 1970s, the public was starting to listen to women's voices.[38] Fred Zinnemann's *Julia* is key in this debate.

Zinnemann was of course not unique in his passion for making films about the Resistance. Film historian Ginette Vincendeau has pointed out director Jean-Pierre Melville's career-long investment in the history of French resistance with his trio of films *La silence de la mer* (1947), *Léon*

Morin, prêtre (1961), and *L'Armée des ombres* (1969). Yet, as Vincendeau argues, his interpretations of the Resistance adhere to conventional trends in French historiography and reinforce the director's faith in war and the Resistance as an inherently heroic, masculine enterprise.[39] Paul Verhoeven's films reproduce similar conservative attitudes toward the wartime past. Although *Black Book*'s (2006) Dutch-Jewish heroine dominates much of the narrative of occupied Holland, Rachel/Ellis (Carice van Houten) remains a sexual object and pawn of her male Resistance colleagues and SS captors. *Soldier of Orange* (1977), with Rutger Hauer in the title role, is even more conventional in its portrait of the Resistance as a man's pursuit with clear-cut differences between collaborators and resisters.

By contrast, Fred Zinnemann's anti-fascist heroes were often solitary heroines such as Gabrielle van der Mal (Audrey Hepburn) and Lisa (Diana Lambert) in *The Nun's Story* or the elusive Julia (Vanessa Redgrave) and her workers (Dora Doll and Elisabeth Mortensen). His best-known Second World War hero, adored in his American hometown, was in reality a quisling who betrayed his unit while interned in a German prison camp (Van Heflin, *Act of Violence*).[40] In stark contrast, the director's major Resistance hero was a German communist, George Heisler (Spencer Tracy). *The Seventh Cross* stands in isolation compared with classic and more recent German films about internal anti-Nazi resistance (*Canaris: Master Spy*, 1954; *Der 20. Juli*, 1955; *Valkyrie*, 2004; *Sophie Scholl*, 2005). While these German films search for and valorize famous "privileged" resisters like Abwehr Chief Admiral Wilhelm Canaris, Count Klaus von Stauffenberg, and, more recently, White Rose student leader Sophie Scholl, Zinnemann's German resisters receive no postwar accolades or recognition, but remain anonymous. All have voices, and though not heard in mainstream historical accounts or public celebrations, their voices resonate with the history of the European resistance to fascism. "Courage needs witnesses," Gabrielle argues in *The Nun's Story* (1959), and Zinnemann's camera and unique adaptation of Resistance history created some of the most powerful witnesses of the twentieth-century struggle against National Socialism.

Over time, historians have come to acknowledge that "the Resistance" is itself an inherently constructed and even suspect term; Zinnemann was already well aware of this when he made *The Day of the Jackal* in 1973. De Gaulle's Resistance legacy was reconfigured in the 1960s with his "betrayal" over Algeria, and the roles of collaborator and resister changed to accommodate a new political landscape of conservative nationalism.

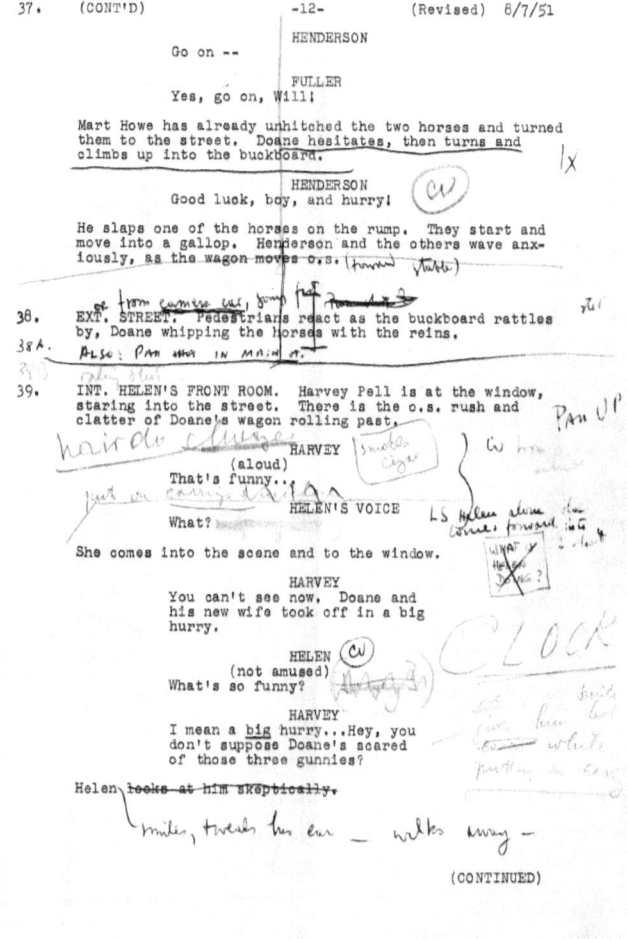

FIG. 9 Fred Zinnemann's annotated script for *High Noon* (1951), AMPAS.

In the film's prologue, the Cross of Lorraine fades, replaced by graffiti of de Gaulle hanging from a gibbet. But even traditional conceptions of French resistance are riddled with the consequences of de Gaulle's sanction that France was "a nation of resisters," when in fact the number of those opposing the Nazi regime was very small. Most were communists, political dissidents, young people, women, and those who would be publically excluded by the Gaullist regime. But the Resistance had to be created in the postwar years as something heroic and full of action. In this, Hollywood was often an active collaborator, releasing narratives, sometimes

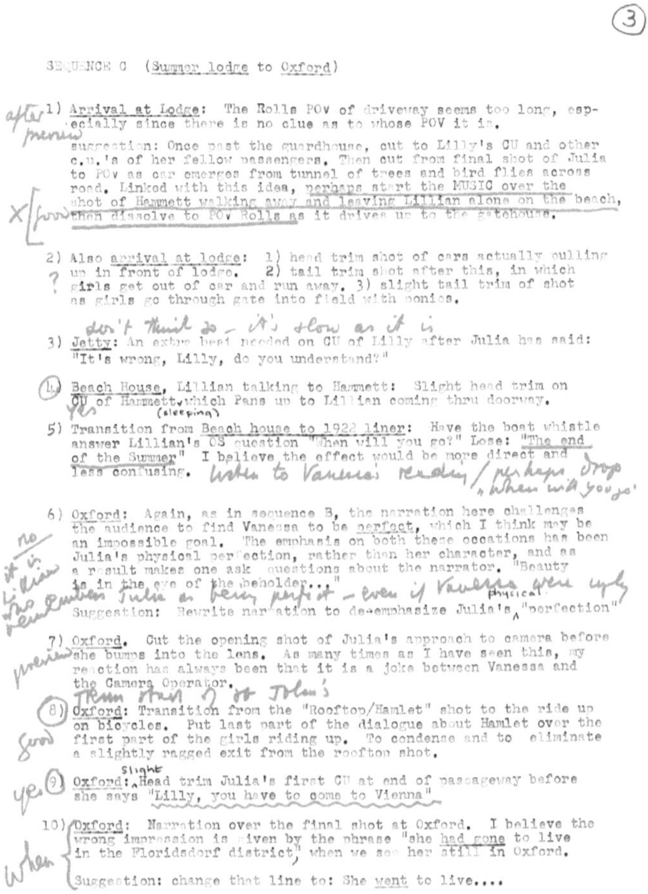

3

SEQUENCE C (Summer lodge to Oxford)

1) Arrival at Lodge: The Rolls POV of driveway seems too long, especially since there is no clue as to whose POV it is.

suggestion: Once past the guardhouse, cut to Lilly's CU and other c.u.'s of her fellow passengers. Then cut from final shot of Julia to POV as car emerges from tunnel of trees and bird flies across road. Linked with this idea, perhaps start the MUSIC over the shot of Hammett walking away and leaving Lillian alone on the beach, then dissolve to POV Rolls as it drives up to the gatehouse.

2) Also arrival at lodge: 1) head trim shot of cars actually pulling up in front of lodge. 2) tail trim shot after this, in which girls get out of car and run away. 3) slight tail trim of shot as girls go through gate into field with ponies.

3) Jetty: An extra beat needed on CU of Lilly after Julia has said: "It's wrong, Lilly, do you understand?"

4) Beach House, Lillian talking to Hammett: Slight head trim on CU of Hammett (sleeping) which Pans up to Lillian coming thru doorway.

5) Transition from Beach house to 1922 liner: Have the boat whistle answer Lillian's OS question "When will you go?" Lose: "The end of the Summer" I believe the effect would be more direct and less confusing.

6) Oxford: Again, as in sequence B, the narration here challenges the audience to find Vanessa to be perfect, which I think may be an impossible goal. The emphasis on both these occations has been Julia's physical perfection, rather than her character, and as a result makes one ask questions about the narrator. "Beauty is in the eye of the beholder..."

Suggestion: Rewrite narration to de-emphasize Julia's physical "perfection"

7) Oxford. Cut the opening shot of Julia's approach to camera before she bumps into the lens. As many times as I have seen this, my reaction has always been that it is a joke between Vanessa and the Camera Operator.

8) Oxford: Transition from the "Rooftop/Hamlet" shot to the ride up on bicycles. Put last part of the dialogue about Hamlet over the first part of the girls riding up. To condense and to eliminate a slightly ragged exit from the rooftop shot.

9) Oxford: slight Head trim Julia's first CU at end of passageway before she says "Lilly, you have to come to Vienna"

10) Oxford: Narration over the final shot at Oxford. I believe the wrong impression is given by the phrase "she had gone to live in the Floridsdorf district," when we see her still in Oxford.

Suggestion: change that line to: She went to live....

FIG. 10 Zinnemann film notes, 1976, AMPAS.

based on actual historical occurrences, which dramatized the solitary heroism of stars Gregory Peck (*Guns of Navarone*, 1961), Burt Lancaster (*The Train*, 1964), and Richard Burton (*Where Eagles Dare*, 1968). Zinnemann was unique as a director of Resistance films in that he focused on ordinary people, eschewed conventional heroism and military action, and also showed resisters in opposition to systems which seemed far too powerful to overcome. Julia, the most obvious and active Resistance heroine in his films, is killed, and remembered only through Lillian Hellman's voice-over. There are no happy endings.

This book is the first to draw upon Zinnemann's papers housed at the Academy of Motion Picture Arts and Sciences Library, and focuses on the nature of Zinnemann's cinema of resistance, his unique approach to the adaptation and scripting of history and heroism, use of voice-over and "oral history," and the gender of history and memory. His archive is perhaps the most extensive of its kind, and this book explores not only his meticulous memos, sketches, and script annotations, but the thousands of pages of production notes which cover every imaginable aspect of research, casting, adaptation, performance, cinematography, editing, dubbing, post-production, publicity, censorship, international and domestic audience analyses, budgets, and criticism. Often Zinnemann did not merely draw a thumbnail sketch of a shot, he noted his reasons for choosing a close-up or a long shot, a low-angle shot, or a backlight, or a composition (figs. 9–10). In rare cases such as these, the gap between the interpretive guesswork of close analysis and primarily text-based historical analysis disappears.

I begin with a comparative analysis of *The Seventh Cross*, *Man's Fate*, and *The Day of the Jackal*, productions which triangulate Zinnemann's complex attitudes toward Resistance history and heroism over his long career as a feature filmmaker and indicate his personal resistance to more standard narratives of anti-fascism. Zinnemann's tendency to conceive of the Resistance and war experience outside of national categories and his exploration of postwar Europe is the focus of Chapter Two, about *The Search*, arguably his most personal film. Chapters Three and Four proceed chronologically to look at American fascism at both a critical and narrative level, in Zinnemann's most popular American productions, *High Noon* and *From Here to Eternity*. Chapter Five returns to the European war with his adaptation of Kathryn Hulme's *The Nun's Story* and an analysis of women's perspectives on war and resistance. *Behold a Pale Horse* again moves outside conventional histories of resistance in its assessment of the life and death of anarchist Manuel Artigas/Francisco Sabaté. Banned in Franco's Spain, a commercial failure, and the source of many of Zinnemann's future battles with film critics, the film nonetheless remains one of the most complex productions about the memory of the Spanish Civil War. And finally, the book concludes with *Julia*, a masterpiece of "Resistance" cinema and arguably one of the most important films about women ever made. Inevitably, some of Zinnemann's works are sidelined, and I discuss many of his unfilmed projects more than the acclaimed costume drama *A Man For All Seasons*, *The Member of the Wedding* (Zinnemann's personal favorite), his extensive work in the MGM shorts department, and his haunting, underrated final film, *Five Days One Summer* (1982). This is not a biography or a filmography; instead, it aims to be an intellectual film history focused on the filmmaker's lifelong interest in twentieth-century resistance movements and anti-fascism. Based on what Zinnemann chose to save and donate to the Academy of Motion Picture Arts and Sciences from his life's work, a startlingly complex picture emerges of his creative process and attitudes toward the legacy of his generation.

Zinnemann's peers had seen the director as a kind of unashamed outsider within the Hollywood film industry, and in his relationship with Hollywood and his search for a truly international cinema, Zinnemann created another dimension of his "resistant" image. Through the success and notoriety of *High Noon* and *From Here to Eternity*, Zinnemann would become one of Hollywood's most honored directors, but, characteristically for him, the more beloved and bankable he became to the studio executives, the farther away he fled to European and Asian locations. In his efforts to achieve his personal vision for each film, he often clashed with others involved in the projects, including writer Lillian Hellman, composer Franz Waxman, producers Lazar Wechsler, Stanley Kramer, Richard Roth, and friends Oscar Hammerstein, Peter Viertel, and Carl Foreman.[41]

But for some critics, Zinnemann would always be a collaborator—the master par excellence of the Hollywood system whose narratives remain ideologically confusing and "uncommitted." This contradiction served me well, for in this way he exemplifies the complexities of the true Resistance director. Part of the Hollywood system, and therefore no stranger to compromise, he was also a solitary European émigré who refused to belong to any school or reflect any ideology. Seemingly modest and unassuming, and recognizing the innately collaborative nature of filmmaking, he was, as Jane Fonda remembered him, "a gentleman and a dictator," who attempted to control every aspect of his work. Though his films remain some of the most popular and critically acclaimed of the twentieth century, he is a shadowy presence in Hollywood lore, traceable only through his camera and archive. Fred Zinnemann was a director of resistant women and unknown, courageous men; a man who preserved the voices of child Holocaust survivors; a Hollywood filmmaker who pushed Hollywood's commitment to Europe and international filmmaking to its breaking point; a politically engaged mind so complex he isolated himself from his generation; a staunch professional who collaborated and fought with the Hollywood system for five decades; and above all, a master director whose consistency was in his resistance.

CHAPTER ONE

From Germany to Algeria, and Other Historiographies of Resistance

> "Just because you were German didn't mean automatically that you were a monster."
> —**Fred Zinnemann, 1976**[1]

> "The weakness of all dictatorships is that they are vast bureaucracies."
> —**Frederick Forsyth,** *The Day of the Jackal* (1971), underlined by Fred Zinnemann in his personal copy

Fred Zinnemann was one of many filmmakers to leave an increasingly fascist Europe for Hollywood. He sailed to New York in the autumn of 1929, following close friend and documentary filmmaker Günther von Fritsch, who had settled in New York City. But, as he recalled, "two weeks in New York convinced me that hardly any 'real' movies were made there; Hollywood, a totally separate world . . . seemed to be the only answer."[2] He headed west, scouting the Hollywood landscape for a job. Trained as a cameraman at Paris's new Technical School of Cinema, one of his first moves was to apply for membership in the Hollywood cameraman's union. Even with the legendary Billy Bitzer (*The Birth of a Nation*, 1915; *Intolerance*, 1916) as his sponsor, he was refused admission. Despite forming friendships with European expatriates Berthold and Salka Viertel, and cameramen Joseph Ruttenberg, Gregg Toland, and Floyd Crosby, Zinnemann found it difficult to adjust to Hollywood in the 1930s. He disliked the production system's inefficiency and lack of attention to historical detail, and was fired from the set of *All Quiet on the Western Front* for arguing with one of the assistant directors. He told Sam Goldwyn point blank that Hollywood pictures were "too slick."[3] Goldwyn was speechless for once. A few years and several mediocre jobs later, while working as an assistant to William Wyler on *Dodsworth* (1935), he disagreed with the director's camera set-up.[4] Wyler was one of the few to find the young upstart's mixture of youthful enthusiasm and artistic distain amusing.

Zinnemann's rebellion against the Hollywood system and a career of anonymity led him to accept a job in Mexico as the director of Paul Strand's new government-funded film. *Redes* (*The Wave*, 1934–36) is the story of a fishing community on the Gulf Coast of Mexico which has been exploited for generations by wealthy oligarchs. When one man attempts to organize a strike and is assassinated, the people unite, cutting the "nets" of capitalism. Zinnemann spent seven months in Alvarado with Strand, writer Henwar Rodakiewicz, and Günther von Fritsch, who edited the film. They used local non-professionals in the roles, and cast university student Silvio Hernandez as the heroic strike leader. Though Strand's interest in making a film about the development of working-class resistance among a group of fishermen was certainly imbued with the aims of Carlos Chavez and Mexico's new socialist government,[5] his tendency to shoot the film as a series of static images infuriated Zinnemann, who, like Sergei Eisenstein, saw cinematic movement as key to embodying revolutionary change. Despite being a staunch defender of photographic objectivity and its ability to engage with social change, Strand's fascination with beautiful images often decontextualized them both in front of and behind the camera, and as art historian James Krippner has argued, betrayed his lack of sensitivity to issues of class, ethnicity, and gender.[6] Zinnemann would later smooth over their ideological differences, remembering only that he and Strand "did not get on too well." But the young director studied the left-wing photographer and his way of maintaining artistic control over the production. Zinnemann had little control over the final cut of *Redes*, but would remain proud of his involvement with the film. Late in life he was fond of pointing out that a few years after its release, "the Nazis found the negative and burned it."[7] It was the first but not the last time that one of his films attracted the wrath of a fascist political regime.

When he returned to Hollywood in late December 1934, Zinnemann was still looking for steady work. His resumé must have worried the conservative studio company men: he was associated with the socialist regime in Mexico and was a close friend of one of Hollywood's biggest critics, Robert Flaherty. While working for Sam Goldwyn and Sidney Franklin on *The Dark Angel* (1935), he met Lillian Hellman and Dashiell

Hammett, Hollywood writers who maintained their political radicalism while remaining on a studio payroll. Greta Garbo and Salka Viertel pulled strings to get him on the set of George Cukor's *Camille*, but after directing *Redes*, he was in no mood to be anyone's assistant again. But a mutual friend of his and Flaherty's, cinematographer Floyd Crosby, got him an introduction to Jack Chertok of the MGM short department in 1937. Chertok admired *Redes*, which had just opened to good art-house reviews. He had an eye for training directors; Jules Dassin, Jacques Tourneur, and George Sidney all learned their craft in Chertok's department. For several years, Zinnemann mastered the shorts system, even winning an Academy Award for *That Mothers Might Live* (1938), the story of an Austrian doctor's cure for childbed fever obviously inspired by Zinnemann's background as the son of a Viennese physician. He made several shorts that tapped into the current industrial trend in history films, such as *The Story of Dr. Carver* (1938) and *The Old South* (1940),[8] but what he really wanted to do was a feature film about Mexican revolutionary Emiliano Zapata. MGM had recently promoted him to direct Van Heflin and Marsha Hunt in *Kid Glove Killer* (1942), but Zinnemann, while praising the talents of Heflin and Hunt, saw the contemporary thriller genre's obvious limitations.[9] Combining his familiarity with Mexico and fluent Spanish, expertise in producing economical historical films, and desire to make an anti-fascist film in keeping with Hollywood's wartime aims, he wrote to Jack Chertok: "Up till now, the film industry has made a few feeble, though costly efforts in behalf of Pan-American solidarity and friendship. We all know how those efforts have failed, how they were booed off screens down there. More than ever, they made the Latin Americans feel that we have no respect for them, that we know nothing about their way of life, and that we care less. No wonder those pictures backfired. Meanwhile, the Germans keep releasing smoothly made films, successfully flattering the Latin American ego."[10] Zinnemann argued that a film about Zapata's life "would be a gesture of respect, provided it is done with dignity and attention to historical truth." According to Zinnemann, Zapata was a greater hero than the macho military icon Pancho Villa, who had been parodied by Wallace Beery in MGM's *Viva Villa!* (1934). Zinnemann would never get to make the Zapata biopic, but his cinematic discovery, Marlon Brando, would star in Elia Kazan's production several years later (*Viva Zapata!*, 1952). Instead, MGM producer Pandro S. Berman offered Zinnemann another project which tested his knowledge of Europe, anti-fascism, and heroism. It also connected with the young director's interest in historical filmmaking and Hollywood's war genre.

But the adaptation of Anna Seghers's *The Seventh Cross* was unique as both a historical film and as an anti-Nazi war picture. Arguably, Hollywood's films about American variants of fascism date back to *Black Legion* and *They Won't Forget* (both 1937), while the studios' early anti-Nazi films, an adaptation of Erich Maria Remarque's *Three Comrades* (MGM, 1938) and *Confessions of a Nazi Spy* (Warner Bros., 1939), followed many months later.[11] With the Nazi occupation of Belgium and Holland, and the French government's collaboration with Nazi Germany in 1940, Hollywood's denunciation of fascist Germany became clearer (*Escape*, MGM, 1940). Yet most Hollywood films about European resistance to fascism focused on the French Resistance (*Joan of Paris, Casablanca, Reunion in France*, all 1942; *Passage to Marseille*, 1943). Germans were cast as menacing military types, from Helmut Dantine's fanatical young pilot (*Mrs. Miniver*, 1942) to Conrad Veidt's menacing Major Strasser (*Casablanca*), who, acknowledging the myth of romantic Paris, slyly asks Rick Blaine (Humphrey Bogart), "Are you one of those people who can't imagine the Germans in their beloved Paris?" Pan Berman wanted a different approach to the emerging war cycle, and was simultaneously exploring the theme of Eastern anti-fascist resistance histories with old RKO friend Katharine Hepburn, who played the anti-Japanese activist Jade in MGM's adaptation of Pearl Buck's historical novel, *Dragon Seed* (1944).[12] But *The Seventh Cross* was an unusual choice for this production cycle since it was set in Germany, had a prewar historical setting, and its principal Resistance hero was, like Seghers herself, a communist political activist fleeing Nazi internment.[13] Spencer Tracy, fresh from his work on *The Keeper of the Flame* (1943), an adaptation of Conrad Richter's bestseller about hidden fascism in America, saw Seghers's work as a way of building on his image as an anti-fascist hero in wartime. Intrigued by Berman's description of Zinnemann, he asked to meet the young director. Their professional chemistry was immediate, and the men became good friends.

Zinnemann, thrilled with the prospect of working with MGM's most revered star, read Helen Deutsch's script with interest.[14] Seghers had employed several recurring first-person voices throughout the novel. Anonymous Westhofen camp prisoners narrate German history and contextualize the escape, George thinks or mutters to himself throughout the massive manhunt, and the voice of Resistance leader Ernst Wallau, who is tortured to death after being recaptured, urges George to persevere in his escape.[15] But for Deutsch and later Zinnemann, Wallau's voice-over, heard even from the grave, became the central feature accompanying George's escape and his political reawakening in the final scenes. Berman, Zinnemann, and Deutsch worried about introducing American audiences to the idea of German resistance to fascism in the 1930s, and were consequently preoccupied with the opening, explanatory voice-over. Deutsch's early scripts expand and contract Wallau's narration; at one point, the script contained multiple versions of the first sixteen pages of narration, and later the narration was considered important enough to merit a separate script composed entirely of the voice-over excerpts.[16] Seghers would later write to Zinnemann saying that she felt Wallau's voice-overs intruded too much in the narrative and were excessive,[17] yet for Deutsch and for Zinnemann, this excess served a historical purpose. Wallau functioned as a crucial historical voice for a vanished group of Germans. George's tendency to be silent in the opening sequences contrasts with both Wallau's voice and George's growing articulateness and political awareness in the second half.

The voice-over developed from the 1930s when it was occasionally used in lieu of a superimposed text foreword in historical films. Both the historical gangster smash-hit *The Roaring Twenties* (1939) and the George M. Cohan biopic *Yankee Doodle Dandy* (1942) used this form of narration in different ways: to link the subject matter to contemporary reportage and to personalize histories with the voice of the protagonist.[18] A few years later, film noir would also tend toward voice-over narration, learning from Hitchcock's *Rebecca* (1940). Voice-over narration would briefly dominate production of noir, from *Double Indemnity, Murder, My Sweet*, and *Laura* (all 1944) to *The Locket* (1946), *Dark Passage* (1947), *Out of the Past* (1947), and *Sunset Boulevard* (1950). All of these noirs were focused on the protagonists' harrowing past lives and complicated the genre's allegedly contemporary contexts. The association between voice-over narration, fraught histories, and claustrophobic personal disaster also links these later noirs with the motifs of *The Seventh Cross*.[19] Yet *The Seventh Cross*'s reliance upon voice-over instead of the more conventional text superimpositions embodied the anti-fascist/anti-Nazi movement's own vulnerability and marginality in a world where official histories and documents were easily corrupted for the purposes of political propaganda. As historian Margaret Collins Weitz has pointed out, "Underground movements do not leave written records."[20] Documents found by Nazis or fascist militia were a death sentence. In *The Seventh Cross*, oral history recovers the narrative of early anti-fascist resistance in Germany—a narrative that, like its protagonists, is all but extinct.

The film begins with what Deutsch described as Wallau's "calm, deliberate, dispassionate" voice, narrating a story almost unknown to the historical records but crucial to remember: "When all the stories have been told, the great stories and the little ones—the tragedies and the melodramas—when all the stories of what happened in Europe have been told, as of course they never *can* be, the seventh cross will be remembered as the story of a few little people who proved *there is something in the human soul which sets men above the animals and beyond them*." Wallau also provides the necessary historical background: "It happened in Germany in the fall of the year 1936 . . . the wars and aggressions had not yet begun, but the concentration camps were filled—the Germans were still purging their own country of rebels—purging their nation of the last traces of human decency."[21] Many of Seghers's prisoners were incarcerated members of the once flourishing Communist Party (the KPD), the Nazi Party's main radical opponent in the late 1920s and 1930s (as opposed to the more established German Socialist Party, the SPD). In March 1933, the Nazis began arresting party members, sending thousands of them to torture and death in the newly created Dachau concentration camp. Until his arrest, George Heisler was one of the party's strongest adherents, and was widely known as a trained demonstrator and agitator. Wallau was his teacher. Yet Seghers was careful not to make her communist persuasions and those of her hero too apparent.[22] There were references to former party officials and demonstrations in the novel, but no doctrine or concrete political history. So, though one might assume Hollywood would divest the film of any communist political content, there was not any to edit in the first place. As Alexander Stephan notes, the character-oriented manhunt and George's successful escape made *The Seventh Cross* a natural for Book-of-the-Month Club and other bestseller lists.[23]

Even though MGM would market the film strictly as a star vehicle for Spencer Tracy, carefully avoiding all mention of Nazis, communists, and concentration camps,[24] Zinnemann was fascinated with the cinematic recovery of this early German resistance. As he wrote to Berman, "I think it is of vital importance to tell the audience *as early as possible* just exactly why George is a hero and a symbol of resistance to oppression."[25] And as he noted, it was important in the first part of the film to "dramatize terror and hunted-animal feeling—cold, hunger—see as much of action as possible from George's point of view: the hunt, as seen through the

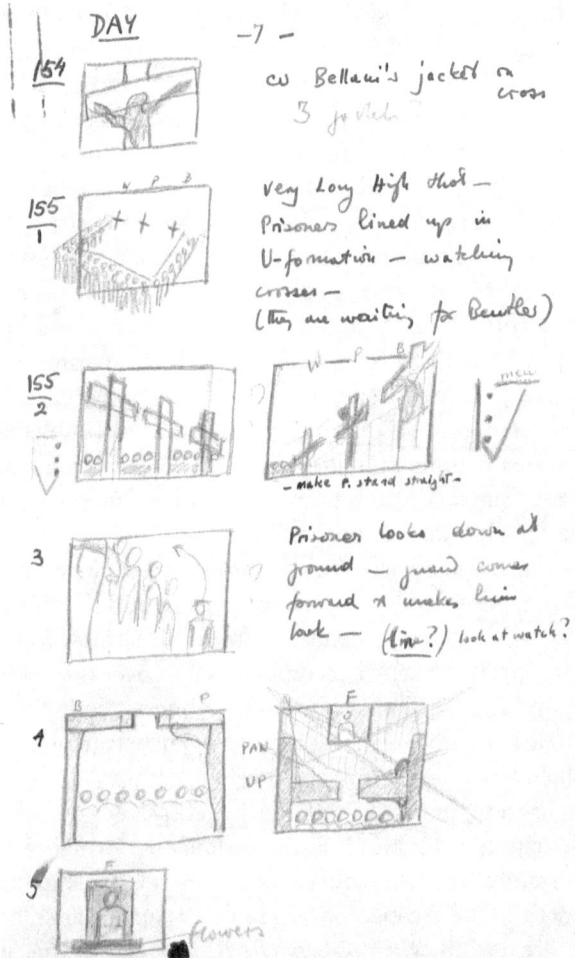

FIG. 11 The Zinnemann sketchbook for *The Seventh Cross*, 1943, AMPAS.

eyes of the hunted—use first-person camera in a few high spots—as he approaches what (to him and to the audience) might be traps—as he walks toward and mingles with crowds—watching whether people are looking at him."[26] Zinnemann positioned the entire narrative from the oral subjectivity of Wallau's voice-over and the visual subjectivity of George Heisler. Zinnemann knew that directing Spencer Tracy had the potential to transform his own career, and did thumbnail sketches of virtually every key sequence. He was particularly drawn to establishing shots where the most important element was the farthest away from the camera—paralleling

George's future escape—and tight close-ups which heightened George's fear and sense of fate and the Nazis closing in (fig. 11).[27]

In July 1943, Zinnemann's script notes prioritized "a clearer sense of George's past" and "a clearer understanding of George's function for the future."[28] Though Zinnemann named no names, George knew working people, his best friend Paul Roeder was an industrial laborer, and many people in the Resistance who helped George were also workers with extensive clandestine political ties. For anyone aware of post-Great War German political history, it was easy to identify George as a member of the once powerful but now hunted Communist Party, and Ernst Wallau as either Ernst Thälmann, the leader of the KPD arrested on March 3, 1933 or Ernst Torgler, the party's leader in the Reichstag.[29] Zinnemann was adamant that George must have a reputation as a troublemaker in the National Socialist regime. Zinnemann's visual construction of George was distinct, and set him apart from the other escapees and the German population.[30] The opening images of the film structure the escape as a series of tight close-ups. Each prisoner runs into the shot like a hunted animal before fleeing. George walks into the frame, and out of it, his face immobile, almost brutish. Later, as he moves from the country to the town, he meets a young girl who silently accompanies him over the fields and along the road. As he ties her hair ribbon, he wonders fleetingly whether he should strangle her with it, echoing a scene in James Whale's *Frankenstein* (1931) in which the monster tosses flowers and then a little girl into the lake (fig. 12). Beside the angelic little girl, George's ragged, clumsy figure and somber, haunted face recall Boris Karloff's performance in *Frankenstein*, and certainly resonate with Victor Erice's relationship between Ana (Ana Torrent) and the escaped Loyalist soldier (Juan Margallo) and monster (José Villasante) in *The Spirit of the Beehive* (1973) (fig. 13). In both these films, the figure of the communist/outcast is ironically linked with that of social "monster." Zinnemann also links George's image intertextually with one of Tracy's more recent roles in *Dr. Jekyll and Mr. Hyde* (1941). As George steals a coat, he looks up into a mirror, seeing his face for the first time in ages. His horror at the new face the Nazis have given him is apparent (fig. 14).

In his notes, the director also wrote that George should "carry out of Germany, to the free countries, the story of what is going on in Germany."[31] While George initially finds inspiration in a church, the plans he forms there to contact a former sweetheart are only "false hopes"—like most hopes that the Catholic Church would oppose fascism and National

FIGS. 12–14 The hunted "monster": German communist leader and concentration camp escapee George Heisler (Spencer Tracy), MGM.

Socialism. Instead, George's only help comes from an old friend and the broken remnants of the communist network. In the end, it is a German communist who brings anti-fascist awareness to the rest of Europe at the end of the film. Zinnemann also cut lines from Helen Deutsch's script in which Paul criticized George's communist friend Marnet: "You wouldn't be in this trouble now if you hadn't taken up with him. He was the one [who] got you in so deep with his meetings and his books."[32] While for Deutsch, Paul embodied ordinary Germans' endorsement of Hitler's regime, Zinnemann wanted the guileless Paul and Liesl Roeder to transform into George's staunch allies. During the production, Zinnemann became close friends with Hume Cronyn (Paul) and Jessica Tandy (Liesl), and each night the young trio would rehearse the next day's shots, enabling Zinnemann to shoot the film his way without interference from Karl Freund, his irascible veteran cinematographer. As Zinnemann once remarked, Freund was the kind of cameraman who asked his assistant to wash his car on Sunday; Cronyn was more blunt and called him "an absolute bastard of a cameraman."[33] Both were delighted when he got sick for a

FIG. 15 Ordinary Germans: George hides with friends Paul and Liesl Roeder (Hume Cronyn and Jessica Tandy), MGM.

few days and Robert Surtees filled in. But Zinnemann had other troubles. Assistant producer Jane Loring was a silent if constant presence on the set, and Helen Deutsch wrote memos to Berman when she saw that the director had changed certain scenes and slashed dialogue. It was hardly a universally encouraging atmosphere for his first major feature film. But Zinnemann had allies in Berman, Tracy, and the Cronyns. His thumbnail sketches also helped him to circumvent any of Freund's suggestions. The film went like clockwork, and under Zinnemann's direction, Tandy and Cronyn's scenes project a warmth and vulnerability made more poignant when viewed from George's point-of-view as a hunted outsider and political threat (fig. 15).

Seghers had deliberately written a story without a conventional hero, and regardless of the fact that he had Spencer Tracy, MGM's most respected star, in the lead, Zinnemann resisted making George Heisler a German version of *Casablanca*'s Victor Laszlo (Paul Henreid). Whatever his committed political past, in the film Heisler was merely "a man possessed, fanatically possessed by one single motive . . . escape . . . he has no use for human relations." Zinnemann wrote that Heisler does not care if he is isolated from people; "he is in a corner all by himself."[34] Only at the end, when he remembers aloud and in an interior voice-over the names of those who helped him, do we understand the extent of his commitment to remember and to articulate political resistance. Zinnemann wrote to Berman, "As I remember in the book, George's and Wallau's prime motive for escape is to attempt to get out of Germany and, if successful, to continue the fight from abroad." He believed that they had to tell the audience "*why* George is a hero and a symbol of resistance to oppression. It is not because he has been important in the Underground, but *because he has refused to give up his dignity as a human being or grovel under torture*" [his emphasis].35 Zinnemann's film was about Heisler's gradual return to political consciousness and activism.

In contrast, Helen Deutsch found the former communist and current Resistance leader Herman the most powerful secondary character in the novel and invested him with a unique brand of masculinity and sexual magnetism. She wrote, "As for Herman himself, he is large, quiet, powerful, perceptive. He has chosen to do the work he is doing and likes it. His rocklike pose is always in contrast with Franz's nervous, intense energy. He has the religious aura of a man dedicated to a cause, without compromise or self-dramatization. Else, his wife, is extremely attractive; she has a sensuous, yet gentle, quality. She worships Hermann, who is at least ten years her senior; she would die for him; she knows him, understands him, and looks upon him as something more than a man—in all the picture, the greatest love, if we were to show it, would be the love of this handsome, intelligent, sexually alive and attractive young woman for this not-very-handsome, not-very-young, rather fat, but supremely fine and strong man."36 Yet Zinnemann was less interested in Herman's "rocklike" heroic image than in following the transformation of George, Paul, and Liesl.

One of the more problematic aspects of *The Seventh Cross* in relation to Zinnemann's future work was that despite the strong presence of women in German anti-Nazi resistance and the book's female author and screenwriter, none of the seven escapees from Westhofen is a woman and none of the official Resistance organization—aside from Herman's wife—is a woman. Though both Mrs. Roeder (Jessica Tandy) and the barmaid Toni (Signe Hasso) help George, they are not part of any organization and do this largely in ignorance of his situation. However, while women are on the periphery of this underground, they are involved in many acts of resistance. Madame Morelli (Agnes Morehead) recognizes George as a fugitive, but provides him with a new disguise and money. Her parting, "Heil Hitler," is distinctly ironic. Of all those who are involved in George's fate on screen, Hedy Sauer (Katherine Locke) articulates a brief but pithy sense of Germany's past and current political resistance. Her husband, Bruno (George Macready), had once been deeply involved in the antifascist resistance and a friend of Herman and George. However, when Paul approaches him to help George, he pretends not to know him. Mrs. Sauer, sexually and emotionally estranged from her husband, attributes their split to his political hypocrisy. "You are a coward," she tells her husband, and Zinnemann's camera stands with her, watching her husband in long-shot.[37] As Zinnemann wrote of this scene: "Mrs S[auer]: Calm, relentless, level, great strength and integrity. She should dominate scene entirely. Calmly."[38]

Women were an important, active part of Hollywood's history of the Resistance in 1940s films, among them Berman's own *Dragon Seed*, *So Ends Our Night* (1941), *Underground* (1941), *Joan of Paris*, *Chetniks* (1943), *Paris After Dark* (1944), and *Paris Underground* (1945). Zinnemann's notes on the final script reveal that he was particularly interested in Liesl Roeder's dilemma in helping George. Though she was risking the life of her family and children and was reluctant to help when she knew the extent of George's predicament, her development of a political conscience was as important to Zinnemann as dramatizing Paul Roeder's obvious courage.[39] Also, when George is nearly free, he intones the names of those who have helped him. His list includes the names of both men and women: "A girl called Toni, Franz Marnet, Paul Roeder, Madame Morelli, Dr. Loewenstein, Fielder, Poldi Schlamm." And when George continues, "There are some whose names I'll never know," and the narrator, Wallau, supplies them to the audience, both Bruno Sauer and wife Hedy make the list.[40] The director's next few films about the Second World War, including *The Search* (1948) and *Teresa* (1951), focused on the articulation of women's voices in the aftermath of the conflict, but it was only in *The Nun's Story*, made some fifteen years after *The Seventh Cross*, that Zinnemann returned to the history of women's resistance, its fragility in conventional definitions, and its remembrance through the mechanisms of oral history.

The director, like most people in Hollywood, was in awe of Spencer Tracy's range as an actor and ability to project silent intensity with economy of movement. Before shooting began, he watched Tracy's films compulsively in order to see what the actor was capable of; he was particularly drawn to Fritz Lang's *Fury* (1936), the historical drama *Power and the Glory* (1933), and William Wellman's historical gangster film, *They Gave Him a Gun* (1937).[41] Tracy was famous for working with a minimum of fuss or even noise. His quiet intensity would "explode" on-screen. Zinnemann worked in a similar way. He liked to do as few takes as possible—something Tracy also appreciated—but would give room for rehearsal and demanded a silent set with a minimum of distractions to help performers concentrate, something that actresses such as Marsha Hunt, Janet Leigh, Audrey Hepburn, and Vanessa Redgrave would remember with gratitude.[42] Tracy

FIG. 16 Zinnemann rehearses with Spencer Tracy and Karen Verne (Leni), 1943, AMPAS.

appreciated the care Zinnemann took with the film, and their off-camera shots together show some of this intense rapport (fig. 16).

Zinnemann asked to screen as many of the current crop of Resistance films as possible: *The Mortal Storm* (1940), *So Ends Our Night, Underground* (1941), *All Through the Night, Once Upon a Honeymoon, Desperate Journey, Berlin Correspondent, The Wife Takes a Flier, Casablanca, Joan of Paris* (all 1942), *Hitler's Madmen, Hostages, Above Suspicion,* and *Cross of Lorraine* (all 1943) all made the preproduction research list.[43] Though Zinnemann did not want George to be like Seghers's hero Herman or a variation of Victor Laszlo in *Casablanca*—fully formed heroic figures—he knew that Tracy's star power and the conventions of major Hollywood pictures demanded a focus on the man who avoided the seventh cross. Zinnemann wrote, "Nazis fear and hate George most . . . As it stands now I feel that the character is described in pretty vague though flowery terms . . . We don't know why Wallau speaks of him in such exalted terms . . . I may appear to be stubborn about this, but it does seem tremendously important to me to give Spencer Tracy a really solid spring-board into the story."[44] Though a political resister to fascism prior to his incarceration,

George's story in *The Seventh Cross* is his development into a Resistance hero. Therefore the film would function less as a perpetuator of the myth of the great Resistance hero and more as a chronicle of the historical development of the Resistance and its geographic spread from Germany to the rest of Europe in the 1930s.[45] This was perhaps Seghers and Zinnemann's most controversial historical proposal—namely, that resistance to fascism developed in Germany itself in the early 1930s and took root in other countries, rather than the rest of Europe having to "cure" German evil. Zinnemann saw a clear connection between the historical narrative and contemporary politics. As he wrote to Berman, "The day of hate pictures is obviously past." Hollywood needs films "that show a new approach toward the beaten Germany," he argued, and directed Berman's attention to famed journalist Dorothy Thompson's article in the July edition of the *Reader's Digest*, "We Must Salvage Germany."[46] The film was popular, and Zinnemann reported to his brother overseas that the two previews had gone well. George later expressed his surprise that the film was made available to the armed forces and populations in Great Britain so quickly, opening at the Leicester Square Theatre in London on September 1. As he wrote, "Just wanted to let you know that we went to see *The Seventh Cross* and we certainly were impressed. So was the rest of the audience for that matter; some people applauded, which is quite unusual in these parts. I bet you feel swell about this and I'm very happy for you. I'm sending you under separate cover a copy of the *London Tribune*, which as you will note is a socialist paper and also has a write-up in it with a different approach than most others, which you might find interesting."[47]

Some American newspapers were more wary. Many critics' skepticism about *The Seventh Cross* resulted from their unease with the filmmakers' account of Germany's history of anti-fascist resistance and its relationship with the present war. Some, like Howard Barnes, wondered whether the added historical dimension of the film might make things too complicated for ordinary American viewers: "One might argue that MGM's *The Seventh Cross* is stymied for popular appeal by the fact that it dramatizes the escape of an enemy of the Gestapo long before the Wehrmacht launched its assault on the democratic world."[48] But Bosley Crowther found the film's historical message of the "good German" "dangerous" since no one wanted Germany to get a soft peace in 1944. "However," Crowther argued, "the people shown in this film—especially the active anti-Nazis—would all likely be dead by now. At the rate they are clipped off in the story, no survivors could remain after eight years. And thus the decent Germans that are shown us are simply historic characters. There are none such left."[49] Some organizations saw *The Seventh Cross* as another contemporary Resistance film, and therefore criticized what they believed to be a false picture of Germany. *Variety* quoted *The Bulletin for the Prevention of World War III* as it attacked MGM's good Germans: "The GIs are not getting any help from the imaginary German underground which exists only in the brains of fiction writers and German refugees—but Hollywood still propagates the good Germans." Mainstream American critics' failure to understand or sympathize with the defeated enemy, even from a historical standpoint, was to trouble Zinnemann deeply, and would certainly influence his decision to make *The Search* and *Teresa*.

Zinnemann's predilection for anti-fascist films put him in potentially dangerous company. In 1940–41, conservatives in Washington labeled Hollywood's growing political awareness as warmongering, and politicians initiated the first of many investigations of "anti-American" tendencies in the film industry.[50] Screenwriters, directors, and producers were especially targeted. Many of these filmmakers were eastern-educated elites and European émigrés fleeing fascist persecution. The US government's fear of anti-fascist propaganda was rooted as much in entrenched xenophobia as in its instinctive anti- communism. With the end of the war and the subsequent purge of left-wing Hollywood, the blacklisting of screenwriters like Lillian Hellman, Dashiell Hammett, Alva Bessie, and Dalton Trumbo and the notoriety of films like *The North Star* (1943) and *Song of Russia* (1944), it is puzzling that *The Seventh Cross*—based on a novel by a known communist writer—escaped press condemnation. Zinnemann, Berman, and Deutsch were unscathed, shielded perhaps by the shadow of conservative MGM, Spencer Tracy's star image, and the innocuous studio publicity which de-emphasized its political and historical significance. Contemporary reviewers saw Zinnemann's film as a powerful, if not subversive, revisioning of the anti-Nazi genre, without directly engaging Germany and the anti-fascist movement's communist history. However, its unspoken communist contexts were problematic. George Heisler escapes Nazi Germany, but so did senior KPD party leaders Wilhelm Pieck and Walter Ulbricht, who went into exile in the Soviet Union. In the postwar world order, George Heisler would have been the West's new enemy. In 1951, while making *Teresa*, Zinnemann had trouble obtaining a 16mm print of the film from his close friend Arthur Loew, a studio executive. As Loew wrote, "Regarding your request for 16mm prints of *The Search* and *The Seventh Cross*, I am going to see what I can do for you, but I am not too optimistic about *Seventh Cross*."[51] In 1954, the Austrian government held a film festival featuring key works of anti-fascist cinema and approached Zinnemann for a print of *The Seventh Cross*. He referred them to MGM, who held the copyright, and was later dismayed to learn that they refused to loan or rent a print, even going so far as to deny that they had one.[52] Fifteen years later, the studio took an even more drastic approach to Zinnemann's "political" films.

Hollywood and *Man's Fate*

Man's Fate is the only unproduced film in Zinnemann's career to merit its own section in his autobiography. As he explained in subsequent interviews, André Malraux's book was the "bible" of his generation. Malraux fought against the fascists in Spain; he fought again in the French resistance. His youthful radicalism was well known. There were obvious attractions for Zinnemann to do a film based on the most famous work of an iconic Resistance hero. But if Zinnemann's liberalism remained unchanged from his radical 30s, Malraux's had not. By the late 1960s, the former Resistance hero had become a cog in the conservative de Gaulle government,[53] and, as Zinnemann noted in his clipping files, Malraux had even banned an Armand Gatti play at the National Theatre because he feared it would offend Franco.[54] Nevertheless, when producer Carlo Ponti approached Zinnemann to direct *Man's Fate* in early 1967, he agreed. But he did not want to compromise the material in the face of the West's current stalemate with China. As he wrote Ponti: "Since the book is pro-revolutionary, the film will have to be of the same kind. Is this approach feasible in the face of the present situation and present public opinion, particularly in America?"[55]

Ponti, however, wanted to skip Chiang Kai-Shek and the party's betrayal of the protagonist Kyo and the radical wing of the workers, and focus instead on the doomed romance between Kyo and his European wife, May. The revolution would serve merely as a colorful backdrop. In effect, he wanted to make another Russian romance like *Dr. Zhivago* (1965), and did not want any of Zinnemann's intellectual arguments about the communist revolution scaring American viewers away. Zinnemann canvassed opinion among screenwriters and commented to Ponti that they all "were of the absolute opinion that it would be wrong to confuse the issue and the audience by avoiding to identify the situation or the characters. They felt that it was vital to speak of Chiang Kai-Shek and of the Communists by name. They said that without any prompting on my part. As you know, I agree with this position. At the same time, I am fully aware of the difficulties which this approach would present vis à vis the English-speaking audience. I know that you and I do not agree on this point and of course I fully respect your opinion. However, I find myself unable to share it."[56]

Jean Cau and John McGrath's early treatments both acknowledge that they were treading on difficult political ground in covering the Chinese Revolution.[57] Yet Zinnemann felt they had less understanding of China and Chinese history. At one point, he toyed with the idea of asking playwright Robert Bolt to write the script.[58] Bolt had worked very successfully for him on *Man For All Seasons* and for David Lean on *Dr. Zhivago*. Yet his recent experience with Bolt over a planned biopic of Gandhi had soured when Bolt said "no Indian actors of remotely the required caliber are known," and suggested Tom Courtenay or Marlon Brando for the title role, "though my word," Bolt acknowledged about the latter, "he'd have to diet."[59] Zinnemann's interest in the project had hinged on casting an Indian actor as Gandhi, but by the time he extracted an agreement for an Indian star, he was involved with *Man's Fate*. Similarly with *Man's Fate*, he emphatically did not want a film made exclusively by Europeans about China, and insisted not only that Asian actors play the principal roles, but also persuaded Ponti to hire Han Suyin (*China in the Year 2001*, 1967) to write the script. Suyin was Dr. Elizabeth Comber, the author of the Twentieth Century-Fox box-office hit, *Love Is a Many-Splendored Thing* (1955). Half Chinese, she traveled often to China and was one of the first "Westerners" to return to the country after the 1949 revolution. Her knowledge of twentieth-century China was both academic and personal. As she wrote to MGM story editor Russell Thacher in the spring of 1968, "I . . . wonder how on earth the Americans could possibly back this as a film . . . I see no way of avoiding the fact that the book is deeply committed to the point of view of the Chinese Communist Party. Of course there is nothing that worries me about this. I just wonder about Ponti and O'Brien. However, I shall simply try to tell the story as strongly and accurately as I can, and let the warlords do the worrying. I want to try a slightly new approach to the epic film, nearer to Eisenstein than David Lean, I think, trying to cover a bigger political canvas with more economical scenes—even trying to get near to Eisenstein's early (but banned) ideas on genuine 'montage.' It's too early to know if they'll work yet, but Fred can tell me what he thinks."[60]

Following her interest in Eisensteinian montage and radical politics, Suyin wrote to Zinnemann in March 1968 after a research trip to Hong Kong that she was especially struck with the *"general tone* of the *workers.* This is where I feel that both Lydia Fang and Tsai Chin [location advisors] may have let you and me down. Let me explain this. In this script we are really talking about revolution. And the success of it is due to the fact that the workers and other minor characters who participate are filled with ardor, hope, and energy. In no way are they dumbly following orders. Now from what I have seen of both Lydia and Tsai Chin, I am not at all sure that their defensiveness (and they are both defensive) against the very idea of a people's uprising may not interfere here. But I know from what your reactions were, and from our seeing the film *Four Days in Naples* [1962] and *The Battle for Algiers* [1966] which you mention, that you feel exactly as I do about it."[61] Writing from China many months later, she affirmed that the "film is about the workers of Shanghai and their heroic struggle against the fascist atrocities of those days," and believed that it was crucial for production crew to realize that as many as 80 percent were child workers forced into sixteen-hour workdays and lived in poverty unseen in the West.[62]

Her outline from May 1968 introduced touches that Zinnemann loved—the conflict between revolutionary men and women, a sense of the international military presence in 1927 China, of barriers keeping Chinese out of parts of Shanghai, the racism, and above all, the fierce poverty. Though Malraux's novel focused as much on the Europeans caught up in the Revolution, Zinnemann and Han Suyin were even more invested in visualizing the struggle of ordinary working people and the way the idealistic revolutionary leaders were separated from those they wished to help. To do this, they pushed contrasts in the city. At one point in her script, Suyin describes "beggars along the walls, surmounted by barbed wire, are strewn with what look like heaps, mounds, garbage, covered with newspaper, with rags, they are immobile, and we feel that they are 'things', dead insentient things, but actually they are people, people folded on themselves, in fetal position. Here a head, sunk on its own knees, drawn up, the face buried between the knees. There we see what may be a hand, but we are not sure, it protrudes from rags and clutches at air. A head peers out of a mound of newspapers. It is the head of a little boy; in the crook of his arm against his breast sleeps a baby. These are the beggars, the destitute, the starving peasants from the countryside lying in heaps in the lands of the Chinese City. The effect is one of terror, of filth and misery, but not of loneliness; on the contrary, 10,000 pairs of eyes, of ears are there, everywhere, immobile. Immediately above are hanging heads in cages, along the wall; the hair is matted, the eyelids upturned."[63]

Zinnemann appreciated the ironic timing of the script. The student protests and strikes in France that May struck at the heart of de Gaulle's last administration and Malraux, once the Chinese Revolution's iconic Western chronicler, was now part of the targeted conservative establishment. Zinnemann's script notes are eloquent in their depiction of the themes of imperialism, communism, and revolutionary conflict. While Suyin captured the details, the director saw *Man's Fate* primarily as a story about the "forces of order vs. forces of chaos . . . Power machine must feed on itself and destroy whoever is in the way. No matter how dedicated, brilliant, idealistic: the individual is expendable. Katov craves martyrdom. He is made expendable by his own character . . . Kyo, Katov, Feral's fates are determined by distant power machines which are totally without emotion. It is an administrative problem." Chiang's betrayal of the more radical communist leaders like Kyo and Katov represents an intrinsic ideological hypocrisy common to any large organization. Both he and Suyin worked closely with the scene in which Kyo tells the workers to lay down their arms, support Chiang, and adhere to party policy, knowing too well that Chiang will murder him and his followers. As Zinnemann concluded, "International settlement is an ivory tower," and he planned that his camera would capture the reality of the sacrifices that the warlords, Europeans, and Chiang himself struggled to obliterate from memory.

Yet he worried that in shooting too many documentary "action" sequences of the workers' uprising, he would lose the sense of just what the human condition was. The personal story and the daily lives of ordinary Chinese workers were what truly interested him: "Show how ordinary workers behave when not observed: eat, scratch, yawn, laugh, squat."[64] Zinnemann did not want a lot of huge establishing shots with coordinated extras. Instead, as he wrote a mental note to cinematographer Ted Moore (*A Man For All Seasons*): "Ted: Narrow angle lens—reveal one thing at a time—sharp focus on important thing only. *Not* important *where* people are—*not* important *what* they do—*Important: Why they do it how they feel what they think.*"[65] Similarly, as he noted of Suyin's script, "Imbalances of personal story vs. documentary—too much documentary, not enough personal story? In any event it is now neither fish nor fowl—neither *Battle for Algiers* nor *FHTE* [*From Here to Eternity*]. What to do? Drop some documentary and action stuff."[66] For Zinnemann, one problem with the established form of political documentary was it not only lost the personal story of individuals, but its massive establishing shots and "objective" chronicling of key events unconsciously mirrored the hegemonic ideologies and manipulative historicism of the mainstream. He wrote: "Picture should not be made as an epic in the grand scale with thousands of extras, huge locations, etc. It should be a tightly knit story of a group of characters, told from their point of view, shot with them almost always present in CUs in the foreground. All the battles, etc. should be a sort of backstory, partly seen through lowered shutters etc. The interest should center on protagonists, *not* on the action."[67]

Zinnemann was trained in the Hollywood tradition and he wanted "a rooting interest" or a hero. He was not ambivalent about heroizing the communist radicals. As he noted, "We must do everything we can to get all possible sympathy for Kyo, Katov, May." While Kyo and Katov had the potential to be the first complex communist activists in a major Hollywood production with whom both Eastern and Western audiences could identify, both Zinnemann and Suyin saw May as an equally powerful heroine. When he first read Suyin's script, he had penciled "Vanessa—Too Late?" in the margins beside her character description, already seeing Vanessa Redgrave's own political identity and persona melding with May.[68] Though Redgrave turned out to be busy with *Isadora* (1968) and *Oh! What a Lovely War* (1969), she would play Julia, Zinnemann's committed socialist leader, some eight years later. Although at the end of Malraux's novel, May is the one radical left alive, and plans to remain in China to spread the true revolution after her husband Kyo's death, she was a marginal figure to Malraux. The author had confessed to Zinnemann in a meeting that "when Eisenstein was planning to make *Man's Fate* he was going to eliminate both women." Zinnemann wrote, "Malraux evidently has no objection to drastic changes because he feels that a film and a novel are two different things. I said that to my mind it would be most important to try and build up Kyo and May, rather than to eliminate them."[69] For Zinnemann and Suyin, women were not expendable in histories of resistance. He was particularly happy with Suyin as screenwriter, not only because of her background and knowledge of Chinese history and society, but also because "it is already evident that as a woman she will get an infinitely better grip on the story of May, Kyo, Valerie, etc., than almost any man could."[70] Suyin wrote to Zinnemann: "I also feel that May is having a raw deal; and it is only when I have 'finished' with the book that I shall be able to re-visualize her. Malraux is very compelling in his making May an unpleasant rather than a fine character."[71]

He disliked some versions of the script in which "May is out of the picture for long stretches—too long,"[72] and in his notes he commented that she needed more context: "May . . . she resents being treated as though she were in a doll's house—she must be aware of what's going on—she must have some political sense."[73] Han Suyin was equally drawn to May, not because she represented a sexual break from all of the masculine politics, but because she was a thinking, passionate woman who articulated the conflict between politically minded modern women and men. As she wrote to Zinnemann, "I don't think the world as a whole is aware of the dynamo of energy which is woman; because so much of this energy is frittered away into menial tasks, time consuming, but not emotionally satisfying or libido satisfying." She hoped May would represent a culture shock as dramatic as Zinnemann's portrait of the Chinese Revolution.

As with all his personally controlled projects, Zinnemann wanted authentic actors and locations. Once he obtained "complete artistic control" from Ponti (something he had to fight for and which David Lean did not receive on *Dr. Zhivago*),[74] he arranged Japanese and Chinese actors to audition for the roles of Chen and Kyo. Hiring Eiji Okada (who was best known for his leading role in *Hiroshima, Mon Amour*, 1959), as Kyo, and Juzo Itami (who appeared in *55 Days at Peking*, 1963, and *Lord Jim*, 1965), as the assassin Chen, caused far less difficulty than his efforts to shoot the film in China. To Zinnemann's credit, he managed to convince the US State Department that he needed a research visit to China. As he wrote William Macomber in January 1968, he wanted to "remain true to the spirit of the novel and to present it without undue distortion. We believe that today's film public expects a degree of authenticity. It would be difficult to make an acceptable film today on the lines of, say, Pearl Buck's *The Good Earth* with Paul Muni and Luise Rainer playing Chinese peasants and the greater part of the production being shot in the interior of a great but remote sound stage."[75] Macomber granted his request, but guessed that the Chinese government would refuse to grant him a visa. It did refuse, even when André Malraux intervened on his behalf.[76] Suyin nevertheless remained hopeful that the Chinese would assist Zinnemann, but in August 1968, MGM ruined their attempt at public relations by linking *Man's Fate*'s shoot in Singapore with Twentieth Century-Fox's anti-communist, Chinese spy film starring Gregory Peck, *The Chairman*. Suyin fumed, "If only MGM spokesmen could shut up, all might turn out well, here (Penang) or in Singapore."[77] Zinnemann contented himself with locations in Kuala Lumpur and Singapore and read his screenwriter's letters as she visited

FIG. 17 The first and last day of shooting: on the set of *Man's Fate*, November 1969, AMPAS.

China again throughout the spring of 1969. As Zinnemann developed casting and locations, Suyin wrote encouraging, carefully worded letters to him from Beijing: "I know you are trying to make a really magnificent and true film about the Chinese Revolution and it is important that all should be true and exact."[78] Even then, she hoped the censors reading her letters would change their minds about cooperating with Zinnemann. Things were proceeding well that fall. The $10 million film was in rehearsal,[79] MGM's publicity department had commiteed no new faux pas, and cast and crew, including Peter Finch, David Niven, Max von Sydow, and Liv Ullmann, were literally ready for the first day of shooting (fig. 17), when MGM canceled the production and held Zinnemann responsible for some accrued production costs.[80] He was appalled, but gamely held a party for cast and crew, optimistically saying they would reunite in a month or so when the studio budget issues were fixed. When things didn't improve and MGM attempted to make him liable for production costs, he sued the studio. As he wrote to Malraux, "I will fight this battle alone. I must say that it doesn't worry me particularly . . . In my opinion this individual case, sad as it is, involves much more than *Man's Fate*. It is a challenge to all people who work in films: for, if MGM's position is not tested in the courts or if it is upheld in law, the industry will never be the same again."[81] MGM settled. Zinnemann's antipathy toward corporate heads deepened. It was perhaps not an accident that his next film imagined a hero who would take on two governments—and almost succeed.

Killing De Gaulle: A British Production

Fred Zinnemann and his wife, Renée, left Hollywood for London in 1959 after he completed *The Nun's Story*. In between film projects in Australia, Singapore, France, and Vienna, it was home until his death in 1997. Although he maintained links with Columbia Pictures in the 1960s, the Academy Award-winning *A Man For All Seasons* was widely publicized as his personally produced production and a "British" film.[82] *Man's Fate*, though aborted by MGM in late 1969, was widely covered in the trade papers as an international production. *The Day of the Jackal* was an important "international" film for a number of reasons. A British-French coproduction produced mainly in London and Paris by David Deutsch and John Woolf, it was also the first Anglo-French coproduction made under the Common Market (Woolf's adaptation of another Forsyth bestseller, *The Odessa File* (1974), which Zinnemann turned down, was the first Anglo-German coproduction). The fact that *The Day of the Jackal* concerned the attempted assassination of de Gaulle was an ironic twist; de Gaulle had been instrumental in blocking British membership in the Common Market in the sixties.[83] De Gaulle may have been safely dead since 1970, but there were many in the United Kingdom who, like Winston Churchill, found the "Cross of Lorraine" the hardest cross to bear.

Many film critics were startled and some even shocked that Fred Zinnemann, the ultimate director of conscience pictures and "principles," would make an apparently amoral film about a glamorous assassin's attempt to kill Resistance icon and French president Charles de Gaulle.[84] As *Time*'s book reviewer had fretted in 1971, "Readers do, inevitably, identify with the assassin, and what he has briefly in his telescopic sights is a heroic and honored chief of state." He worried what would come next— "*Tell Them Willy Brandt Was Here?*"[85] Reviewers were disturbed that on-screen and in interviews, Zinnemann did not condemn the OAS (Organisation de l'armée secrete) or endorse de Gaulle. Of course, it was unthinkable that he would sympathize with the killer or advocate the OAS against the French establishment.[86] Or was it? Was *The Day of the Jackal* all that different from Zinnemann's other films about the Resistance and outsiders battling corrupt and violent systems? In 1944, he had shown that all Germans weren't monsters, and that anti-fascist resistance may have started in Germany. Although he had failed to bring ex-Loyalist pilot-turned-establishment minister André Malraux's revolutionary novel to the screen, Malraux was not the only Resistance hero of his generation accused of betraying his past principles. In the 1950s and '60s, there were few men more hated than Charles de Gaulle. Elected because of his promise to keep Algeria French, he almost immediately reversed his policy, incurring the wrath of the army and French citizens of Algeria. The British had no love for him either. A man who fought the war from a comfortable distance in London, he shaped public remembrance of the Resistance as predominantly French, while editing the participation of French communists and women. Even historians as admiring of the general as Régis Debray have acknowledged that he was, for many, an "archaic, ungrateful xenophobe, authoritarian, and vaguely fascist."[87] Though the OAS was certainly a right-wing nationalist movement, formed in Franco's Spain, de Gaulle and much of France were nearly as conservative. To a certain extent, *The Day of the Jackal*'s French political canvas was a study in political relativism. Zinnemann's own attitudes toward France were equally complicated. While he had trained as a cameraman in Paris, he couldn't work in France as a foreigner. Anti-Semitism was rife. Throughout his Hollywood career, French film critics were ambivalent and—in the case of *Cahiers du cinéma*—even hostile to his work.

It was characteristic of Zinnemann that in making a film featuring one of the Second World War's iconic heroes, he would focus not on the war against the Nazis, but on the postwar clash over Algerian independence. In this struggle, the members of the OAS were the hunted resisters, and de Gaulle was the establishment chief protected by the thuggish Action Service. Though author and initial screenwriter Frederick Forsyth had covered de Gaulle over many years as a reporter and was not about to criticize the leader in print, Zinnemann's film was very obviously focused on the perspective of the OAS and the enigmatic persona of the Jackal (Edward Fox). Rather than being a stylish thriller and thus an anomaly in the Zinnemann oeuvre, *The Day of the Jackal* is a startling film about political assassination and resistance in the post-national world. The Jackal's easy ability to pass as a Frenchman, Dane, or an Englishman; to produce false documents of nationality; and to cross borders unrecognized reflected the director's global interests and discomfort with nationalism. In the Jackal's attempt to thwart two major governments alone, the director's long exploration of the individual versus the machine found full expression.

The film opens with the Algérie Française theme of four quick drumbeats followed by one longer beat—telegraphically four dots and one dash—deliberately reminiscent of the wartime three dots and one dash of "V for Victory." The proponents of a French Algeria used the wartime Resistance code against de Gaulle, casting the establishment in the role of Nazi occupiers and collaborators. The Cross of Lorraine fades in and out as the voice of BBC Europe's reporter begins: "August 1962 was a stormy time for France. Many people felt that the President, Charles de Gaulle, had betrayed the country by giving independence to Algeria. Extremists, mostly from the army, swore to kill him in revenge. They banded together and called themselves the OAS." The narrator's tone—tough, terse, and matter-of-fact—nevertheless emphasizes the word "betrayed." The first shot appears showing de Gaulle's image hanging from the center of the "O" of a graffiti "OAS—Algérie Française," which forms the opening title of the film. The camera follows a lone motorcyclist as he speeds to the Elysée Palace. When the officials leave after a late meeting, Zinnemann shoots them passing through the gates from above in a remarkable assassin's-eye-view shot. This is the first of many such shots in the film which survey the political landscapes as the Jackal or another assassin might: high-angle shots from 50 to 150 yards away. Over the next few minutes, Zinnemann's camera follows the motorcyclist as he shadows the president's car and alerts his OAS conspirators. The director's credit is superimposed over the shots of the assassin tracking the president's car, accompanied by the repeated music cue of the Algérie Française. Zinnemann also planned the assassination sequence from the perspective of the assassins as they nervously wait for the black Citroen. This sequence deviates completely from Frederick Forsyth's original script, which opens with shots of de Gaulle's ministers and de Gaulle's departure, and then picks up the motorcyclist en route.[88] Bastien-Thiry's death by firing squad (the last execution in France) was to have been followed by Zinnemann's directorial credit—almost a directorial endorsement. Instead, Kenneth Ross and Zinnemann's revised script focuses on the motorcyclist rather than the establishment,[89] and Zinnemann's shots emphasize a collusion of points of view between the filmmaker and the OAS. As for the very few shots of Adrien Cayla-Legrand's Charles de Gaulle, Zinnemann wanted no warm and rosy close-ups: "It seemed to me that the colder the tone, the better the likeness to the General."[90]

Quickly following Bastien-Thiry's execution, in the Fort D'Ivry, the same BBC narrator smugly predicts the end of the OAS. His tone on the radio is starkly different from the foreword, a pro-de Gaulle media tone which praises the French security forces. Eric Porter's Rodin switches it off abruptly, already planning to use a foreigner to kill de Gaulle. His decision to abandon the idea of a French assassin is a masterstroke, and the Jackal will concur, giving an opinion of French nationalism that could have doubled for the "loyalty" of the French wartime resistance: "Your organization is so riddled with informers that nothing you decide is a secret for very long." The OAS's decision to hire internationally also strikes at the heart of de Gaulle's highly publicized image as the embodiment of the French nation. But Zinnemann's decision to hire a British actor to play the Jackal contained another pointed irony, and certainly resonated with the British dislike of de Gaulle and the country's only half-joking assessment of foreigners: "The wogs start at Calais."[91] *The Day of the Jackal*'s "foreigner" was not played by a tough assassin in dark glasses, as Forsyth had planned in his script,[92] but a genial, smiling, and impeccably dressed upper-class Englishman (more in line with Forsyth's original characterization in the novel).[93] Edward Fox was then more or less unknown, save for his performance in Joseph Losey's *The Go-Between* (1971), but Zinnemann immediately recognized his intense charisma. He did not want a thug or a tall, dark, and steely assassin. Instead, his preference being for someone comparatively ordinary and disarming, Zinnemann decided him to cast against the traditional Hollywood type, and made an instant star out of Fox.[94] The two worked brilliantly on both a professional and personal level; years later, Fox and his wife, the actress Joanna David, named their son "Freddie" after Zinnemann.

Zinnemann also refused to make Rodin (Eric Porter) into a terrifying fanatic. In contrast to earlier versions of the script by both Forsyth and Ross, which had Rodin and his two colleagues Montclair and Casson rail about "traitors" and "wogs,"[95] Porter's spin for the Jackal is reasoned and intelligent. As he explains the OAS's raison d'être ("We are not terrorists, you understand. We are patriots"), Zinnemann positioned his camera at Casson's elbow, lining up with the OAS top brass. When the Jackal responds coolly, dismissing any patriotic pretentions, "So, you want to get rid of him," the camera shares Rodin's surprise, positioned behind his shoulder, looking at the Jackal seated in a long shot. Similarly, when Victor Wolenski (Jean Martin) is kidnapped by Action Service in Italy (unlike Forsyth's novel and script, which had had the ex-Legionnaire legally picked up at a French airport), Zinnemann follows ahead of Wolenski, showing the viciousness of the attack. He quickly cut to the interrogation

FIG. 18 Star assassin at work: Edward Fox in *The Day of the Jackal*, United Artists.

room, where a single light illuminates the room. Again, Zinnemann places his camera with Victor, stripped, cringing, and beaten, as he faces a row of Action Service interrogators. "Tell us, Victor," the leader says (Vernon Dobtcheff), and the audience effectively waits with Victor for the torture of the electric shocks. Later, as sound experts go over the dead man's testimony in a white, impersonal office, even the man listening on headphones reacts in angry dismay to the screams, "What the hell did they do to the bastard?" Zinnemann has shown us what happened, up close, yet when the OAS attacks de Gaulle, we never get inside the Citroen to see the personal impact of the attack on the President and Madame de Gaulle.

Much of Zinnemann's most intriguing material focused on the Jackal's research for his assassination. We see him in the British Library, as a tourist in Paris, hunting for the best locations (like Zinnemann and production assistant Julien Derode), in Genoa arranging for documents and guns. We see the Jackal at home, making his birth certificate late at night and reading up on de Gaulle (the books on his coffee table were very likely read by Derode and Zinnemann for their own research; fig. 18); we see him chatting up a pretty chemist's assistant, looking for hair dye; we see him in the English countryside, looking at gravestones in a churchyard. In effect, we see him "out of the office," intent on seemingly everyday tasks which have a dual significance. The men sworn to find and kill him around the table at the Minister of the Interior's office are not so accessible. They are known only in their official capacity—with two exceptions. St. Clair (Barrie Ingham), the de Gaulle fanatic, is shown with his mistress, the OAS operative (Olga Georges-Picot). Commissioner Claude Lebel (Zinnemann veteran Michael Lonsdale), the ordinary, put-upon detective, is seen at several points during the investigation, fighting not only the Jackal but also his government colleagues' class-based distain for an ordinary detective with crumpled clothes. Aside from Zinnemann's initial sympathetic treatment of the OAS and his detailed focus on the Jackal's near-perfect plan, Zinnemann's sympathy was with the little working-class cogs in the administrative networks of government.[96]

Forsyth's decision to stage the Jackal's assassination attempt at the Resistance commemorations on August 25 embodied an irony that appealed to Zinnemann. He bracketed his copy of the novel: "There was something about this square, with the bulk of the Gare Montparnasse on its southern side, full of memories for the Parisians of the war generation, that caused the assassin to stop."[97] Practically speaking, it was where de Gaulle could always be expected to appear each year, like clockwork. Zinnemann showed facets of the Resistance history and its future importance to the assassination: the forger's mysterious comment about a disabled Resistance veteran's card ("The other one—I don't think I've ever seen what they look like—let alone copy it"); the gray wig and advice about swallowing cordite to simulate illness and age; the Jackal's concentration on the war medals in the flea market; his long reconnaissance at the renamed square; the drumroll for the national anthem which brings the Jackal/Resistance veteran to his feet with ironic solemnity. Yet Zinnemann did not have the Jackal shoot de Gaulle while he stood at attention for the Marseillaise. However fitting (and practical) this may have been for the OAS who saw de Gaulle as a traitor, Zinnemann instead staged the Jackal's shot at the moment when he awards a medal to a long-neglected Resistance fighter. In this symbolic moment tied to de Gaulle's arrogation as head of the Resistance, de Gaulle was to have fallen. Ironically, he modeled the Jackal's costume on a Henri Cartier-Bresson photograph of a highly decorated older résistante at an earlier Liberation Day ceremony.[98] Only six women were decorated with the Médaille de la Résistance, and many historians have drawn attention to de Gaulle's exclusion of key female leaders. Fox's makeup was based on a news photo Zinnemann kept of Jean Gabin as he left actor Fernandel's funeral.[99] Giving the aging face of 1930s Popular Front cinema to de Gaulle's potential assassin adds yet another layer of political irony to the film. Zinnemann also bracketed sequences in the novel where characters allude to Action Service as "the French Gestapo" and compare the current French government with the Nazis in their violation of human rights.[100]

Zinnemann's ambivalence toward French nationalism and de Gaulle was even more pointed in his casting decisions. Despite using extensive French locations and several prominent French actors, he cast British actors in the majority of the roles (Ingham, Derek Jacobi, Alan Badel,

Maurice Denham, and Samuel West all played French officials) and shot the whole film in English. Though an admirer of Pontecorvo's bilingual *Battle for Algiers* (1966)—he hired Jean Martin, one of its stars, to play ex-Legionnaire Victor Wolenski—Zinnemann made a conscious decision to make a predominantly British film about the assassination attempt. He made a star out of his British-born Jackal. Even Rodin was played by British television star Eric Porter (*The Forsyte Saga*, 1969). Aside from the patient, low-key performance from the unassuming Michael Lonsdale, it was Tony Britton's dogged Inspector Thomas, with his working-class Northern accent and humor that drew Zinnemann's greatest attention in the script and film, and who remains one of the most memorable characters.

Zinnemann's hunt for locations occurred at an interesting time for commemoration of the French resistance. The ceremonies in August had long taken place under the façade of the Gare Montparnasse, but the old building had been demolished and a new, unpopular station building sat on the square. As Julien Derode wrote to Zinnemann: "Most unfortunately for us, I have been surprised to hear that, although there is no relationship between the Gare Montparnasse and the surrender of the Germans, the ceremony on August 25th does not take place there any more as the commemorating monument of the Liberation of Paris disappeared with the pulling down of the former station, as it was inside it. They will probably erect a new monument, but it is not known when yet."[101] As Derode pointed out, the French were not really invested in the liberation celebrations so it would be ineffective to shoot documentary footage: "From our investigations with the Hôtel de Ville and the Ministères Anciens Combattants, it appears that, except for 1964 when it was the 20th anniversary, and for 1969 being the 25th anniversary, there have been very small ceremonies lately, and their importance is decreasing every year. It seems that they now only organize a symbolic ceremony, at all the different spots, with a few officials, but not very important personalities of the Government (except at the Hôtel de Ville where one Minister usually attends), no military parades, and no large crowds."[102] He concluded, "I doubt that we can shoot any interesting material next August." They ended up shooting locations for the final assassination attempt on Bastille Day.

The Day of the Jackal performed well everywhere in Europe—except in France.[103] Though André Malraux was invited to a special screening and was said to love the film, by and large French citizens did not go to see it. Whether they resented a predominantly British film about Le Grand Charles's near-assassination or were upset that he lived through it is uncertain. But France carefully guarded its myth of the Resistance, and many critics drew attention to the fact that Zinnemann showed the French police breaking international law and torturing suspects.[104] Censors forced Alain Resnais to cut a scene from *Night and Fog* (1955) showing French policemen collaborating in the notorious deportation of French Jews at the Vélodrôme d'Hiver in Paris. Marcel Ophüls's *The Sorrow and The Pity* (1970), which revealed widespread French collaboration with the Nazis, was made for West German television, and was banned in France for at least a decade. Zinnemann had arranged to cut *The Day of the Jackal*'s opening voice-over because the information was already familiar to French audiences; possibly the OAS music cue and the opening image of a hanging de Gaulle were too much for conservative film audiences intent on protecting their Resistance heritage from "foreigners."[105] They may well have agreed with *Variety*, who noted, this "quasi-documentary" has "a predominantly British feel to the film (in dialogue, dialect, idiom, manner, and form), underlined pointedly by occasional story cuts to England which make virtually no cultural contrast, that the film almost loses its French flavor."[106]

Yet the film grossed impressively worldwide, and film critics in Britain and, to a lesser extent, the United States responded to Zinnemann's first "thriller" since *High Noon*.[107] Zinnemann may well have agreed with the *High Noon* connection. In his production notes for the film, he noted frequent close-ups of clocks to intensify the Jackal and Lebel's contrasting efforts.[108] Yet while the Jackal, like Will Kane, is the obvious focus of the film narrative, critics were uncomfortable seeing a political assassin as a blond, glamorous film star and reacted angrily in the US to the prominent sight of President Kennedy on a magazine cover in the gunsmith's offices. As Zinnemann recognized, "the assassin is the world's outlaw," but by 1973 the "law" was no longer represented by Will Kane. That outlaw was enormously attractive—even heroic. When Zinnemann read Forsyth's first treatment, he scrawled in the margins next to the description of Bastien-Thiry's death by firing squad, *"Bonnie and Clyde,"* seeing the OAS leader (played by the stunning Jean Sorel) as another young and dashing outlaw.[109] Yet while evil and menace may be more definitive in the nineteenth-century Western, Zinnemann's positioning of the Jackal as the film's protagonist in 1960s Europe drew an unusual parallel with the nature of society's "hired guns" in a postwar economy of power. *Variety* reasoned, "European and Asiatic audiences, whose older national cultures are replete with periodic incidents of scandal, intrigue, and subversion, may comprise the more popular commercial centers. The US, now in the midst of one of its rare exposed political intrigues, is another situation which (it is to be noted again), the book's popularity may serve to mitigate."[110] Edward Fox put it very well in an interview: "It's a much better part than James Bond. Bond is a known quantity. You can predict what he will do in any situation. This man is totally unpredictable. Not only do you not know what he will do . . . you never know where he is."[111] He could not belong to one nation or ideology. Yet Zinnemann was demonstrably fascinated with the Jackal and it intensified in the final stages. In his editing notes, he wrote, "Stay with Jackal for longer periods?" and "Too much de Gaulle in and after Nôtre Dame, Champs Elysées, Arc de Triomphe, Rennes."[112] He had second thoughts about the abruptness of the Jackal's death, and was reminded of the antiheroism in Manuel Artigas's (Gregory Peck) death in *Behold a Pale Horse*. The Jackal turned out to be a "resistance" hero not unlike the anarchist leader Artigas. Coming out of the past to haunt France's constructed legacy of national unity, wearing the Resistance costume, someone who appeared aged and crippled could strike, and, as Zinnemann slyly commented in an interview, "The fact that he challenges single-handedly the enormous bureaucracy of the French government and almost gets away with it," was, as he put it with disarming simplicity, very "cinematic."[113]

CHAPTER TWO

Surviving Voices and the Search for Europe

"During all the time when we were obstinately and silently serving our country, we never lost sight of an idea and a hope, forever present in us—the idea and hope of Europe. To be sure, we have not mentioned Europe for five years. But this is because you talked too much of it. And then, too, we were not speaking the same language; our Europe is not yours."
—**Albert Camus**, 1944[1]

"I knew what was happening in those years, but it was not quite clear to me how it would develop. I left Vienna—not for political reasons—but because I had some wild ideas about becoming a film director. Sometimes I wonder what would have happened to me if I had stayed—chances are that I would have ended up in Auschwitz, as did practically my whole family. And to yourself it means that you feel guilty about being alive . . . I can make films about it, yes, but I do not get rid of the ghosts—so I am not a happy man."
—**Fred Zinnemann**, 1978[2]

When Fred Zinnemann finished *The Seventh Cross* in 1943, his position at MGM was still uncertain. However, Spencer Tracy enjoyed working with him, and when the strong reviews began to appear in the trade papers, Zinnemann was assigned other A-feature projects seemingly at random. A director at MGM was expected to complete any project without complaint. But Zinnemann knew the particular type of motion pictures he wanted to make. They were not films like *Little Mister Jim* (1946) and *My Brother Talks to Horses* (1947), and several rejected scripts later, he voluntarily went on suspension.[3] Executive Eddie Mannix had never seen anything like him.

Zinnemann was not one to discuss personal concerns with others. Yet his dedication to films about war and resistance to fascism was intensely personal. For several years prior to the war, he had tried to persuade his parents to leave Vienna and join him and his younger brother George in America (one of his early short films, *Forbidden Passage*, 1940), documents the tragic attempts of one Austrian refugee to join his family in America under the current immigration schemes). The Zinnemanns initially refused to leave Europe, but finally agreed to take passage on a Spanish ship once their US visas arrived. The visas arrived, but they did not. Much of George Zinnemann's V-Mail correspondence is caught up in their efforts to locate their parents. When Fred Zinnemann contacted the State Department in 1945, he was sent almost inhumanly bureaucratic replies advising him to "try telephoning Poland."[4] Their son was not to know about their fates until after the war when he was making *The Search*.[5] He never spoke about his parents or the deaths of his other Zinnemann relatives, but more and more, he retreated to his study on Mayberry Road, closed the door, and concentrated on his films.

UNRRA and Child Survivors

But in 1944 he still did not know whether his parents were dead or alive. Like millions of European Jews, Roma, members of political resistance groups, communists, and homosexuals, following the Allied liberation they were increasingly classified as "displaced persons" or "DPs." An estimated 12 million Europeans were displaced as internees and forced laborers during the war, and the crisis escalated as Germany and Poland's boundaries were redrawn to accommodate Soviet demands.[6] The Supreme Headquarters of the Allied Expeditionary Force (SHAEF) controlled the repatriation process and in 1945 gave control of the humanitarian aspects of displaced persons to the newly created United Nations Relief and Rehabilitation Administration (UNRRA). SHAEF and UNRRA had a titanic task, but in the spring and summer of 1945, the organizations repatriated between 30,000 and 100,000 people per day, including thousands of German POWs.[7] But most of the repatriates were French, Russian, Polish, Belgian, and Dutch. There were over 250 repatriation centers in the American zone alone.[8] Though SHAEF and UNRRA processed staggering numbers of people, unrepatriable DPs would remain in camps in Germany until the fifties. Most were from Eastern Europe, and until the creation of Israel in 1948, many were Jewish.[9]

Many of the DPs were children. The Red Cross estimated that 13 million European children had lost parents, and within days of the war's end, UNRRA was in charge of over 50,000 displaced children.[10] While over 1.5 million Jewish children were murdered in the concentration camps, thousands of babies were abducted for Germanization as *lebensborn*, and those younger than five were kidnapped for forced labor, hostages, and medical experiments. Older children were often forced recruits for the SS. By 1946, over 200,000 queries for lost children were received by Polish relief organizations alone.[11] Lucky ones, including a young Audrey Hepburn, worked for the Resistance or the partisans, and managed to stay in contact with a family member or protector. And against the odds, once UNRRA organized child-search teams in 1946–47, over 15,000 children were reunited with their families. As time passed, however, the number of traced children declined to under 2,000 in 1948 despite over 40,000 new tracing requests.[12] For the others, children's homes, including UNRRA's twenty-five children's centers in the British, American, and French zones of Germany, became home before repatriation, adoption, or one-way voyages to Palestine.

Zinnemann concealed his long-held fears over his family's safety and began collecting copies of major articles about the Nazis' treatment of civilians and the Final Solution. The American press coverage of the Nuremberg trials slowly revealed the horrifying details of the Holocaust, and Zinnemann kept clippings of some of the more sickening reports, including the trial of Auschwitz camp commander Rudolf Höss, who blandly corrected a prosecutor asking him how it felt to murder 4 million people: "It was only 2 million."[13] When the surviving perpetrators of the Lidice massacre were tried in Czechoslovakia, Zinnemann scissored the article covering the trial in which sixteen Czech mothers faced the men who were responsible for the deaths of their children.[14] The report noted that following the destruction of the town and the murder of all male inhabitants in June 1942, "the Gestapo then scattered 104 children to various parts of Europe and that most of them never were found or returned." Lidice returned to the headlines as fifteen of the children, including one family of two sisters and a brother, were located in Germany and Prague by child-search teams.[15] Zinnemann kept another article by UNRRA's Ruth S. Fede, who described the experiences of 276 Jewish youngsters near Mannheim.[16] Hadassan Rosen was shot and left for dead; Mosheh Tompkin watched his mother die; and Daniel Burstein, son of the well known Yiddish author, jumped from the train taking him to Auschwitz. Zinnemann would later visit this center. He also kept one unmarked press clipping from a Nuremberg paper quoting Isray Biesky, a Polish journalist and survivor of Auschwitz, who stated that children "were thrown alive into the fires" of the crematorium when the Nazis ran out of gas.[17]

There were numerous articles in the mainstream American press about Europe's murdered, kidnapped, abused, and starving children; popular writer I. A. R. Wylie wrote of horrific medical experiments carried out on children by Nazi "doctors" in the *Ladies' Home Journal*, and international conferences in Zurich and Geneva in 1945–46 addressed the plight of child victims.[18] But as Dorothy Macardle would point out in her exhaustive study, *Europe's Children*, the American public tried to shelter itself by ignoring or denying many of the appalling stories. By 1946, relief workers and humanitarians were less concerned with persuading comfortable Americans to believe the horrors of the Holocaust than in getting children enough food, milk, and clothing to survive the winter. UNRRA would close by the summer of 1947, and the International Refugee Organization (IRO) and UNICEF would take over, but in its early stages UNICEF nearly collapsed due to lack of funds and private donations.[19]

As both Macardle and historian Mark Wyman document, European nations such as Denmark, Sweden, the Netherlands, and Great Britain sent swift and effective relief to stricken countries Greece, Italy, France, Austria, and Czechoslovakia, as well as facilitating emigration of DP children and adults. Despite contributing to UNRRA, the US was slow to admit DPs, and in the first few years after the war, was still using the restrictive and racist laws instituted in the 1920s which permitted only miniscule numbers of Southern and Eastern Europeans to immigrate.[20] Compared with European nations and Canada, the US was also initially less effective with private charitable donations. The American public needed to become involved in Europe's regeneration. American UN worker Kathryn Hulme (who would later work with Zinnemann on *The Nun's Story*, 1959) noted that in 1946 and 1947, increasing numbers of DP workers and families left for Belgium, Canada, Great Britain, Holland, France, Venezuela, Australia, and many other nations "until at last there would seem to be no place on earth to which those tread marks did not point, except to the United States of America."[21] Hulme was aware of how the US Army viewed the DPs with suspicion and disdain; behind the occupying army's attitude was the entrenched xenophobia of the middle-class American public.

During the war, American photojournalist Thérèse Bonney published a book on displaced children, which chronicled the deprivation of French, British, Finnish, and Spanish girls and boys.[22] Bonney was influenced by the work of Jacob Riis and Lewis Hine, whose photographs of America's poor, working, maimed, and homeless children made headlines and fueled progressive legislation to end child labor decades before.[23] Yet however moving Bonney's photographs were, her subjects were the most fortunate of the hordes of displaced children, and it was apparent that the images were marketed for a softhearted but largely anti-Semitic middle-class American public. The cover of Bonney's book showed a French mother holding her exhausted daughter, whose long blond hair catches the light as it hangs from her shoulders. Most images were of individual or small groups of children in rags, on refugee trains, or hiding in bomb shelters. The most unsettling images of starving young camp survivors were placed at the back of the book, long after the plucky, big-eyed charmers would have captivated a casual American viewer. Many were captivated. Bonney made a lot of friends in SHAEF who recognized the value of her book as a public relations tool for galvanizing refugee aid. Zinnemann immediately saw the cinematic potential of Bonney's material, and despite the book's somewhat sanitized images, appreciated its final textual challenge to the reader: "The danger is so near—how can we ignore it?"

Polish-born Lazar Wechsler, head of the Swiss-based Praesens Films, also saw Bonney's book, and was aware of the impact the images could have on a generous American public. Praesens's production facilities were unaffected by the war, and Wechsler realized that Germany's defeat would enable him to dominate film production in Central Europe. He began by raising Praesens's profile in the US, and planned a major feature film about Europe's children and the positive influence America could have in easing their plight. He found one of Bonney's photographs particularly arresting. It shows a French schoolgirl of perhaps nine or ten carrying a bedroll, rucksack, and doll in her arms as she and her mother are sent to an unknown destination after the fall of France. Bonney writes, "They tried so hard to save what they loved if only—a doll."

Marie-Louise (1945) narrated a refugee child's desperate attempt to protect her little brother and keep a treasured toy with her during her ordeal. Appearing in the US in November 1945, it was America's first film import from continental Europe since the war began and critics applauded the film for being "direct and simple in its graphic assembly of details expressing the heartrending pathos of the impact of war upon a child."[24] It was refreshingly free of Hollywood heroism and melodrama. Richard Schweizer went on to win an Academy Award for his original screenplay. Yet the film only played in art-house cinemas in big cities and had little impact beyond the awards ceremony. European cinemas were still re-establishing themselves, and aside from the occasional British prestige film (*Henry V*, 1945), Americans saw only films produced in Hollywood. Wechsler was ambitious and imagined a film that could bridge both American and European audiences. His next film, *The Last Chance* (1945), told of a desperate escape of two prisoners of war—one American and one Italian—and chronicled their growing friendship. It was another partially successful attempt by Wechsler to imagine America within the European community. Studio heads in Hollywood now recognized Wechsler's name and Praesens Films, yet the feature had limited US distribution.

Wechsler wanted to develop not only America's interest in Europe's postwar plight but also the financial connection between his small studio and Hollywood. To that end, he invited American writer Betty Smith (*A Tree Grows in Brooklyn*, Twentieth Century-Fox, 1945) to write treatments for him.[25] But he was fighting a difficult battle in 1945. Only a handful of Hollywood's feature films had been shot in Europe (all before 1939), and the studios were extremely cautious about bankrolling films or renting their employees to European studios. By August 1945, of all Hollywood's major filmmakers, only Billy Wilder had returned to Germany to assess the state of the German film industry and to work in the "re-education" of German citizens by editing and directing films like *Die Todesmühlen* (*The Death Mills*, 1945). But instead of telling his American bosses in the army's Division of Psychological Warfare that Germans were again making films at DEFA and in the western zones, he argued that the film industry in Germany was ripe for Hollywood conquest.[26] As he argued, no film yet exists in "our program of re-educating the German people." He continued, "Now if there was an entertainment film with Rita Hayworth or Ingrid Bergman or Gary Cooper, in Technicolor if you wish, and with a love story—only with a very special love story, cleverly devised to sell us a few ideological items—such a film would provide us with a superior piece of propaganda; they would stand in long lines to buy, and once they bought it, it would stick. Unfortunately, no such film exists yet. It must be made. I want to make it."[27]

Wechsler was wary of Hollywood types like Wilder. The Swiss producer wanted a Hollywood name and some Hollywood money attached to his film, but didn't want to be swallowed up as a subsidiary bent on the re-education of Europe and the glorification of America. When Wechsler saw *The Seventh Cross*, he knew he had found his director for the film on Europe's children. Zinnemann, languishing in suspension after making *My Brother Talks to Horses* with the popular American child star Jackie Jenkins, jumped at the chance. They met in Hollywood in late 1945, and though Zinnemann enthusiastically agreed, he stipulated that he would have to do substantial research in Europe, influence the script, and control the final product. He also warned Wechsler that MGM had to release him for the project.[28] Wechsler tried, but for many months in 1945 and 1946 the studio refused. His close friend and agent Abe Lastfogel and Loew's president Arthur Loew did their best to negotiate something before he was fired. Zinnemann, increasingly scornful of the postwar Hollywood product, made himself very unpopular. Meanwhile, the production of Vittorio de Sica's *Bicycle Thieves* (released in Italy in November 1948) and Rossellini's *Germany Year Zero* (released 1948–49) were underway, and Zinnemann, understandably worried that Wechsler had missed the novelty factor, nursed his "pet idea" to do a location film about the European underground.[29] However, eventually in October 1946, both Nicholas Schenck and Louis B. Mayer changed their minds. Arthur Loew was charged with keeping an eye on Zinnemann and the production. Although the studio was undoubtedly happy to be rid of Zinnemann for several months, executives were most likely persuaded by Paramount's decision to back Billy Wilder's *Foreign Affair* (shot in Berlin) and RKO's planned *Berlin Express* (1948), directed by Jacques Tourneur and shot mostly in Frankfurt. Studios were slowly realizing the tax benefits of funneling their "frozen" European assets into overseas productions. Wechsler's payment of $30,000 and control of US publicity and distribution in exchange for Zinnemann's services sweetened the deal for MGM even more.[30] Visas were procured in November and the Zinnemann family, including six-year-old Tim, took passage for Europe aboard an almost empty *America* in December 1946.[31]

Europe's Children: Researching Survivors of the Holocaust

Writer Peter Viertel, lately released from service with the OSS, was not at the studio's beck and call. In the summer of 1946, he and Zinnemann drafted some preliminary storylines, and in October, the writer returned to Davos, Switzerland, to work on a treatment for Wechsler. However, Viertel remained mostly in Davos, telling Zinnemann that the French authorities were making difficulties for those wishing to go into the American zone. He wrote, "As the basic adventures of our two heroes have to be invented anyway, it would be better if I started to write a first draft, which you and I can then later tear apart." Zinnemann underlined this and scrawled "Why?" in the margins.[32] He and Peter Viertel had been friends for a long time; after all, it was Peter's father, Berthold, who had employed Zinnemann in the 1930s, and the Zinnemanns were frequent guests at his mother's salon on Mayberry Road. Although Zinnemann valued Peter Viertel's talent and sense of humor, he became uneasy as he realized that Viertel shared less than his commitment to on-site research or authenticity. Viertel also seemed to have a grudge against Thérèse Bonney (Wechsler had hired Bonney as liaison to the US Army and UNRRA organizations) complaining jealously that she "is a bullshit artist from way back . . . a sort of official army gal, decorated from ass to elbow, but she's an apologist for the US army, which is swell for her but wrong for us."[33]

Viertel may have had a point; as a lieutenant in the OSS, he had seen firsthand the army's inability to cope with the child refugees and especially Jewish survivors. He had also witnessed a disturbing lack of repentance in mainstream German populations. Historian Atina Grossman has chronicled varied reactions to German apathy and feelings of victimization from army officials and journalists.[34] As American photojournalist Margaret Bourke-White famously wrote, "The Germans act as though the Nazis were a strange race of Eskimos who came down from the North Pole and somehow invaded Germany."[35] Yet coupled with this resistance to facing Germany's recent history was the very real need of ordinary German children and especially displaced peoples within the former Reich of milk, food, medical supplies, and shelter, something publisher Victor Gollancz, Dorothy Macardle, and Kathryn Hulme wrote about at length. Here, the American military was woefully inefficient and even callous.[36] Yet in 1945–46, when Viertel was writing his first outline of "The European Children," press coverage was focused on Earl Harrison's report to President Truman on the army's mismanagement of the Jewish refugees and its resonance with the Nuremberg trials later in the fall of 1945. Harrison drew attention to the poor food, clothing, and living accommodations in the camps and condemned the US's role: "As matters now stand, we appear to be treating the Jews as the Nazis treated them except that we do not exterminate them." Grossman has pointed out Harrison's emphasis on the contrast between the relatively well-fed, free German population and the cadaverous, still-interned DPs nearby.[37]

Viertel would also focus on this contrast. Although he had made no trips into Germany for specific research, he was careful to note: "All the actions and backgrounds in this film will be checked against actual conditions existing in Germany and in all countries in which the picture plays, so that no misconceptions or untruths will be presented."[38] The outline began with an old man, himself a camp survivor, watching DP kids beginning to play again in the camp. He mused, "They had never known anything but this; living in camps, in fear and squalor, their lives and the lives of their parents constantly threatened. It was amazing that any of them had survived." Viertel continued, "The Germans were going to church, to ask God forgiveness for their sins . . . They were being forgiven all too quickly. The world pitied *them*." While the man watches the kids, he recognizes a former guard at Buchenwald, but the German townspeople protect him and scream anti-Jewish threats, which the foreign soldiers do not understand. At one point, the soldiers actually fire into the crowd of protesting DPs and kill one. This was quite a condemnation from a former member of the OSS.

But the bulk of Viertel's story was to focus upon a little girl and boy from the camp who escape together and plan to return to Czechoslovakia. This idea was developed between him and Zinnemann in the summer of 1946 before Viertel left Hollywood for Wechsler's studio in Switzerland. Viertel shared Zinnemann's interest in Czechoslovakia and wrote to Wechsler, "We chose Prague because of all the countries that I visited in Europe, this one seemed to be the one with the greatest hope for the future."[39] The Czechoslovakian "nation" had also been the greatest affront to Hitler's plans for both greater Germany and the Nazis' imposed European order. In focusing on Czech children, Viertel and Zinnemann imagined the beginnings of a new European community, an idea famously described by Albert Camus as an act of resistance against German nationalism. Early on in the children's adventures, the little girl, Susan, still has a photograph of her house in Plzen and so "the photograph became their hope."[40] Viertel focuses on Carl, an eleven-year-old Polish boy, whose "young brain was still tortured by a hundred pictures of brutality and fear," who remembered his parents being taken away from him, hunger, and cold. Eventually they meet up with a gang of *wolfskinder* (wild children) in the woods (the basis for Géza Radványi's *Somewhere in Europe*, 1947, then in production). The young leader runs the group like an incipient Hitler and at one point, he makes contact with a former Wehrmacht officer, "a cynical Nazi diehard" and black market Fagin, who runs gangs of thieving children. Carl and Susan escape at last and American soldiers try to protect the children, but the German people are unsympathetic. When Carl tells of their treatment in the gang, the Germans treat the young boy "as a spy." One Nazi reminds him that "Germany is not such a large country and one day the Americans will be gone."

In his treatment, Viertel tries to show the American officer Patterson's development from an uninvolved occupier to a human being concerned with the fate of the two children. As he wrote to Wechsler, "In many ways America is the hope of Europe today. We have food, materials, and a general welfare which exists nowhere else. We cannot disappoint those Europeans who still think of our country as a paradise from which they are barred by immigration quotas. We cannot be satisfied to be Sir Galahads in shining armor, who kill the dragon and then go home, to forget the battle, for we have learned that this is one world and if disillusionment and cynicism spread again the children who today scurry through Europe's gutters will become new *führers*, new scourges of humanity."[41]

When we first meet him, Patterson has only a surface "Sir Galahad" involvement with Europe. Patterson's German girlfriend cares only about German kids and complains that Americans "always manage to go back across their ocean, to their easy life and stop worrying about the rest of the world." Patterson eventually sees that behind her façade of sexy apathy, she is nothing but an apologist for National Socialism. The American officer tries to take the kids to Susan's old home in Plzen, but, inept and increasingly thwarted by the unfamiliar environment and visa problems, he gives up, leaving the kids in a DP camp. The girl is quickly adopted but a "physical examination" reveals that Carl is Jewish and families do not want to adopt him. The officials try to explain to a distraught Susan, who does not want to be separated from him, that "there were certain complications ... not for children." But Viertel's script planned that Carl would be honest with her: "He is a Jew. People don't want him as readily as they want her. The little girl doesn't understand." When Susan is sent to her new home, he escapes, and comes to a crossroads. Here Viertel ended his outline. The story managed to touch upon many controversial areas, including German citizens' protection of war criminals, the persistence of violent nationalism, America's halfhearted involvement in European affairs, the sexual exploitation of German women, and the continued segregation of Jewish children (though Viertel avoids the controversial efforts of Jewish groups to maintain the segregation of Jewish unaccompanied children in order to export them to Palestine).[42]

Zinnemann seemed fairly happy with Viertel's outline, although the scenes with the gang of children and corrupt former Wehrmacht officer would become conventions of German rubble films such as *Irgendwo in Berlin* (Gerhard Lamprecht, 1946) and Roberto Rossellini's *Germany Year Zero*.[43] Unlike other screenwriters of the rubble films, Viertel did not avoid the issue of Jewish children and there was no "Hollywood" ending for Carl. Zinnemann originally envisioned a tragic boy-hero along the lines of Robert Lynen's performance in Duvivier's *Poil de Carotte* (1932), and Viertel concurred, thinking they could take the suicide theme to an affecting conclusion.[44] Viertel argued: "It might be a terrific sock . . . It might be too tough, too gruesome."[45] But as Zinnemann's knowledge of the Holocaust developed, he grew impatient with Viertel's "Hollywood" conventions, the stock occupier romance, the children's escape from the "little Hitler" gang, and avoidance of the details of the children's horrific lives prior to the liberation. As he wrote: "I'm convinced you and I have a hell of a chance to make an honest and strong movie about Europe today. If we muff it, then both of us deserve to get our balls cut off."[46]

He countered Viertel's worry about sugarcoating the script for an American audience: "[I]t doesn't matter if the film is 'depressing.'" He reminded Viertel that both Rossellini's *Rome, Open City* (1945) and his own *Seventh Cross* were "depressing" films. "And if we can't find any hope, then at least we should try to arouse a very strong feeling of indignation," he argued, ironically echoing the words of Jacob Riis fifty years before him. Though Zinnemann was deeply influenced by the work of documentary filmmaker Robert Flaherty and was a great admirer of Rossellini's wartime films *Rome, Open City* and *Paisà* (1946), he did not want his audience to have any doubts about his position on Europe's displaced children. Flaherty had often been criticized for making artistic documentaries like *Moana* (1926) that avoided social realities and the filmmakers' exploitation of ordinary people. Similarly, a "balanced" documentary approach was the last thing he wanted: "I don't see how any film about Europe today and be neutral or detached without also being dishonest," he wrote. He urged Viertel not to "sidestep the so called Jewish problem if it wants to come up in the story. Not for one moment." But Zinnemann also wanted a strong point to be made about America's obligation to Europe and the historical consequences of isolation: "Maybe there should be some character in the story somewhere, some old guy maybe, only a bit, who could point out the growing parallel between 1919–20 and today—when the first peace was sold out from under the nose of a fat, dumb and happy America, that wanted nothink [sic] but to go to sleep again, just like today. Maybe he could tell how the French in 1917 knelt down in the mud where the first doughboys had just passed through and how they had kissed the mud— and how a year later those same French hated the Americans' guts—and maybe he should wonder why. If that doesn't fit, forget it."[47] Zinnemann knew that these images needed a powerful voice and a sense of history to guide American viewers into action. His attitude toward US involvement in Europe differed from Billy Wilder's. While Wilder had initially planned a straight patriotic *Foreign Affair*, exalting the virtues of the army's impact on Germany, from the beginning of *The Search*'s production, Zinnemann seemed skeptical about America's past and present commitments and more interested in the US's future relationship with Europe.[48]

Viertel was happy enough to add these touches and to leave the research and liaison with the army to his bête noir, Thérèse Bonney, and to Zinnemann. Zinnemann was anxious to get to Germany as soon as possible and knew Bonney was a good friend to have in this regard. Wechsler, for his part, was also encouraging.[49] But as Viertel cautioned Zinnemann, the producer "worries about it being depressing, about mixing into the problems of the occupation army etc."[50] Wechsler had hired Thérèse Bonney as liaison to the US Army and UNRRA organizations, and she arranged Zinnemann's passes to the German zones in early January by arguing that Zinnemann was a "documentarist" rather than just a run-of-the-mill Hollywood filmmaker.[51] Zinnemann's initial research visit would be followed by substantial location shooting in March and April. The application argued that it was crucial to make the "public aware of one of most vital problems and responsibilities of post-war world" and that "time an important and urgent factor because character and physical aspects of UNRRA children's camps as background documentary material very soon to undergo radical transformations."[52] The people at UNRRA didn't need convincing. They realized that Zinnemann's film would raise public awareness about their work (which had been coming under recent political fire due in part to the fallout from Harrison's report). Soon, UNRRA itself would cease to exist and the International Refugee Organization (IRO) would take charge and national governments would have sovereignty over DPs. UNRRA officials put the necessary pressure on the military to help supply the passes. Zinnemann, argued William Wells of UNRRA, "needs to do research and perhaps some background shooing in DP camps in the

Surviving Voices and the Search for Europe [69]

US Zone, and I have told him to get in touch." He mentioned that although Zinnemann was an Austrian-born German speaker, he was now a US citizen and "is a very good man to work with."[53] The passes came through for Zinnemann to tour Germany's ruined cities and numerous DP camps in late January and February 1947.

While the director was preparing for his trip to Germany, he had come across an article on fellow Austrian Albert Schweitzer, whose creed of moral responsibility deeply influenced him. When asked why he did what he did, Schweitzer replied, "Whatever more than others you have received in health, natural gifts, working capacity, success, a beautiful childhood, harmonious family circumstances, you must not accept as being a matter of course. You must pay a price for them. You must show more than an average devotion to life."[54] Zinnemann took this creed to heart. Although he had initially told his agent Abe Lastfogel and MGM that he would be in Europe only a few months, he would be gone for over a year researching, writing, and filming. As he wrote to friend Arthur Loew, he knew those additional months away from the studio put his career in jeopardy, but "I feel that the subject is of tremendous importance and that it should be made even at a certain personal sacrifice."[55]

So what did Fred Zinnemann see that would change his outlook and challenge his commitment to intellectual balance and detachment? He did many interviews with Jewish and non-Jewish children at the camps, including Christina Zamoyska. She was in a camp in Munich and survived the SS "clearance" of the Krakow ghetto in 1940. She remembered a horrific incident, and Zinnemann transcribed: "Mother on knees holding baby pointing save baby kill me—SS man one dog and cigar—listening casually, kindly—CZ [Zamoyska] wants to run, take baby, friend holds her back—SS man waits, watches, very kindly takes baby, pats it, smashes brains on wall—shoots mother—walks off—scrapes brains off wall and feeds dog." At the Prien International Home, there were a lot of young Czech boys from ages six to twelve. Zinnemann took particular note of one, "George Milon, 4½—hugs my legs—looks deep into my eyes—touching both my cheeks with his hands... 'Du bist mein Vater' he says to me."[56] He also took notes on some shocking things done by an Aglast Evangelical Church group. Every week the minister "made selections from list, so many a week to be exterminated... Kids killed in Karlsruhe and Stuttgart by injections." His cynicism with churches deepened.

He heavily annotated one account of a German atrocity in Sambor, Poland, in April 1943, involving the massacre of infants and children.

[70] Surviving Voices and the Search for Europe

Warsaw, Ghetto

FIGS. 19–20 From Zinnemann's research archive. Inspirations for the children and Karel's last kiss with his mother, AMPAS.

He bracketed the following segment: "Oh, Jewish People! Where is your honor? Where is your ambition? How will you explain it to the world, if a few of you will remain in Europe."[57] The agonized exhortation drove him on. He heard children and UNRRA officials tell of Nazis gassing children in ambulances and trucks and that therefore the children would not enter Red Cross ambulances, of mothers who strangled their babies so they would not die of hunger in the camps, of tiny children working in slave labor, of teenagers who had to sign "with a cross" because there "were no schools in KZ for five years," and was shattered by the narratives.[58] He compiled a photographic archive which would inspire many of the shots from the concentration camps and children's centers (figs. 19–20). UNRRA also supplied him with their reports since 1946, and he learned about the history of the child-tracing teams and their success. Initially no one thought of DP children until parents forced to do slave labor told their liberators that their children were still alive in Germany. One UNRRA report described how everything began when 10,000 DP children were found after "a few of these DPs, unable to contain their paternal and maternal instincts, took matters into their own hands and set out to find their children."[59] As Zinnemann compiled more and more dossiers, he scrawled, "Get detailed case histories—the most moving ones—get detail on kids' first reactions upon arrival." Although he knew that the narrative would hinge on the experience of one child arriving at a new camp, he wanted to cover as many poignant and horrifying histories as possible to show the scale of the crisis. He did not want a "national" story either, which focused on children of one favored country. The concept of the geographically and ideologically resilient nation preoccupied not only Nazi Germany, but also the US and many European nations in the postwar era. Even as he worked, European governments were banning international adoptions of DP kids and UNRRA's international child centers were disbanded as children returned to the care of their birth nations.[60] As Germany's film industry staggered to its feet, DEFA and film companies in the western zones began to make films which focused on Germany's non-Jewish children and largely ignored the lives of DP children in Germany or any international presence.[61] Even the remarkable Hungarian release *Somewhere in Europe* focuses on the experiences of a group of Hungarian children after the war as a way of envisioning European reconstruction.[62] Zinnemann would continue to resist the reappearance of nationalism in Europe, opting instead for a uniquely European perspective. He scrawled in the margins of the reports, "To make the film big it MUST show wandering of kids across the face of Europe—at least 3 countries!"

Scripting *The Search*

Lazar Wechsler had initially suggested to Zinnemann that the project might attract more international attention with the participation of a major Hollywood star. But even before visiting the camps, Zinnemann had been wary of involving even the most potentially dedicated Hollywood actors. In early December 1946, he wrote to Wechsler, who had hoped to build the role of Patterson around a big Hollywood star like John Garfield, "Would it not perhaps be best to concentrate on writing the story we want, and to say what we want in the most effective way, without committing ourselves a priori to a starring vehicle for Garfield or some comparable Hollywood personality?"[63] Zinnemann argued that although the American connection was important, he did not want the role to diminish the importance of the children's stories. "I believe—perhaps wrongly—that in order to interest a star, the story would almost certainly have to be primarily about *him*." He continued, "Either we would like to make a film about displaced European kids—and the world as it appears to them—including their friendship with a young GI, or the film could be about a young officer, reluctant and disinterested in Europe, who grows to understand what is at stake through his friendship with the two displaced children."[64] He also wrote to Viertel, enclosing a copy of his letter to Wechsler, and asked, "Which character do we emphasize? The kids or the GI? The outline is sort of indecisive ... Personally I like the kid story much better." Viertel, who had initially been flattered by Garfield's interest (as one of the most prominent Jewish stars in Hollywood), soon grew to agree with Zinnemann because of the potential power Garfield might wield in molding the script to flatter his star image: "Garfield is not as cagey as he is dumb, but unfortunately our business is set up so that his little mind can govern lots of money."[65] Ironically, Viertel would work with Garfield a year later on John Huston's ill-fated *We Were Strangers* (1949). Both Viertel and Zinnemann worried that the focus would shift from the saga of the two children to the political and personal reawakening of the American soldier. Eventually, Zinnemann would hire the unknown New York actor Montgomery Clift for the part. Later in life, Zinnemann loved telling the story of a fan who wrote: "Where did you find a soldier who could act?"[66] Clift's status as a newcomer gave his performance an authenticity the director craved.

But soon Viertel would be another casualty of Zinnemann's commitment. Viertel felt slightly bewildered by Zinnemann's zeal and his determination to make a non-Hollywood film about Europe's displaced children.

While the writer wanted to get back to Hollywood and his wife Virginia by the beginning of March at the latest,[67] Zinnemann let his contract lapse so he could remain in Europe to finish *The Search*.[68] Never again in his life would Zinnemann feel so committed to a film and its impact on the public. His passion and rage are palpable in the hundreds of pages of handwritten notes about the children's experiences and the records of displaced persons. When he came back from his first trip to the camps, he spoke with Wechsler, and the producer severed Viertel's contract. Initially, there seemed to be no animosity. As Zinnemann explained to Abe Lastfogel, "The script itself was a good job of writing and would undoubtedly make the basis of a fair movie but to me it did not seem to encompass the tragedy of European children of today."[69] Richard Schweizer (*Marie-Louise*) was brought in to work with Zinnemann, and a new story was constructed with some input from the producer's son David and Thérèse Bonney. But Zinnemann had talked about his experience with several UNRRA people, including William Wells. Wells gave a candid interview which reached Hollywood's *Variety*, and Viertel was outraged. One of Zinnemann's letters to Wells was quoted at length: "The story originally written was rejected upon my arrival in Zurich, because it seemed too remote from reality and because it lacked inner truth and strength." Staff writer Florence Lowe speculated, "It is that paragraph about stories lacking inner truth and being too remote from reality which might be the crux of many of the eggs laid by Hollywood in 1946. The script which did not have the stuff was a Hollywood project."[70] This was more than embarrassing. While initially he may not have given a damn about MGM's feelings, he hastily explained to Viertel that "it was not until late January, when I went to Germany for the first time, and was literally hit over the head by things of enormous, you might say monstrous emotional impact, that my feelings in regard to your script began to change. You see, there are things happening there which I saw or heard of first-hand, that defy the imagination of any essentially normal person, no matter how talented."[71] He continued, "I don't believe that any writer, no matter how great, could possibly get the feeling of those things across, or even set them down adequately, unless he had seen them, smelled them at least, if not suffered through them himself. No one's imagination could produce the situations, incidents, characters that make up the brew in that witches' cauldron called Germany." His letter saved their friendship. Seething, he wrote a careful letter to Wells, in which he asked him not to send any personal letters to the press as it appears "as though I had taken an underhanded crack at the

US film industry as a whole and in doing so had combined disloyalty with very poor taste."[72] Zinnemann may have toyed with remaining in Europe after completing *The Search* but was too intelligent to burn his bridges. "Don't mention my name in connection with remarks about or against Hollywood and US films," he asked, "because I intend to continue to work there and it is home, so far as I am concerned."

Zinnemann would shape *The Search* himself. Schweizer, the principal screenwriter, spoke no English, so the script was initially written in German and subsequently translated by Zinnemann, David Wechsler, and a studio secretary.[73] By March 7, 1947, he had his story and knew how he wanted to integrate his weeks of research. His main passion was to give the story of one child context and substance through the additional experiences of other children and to provide the audience with some sense of the children's lives during the war and afterward under UNRRA's care. His main character would have to symbolize the trauma and horror experienced by thousands of children whose stories would never be told, he wrote Wechsler.[74] Initially, he wanted to include shots of concentration camps, the Death March, the liberation, and several UNRRA camps, but eventually he honed his historical material, abandoning mainstream stock images so that the script concentrated purely on the children's experiences.[75]

Although toward the end of his career, Zinnemann would repudiate the film's opening narration, claiming it was a clumsy, cumbersome fabrication of Lazar Wechsler's and "untrue" to the shape of the film, the screenplays and production notes tell a different story.[76] Zinnemann and Wechsler both agreed that audiences needed to be taught about the children's situation; it could not simply be filmed without context.[77] Though in later years, he may have wanted the film to resemble the voice-over-less *Shoeshine* (De Sica, 1946) and *Germany Year Zero*, *The Search*'s historical and social stakes were simply too high to sacrifice the "non-diegetic" voice for the trendiness of a contained neorealist style. Projected text was too impersonal, too reminiscent of political bureaucracy, and too recognizable a tool of traditional "historical" films made in Hollywood. The narration, later assigned to the female UNRRA director Mrs. Murray (played by veteran Warner Bros. actress Aline MacMahon), was to begin shortly after trains carrying the new DP children arrive in the station. Although the voice-over provides some historical context for the narrative, the film acknowledges that "this is only one detail, one small detail, of the chaos left behind by the war. The war is over, but the wreckage remains. . . .

And this is but a handful, a tiny almost commonplace handful, of the millions of children who are orphaned and homeless in Europe today." While "forewords" usually provided a conception of the whole, the voice-over indicates that a universal history of Europe's children during and after the war is impossible to conceptualize or describe. Grand narratives no longer function in these historical conditions; instead, the value is in voicing individual stories and resisting the conspiracy of Nazi silence about the Holocaust. The voice-over continues: "If only one of these children would speak! If only they would break their dreadful silence."[78] The issue of the voice and breaking silence was a moral imperative within the film. While the voice-over, with its links to oral history and validation of "marginal" lives, in some sense provides a historical framework for the "search," it provides only "a small detail" or fragment.[79] The main issues of voice and silence are articulated through the experience of the DP children and Karel Malik (Ivan Jandl), who has no memory of his past life and cannot even speak.[80]

But if the female voice-over articulates the failure of postwar grand narratives, it is even more wary of a kind of visual relativism wrought by the war: "Their spirit is broken. Terrified, they obey every order . . . Nor can they understand that UNRRA, which has now taken charge of them, is there to help them, for the UNRRA people wear uniforms. And the men who beat them, the men who persecuted and tortured them—they wore uniforms too."[81] European publicity emphasizes this ambiguity and the slippage between the children's experiences with uniforms during and after the war. Uniforms, whether worn by Nazis or UN workers or even American GIs like Steve (Montgomery Clift), terrify the children. Later the "universal" symbol of mercy, the Red Cross, panics the children who believe their erstwhile protectors are about to gas them like the Nazis. Only one boy, the unknown Karel Malik, escapes successfully. When Steve takes Karel from the rubble to his army digs, the boy fights tooth and nail against this "help." As they enter the house, Zinnemann shoots the struggling pair against a chain-link wall motif, recalling Karel's earlier experiences at Auschwitz with other soldiers. When Steve tries to doctor Karel's injured feet, the child recoils, and Steve realizes, "Probably thinks we're SS men or something . . . And I go and lock him up! And show him that hypodermic. You know what they DID to these kids in the concentration camps!"[82] As Steve teaches Karel to speak English, he cuts images out of magazines and drills him on the single definition of each image. Furthermore, Karel's and his mother's searches for each other are personal variations on the search

FIG. 21 *The Search* (1948): Fred Zinnemann on location in Munich with the children, 1947, AMPAS.

FIG. 22 Zinnemann with Ivan Jandl (Karel), Claude Gambier (Raoul), and the other children preparing for the ambulance sequence, 1947, AMPAS.

for the definition of the "one face" and their reunion concludes the film. The recovery of personal histories and memories resists the impact of the Nazis and restores the order of language and image.

Yet as Zinnemann circumvented the perceived necessity of a Hollywood star like Garfield, so he also avoided the tradition of the single "heroic" child protagonist. One of Zinnemann's concerns was presenting both the immediate needs of many DP children with their historical experiences. Holocaust victims' testimonies were a major issue in the aftermath of the war yet few initially considered the testimony of children. Zinnemann focused on a number of stories, setting one sequence in the

Surviving Voices and the Search for Europe [77]

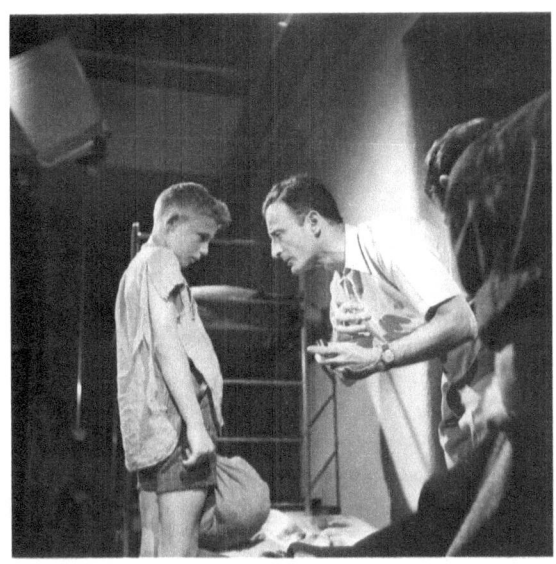

FIG. 23 Making a former child survivor relive the past, 1947, AMPAS.

UNRRA children's home where a series of UN interpreters act as a kind of tribunal hearing the children's individual histories. Here Zinnemann incorporates some of the research he did in the children's homes in Germany. In fact, these filmed sequences show real DP camp survivors instead of child actors. Most were Jewish children, unwanted in Europe, who Zinnemann arranged to travel to Switzerland for filming.[83] UNRRA later authorized the use of mostly Jewish children from the Rosenheim children's summer camp and 600 DP children for filming around Nuremberg and Inglstadt (figs. 21–22).[84] Years later, Zinnemann would write movingly about working with the children. Many submitted to re-shaving their heads, wearing rags, and expressing looks of terror that were only too real. In some of the off-camera shots of the rehearsals, Zinnemann looks almost terrifying as he looms over the children, one hand outstretched, his gaze relentless, in his efforts to make them relive the horrors of the camps (fig. 23).

In the opening "processing" sequence, UNRRA director Mrs. Murray tries to turn blank sheets of paper into one-page biographies of each child. Zinnemann emphasizes the multiple effort of translation. Murray asks the children questions in English through interpreters, and their responses are orally retranslated into English and then typed up. The mise-en-scène separates the UN adults from the children behind a long desk, and the camera also separates them in the establishing shots and between each interview. But as a child testifies, he or she becomes part of a shot with the

UNRRA officials and the other children awaiting their turns, unifying victim, witness, and audience. The voice of the child unites people and space. A typewriter clicks away as each tells his story in his original language, though Zinnemann eschews subtitles and shots of the documents. It is the oral testimony that counts.

In the earlier screenplays, the first child to be interviewed is Serbian, Mikhail Jovanovich. He relates in his native language that the Nazis took his mother away to another camp while his father "went into the mountains. My father was a hero—everybody said so. But they shot him."[85] The boy was later taken to Mauthausen; Mrs. Murray understands this without the need of the translator. But the cutting continuity shows that they later changed the boy's name and nationality to "Raoul Dubois, French."[86] Was this because too many of Zinnemann's children were originally scripted from Eastern Europe? Was it necessary to have the archetypal child of Western Europe with a Resistance father in order to garner American sympathy and glamour? The second child interviewed is Marjorie Luthgen, but Zinnemann wanted a more Polish-Jewish name and would change it to Ludwiga Brownoski. Her parents were killed in Bergen-Belsen, while she was slave labor and managed to find her brother after the war. Another was Mirjam Szigeti, from Budapest. Early screenplays note that the little girl's back should be to the camera as she tells the story: "Her job was to sort out the clothes of the people who'd been gassed—she had to sort them according to size, in a room next to the crematorium. She found her own mother's blouse among them." While Zinnemann and Schweizer may have initially believed that showing Mirjam's back as she spoke universalized her horrific story, Zinnemann abandoned this approach for filming the "voice" of the survivor. It was more important for him to show each child speaking his or her horrific personal tale. As each speaks, the camera seems to sit with the children like a silent observer or another UNRRA official, filming them at eye level, and facing them at either a side angle or frontally. Their succinct narratives, even, unemotional voices, and expressionless faces have the most horrifying impact of all. Although Vittorio De Sica's *Shoeshine* and Géza Radványi's *Somewhere in Europe* (1947) were notable for focusing almost entirely on boys (De Sica's original script title was *Ragazzi* or *The Boys*),[87] Zinnemann had Richard Schweizer include a number of girls in the testimonies despite the fact that so many were killed outright at the camps due to their assumed inability to work as slave labor.[88] Yet this sequence was crucial for him because he wanted

FIG. 24 Boys are not the only victims: *The Search*, Prasens/MGM.

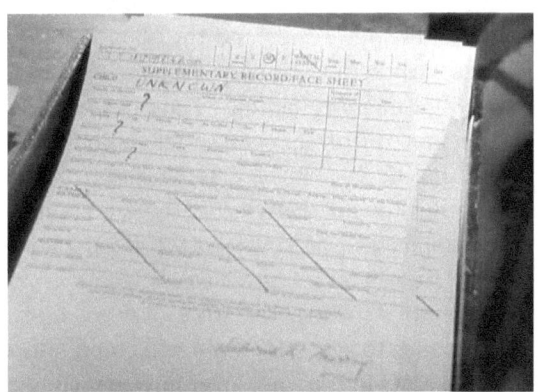

FIG. 25 The search for Karel in the absence of documentation, Praesens/MGM.

to preserve the stories—even those which could no longer be told by the victims (fig. 24).

After some of these testimonies, the camera lingers on Karel Malik, the boy with no memory of his past life. As officials are busy documenting another child's testimony, Karel's Auschwitz number shows through his rags and he tries to cover it as another boy stoops to look. When Mrs. Murray and the translators call him over, Karel cannot speak or remember like the other children at the camp; he doesn't know his own story and only replies in terror to the UNRRA officials in German: "I don't know." Karel's identification document, covered only with question marks, is the only one to be filmed in close-up. UNRRA workers do not even notice his tattooed number. The official, textual document, so essential in wartime and postwar Europe, fails to historicize any part of Karel's life (fig. 25).

As Dorothy Macardle points out in *Europe's Children*, many young people reacted to the horrors they witnessed by either suppressing all memories or refusing to engage with anyone, like Karel. Child-search investigators had to use a variety of techniques to reconstruct the memories of many children. Here Aline MacMahon's voice-over returns to ask, "Have you really forgotten?"[89] The voice then triggers an apparently accurate flashback to Karel's childhood, an oral and filmic witnessing of the events prior to the arrest and deportation of his family. The screen itself is likened to a sheet of paper, but one far more adequate than UNRRA's blank document: "A dark spot appears in the middle of the form, spreading rapidly like a blot of ink, until the form is obliterated." Some thirty years later, Zinnemann would again explore the power and ambiguities of the voice-over in *Julia*. In *The Search*, the voice-over describes Karel's house and happy family and the Nazis' attack on "Czech intellectuals."[90] On one early script, Zinnemann penciled in his revisions to a final voice-over about memory fading: "Time passed and from the time little Karel was separated from his mother, his mind started going blank. Bit by bit, everything he ever knew was blotted from his memory. He's forgotten his mother tongue. He's wandered far, come across many people, heard many languages—picking up a word here; a phrase there. But he seldom speaks. He has found how useless words are; how little they can help."[91] The director's constructed voice-over acted like a narrative balm, helping the audience to see what Karel still could not remember. Yet Zinnemann acknowledges in the voice-over how inadequate all words are in indirectly reconstructing Holocaust survivors' experiences. Mrs. Murray's narrated flashback is deliberately not Karel's personal flashback, but a discourse reconstructed by UN caseworkers retrospectively, including the charming scenes of Karel's middle-class home life before the Nazi occupation. Later, when Karel does remember his mother, he simply asks his American protector Steve, without any flashbacks or voice-over, where she is. His suspicious and fearful stare evokes the horrors of his past.

Neither official documents nor retrospective oral histories could replicate Karel's own testimony. In fact, written official documentation always fails Karel. While Steve attempts to write to various UN and US Army organizations about Karel, identifying him only by his Auschwitz number, the bureaus respond: "There is no record of anyone so far having inquired at any of our offices for a boy with the number A24328. We were able, however, to conclude from the number that he was one of a group of children who were all separated from their mothers. Practically all of these women are known to be dead. They were gassed."[92] Zinnemann had recent, firsthand knowledge of this kind of uncaring, bureaucratic biographical "search," and deliberately contrasts its tone and inaccurate evidence with Steve's own postwar reconstruction project: he teaches Karel (renamed "Jim") to speak English using images cut from magazines. While Steve does attempt some American history through his explanation of Abraham Lincoln's picture, Karel's real interest is in images of mothers and children.[93] These images trigger the recovery of Karel's past, and Zinnemann's camera, rather than any UN or army typewriter, documents this process.[94]

The Legacy of Lidice

Zinnemann's interest in keeping his young protagonist a Czech was maintained by reports from UNRRA newsletters describing Czech children who had forgotten their own language since they were interned in Germany. "'There are young children in Czechoslovakia today, children ten and twelve years of age, who are struggling to unlearn German, the only language they know, and re-learn Czech, the language they have forgotten," noted one such report.[95] Most of them were Jewish or children of those suspected of political resistance. The article explained, "Six-year-old children were often put to work that way and forced to speak only German. They were given German names. Or only numbers branded on their little arms. And many of them hardly remember their own names or their mother-tongue. The difficulties of tracing such children and reuniting them with the remains of their frantic families after so many years, can easily be understood."[96]

Czechoslovakian children endured deprivation the longest of any occupied and resistant European country. Once a model of ethnic tolerance and broad-based educational reform, the Czech nation was targeted by the Nazis with systematic persecution of Jews, communists, the country's educated elites, and political refugees from Austria and Germany. The Nazis implemented forced child labor, and executed hundreds of students and professors following Britain's declaration of war, but Czech resistance continued even after the Lidice massacre on June 10, 1942. Later, other countries would experience similar horrors, but Lidice was the first. Though the Germans would claim that "the very name of the village has ceased to exist," this boast fueled worldwide remembrance of Lidice. After the war, public energies concentrated on finding the village's lost children and reuniting them with surviving mothers. In some sense, Karel's experience, eventual recovery of his memory, and reunion with his mother (Jarmila Novotna) can be seen as a metaphor for remembrance of Lidice.

Ivan Jandl was one of the handful of "professional" actors involved in the film, although as a Czech radio actor, he had had very little experience prior to meeting Zinnemann. They met during the director's research trip to Czechoslovakia. Jandl's personal knowledge of the Nazi occupation was deep. But historian Atina Grossmann has argued that in making *The Search*'s child hero "little blond Karel the child of anti-Nazi Czech intelligentsia parents," the film was part of a pattern of the "universalization and dejudaization of the Holocaust" in the postwar era.[97] Grossman's assessment oversimplifies Zinnemann's position. Zinnemann was himself Jewish, interviewed many Jewish child survivors, and wanted to focus on the unique plight of Jewish children, but was well aware that there were tens of thousands of non-Jewish child victims under UNRRA's care as well. Between 1.5 and 2 million Jewish children were killed in the Second World War, but another million children died in Europe between 1938 and 1945, including tens of thousands of German children killed by Lancaster bombing raids on major German cities. Thousands more perished from famine and neglect in 1946–47, and the UN reported that in 1947, 20 to 30 million children were at risk of starvation.[98] Zinnemann was equally "guilty" of universalization and particularization simply because he wanted to accommodate the stories of as many European child victims as possible. Karel, as a non-religiously affiliated son of Czech intellectuals, was part of a resisting group that experienced some of the longest oppression of the war. Although not a Lidice child, his separation from his mother, miserable silence, and lack of memory attest to a national psyche overpowered and nearly obliterated by the Third Reich.

The fate of the children of Lidice was particularly in the news and during the immediate postwar period, had acquired mythic symbolism of German atrocities and the wanton destruction of the family. Zinnemann seems to have considered making the story focus on the fate of Czech children in a Lidice-like situation. In his research notes, he writes: "Possible story: Kids caught in Czech village on street—put into institute—one can't make grade—in slave labor—one resists—experiment."[99] Zinnemann continued, taking notes on UNRRA worker John Troniak's report on Lidice and kidnapped Czech kids: "1449 Czech kids taken to Germany; 390 dead; 289 found and sent home; found 73 = 697 missing."[100] In addition, Czech children were particularly vulnerable to starvation and neglect, and in 1945–46, Jan Masaryk had appealed to the Allies for additional emergency relief for the children.[101] In his research at the Jewish Agency for Palestine Child and Youth Immigration Bureau Zinnemann found a potential protagonist: Czech-born Jichak Grosz, who was separated from his parents and sent to Deutschkreutz. He survived, but his parents' fates were unknown.[102] Yet however much the Czechs' plight interested Zinnemann, he was as suspicious of focusing on one particular "group" of children as he was of focusing on one particular nation's experience of the war. In order to make the truly European, multistoried film he wanted, the children had to be diverse.

Karel has a unique and tragic past, but he represents a mixture of many horrific events in the lives of Europe's children. Though unlike his parents and sister, Karel is blond and pale-eyed, so were many Polish and Eastern European Jews (recall Sol's/Rod Steiger's golden-haired children in *The Pawnbroker*, 1964).[103] Initially, Karel is not identified as Jewish or Gentile. Only later, after discovering that a Jewish boy, Joel Makowsky (Leopold Borkowski), attempted to assume Karel's safe identity while in a camp, Mrs. Murray mentions that Karel is not Jewish. But in the flashback, Karel's home is presented as middle class and prosperous, and heavily invested in music, something common to Zinnemann's own background in Vienna and the representation of many European Jewish homes in film (*Golden Boy*, 1939; *Humoresque*, 1946).[104] Karel's knitted cap may be treasured because his mother made it for him and kept it in good repair even in the concentration camp, but the small cap has visual connections to both the kippah worn by Jewish men and boys and the ubiquitous cap of a schoolboy. More broadly, in the initial filmed interviews, the UNRRA officials avoid designating the children as Jewish. Instead, their parents' names, original country, and fate in the concentration camps identify them only as victims of the Nazis.

But while Zinnemann's little protagonist is not Jewish, Zinnemann does give some of the children names with Jewish connotations like Mirjam. When Mrs. Malik searches for her son in a convent, she discovers one Jewish boy posing as a Catholic choirboy to avoid persecution. Later, when Karel returns with Steve to the UNRRA camp, Mrs. Murray explains that only the Jewish children leaving for Palestine are left; the others have all been returned to their original countries. Here Zinnemann hints at the plight of Jewish children in the DP camps, though Mrs. Murray is not accosted by Jewish leaders demanding the separation of Jewish children from the other young DPs. Instead, the children view their trip to Palestine as a joyful event and sing as they depart. Only the mostly female UNRRA workers, including Mrs. Malik, are sad at their departure.

Collaboration with Hollywood

Initially, Zinnemann seems to have enjoyed working for Wechsler, and up until the early stages of shooting, it was a happy set. Zinnemann and cameraman Emil Berna got along famously, and old friends William and Tally Wyler visited during the initial UNRRA-child interview sequence in the summer of 1947. Zinnemann envied Wyler his career in the army air force, where he not only directed two documentaries (*The Memphis Belle*, 1944, and *Thunderbolt!*, 1947), but took part in bombing missions on Nazi Germany. But after directing the Academy Award-winning *The Best Years of Our Lives*, he took a break from feature filmmaking. The story of American's postwar readjustment was arguably the Jewish émigré director's most personal film, but unlike Zinnemann, he avoided stories dealing directly with the Holocaust and Nazi atrocities. At first, Wechsler let Zinnemann do his extensive research and location searches in peace, and, with son David involved in retranslating and writing Wechsler's work, did not interfere unduly with the construction of the script. When Zinnemann decided to hire Montgomery Clift and opera star Jarmila Novotna for the principle adult roles, Wechsler quickly made up the contracts. Wendell Corey and Aline MacMahon were appearing in London theaters and were also hired at Zinnemann's request. Wechsler ostensibly hired writer Paul Jarrico at Zinnemann's suggestion to tighten the American dialogue. Zinnemann may have worried about Schweizer's inability to understand English, or he may have wanted an ally in the screenwriting process. Regardless, Jarrico undoubtedly did more than expected. He did an initial report on the entire script. Many of his changes to the script outraged Wechsler, particularly Jarrico's removal of individual children's names ("In Mr. Jarrico's script no children are given names. I would prefer, as in the original version, that each child is given a name as it is more personal and kinder to the children.")[105] He also disliked Jarrico's tendency to insert a more interrogative tone to the exposition, edit narration, and cut any flashbacks.

The writer's interests were less in contextualizing the situation in Europe than in targeting American involvement. Jarrico wrote to Zinnemann, "The theme implicit in this treatment, as I understand it, is the responsibility that mankind must feel for the refugee children of Europe. Whilst I agree with this theme, I should like to see it focused a little for the American audience so that the corollary of the theme is clear: American responsibility for the refugee children of Europe."[106] He wanted to focus more on the GIs and less on the story of the mother and child. He also felt that one of the major problems was with the narration, which at that point had not definitively become the voice of Mrs. Murray: "Though I am not against narration I feel it should be avoided when possible. I also feel the desire to know who the narrator is. Is he Mr. Schweizer? Is he Mr. Wechsler? Is he Mr. Zinnemann? How does he happen to be omniscient?" He also disliked the flashback to Karel's life in Czechoslovakia: "Here again I feel a flashback is not bad if it is really necessary but it should be avoided if possible. In this case it seems rather mechanical." Schweizer and Zinnemann had created a scene based upon Zinnemann's research in which the children refuse to enter trucks to the new children's center because they are reminded of the gas chambers. It was a powerful way of reminding audiences about the horrors the children endured during the war and the persistence of these memories. Yet Jarrico merely thought the device made the children look "stupid." He didn't like Karel's cap as an identifying feature (and the one fragment of his past he struggles to keep, as in *Marie-Louise*), and he disliked having a woman in charge of the UNRRA facilities, saying Mrs. Murray "preaches too much."

Wechsler was irritated when he read the document and further incensed when Jarrico tried to remove specific elements from the script, complaining to Zinnemann that Jarrico's writing was "grob" or crude.[107] Zinnemann may have agreed with Wechsler's instincts about keeping the existing contextualized narrative, but he resisted Wechsler's growing efforts to control the script at any cost: "Forgetting the narration for a moment . . . I frankly believe that your existing contract with Mr. Schweizer whereby he has full and exclusive control over his material infringes upon and alters my status as a director."[108] The two began a heated correspondence about their relative control of the production, with Wechsler asserting the authority of his screenwriter. An already resistant Zinnemann was outraged when Wechsler attempted to view rushes before the director saw them and went to the developing labs on the sly to order separate prints.[109] Zinnemann fumed that this was "intolerable" and the "most unprofessional way of working I have ever heard of."[110] Though Wechsler may have initially hoped for a purely collaborative Euro-American production, he increasingly saw Zinnemann as the Hollywood enemy. In particular,

Wechsler saw Zinnemann's use of Jarrico as a part of the "vulgarization" of the script and said, "Don't ever let any American dialogists spoil his [Schweizer's] writing."[111]

Wechsler's fears were mostly unfounded. Zinnemann ignored almost all of Jarrico's complaints about the script's European context, flashback, narration, and female-directed UNRRA content. But Clift's spontaneity and interest in both rehearsals and alternate takes kept much of the dialogue fluid—something Wechsler detested and complained about to Clift.[112] With Zinnemann's encouragement Clift rewrote much of his dialogue on the set to make the colloquialisms of a young GI more natural for US audiences. Clift's opinion of the writers was expressed in a letter to Zinnemann: "I told [Arthur Loew] the three of us ought to work together sometime and soon. Now it's up to some untalented author to give us a reason to get together. Why aren't authors as talented as you and I? All authors are nudnicks. Give my love to Renée and your cowboy son."[113] Zinnemann was more cautious (he liked Richard Schweizer very much), and tried to maintain a balance between America and Europe at both the script and production level. But it became increasingly difficult for him when he discovered that in addition to sending daily peeved memos about Clift's changes to the dialogue and snooping around the developing room, Wechsler was also complaining to MGM that Zinnemann was obstructing the film production and refusing to come to work. The director sent seething replies to Wechsler and his agents at MGM, saying that he had been acting as everything from director to writer to casting agent, grip, and prop man.[114] By the end of filming, he and Wechsler were barely speaking.

If Zinnemann and Wechsler represented the behind-the-scenes breakdown of European and American relations, then Zinnemann, Clift, and Jandl were a model of friendship and collaboration. Clift had a gentleness, spontaneity, and sense of fun that made him instantly popular with children. "He took the time to listen to you," Tim Zinnemann recalls. "I saw more of Clift in Switzerland that I did of my father."[115] Zinnemann recalls a particularly fun Fourth of July, when Clift brought all the fireworks he could find from the BX to their hotel in Davos and had Tim line them up on the roof, before igniting them all in one go. The police, fire department, and MPs must have thought World War III had started. Clift became close friends with Tim, Ivan Jandl, and other DP kids on the set. Jandl spoke no English prior to making *The Search*, and at first, learned all his lines by rote with Zinnemann and Clift, as Karel/"Jim" learns English words in Steve's house. As Steve notes sagely, "You can use English all over

FIG. 26 Karel's search for his mother through another fence, Praesens/MGM.

the world . . . everyone understands you. Even in England they understand you. Well, almost."

But the tragedy for Karel and for Ivan was that the fluidity of language and culture did not permeate the geographical boundaries of the United States. Steve's efforts to adopt Karel are met with heavy resistance, and at the end of the film, had Karel not been reunited with his mother, Steve would have had to leave him at an UNRRA camp with no guarantee that he could arrange his emigration. But Steve cares about what happens to Karel, and delays his return to the US in order to facilitate adoption. American and European audiences responded to Clift's energy and compassion. Steve's ability to truly see Karel in the rubble of Munich and not simply run away after tossing him the remains of his lunch was a telling metaphor for what American commitment to Europe could mean. It was significant that Zinnemann changed Steve's occupation from army journalist (intent on using Karel's story for career advancement) to an engineer (in the business of German reconstruction).[116]

But in *The Search*, the dominant images in Karel's life are wire fences and gates. He slowly learns to place word with image as Steve talks over his efforts to bring Karel over to the States. Karel stares at a wire fence in a zoo, then later draws his own fence on a blank sheet of paper. His own drawing triggers his memory of his mother in a camp and a visit to a Munich factory, where he observes women leaving the plant through the links in the wire fence. Arguably the most heartrending image in the film is of Karel behind the barbed wire fences of Auschwitz watching his mother being taken away in a truck. But fences also dominate his life in the postwar era (fig. 26). As a stateless DP child trying to get to America,

Karel faced fences as impenetrable as those at Auschwitz. Zinnemann's evocative shots of Germany's ruined cities and desolate, empty streets, contrasted with the throng of refugee children in box cars and train stations, are repeated again at the end of the film. This process has no end. Although his reunion with his mother creates a nominal sense of narrative completion, Zinnemann deliberately leaves the rest of his narrative unresolved.

Ivan Jandl faced something as tragic soon after. With the assassination of Jan Masaryk and the Soviet takeover of Czechoslovakia, Czech immigration to America ceased. America had been the slowest nation to offer DPs asylum, and the DP Act/Public Law 774 (1948) had exclusions that effectively barred Czech immigrants (since refugees from the communist regime would have left after December 1945).[117] When Jandl won a special Academy Award (1948) for his performance as a child actor, the regime ended his acting career. He was barred from the film industry, from the theater, and from immigrating to the US. The communists even broke his Golden Globe and confiscated his Academy Award. Zinnemann arranged to send him another. As he wrote Margaret Herrick, secretary to the Academy, "Ivan is very unhappy because to date he has not received the award ... You can well understand how strongly a child feels about such things. Perhaps it was sent to someone else who might have failed to forward it. At any rate, knowing how much this means to Ivan, I beg you to investigate the matter and to inform me at your earliest convenience ... Should it prove necessary, I would be glad to pay personally for a replica of the Award—because I feel very strongly that a joy such as this should not be withheld from a child who may not be leading a very joyful life at present." Soon, even his letters to Jandl were confiscated.[118] The same happened with Clift and Aline MacMahon's correspondence. Peter Viertel and Fred Zinnemann's original hope—that Czechoslovakia was the future of European regeneration—was over.

The Impact of the New International Film

Although by the 1950s Hollywood's European productions would become set pieces of the studios' annual prestige output, in the second half of the 1940s, filmmakers contemplating foreign locations encountered massive logistical problems and ideological resistance from studio bosses. Billy Wilder's case, in which he used his military appointment to pitch *A*

Foreign Affair to American occupying forces and Paramount, was unique. The outcome of the *Paramount* case had not yet made the financial benefits of shooting in Europe apparent, and by late 1946, despite efforts by Wilder and others within the US government to corner the German film market, most of Hollywood still refused to emerge from its entrenched filmmaking isolationism.[119] When MGM began to churn out publicity for *The Search* for its March 28, 1948, release date, one of its advertising tags focused on the novelty of the studio bankrolling any European-based production. *The Search* was one of only a handful of films made in Europe and backed with MGM's money since the silent era—a list which included the silent *Ben-Hur* (1925) and *Goodbye, Mr. Chips.* (1939).[120] The film was the first release of a growing trend. *Berlin Express* was released May 1, and *A Foreign Affair* was on American screens in late August. By the early 1950s, European production would become the norm for the Hollywood studios' most prestigious productions, peaking in the 1950s with *Quo Vadis* (1951), *Roman Holiday* (1953), *Three Coins in the Fountain* (1954), *Around the World in Eighty Days* (1956), *Funny Face* (1957), *Gigi* (1958), *The Young Lions* (1958), and Zinnemann's own *Nun's Story* (1959). Yet *The Search* remained unique because it was a truly international film, produced by a Swiss film company, bankrolled with Swiss and American money, with a Swiss, German, French, Czech, and American production team, and featuring child DP "actors" drawn from all over Europe.

But *The Search* was even more unique in its ability to connect America and Europe. At first, it seemed as if European publicity and box office returns would completely outstrip its impact in America. MGM executives were delighted to find that the film quickly cleared a million dollars in net profits within a few months in European theaters. Initially, MGM's image layouts focused bizarrely on a lone woman (not obviously Jarmila Novotna) pursued by a man in unmarked alleys and variants of the pursued woman.[121] The children's angle and the war context were completely ignored. Since the film had no recognizable stars (Clift achieved stardom with *The Search* and his subsequent release, *Red River*, 1948) and few professional actors (Corey and MacMahon), few faces appeared in initial posters and newspaper ads, contributing to the general sense that *The Search* was more of an orphan than an MGM release.[122]

The United Nations and other relief organizations were instrumental in generating US interest in the film. Journalists took photographs for the "Save a Child, Save a Future" march in New York City's Times Square where *The Search* was prominently displayed on a theater marquee.[123]

Worldwide events like UNAC's appeal for children in the Philippines featured a benefit premiere of *The Search* on August 17, 1948, in Manila.[124] *The Search*'s release in the US also coincided with a recent UN report which stated that 30 million children were in desperate need of food and shelter. The film's prominence in the big cities was used to generate donations to the American Overseas Aid (AOA)—UNAC's $60 million appeal.[125] In addition, the director of the United Nations insisted that all of his staff see the film, and MGM made special tickets available for a dollar.[126]

The film's success in Europe and its prominence as a UN film made certain American critics take notice. Spreads in the *New York Times* focused on the film's unique origins as a collaborative project between European and American filmmakers, and Wechsler did his utmost to describe the film's main impetus: "The genesis of *The Search* which dramatizes the plight of Europe's war orphans, goes back to Thérèse Bonney's book of photographic studies, *Europe's Children*, and to the trip Mr. Wechsler made here from Switzerland in 1945 . . . Mr. Wechsler also was disturbed to find that we did not 'really comprehend' the extent of human suffering abroad and especially the 'sad plight of innocent children.'"[127]

Zinnemann acknowledged Wechsler's role, and Wechsler would go on to address a range of children's issues in subsequent films, from the saccharine *Heidi* (1952) and *Heidi und Peter* (1955) to *The Village* (1953), a fictionalized story set at the Pestalozzi children's village. In 1947–48, Zinnemann's efforts with the press were less about authorship and more focused on deemphasizing the film as a fictional narrative and in giving UNRRA the good press it deserved. As he wrote in *The Screenwriter*, "No writer in his office could be trusted to dream up the story. These children must be seen. They cannot be imagined . . . From the lips of these workers and from the children themselves came the raw stuff from which *The Search* was made. Without drama, without emphasis, these people gave us material sufficient for ten such films." Zinnemann also defended UNRRA, saying that while conservative US critics have argued that UNRRA "mainly wasted the taxpayers' money and that it was a front for black market activities besides," this was not true.[128]

With MGM's money behind *The Search*, Wechsler could do little to minimize its public perception as a Fred Zinnemann film. In fact, Zinnemann's reputation as one of Hollywood's most socially and politically committed directors dates from the critical reception of *The Search*. Zinnemann was honored with his first award from the Directors Guild of America for his work. The usually cantankerous Bosley Crowther called it "a major revelation in our times," and became a staunch advocate of Zinnemann's pictures.[129] Archer Winsten and Alton Cook named it as one of the year's ten best films, and it came in second on the prestigious *Film Daily*'s top ten for 1948.[130] Reviews always headlined Zinnemann's work as a director and his meticulous research and sensitive use of actors.[131] When he had left Hollywood for Europe to make *The Search*, it looked as though both Hollywood and Zinnemann had had enough of each other. As Jay Carmody noted in August, "Before his brilliant achievement in that screenplay narrating the plight of Europe's lost children, Zinnemann was merely a bright young man lost at the bottom of his studio's personnel chart."[132]

The Search reconnected Hollywood to the potential of European locations and profits, though sadly not to serious social issues. Shortly after completing the film, Montgomery Clift, Zinnemann, and writer Seymour Stern (*Benjy*, 1951) traveled to Palestine on an extensive research trip about the new Jewish communities and their relationship with indigenous Arabs. In some sense, it represented their continued interest in the lives of the former DP children. In his notebooks, Zinnemann planned that their film would "show tenderness of people—especially soldiers (men and girls) for children—the feeling how precious they are—as a symbol of the future—the few surviving ones form Europe will be start of a new nation." Yet *Sabra* came to nothing, perhaps due to Zinnemann's uneasiness with the ideology of the kibbutz: "They're not individualists. They think in terms of the NATION; the smallest unit they think in is NOT the individual, not even the family. It is the group. Kibbutz: It's group conscious and group motivated."[133] The militant emerging nation had an emphasis on physical health, prowess, a mantra fixed on the future ("Stop thinking about the past"),[134] and the sentimental attachment to children—these were all qualities of other wartime regimes seemingly positioned at opposite ends of the political spectrum. Staring relativism in the face was particularly hard for a Jewish filmmaker, but Zinnemann did it.[135] Throughout his career, Zinnemann focused on the individual and his or her resistance to a group, system, or doctrine. Through the script, mise-en-scène, lighting, close-ups, dolly shots, he worked to "reveal one thing at a time," to focus on the human face moving in and often against, prevailing historical forces.

As a result of *The Search*, Zinnemann would also remain on good terms with the UN Film Board and former UNRRA officials. While Zinnemann was on location for *The Nun's Story*, the UN's chief of film services, Thorold Dickinson, told him "the UN High Commissioner for Refugees has an urgent subject—the drive to clear all the refugee camps in

Europe by the end of 1960. It is a subject of settling the 'difficult' refugees that nobody wants, the old, weak and sick, mentally and physically."[136] But, as child DPs would not be an issue in this documentary re-evaluation of *The Search*'s refugee context, the director balked, and instead suggested other projects. He approached them several times between 1958 and 1965 about making documentaries to spread knowledge of world hunger, decolonization in Africa, and even a semi-fictional feature about the Muslim-Hindu conflict in Northern India and the UN's efforts to maintain the peace without demonstrably interfering with non-Western governments and cultures.[137] The UN warned him that these were potentially dangerous topics to negotiate with the bureaucracy and that they couldn't guarantee him the final cut ("we would not want work of your quality getting caught in the machine").[138] He replied to Dickinson: "I was particularly interested in your observation that certain controversial subjects could be best handled by a private firm, without official approval of the UN."[139] The shadow of censorship, as much as the Film Board's limited resources, forced him to abandon the projects. The Hollywood system not only provided the financing, but also, ironically, the artistic environment in which he could say what he liked. The UN's documentary filmmakers had neither of those luxuries.

Once Wechsler obtained MGM's grudging loan of Zinnemann and partial financial backing, Hollywood unintentionally sanctioned a unique international film that paved the way for future Hollywood ventures in Europe. Historical assessments of Germany's rubble films and the Hollywood and international productions shot in bombed German cities treat *The Search* as either part of a cluster of Hollywood films about Europe (with *Berlin Express* and *Foreign Affair*) or a "neo-realist-influenced" Hollywood shadow of Rossellini's *Germany Year Zero*, Vittorio de Sica's *Shoeshine* (1946) and *Bicycle Thieves* (1948), and Géza Radványi and Béla Balázs's *Somewhere in Europe* (1947).[140] But *The Search* is unique. Conceived in 1945, *The Search* anticipates and is set apart from all of these major narrative films in its international pedigree, avoidance of a "national" narrative basis, and rejection of conventions of traditional heroism and American involvement. And unlike Hollywood's future location films, Zinnemann's two years of work on *The Search* represented a commitment to not only Hollywood's involvement in the regeneration of European cinema, but also to America's role in the reconstruction of Europe. While Tourneur exploited ruined Germany's potential for espionage thrills and Wilder, via Jean Arthur's uptight American politician, poked fun at America's fear and fascination with the former enemy in *A Foreign Affair*, Zinnemann avoided genre clichés and generating the postwar binaries of enemy-conqueror. He also created a fictional soldier who embodied America's efforts to define international citizenship. Montgomery Clift's role as an American soldier posted in Germany who helps a nameless "displaced child" focused United Nations' efforts to target American isolation from Europe in 1947–48. But most importantly, were it not for Zinnemann's commitment to research and the visualization of oral history, Karel's and many other child testimonies would have been lost to history. He was the only major filmmaker to be invited by UNRRA and the US military to interview child survivors of the Holocaust held in camps in occupied Germany. More than any other director of his generation, Zinnemann's commitment to international filmmaking was a moral and ideological choice. While his future ventures would be stamped with a Hollywood studio label, the contents would be marked by the memory of *The Search*.

CHAPTER THREE

The Un-American Western

"We wanted to see whether we could take the rigid classic
form of the Western and give it new meaning."
—**Fred Zinnemann** (1954)[1]

"'May, are we going to part on a misunderstanding?'
'Have I lived like a woman who needs protection?'"
—**André Malraux,** *Man's Fate* (1933)[2]

MGM was stunned by the domestic and international success of *The Search*, and studio executives attempted to renew Zinnemann's contract instead of firing him. But after fulfilling the terms of his original, reinstated contract with *Act of Violence*, he quietly left the studio, eventually signing with independent producer Stanley Kramer for a three-picture deal.[3] Zinnemann's first project for Kramer also brought Marlon Brando to Hollywood. In many ways, *The Men* (1950) resonates with Zinnemann's interests in the social consequences of the Second World War; Brando's character was based on the experiences of a real wounded soldier and his agonizing rehabilitation. Zinnemann and writer Carl Foreman spent a lot of time researching the backstory and became good friends, and Zinnemann was able to manage Brando's type of Method acting, even though it differed substantially from Montgomery Clift's easy, accommodating style. Yet Kramer's interference with *The Men*'s postproduction music editing irritated him.[4] He found Dimitri Tiomkin's score superfluous and distracting, and more and more, planned for the time when he would control the final cut. In his next project for Kramer, Zinnemann would be especially careful to camera cut, leaving no extra footage or options for the producer so that the film would be assembled as the director intended. With *High Noon*, Zinnemann may have breathed a sign of relief. Carl Foreman's adaptation of John Cunningham's short story in *Colliers* was just an ordinary, small-time Western, and Kramer showed little interest in the project, even when aging Western actor Gary Cooper agreed to play the starring role of Doane, a retiring sheriff who refuses to run from a killer he once put behind bars. Having been abandoned by the town and all of his former friends and special deputies, he kills his old adversary and his gang with the last-minute help of his wife (who shoots one of the gunmen in the back). It would be a short, inexpensive project, shot in twenty-eight days on the Columbia ranch.[5]

Zinnemann had loved Westerns since reading Karl May's *Winnetou* novels in Vienna as a boy, and knew that they were one of the few Hollywood genres that enabled filmmakers to get out of the studio on location shoots. As he recalled, "Friends were quite puzzled by my enthusiasm over what they thought to be the script for just another Western,"[6] and their bewilderment is somewhat understandable. Why would an urbane, educated European want to direct a Western?

It would become his most controversial film. When *High Noon* was released in April 1952, critics praised Zinnemann's direction, even arguing that it was the equal of *Stagecoach* (1939) as the all-time best Western. But as time passed, some politically conservative filmmakers and auteurist critics would attack his work for its failure to conform to the traditions of the genre, targeting the actions of the sheriff (renamed Will Kane), the roles of the two women (wife Amy Kane and Helen Ramirez, local businesswoman and Kane's former lover), and even the cinematography.[7] As Zinnemann found out, film criticism of the Hollywood Western has a particularly rigid code, and when Westerns are said to "violate" the rules of the genre, since the 1950s critics have used a very simple tactic: the offending film is not a "pure" Western.[8] *High Noon* (1952) became Hollywood's most high profile renegade, a true genre hybrid that unsettled critics Robert Warshow and André Bazin and offended conservative filmmakers Howard Hawks and John Wayne. Despite popular and academic interest in postwar Hollywood Westerns, structuralists and auteur-driven connoisseurs continued to sideline *High Noon* through the 1990s, and even today, with genre criticism allegedly more historically engaged and willing to embrace "hybrids," the film remains a prominent outsider in a community of classic Westerns.[9] This might surprise some, given the film's initial industrial praise (four Oscars and seven nominations), popularity with mainstream audiences (one of the top ten grossers of 1952),[10] and its story of a small-town sheriff, abandoned by his former friends and townspeople, who faces some former enemies alone at high noon. Film historian Phillip Drummond puts it innocently enough; despite its setting, boots, saddles, spurs, star, and gunfight, *High Noon* "gets its content from elsewhere."[11]

Many, including *High Noon*'s screenwriter Carl Foreman, have argued that the narrative was an allegory of Hollywood's cowardice during the HUAC hearings, and indeed this is what motivated André Bazin to note "the great skill exemplified in Foreman's adaptation was his ability to combine a story that might well have been developed in another genre with a traditional Western theme. In other words, he treated the Western as a form in need of a content."[12] Because the Western's content is the epic of American individualism and freedom—the image of wide-open spaces marked only by the lone man on his horse—Foreman's decision implies that Western history is not complete and that its narrative lacks something. That Foreman's "something" was the contemporary anti-communist witch-hunt was more than controversial. Furthermore, Western historians Frederick Jackson Turner and Theodore Roosevelt, with many of their less well-known followers, created the sense that the frontier experience was something specific to the nineteenth century. Ensuing popular and academic writings on the West tended to reinforce the idea that with 1890 and the "closed" frontier, Western history simply stopped. But *High Noon*'s Western history was not safely dead; the adage "better dead than Red" had a new meaning. Although not a self-consciously historical Western (there are no text inserts or dates which reference a specific time and place and none of the characters is a recognizable historical figure), *High Noon* is not a self-contained myth—it relates to contemporary events of the Cold War. The conflicts aren't timeless but timely.[13] Writing later in life, Zinnemann, while acknowledging the impact of the Red Scare on the film's reception, felt that "the nervousness about subversion was perhaps not even political, but rather a subconscious worry that the classic myth of the fearless Western hero, the always victorious superman, was in danger of being subverted."[14] In its very look and alteration of key Western genre traditions, Zinnemann would argue that *High Noon* was truly "subversive." Yet Western history and myth are to an extent inextricably bound to American political consciousness. In any case, from its release, *High Noon* refused to be "contained" on the level of American Western content, history, and genre conventions, though Foreman was exiled to Britain and cinematographer Floyd Crosby and others involved with the project suffered the impact of the Hollywood blacklist.[15] Zinnemann, a workaholic with a low social profile and an innate reluctance to join any group, remained watchful but unscathed.[16]

Although the film's resonance with the blacklist has impacted its critical status as a "true Western," the European-born, Jewish director, perhaps even more than the screenwriter, is the "outsider" in this American Western debate and the key to understanding much of the critical unease surrounding *High Noon* for sixty years. When Zinnemann left Europe for America in 1929, he remembered with affection his cross-country bus ride with the passengers, who, although "curious about a foreigner," were warm and trusting: "Never mind who or what I was, or where I came from."[17] Zinnemann's memories evoked an America familiar from Frank Capra's *It Happened One Night* (1934), where people helped each other regardless of their differences. But with *High Noon*'s release in the spring of 1952, Zinnemann faced another America which could be every bit as intolerant and vicious as the fascist Europe he had left. This fear of foreign influences, either politically or culturally imagined, impacted critics' understanding of both *High Noon* and Zinnemann's work, and the director came to realize that fascism was not just a European disease.

Authorship: Or, Why Only Native-Born Directors Can Make Westerns

As Drummond mentions, *High Noon* is not as frequently cited in genre criticism of the Western, which from John Cawelti and Will Wright's structuralism to the neat genre studies of Philip French, Jim Kitses, and Edward Buscombe, tends to focus on the work of John Ford, Howard Hawks, Anthony Mann, and Budd Boetticher—all of whom were directors prized by *Cahiers du cinéma* and the postwar European auteurist critical tradition popularized in the 1960s by American film critic Andrew Sarris.[18] While they tend to use words like "symbolic," "lyrical," "romantic," "expansive," and "metaphoric" to describe the power of the genre and its code, what one also notices in their approaches is that the films discussed and praised are largely directed by native-born Americans, despite the clear evidence that foreign-born directors such as William Wyler, Fred Zinnemann, and Fritz Lang could make Westerns acceptable to mainstream audiences. As Philip French blithely claims, when critics condemn Westerns, "the real judgments are aesthetic, and as a result even Marxists and the structuralist critics finish up celebrating the Westerns of Howard Hawks, John Ford, and Sam Fuller and rejecting (or denouncing) liberal Westerns such as *High Noon* or William Wyler's United Nations hymn to peaceful coexistence, *The Big Country*."[19] According to Will Wright, German-born William Wyler, who made the occasional Western beginning in the 1930s, "made the error (with respect to the myth) of making the hero [Gregory Peck] an eastern dude" in *The Big Country*.[20] Fritz Lang often stood out as the foreign director of historical takes on the genre, like *Western Union* (1941), but reviewers usually ignored Lang in favor of the screenwriter.[21] Lang's use of Marlene Dietrich in *Rancho Notorious* (1950) was just not the way things were done, according to Bosley Crowther. This unease has persisted in more recent assessments of Lang's Westerns, which tend to segregate their style in terms of the director's other work in melodrama and film noir, rather than to compare them with other Western films.[22] In Hollywood, John Ford and Howard Hawks were the most articulate about their personal investment in the American frontier, and film criticism beginning in the 1950s amply supported the belief that the genre was created and sustained by a group of men who "knew the West."[23]

In *The Cultures of the Cold War*, historian Stephen J. Whitfield perpetuates the sense that *High Noon* is not "a director's film" or the work of a Western auteur like Ford or Hawks because Zinnemann was not a native-born American. As he remarks, "Perhaps because its director, Fred Zinnemann, was born in Vienna (where chuck wagon grits are not part of the cuisine) and was never to direct another [W]estern, scenarist Carl Foreman has usually been credited with primary responsibility for this 1952 movie."[24] Whitfield's omission of *Oklahoma!* (1955) from Zinnemann's Western credentials is a mistake many critics make, perhaps innocently, given its crossover status as both a musical and Western and its close association with Richard Rodgers and Oscar Hammerstein II as its principal creators. However, as Zinnemann pointed out, "I tried to make the heavy, Rod Steiger [Judd Fry], understandable as a human being, and Rod did a marvelous job. He became totally understandable, and it threw the whole film out of kilter, because everyone suddenly became terribly beastly. They hounded him to death, and it was very nasty if you look at it that way."[25] The fact that Zinnemann cast the only Jewish actor in the cast as the dark working-class outsider in the golden West made this "mistake" even more interesting.

Stephen Prince has made a convincing argument that "Zinnemann's experience as a Jew in Austria may have made him exceptionally keen to the agonizing dilemma faced by Kane" when he is made a scapegoat in *High Noon* and abandoned by his friends.[26] More often, when critics have focused on his Jewish émigré status, they have avoided discussions of Zinnemann's understanding of Western history and the touchy issue of "foreigners" making important critical Westerns. But Whitfield's critical nativism diminishes Zinnemann as the "foreign" production element, a filmmaker who got his exposure to the West via Karl May rather than the nationally approved Theodore Roosevelt or Zane Grey.[27] This nativist strategy, which grants the native-born American Foreman priority of authorship, also dovetails with US historians' interests in Cold War culture. For Whitfield and many other cultural and film historians in the 1980s and 1990s, *High Noon* is not necessarily important as a Western so much as it is a fairly self-conscious critique of McCarthyism in the 1950s.[28] Foreman is therefore critical to this debate, since he "wrote" the political subversion into the script. More historically oriented film critics like Michael Coyne have subsequently described *High Noon* from a similar perspective.[29] Yet *High Noon*'s critique of anti-communist rhetoric, explicitly stated by Foreman in interviews, has impacted the film's status as a Western precisely because it gets its content "from elsewhere."

The critical focus on Foreman and even executive producer Stanley Kramer over director Fred Zinnemann as the film's principal auteur is another unsettling element in the predominantly director-based film criticism of the 1950s and beyond. It also underscores the film's aberrance as a Hollywood Western.[30] Although screenwriters and producers are normally ignored in prevailing auteurist debates in Hollywood cinema which has tended to canonize directors, Foreman and producer Stanley Kramer were invested in controlling the public response and authorship credit for the film. Foreman's position is arguably more credible than Kramer's. He owned the rights to the original magazine story, *The Tin Star*, upon which he based *High Noon*.[31] Foreman wrote all versions of the script—which differ significantly from the original story—and without input from Kramer.[32] Originally, Foreman's role was considered substantial enough by Kramer to warrant making Foreman the film's associate producer. Both Zinnemann and Foreman recall that Kramer had little day-to-day interest in the development of the script and shooting, and Zinnemann's relationship with Kramer visibly deteriorated on the set (fig. 27).[33] Foreman recalls having productive discussions with Zinnemann about the staging and look of the film. The writer's appearance as a non-friendly witness for HUAC in 1951 devastated his Hollywood career, despite the efforts of

FIG. 27 Zinnemann trying to ignore Stanley Kramer on the set of *High Noon*, 1951, AMPAS.

Gary Cooper and Zinnemann to publicly support him. However, Kramer severed all contact with Foreman upon learning his testimony to HUAC and fired him. The screenwriter left for Great Britain. When he did return to America in the post Cold War era, Foreman titled his new production company High Noon.[34] His public remarks about the film, particularly in the 1960s and 1970s, reinforce the public perception of the film as an allegory of American political life, where Sheriff Will Kane (read Foreman) gets no help from the town (Hollywood) in his efforts to combat the threat of the Miller gang (HUAC and Senator Joseph McCarthy).

With Zinnemann's input in the summer of 1951, the shooting script became the blueprint for the film's narrative structure, although Zinnemann cut Foreman's dialogue down to a bare minimum, preferring to structure the film around Kane's series of silent, lonely walks or "plods" around the town.[35] Only two of Foreman's small scenes involving a second deputy bringing in a prisoner were cut during production, yet Kramer would later claim that he edited the film and saved *High Noon*.[36]

Zinnemann, who planned the day-to-day shooting long in advance and shot sparingly throughout the project, rejected this, and when one compares script to film, Zinnemann's position is clear. From page one and the opening shots, there is nothing to cut or rearrange. "There is simply no fat on the narrative and nothing to edit," concurs son Tim Zinnemann. Yet Kramer, intent on taking production credit for a film in which he had initially little interest, created the sense that *High Noon* needed handling after Zinnemann's inexperienced work. Other executives at Kramer Productions and United Artists may have been willing collaborators. As Tim Zinnemann recalls, executives had walked out at the studio preview, complaining loudly about the film and the music (Kramer should at least take the credit for commissioning Dimitri Tiomkin's score). Yet Zinnemann took the blame that night. As one executive remarked to another in the men's restroom, "What does a European Jew know about making a Western anyway?"[37]

Zinnemann's Reshooting the Western in Twenty-eight Days

Before film criticism focused on debates surrounding Foreman and the film's political aberrance, Bosley Crowther would be one of Zinnemann and *High Noon*'s staunchest advocates:

> He has constructed a real pictorial ballad with imagination and skill—a ballad of poetic rhythm that flows from realistic images paced to the strolling-minstrel measures of a fine Dimitri Tiomkin score. Mr. Zinnemann has so made his picture that you get the dusty feel of a Western town, the lean and solid nature of its people, the loneliness of the plains and the terrible tension of waiting for violence and death in the afternoon. This is no story-book Western; this seems a replica of actuality. It is a picture that does honor to the Western and elevates the medium of films.[38]

Crowther normally rejected Westerns that ranged too far from the norm, so his praise for *High Noon* is noteworthy. Yet Crowther saw the film as part of a tradition going back to John Ford's *Iron Horse*, and was willing to embrace its new Western hero and narrative, Foreman's unique political perspective, and Zinnemann's unique composition of each shot and "realistic" vision of the West. Not everyone was so disposed, perhaps preferring the "story-book Western" Crowther mentions.

Presbyterian Church, oldest church building still standing, built 1867

FIG. 28 Inspirations for the cinematography and set: Pictures of Virginia City, AMPAS.

Both Zinnemann and Foreman knew that there were rules for the representation of the Western hero and rules for the representation of Native Americans, women, the townspeople, and especially the landscape and overall "look" of the space. But they deliberately chose to revise the generic formula. For Zinnemann, this began with the cinematography. As he commented to film historian Gene Phillips, "Up to that time there was almost a religious ritual about the way that Westerns were made. There was always a lovely grey sky with pretty clouds in the background." The cinematographer Floyd Crosby "had the courage to give it the style that we had agreed upon. Floyd and I thought that *High Noon* should look like a newsreel would have looked if they had newsreels in those days, and we studied Mathew Brady's photographs of the Civil War as an aid . . . Crosby used no filters and gave the sky a white, cloudless, burnt-out look. He used flat lighting and that gave the film a grainy quality. From the first day the front office complained about the poor photography. Most cameramen might have struck their colors, but Floyd went ahead anyway. Subliminally the photography created the effect we wanted; it made the film look more real."[39] What Zinnemann does not say was that Crosby was nearly fired by Stanley Kramer, and would have been were it not for Zinnemann's backing. Zinnemann's position defends the photography in terms of its greater historical accuracy and reality compared with the films of John Ford, where the director would wait hours for the right cloud formation. He was also rejecting the pretty picture legacy created in part by painter Albert Bierstadt.[40] Zinnemann went for the slightly overexposed, bright desert-like quality of the black-and-white footage, a place which, like its hero Will Kane, showed its age up close. He didn't want the settled West looking like a garden or like a beautifully maintained Native American wilderness. Although Brady and his studio developed a style very similar to *High Noon*'s medium- and long-shot compositions, Zinnemann was equally interested in the kinds of images of Tombstone and Virginia City displayed by local historical societies in pamphlets and brochures. One of these, saved in his archive, contains photographs of the Presbyterian Church and fire station very similar to those in *High Noon*'s Hadleyville [fig. 28].[41]

Zinnemann's comments in interviews about *High Noon* consistently create a sense of the foreign outsider cutting away the fat from the national myth. This is witnessed in Zinnemann's opening shot of the frontier horizon, where Colby (Lee Van Cleef) looks out to see his partner riding towards him from an angled horizon. The first time we see the frontier space, the horizon line is at a sharp angle (fig. 29). One would almost think it was a canted frame, but no, the horizon is askew. Zinnemann also shot the meeting of Colby, Pierce, and Ben Miller as a silent sequence that would appear with the opening credits. The actors move in a coordinated, almost balletic manner, with Colby's eyes refocusing in anticipation as he first sees Ben Miller on the horizon, Miller's loose-limbed stride toward Colby as he joins him in the frame, and the grim Pierce waiting for Colby and Miller to ride with him, fitting themselves into the shot he dominates. As the three riders jog down the path toward Hadleyville like the horsemen of the apocalypse or of some distant silent Tom Mix Western (or as Zinnemann called them in the script, the "witches" from *Macbeth*),[42] we still don't know who they are. The references to the old-style Western are there, the stories that need no words, the simplicity and the coordinated flow of masculine movement. It's all there, only really broken as the discordant notes of the church bell take us out of that silent past, and into a new concept of "real time" (the film is shot and staged roughly from 10:20–12:05).

FIG. 29 The canted horizon in *High Noon*, United Artists.

Zinnemann's repeated use of time deliberately transgresses the reputed timelessness of the Western myth. While Foreman had initially scripted several inserts of ticking clocks showing the advancing time toward Miller's arrival on the noon train, Zinnemann doubled the number of clock inserts, writing each into his script and even outlining the twelve clock inserts on a separate page (fig. 30).[43] He would do something similar with frequent inserts of empty train tracks stretching directly into oblivion. Rather than showing motion, and the ultimate image of Western movement and progress associated with the frontier, Zinnemann shows them static. He even drew the shot for an interviewer shortly after the film opened: "Pencil in hand, Zinnemann bent over the tablecloth, murmuring briefly about restaurant proprieties. A small rectangle took shape. Halving it, he drew a railroad track tapering upward to the horizon, which he pinpointed. 'Eternity. My idea here was to have a conflicting flow of visual concepts. Take this white sky with no clouds, bearing down on the sheriff, Cooper. You have the contrast of this guy's loneliness, in the sky, the movement around the station and this skeleton story in the background.'"[44] He later said to critic Otis Guernsey, "Yes, there was a feeling of excitement that crept into people on the set . . . It was when we did the scenes at the railroad station. I began to feel good about those tracks as a symbol of nameless evil approaching from the point in infinity where the tracks meet. I must admit, though, that I relished the symbol for my own private enjoyment—I never dreamed it would get across so strongly to every one else" (fig. 31).[45] Zinnemann's sense of the railroad as a harbinger

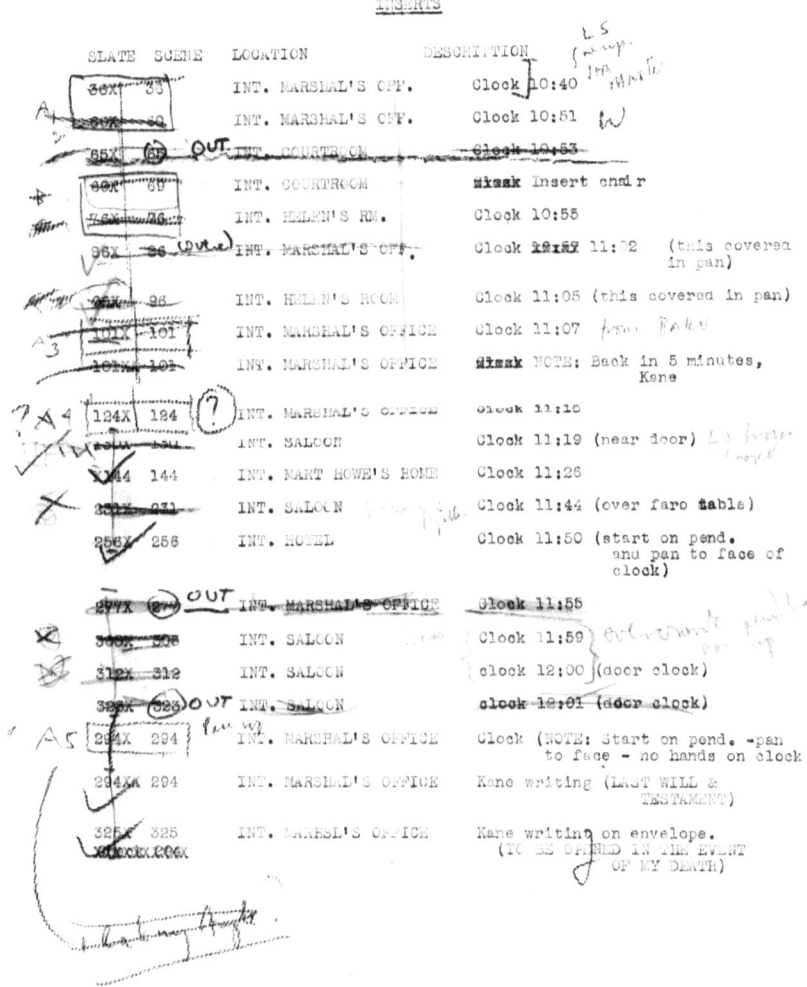

FIG. 30 Zinnemann's clock notes, AMPAS.

of evil certainly had more modern visual resonances; most famously, the shot of the tracks leading to Auschwitz's main gate (fig. 32).

In another revision of the formula, the town, eventually so demonized in the narrative, is initially a haven for Will Kane, in contrast to the open country. When Kane and Amy are fleeing Hadleyville, Zinnemann and Crosby's camera keeps tight on the turning wheels of the buckboard, resisting the temptation to show dramatic long shots of the grasslands.

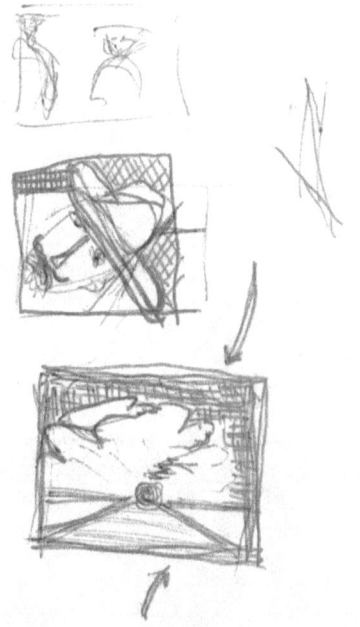 

FIG. 31 Zinnemann's image of infinity, sketched in the spring of 1951, AMPAS.

FIG. 32 And at the back of his mind, another pair of menacing tracks leading to Auschwitz, 1945, AP.

Instead, when Kane pulls up and surveys the openness with unease, Zinnemann uses only a medium shot before closing in for a closer shot revealing Kane's fear of Miller's closeness. In the buggy, he tells Amy that the prairie and open landscape are not a source of freedom but will leave them defenseless and alone. Figures inevitably become the focus of any Zinnemann long shot; when Zinnemann shows a landscape in long shot, it is, as he revealed to interviewers, a source of evil.

And what of the great uniqueness of the Western experience? In Foreman's script, Judge Mettrick lets him know that this betrayal of the town's sense of justice is not only something that reminds him of ancient Greece and its dictators, but of a small town in Indian Falls, where his only help came from a prostitute. Far from being the uniquely American democratic experience, Hadleyville's settled frontier community is neither unique nor democratic. But Zinnemann significantly altered Foreman's tone; while Foreman had scripted the judge's sense of shame in revealing this history lesson, Otto Kruger's performance projects a matter-of-fact, unrelenting cynicism.[46] Zinnemann would later expand on this position

[108]   *The Un-American Western*

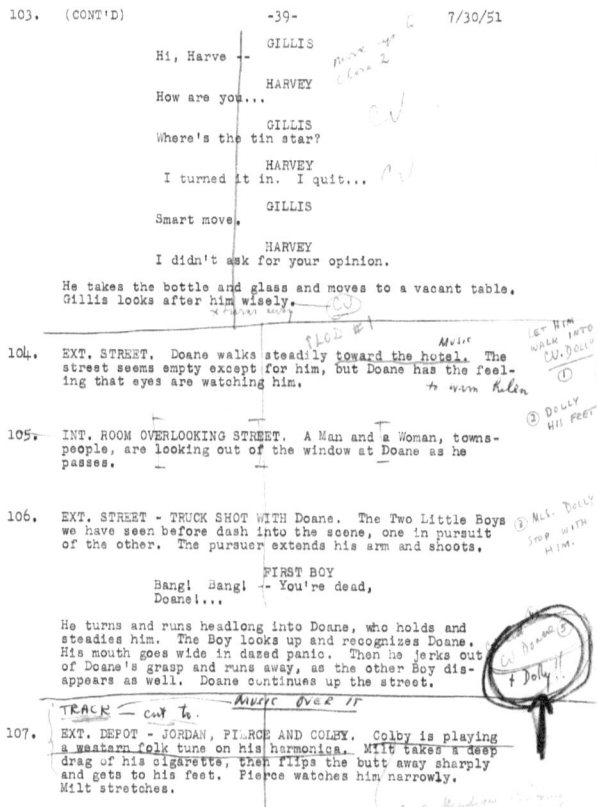

FIG. 33 The annotated script, 1951, AMPAS.

FIG. 34 One of the close-ups, *High Noon*, United Artists.

in interviews, arguing against Howard Hawks's passionate American exceptionalism and the stories of unchanging superheroes. In addition, Zinnemann would also connect themes in *The Seventh Cross* with *High Noon* in the way the heroes' contact with friends damages them, and in the way both seek the help of friends when they are in danger.[47] In Nazi Germany, George Heisler's friends and even complete strangers help him from the Gestapo, but in the American West, not one of those upstanding citizens helps Will Kane—with the exception of the other outsider, Quaker wife and "feminist," Amy.

But arguably it was Zinnemann's decision to use short cuts, stark shot-reverse shots, and tight close-ups, which turned the Western form inside out. From André Bazin to Gilles Deleuze to Edward Buscombe, the Western is epitomized by a galloping horse and rider in a vast landscape. The Western's essential visual element was the long shot, and to a certain extent, Bazin's certainty about this mirrors the historiographic metaphor codified by Frederick Jackson Turner of the glorious frontier procession seen from the distance of Cumberland Gap.[48] But Zinnemann composed *High Noon* as a series of dramatic montages of close-ups rather than the Western's traditional long takes and long shots. His annotated shooting script is covered with blocking for each scene arguing for close-ups "CU" and close shots "CS" (fig. 33). Foreman was less interested in scripting the type of shot; he left this decision to Zinnemann and Crosby. Though over his career Zinnemann would occasionally mention Ford as an early film influence, Vsevolod Pudovkin and Sergei Eisenstein were the director's inspirations for *High Noon*. The final moments before the noon train's whistle are built entirely of tightly composed, static, silent close-ups before the explosion of steam, sound, and gunshots (fig. 34), significantly altering the tempo of Foreman's script.[49]

The Significance of 1952: Genre Cleansing and *High Noon's* Women

Phillip Drummond's comment on *High Noon*—that it gets "its content from elsewhere"—resonates strongly with a long tradition in structuralist and auteur-based film criticism of the Western going back to the work of Bazin, Warshow, Sarris, Wright, and Cawelti, in which Westerns were graded on their generic "purity" and degree of conformism to timeless, masculine mythology. The basis for this search for the "pure" Western seems to be as murky as Americans' searches for that equally "pure" and elusive white, Anglo-Saxon race in the nineteenth and twentieth centuries, a loose combination of Owen Wister, Frederick Jackson Turner, and Theodore Roosevelt's writings, the images of Frederic Remington, and the B serials of Gene Autry and William Boyd (Hopalong Cassidy). Though Gene Autry did codify a list of "dos" and "don'ts" for boys wanting to be cowboys, Hollywood filmmakers were not always so careful, making a number of Westerns about women, racial minorities and lesser-known historical incidents from the mid-1920s onwards.[50] While overtly historical Westerns that used projected text and extra-textual references broke with the self-enclosed, mythic world of the Western ideal, films with women and minority characters told other narratives which conflicted with the great story of white masculine conquest. Consequently, many of these Westerns, however popular with their original audiences, were neglected by ensuing film criticism as aberrations within a perfect form.[51] Instead, films that focused on masculine professionalism and friendships with other white men (directed by Ford, Hawks, Anthony Mann, and later Sam Peckinpah) became the preferred genre currency.

This brand of genre "cleansing" in film criticism parallels Western historians and literary critics' efforts to maintain the borders of the Western "story." Historian Julie Des Jardins has discussed the ways in which popular nineteenth- and early twentieth-century American women's histories were ignored by the mainstream male world of Western historiography.[52] Angie Debo's writings dating from the 1930s on Native American history and culture were only noticed in the 1980s by "New Western" women's historians. Best-selling historical novelist Edna Ferber enjoyed writing about pioneering women and exposing controversial areas in the national past. Western cultural critics viciously attacked her work on two occasions: in 1929, when she published *Cimarron*, an exposé of white treatment of Native Americans in Oklahoma, and in 1952, when she published *Giant*, which turned attention on the treatment of Mexican Americans in Texas and the persistence of Jim Crow laws (something which *High Noon* also addresses in Helen Ramirez's comment about "what it's like being a Mexican woman in a town like this").[53] Both Western novels committed the further offense of having strong female protagonists. The controversy over *Cimarron* highlighted the indignity of a woman and a "foreigner" (Ferber was from New York and was Jewish) writing about the West. In 1952, when *Giant*'s publication coincided with *High Noon*'s release, these criticisms were repeated, and Ferber was also accused of being a communist dupe.[54]

FIG. 35 Amy (Grace Kelly) helps Will (Gary Cooper) kill Frank Miller, United Artists.

As others have noted, Foreman's most significant changes to *Tin Star* involved creating two prominent and articulate female characters, Amy Kane and Helen Ramirez.[55] Both women are outsiders in the white religious community of Hadleyville. Amy is a Quaker and, in the script, a self-proclaimed "feminist," whose rejection of violence and her husband's authority set the pace of the film in that she is the first of many people to reject Kane's decision to face Miller and help him. Helen Ramirez, the only Mexican woman in the town, is also one of its key business people and Kane's former lover. Both women have escaped unpleasant pasts and speak to each other about their experiences. Helen sells her businesses and leaves town not because she's afraid of Frank Miller, but because she doesn't want to see Kane die. At first Amy rejects Kane's decision to fight, and plans to leave on a train for St. Louis, but she returns to shoot Pierce in the back and claw the face of Frank Miller so her husband can get in the final shot (fig. 35).

Film historians Joanna Rapf and Gwendolyn Audrey Foster have examined the film and Jurado and Kelly's performances as feminist subversions of Western masculinity.[56] At one screening during the height of the women's movement in 1978, cinematographer Floyd Crosby gleefully wrote to Zinnemann that the young female audience cheered when Amy shot Pierce in the back.[57] Helen and Amy were by no means the typical binary opposites so dear to structural critics of the Western: the whore and the Madonna, yet historians in particular have persisted in seeing Ramirez as a whore and Amy as a compliant, virginal wife.[58] One film historian has claimed that in *High Noon*, "youth and women offer little hope for redemption; the civilizing female can only endorse fleeing from responsibility and is herself converted to the need for violence by her husband's predicament."[59] Molly Haskell also sees the film as "monolithically male," and one wonders whether she closed her eyes through most of the film.[60] These views ignore Foreman and Zinnemann's unique construction of Helen Ramirez and Amy Fowler Kane as two "active" and even transgressive agents who pursue their own forms of independent judgment. While Helen can give Kane stare for stare and demand, "What are you looking at?" Amy is responsible for killing Pierce and attacking Miller so that Kane can shoot him. Zinnemann's annotations on his shooting script indicate how anxious he was to make audiences "like" Amy in spite of her rejection of Kane, and to convey Helen's easy dominance over current lover Harvey, business associate Mr. Wheeler, and even Frank Miller.

Amy and Helen are two of many powerful roles Hollywood filmmakers created for women in Westerns from roughly 1930–60, yet there is a critical tendency to edit these films from the Western canon. According to critic Phillip French: "Westerns of course have to feature women if only because commercial movies must offer some so-called romantic interest. When women take the center stage in this most masculine of genres, the result is less likely to be a blow in favor of sexual equality than a strong whiff of erotic perversity."[61] French's remarks indicate an interesting dichotomy; Hollywood creates strong roles for women in Westerns, but these are "unnatural" and violate the principles of the genre. Whose principles, one might ask, given that there was historical basis for women's prominence in both written and cinematic Western narratives? They were prostitutes and saloon girls, wives and teachers, certainly, but even in the hallowed nineteenth-century West women were homesteaders and heads of house, business owners, cattle ranchers, bandits, and even politicians.[62] But Western historiography—at least until the "New Western History" of the 1980s—was invested in the story of the lone white Westerner.

However, the jacket advertisement of Frantz and Choate's "demythologizing" of *The American Cowboy* (1952) reveals an interesting strand of the debate over women's history in the West. It asserts that after reading the *real* history of the cowboy, they will realize that "the beautiful cowgirl probably originated in a Hollywood studio."[63] Hollywood, therefore, was allegedly complicit in creating a space for women in the West of which historians of the 1950s disapproved. But if French and, by implication, historians like Franz and Choate disapproved of these feminist aberrations, Hollywood's audiences paid to see them. Though late twentieth-century critics would lionize John Ford's *My Darling Clementine* (1946) with its compliant and marginal women, the film made a relatively poor showing at the box office. It was *Duel in the Sun* (1946), with its mixed race female protagonist Pearl Chavez (Jennifer Jones), which dominated all box-office records and continues to be one of the highest grossing Westerns on record.[64] But *Duel in the Sun* wasn't just an exception to the rule. The prominence of novelists like Ferber, prestige women's Westerns, and producers' interests in catering to large female audiences in the studio era may have contributed to this cultural phenomenon, a popular prequel to "New" Western women's history. Things began to change in the 1950s, partially due to the response to *High Noon*. Howard Hawks was one director who didn't approve of *High Noon*'s women. As he stated to Joseph McBride, "I didn't think a good sheriff was going to run around town like a chicken with his head off asking for help and finally his Quaker wife had to save him."[65] As Zinnemann dryly responded: "I'm sure he's a great scholar."[66]

The Studio Politics of the Revisionist Western

John Wayne and Howard Hawks were the most prominent critics of *High Noon*'s alleged subversion of American masculinity and frontier individualism, and late in life, John Wayne would publicly state that women's roles and concerns had no place in the "real" West. But Wayne and Hawks had more complaints about the film's content. As Fred Zinnemann recalled in an interview with Gene Phillips, "I'm told that Howard Hawks has said on various occasions that he made *Rio Bravo* as a kind of answer to *High Noon*, because he didn't believe that a good sheriff would go running around town asking for other people's help to do his job. I'm rather surprised at this kind of thinking. Sheriffs are people and no two people are alike. The story of *High Noon* takes place in the Old West but it is really a story about a man's conflict of conscience."[67] Zinnemann's response is striking in that he articulates variety and difference in the Western hero ("no two people are alike") rather than admitting any generic formulas. He also demystifies the American exceptionalism inherent in American formulations of the frontier by claiming that the story and the conflict could have happened in another time and place (hence his reference to *High Noon*'s three "witches" and Foreman's reference to Greek history). Zinnemann would continue this generic brinksmanship for five decades, maintaining *High Noon*'s *revision* and *transcendence* of Western traditions.

Hawks and Wayne, who also damned the film for the final scene in which Kane flings his sheriff's star in the dirt, were arguing that the Western had a code of practice and conventions, a list of dos and don'ts, which were specific to the American Western tradition. Ironically, the fiercely right-wing patriots held views of the Western as detailed as any structuralist film critic; Andrew Sarris denounced Zinnemann as a maker of "false Westerns" and preferred Hawks's conservative rebuke to *High Noon*, *Rio Bravo* (1959).[68] Foreman, instrumental in framing Kane's relationship to the townspeople and his final rejection of them, bore the brunt of the un-American criticism due to his past political persuasions, yet Zinnemann, as a "foreigner" unschooled in the rules of the Western, was also targeted. Yet many left-leaning Hollywood citizens saw Zinnemann as a courageous Hollywood outsider in the tradition of that other "foreigner," Charlie Chaplin, who was expelled from the US shortly after *High Noon*'s release. Zinnemann and Chaplin had met at Berthold Viertel's afternoon gatherings back in the late 1920s and had remained on good terms since.[69] Shortly after Chaplin was denied reentry to the US in 1952 for his alleged communist politics, Chaplin's longtime friend Tim Durrant wrote to Zinnemann:

> Through the courtesy of George Glass I had the rare and thrilling experience of seeing yesterday, one of the best so-called "Westerns" ever made. I've seen them all from the days of Bronco Billy, and if my judgment is worth anything, *High Noon* will take its permanent place among the classics in that field ... Nearly everyone experiences at least once in their life a time when they must face the impending and all-terrifying crisis absolutely alone. It is an enriching emotional and spiritual experience to vicariously feel the example of one mere human who accepted the challenge. May his acceptance inspire others to do likewise. I would love to show this picture to Chaplin, not only for aesthetic reasons, but for the satisfaction of a certain amount of self-identification.[70]

Zinnemann's friend from the production of *The Search*, former UNRRA chief William Wells, wrote similarly: "*High Noon* will not be imitated because it cannot be, any more than Chaplin's pictures can be."[71]

In the 1970s, Carl Foreman's interviews contributed to the Cold War context of *High Noon*, but it is untrue, as Phillip Drummond has argued, that "in the public sphere" *High Noon* was "airbrushed of its politics" and that in 1952, America viewed it merely as another Western.[72] Some inside and outside Hollywood made the connection between Chaplin and Zinnemann, but everyone in the industry knew of Foreman's fate in 1951. The national papers covered the HUAC enquiry extensively, and despite Kramer removing him as associate producer and firing him from the company, Foreman's name remained on the title cards as writer. Luigi Lurashi, head of domestic and foreign censorship at the rival studio Paramount, tried his best to stop *High Noon* from getting any Oscars and complained to the CIA that it was "un-American" and only "dressed up in Western clothes."[73] Furthermore, reviewers like Jesse Zunser in *Cue* noted that the central theme in the "drama of character and communal responsibility" was "No citizen is worthy of liberty who is not willing to fight to preserve it."[74] Even the *New York Times*'s Bosley Crowther took aim at the political contents of the drama, by singling out Foreman for portraying "the thorniness of being courageous in a world of bullies and poltroons." He continued, "How Mr. Foreman has surrounded this simple and forceful tale with tremendous dramatic implications is a thing we can't glibly state in words."[75]

Yet Zinnemann was also involved in these debates. Though never called to testify before HUAC, Zinnemann's liberalism was well known since his work on *The Seventh Cross* (1944) and *The Search* (1948). Several prominent critics hinted that John Ford had a competitor as a top director of Westerns.[76] Zinnemann received the New York Film Critics Circle Award for direction and was heavily touted to win the Academy Award that year. However, in an upset that many critics underscored in their columns, John Ford received the director's award for his Irish fable, *The Quiet Man*, starring John Wayne. Crowther and Guernsey noted the irony of Ford's "stock direction" winning over Zinnemann's "extraordinarily artful" work, and that "studio politics" as well as national politics, may have played a role in robbing both Zinnemann and Foreman of prizes (Foreman's script lost to Charles Schnee's workmanlike Hollywood drama, *The Bad and the Beautiful*, 1952).[77] As Crowther wrote, "The awards were not only pedestrian and conventional in the main, but the whole atmosphere of the occasion was retrospective and rococo." That Ford's semi-rare non-Western turn won over Zinnemann's revisionist Western was no coincidence for the "stodgy" and politically conservative elements of the Academy. Though Zinnemann paid tribute to Ford as an influence on his work in his acceptance speech when he won the Academy Award for *From Here to Eternity* the following year, they were not friendly.

Permeable Frontiers and the Body of the Cold Warrior

For all the public drama over Foreman, which later involved Wayne and Hawks, *High Noon* has provoked alternate readings of its Western narrative, most notably by Harry Schein in 1955, who argued the film was a metaphor for Cold War containment and the reluctance of certain Western powers to confront the menace during the Korean War.[78] Cultural historian Richard Slotkin, while acknowledging that *High Noon* can appear "anti-canonical" in making frontier progress (mouthed by Thomas Mitchell's mayor) as "motives for cowardice," underscores its "ideological structure that devalues 'democracy' as an instrument of progress and declares that the only effective instrument for constructive historical action is a gun in the hands of the right man."[79] More recently, film historian Matthew Costello pointed out that in its demonization of the community, *High Noon* reinforces some of anti-communist discourse's attitude toward group leadership (the town).[80]

The history of *High Noon*'s critical reception since 1952 certainly recalls the instability of the text in the face of modernist and deconstructive interpretations, yet one has to stop somewhere. Neither historically nor visually can one justify interpreting *High Noon* as a defense of Cold War discourse (where Miller is the communist threat and Kane the lone warrior). Suzanne Clark's brilliant delineation of Cold War ideology's appropriation of Western discourse and its links with fascist ideologies of containment and extermination begins by focusing on the body of the "Cold Warrior." She writes, "The Cold War made the historical drama of the national subject its center." That center of consensus was dramatized by narratives of defense focusing on the decay of the body. George Kennan's infamous telegram becomes the starting point for images of disease and fluidity, qualities often used to describe women, communists, and Jews. Clark notes, "It is the waste of bodies—the growing hair and nails, the excrement, menses, saliva, spilled semen, excess of nursing milk, blood—and their final reduction to waste, as corpse, that marks the act of definition, and difference, in the Cold War—the body as abject."[81]

With regard to Cold War rhetoric and its rejection of the permeability of the Cold Warrior's body, Clark should also have included tears and sweat. Zinnemann's filming of the visibly aged Cooper as he sweats, winces in pain, and cries in desperation articulate what Clark has identified as the Cold War battle over Western masculinity. Rather than being the contained, impregnable bastion of the Western hero like John Wayne,

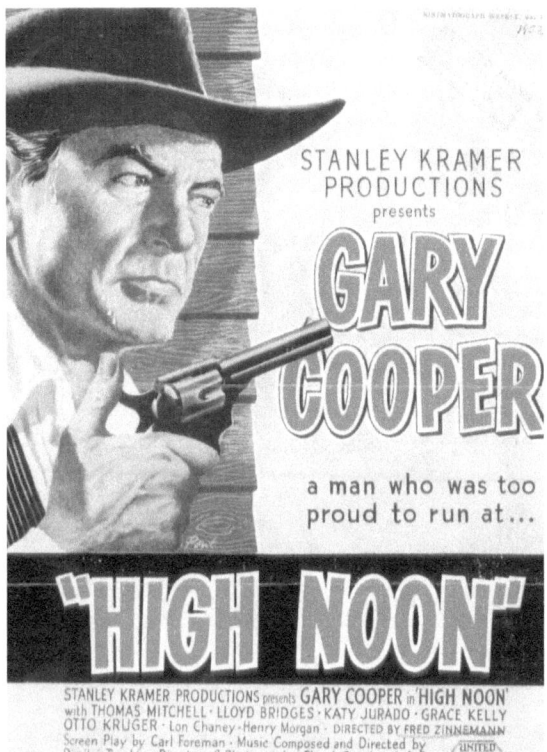

FIG. 36 Cold War sweat: Publicity for *High Noon*, 1952, AMPAS.

Cooper's performance as Will Kane and the hero's physical borders have a permeability usually reserved for the projection of women in Cold War Westerns. Cooper's sweating face was even marketed by the studio publicity machine as a key public image in 1952, making the cover of *Kinematograph Weekly* (fig. 36).[82] This permeability, as Clark and Susan Jeffords point out, is often coded as a political threat: hence the need for tough cold warriors from Mike Hammer (*Kiss Me Deadly*, 1955) and Ethan Edwards (*The Searchers*, 1956) to Harry Callahan (*Dirty Harry*, 1973). Others have noted Cooper's ambiguously gendered image of stardom,[83] and in many senses, Cooper's performance of Kane with Zinnemann's input reformulated the image of the Western hero as one who didn't have to project a hyper-violent, impregnable façade in order to articulate his American individualism and masculinity. His borders could be broached and he could display physical and emotional vulnerability, moral ambivalence, and political differences from the typical Western hero without compromising his personal integrity.

FIG. 37 Watching baseball, AMPAS.

FIG. 38 The Western hero and his Jaguar, July 1951, AMPAS.

FIG. 39 Gary Cooper clowning with Grace Kelly, July 1951: a hero unafraid of challenging his image, AMPAS.

This happened off the set as well. There was an intense camaraderie on the set, visible in the many off-camera shots of the cast and crew eating together at one table, watching a baseball game on television (fig. 37), and grinning at the camera. Though the film was responsible for graylisting him, Floyd Crosby would write to Zinnemann at the end of his life, remembering the twenty-eight days on *High Noon* as the "happiest" of his life.[84] Cooper and Zinnemann developed an intense mutual respect and friendship. Of Cooper, Zinnemann recalled, "Audiences watched him as they would watch a baby or a white kitten on screen; 'the camera loved him,' the prototype of the vanishing American."[85] For his part, Cooper was relaxed and happy on the set, and attended rehearsals, a rare thing for a star of his caliber. He was photographed under a tree with his Jaguar (not a horse), resting his arthritic back on the ground (fig. 38), feeding his teenaged daughter Maria ice cream, and in one of the candid publicity photos, rarely seen now, Cooper clowns with Grace Kelly between takes, wearing her beflowered bonnet with a sly smile (fig. 39).[86] Later in 1951–52,

Cooper famously defended Carl Foreman in the midst of the HUAC hearings despite his conservative political background. Foreman never forgot this act. Cooper's friendship with Zinnemann lasted until the actor's death of cancer in 1961. For a number of years they searched for another chance to work together again—either on a Western or an adaptation of Hemingway's work.[87]

In his very fluidity and openness as a hero, Kane resists the links Western frontier rhetoric has with fascist ideology's fantasies of containment. The Western writings of Mary Sandoz, particularly *Cheyenne Autumn* (published 1953; later an unpopular 1964 film directed by John Ford), connect the legacy of American fascism and the Native American holocaust with the more recent horrors of the Second World War. This connection between American fascism and the frontier ideology is particularly applicable to *High Noon*. In the years after the Second World War, *High Noon* was the most prominent Western directed by a Jewish immigrant. Anti-Semitism was rife in 1950s Hollywood, with Cecil B. DeMille and Howard Hawks being some of the most vocal anti-Semites and xenophobes.[88] Though *High Noon* has had many advocates over the years, *Cahiers du cinéma*, Andrew Sarris, and Hawks (beloved by both *Cahiers* and Sarris) perpetuated this view that *High Noon* was the odd-man-out in the genre.

Zinnemann, who rehearsed closely with Cooper for a week prior to shooting and filmed him frequently wiping the sweat from his brow, also used a series of close-ups revealing his face in pain and desperation, writing them directly into the blocking of all of the major scenes. He also refused to use light filters to soften the harsh shots of his aging face. But Zinnemann's influence on the look of the film and its short, rhythmic cuts (strongly reminiscent of his work on *The Seventh Cross*) reveal a unique approach to the cinematic representation of the West and American myths. While Foreman broke with the structures of the Western narrative and their intense glorification in Cold War ideology, Zinnemann fundamentally resisted the traditional look of the frontier that reinforced this cultural and political mythology. This, he felt, was even more subversive than any claims about its political subversion: "The Marshal was not *fearless*, he was scared; he was not a mythical figure—he was human."[89] Gary Cooper saw Will Kane and his dilemma as a more *historically accurate* version of Western history. The actor's father had been a trial lawyer and judge in Montana, and according to Cooper, "Dad knew sheriffs all over the West, and he knew what they were up against. Law enforcement, as he taught it to me, was everybody's job. The sheriff was not a lone figure, but the representative of the people's desire for law and order, and unless he had the people behind him, he was in poor shape. Such a man was the sheriff I was asked to portray."[90] Will Kane's looks, actions, and the film's cinematography may not have been pretty but they were real.

While Cooper saw *High Noon* in contrast to the many generic, mythic, and inaccurate Westerns, Zinnemann persisted in articulating the film as both a revisionist American narrative and a Western with transnational appeal. As with *The Search*, he balked at strictly national narratives with neatly policed boundaries of content and style. Ironically, in looking at the West and its ideological conflicts up close, *High Noon* not only revealed Cooper's age and his physical weaknesses coexisting with heroism, but also introduced a deliberately un-Hollywood, un-American style and use of montage to convey the ultimate American frontier conflict: the gunfight.[91] The Russian filmmakers' theories on the political impact of close-ups and montage may not have been familiar to most Hollywood filmmakers in the 1950s, but the European-born Zinnemann was well schooled, and knew a bit about both Soviet filmmaking and the "frontiers" of that country. Twenty years earlier, he and Robert Flaherty nearly made a documentary Russian "Western" about the experiences of a nomadic tribe in the Urals. Unfortunately, the Soviets were suspicious of "foreigners" making a film about their frontier peoples, and the project had to be abandoned. As Zinnemann remembered, "'The Russians wanted to show how primitive it all was until the Soviets came and created a paradise, and Bob [Flaherty] wanted to do a picture about a culture that was being gradually submerged by something alien."[92] Soviet frontier ideologues seemed to function not unlike their American counterparts, who wanted to show the conquest of "savage" Native Americans by Euro-American civilization as a natural part of history and progress. In the ultimate irony, *High Noon* got its content, form, and principal filmmaker "from elsewhere." But in spite of the notoriety generated by *High Noon*, Zinnemann was not yet finished exploring the American past and present, its legacies of violent patriotism, and its dread of difference.

CHAPTER FOUR
American Fascists

"Roll with the punches, if you know what I mean, but keep a firm hold onto your courage. A great deal of talent has been lost to the world for want of a little courage. You have the courage of your convictions. Courage is the first of all human qualities because it is the quality that guarantees all the others."
—**Jerry Wald to Fred Zinnemann**, 23 July 1953[1]

"Warden had a theory about officers: Being an officer would make a son of a bitch out of Christ himself."
—**James Jones,** underscored by Zinnemann in his personal copy of *From Here to Eternity* (1951)[2]

Between 1952 and 1953, Zinnemann became one of Hollywood's star directors. His ambition and rebellious need for artistic control over his work were often at odds, but for a few years, he took Jerry Wald's advice and prospered. Years before, when he made the transition to A features, his brother George kidded him over the future compromises he would have to make as he climbed the Hollywood ladder (only George would dare to call him an "anemic little prostitute").[3] Directing *High Noon* brought him an industry-wide recognition and public notoriety, but his two collaborators, Carl Foreman and Floyd Crosby, had not been so fortunate. While Zinnemann used his pull as *From Here to Eternity*'s director to hire Crosby, the cinematographer only shot some location exteriors in Hawaii before Columbia fired him. Crosby's politics were allegedly to blame, yet there is no indication that Zinnemann protested this action against his closest friend. Arguably it was a dangerous time to enter Hollywood's big league; when Zinnemann and other left-leaning members of the Screen Directors Guild signed a document calling for a general meeting to protest a recent loyalty oath, red-baiting Cecil B. DeMille pointedly mentioned the interference of "Mr. Vyler, Mr. Vilder, and Mr. Zinnemann."[4] Years later, he would remember the incident with pride, but he never mentioned what happened to Crosby. Close friend and *From Here to Eternity* star Montgomery Clift noted a change in Zinnemann from his days on *The Search*. While shooting on location at the end of April, 1953, Clift wrote him a note, inviting him for a birthday drink, gently needling him: "Ask your social secretary to confirm or deconfirm."[5]

But if Zinnemann had always "looked out on the world with the instinct for resistance," he knew when it paid to be diplomatic with Columbia. James Jones's book was the number one bestseller of 1951 and the biggest Hollywood production of 1953. And while Zinnemann had directed a number of well-received films about Second World War veterans and misfits (*The Seventh Cross, Act of Violence, The Men, Teresa*), he had never made a World War II combat picture. A year before, *High Noon* challenged all previous conventions of the Western; *From Here to Eternity* would attempt to be as controversial on screen as Jones's novel.

James Jones and the Army

Like many others in 1951, Zinnemann spent some time reading *From Here to Eternity*. James Jones would spend his career writing about the average American soldier's experience immediately prior to and during the Second World War, from his "fictional" combat trilogy *From Here to Eternity* (1951), *The Thin Red Line* (1962), and *Whistle* (published posthumously in 1978) to his popular history *World War II* (1975). To a certain extent, *From Here to Eternity* as both novel and film can be positioned within the "history from below" trend in social history and studies of war experience popular since the 1930s. Frederick Lewis Allen's popular histories of everyday life in America and Bell Irvin Wiley's studies of the lives of ordinary Civil War soldiers were significant parts of a wider movement away from the diplomatic and political history and "Great Man" biographies which had defined serious history for so long.[6] But *From Here to Eternity*'s historical revisionism operated on more than one front. Its main protagonist was a poor, white Southerner, who enlisted in the army during the Depression. In the opening chapters, Prewitt is involved, like many other US soldiers, with an immigrant Japanese woman. Later, he and his best friend, a working-class Italian American named Angelo

Maggio, are so broke as privates they go out with wealthy homosexuals to have a good time. Both men are eventually thrown in the stockade (Prewitt merely refuses to box on his vain company commander's team), and Maggio is killed by the sadistic sergeant-at-arms. Jones shows an army rife with incompetence and abuse of individuals. But the novel had many significant characters, and although focused on military life, two of them were women enmeshed in its brutalizing system, the prostitute Lorene and army wife Karen Holmes.

Nevertheless, literary historians and film critics have tended to downplay *From Here to Eternity*'s investment in the Second World War as a site of historical speculation and critique, and have instead emphasized the more limited discourses of personal memory controlling the popular novelist's creative drives.[7] Jones's "memories" are material for creating an imagined, mythic space which reflects and soothes postwar anxieties about American masculinity.[8] Cultural historians of the Cold War and the US military have been equally resistant to seeing Zinnemann's *From Here to Eternity* as an antiestablishment film, despite the fact that Jones's novel, publicity, and contemporaneous reviews of the book and film emphasized *From Here to Eternity*'s controversial critique of prewar masculine institutions, American empire, and class.[9] So in one interview, Lawrence Suid attempted several times to trap Zinnemann into admitting the army and its technical advisor had persuaded the studio to drop many of the novel's controversial aspects.[10] Historian Stephen J. Whitfield also claims that Zinnemann wanted to cooperate with the establishment when filming *From Here to Eternity*; the historian justifies this by arguing that "if it had been critical of the military, a movie version would have been not only intolerable, but, in the 1950s, also inconceivable."[11] These remarks are typical of a generation of cultural historians who have persisted in seeing studio-era Hollywood films as complicit in cultures of conformity and, during the 1950s especially, of upholding the establishment's status quo. Whitfield seems blind to Columbia's engagement with Jones's stinging critique of the army and prewar American society, and also ignores contemporary perceptions of both the novel and film as being rigorously antiestablishment to the point of subversion.[12] As *Los Angeles Times* reviewer Edwin Schallert remarked in 1953, the "subversive" film "goes all out in making the military situation look its worst, and could probably be used by alien interests for subversive purposes if they happened to want to make capital of this production."[13] But Schallert frankly admired the "great technical coup" that brought such a controversial story to the screen intact.

From Here to Eternity's hero, Robert E. Lee Prewitt, is doomed because he is an individual in a mechanistic society and military organization which demand complete subservience to the group's needs. America's peacetime army is obsessed with sports competitions, military drill, and company lore. A closely knit, powerful group unquestioningly supports the company commander. National feeling is as natural as breathing. The bureaucracy discourages politics and individualism, homosexuality is secretly tolerated, and sadism and even torture are rife in the confines of the stockade. The novel's other heroic figure, Jack Malloy, becomes a close friend of Prewitt and urban ethnic recruit Angelo Maggio while in the stockade. Malloy is a communist, and his eventual murder by the stockade commander is particularly brutal.[14] All three of these men are doomed. Though the peacetime army is drawn from the lower classes of American society, class is less important than one's position within the new bureaucracy. Women remain outside the military society but are integral as sexual objects. Racism is rife; there are almost no African American officers in the peacetime military and segregation is taken for granted.

All of the classic characteristics of fascism are in *From Here to Eternity*'s portrait of the US military and society. Jones was not the first to suggest that the US had its own brand of fascism. During the 1930s, many Americans compared FDR's New Deal and cult of personality with that of his peers in Italy, Germany, and Franco's Spain.[15] Britain and France had flourishing fascist parties prior to the war. Even Stalin's Soviet Union had been called fascist, despite fascism's intrinsic opposition to communism. Historians and political activists have drawn uncomfortable parallels with the US passion for eugenics in the early twentieth century, its harsh immigration laws, widespread anti-Semitism, racism, the power of the Ku Klux Klan and later the Black Legion, and not least, the US government's fear of communism.[16] Hollywood had also confronted America's fascist heritage on more than one occasion; in addition to Warner Bros's *Black Legion* and *They Won't Forget* (loosely adapted from the story of the Leo Frank trial), Zinnemann's *Seventh Cross* colleague, Spencer Tracy, had starred with Katharine Hepburn in *The Keeper of the Flame* (1943), a story of a deceased American political hero who was actually a closet fascist plotting a military coup.

There are obvious dangers in taking this relativism too far; the United States and Nazi Germany were not twins, although during the anti-communist witch-hunts, both book burning (including the work of Thomas Mann, whose work had also been burned in Nazi Germany) and anti-Semitism (largely directed at some of the Hollywood Ten) were rife.[17] Although fascism has been equated with German National Socialism, the two are not synonymous. Yet critics of *From Here to Eternity* noted the brutality of the stockade sequences, the corruption and sadism behind closed doors, and the toleration of these abuses. Jones's working-class, antiestablishment perspective, his frank discussion of communism and individualism as equal "threats" to the American system, his critical attitude toward national history and the military—these were all issues which challenged Columbia's filmmakers, and in particular, Fred Zinnemann. Under his direction, *From Here to Eternity* would be more than a successful adaptation of a controversial bestseller, and more than a reflection of contemporary gender conflicts. The film represents a major revision of the World War II film genre and the visual and textual establishment histories of America's "Good War." Within the heart of that establishment lay a glaring streak of physical brutality and abusive bureaucracy that was uniquely American.

Controversy and Compromise

In 1951, Jones's agent, Burroughs Mitchell, and the staff at Scribners touted the young writer as a new Fitzgerald or Hemingway, and as soon as it appeared in bookstores, critics began laying odds as to how much of the content Hollywood would censor in the screen adaptation. As with Margaret Mitchell's *Gone with the Wind* fifteen years earlier, studio executives approached the bestseller with caution. The book was infamous for its accurate barrack-room language, sex scenes, adultery, and sadism. Mitchell, who over the years had seen what the Production Code could do to a good novel, wrote to Jones, "God knows what Hollywood would do with your book, but you never can tell." Jones, preparing himself for literary stardom in New York, initially replied that he only wanted two things from Hollywood and the "main one is that I get as much money out of the sale as I can, and to hell with how they butcher it up. I'll never try to buy it back after I see what they do to it, as Hemingway is supposed to have done with *A Farewell to Arms*. I don't give a damn what they do to the movie; the book will stand by itself after the movie is forgotten."[18] However, Hollywood evidently cared. Harry Cohn not only paid $82,000 for the screen rights,[19] but, with producer Buddy Adler's approval, hired Jones to write the first screenplay.

Ironically, Jones's script reveals how little he cared about an "accurate" adaptation of his own book. Instead of beginning, as had the novel, with Prewitt's move from the elite Bugle Corps to the proletarian infantry in 1940, Jones's preliminary script begins with a flashback to Prewitt's youth and early army experiences.[20] In transposing his book to film form, Jones saw *From Here to Eternity* as a historical film focusing on the "life" of Robert E. Lee Prewitt. The narrative opens with a flashback to Prewitt's birthplace, Harlan, Kentucky, in 1932, when Prewitt was thirteen. Sergeant Warden supplies the voice-over narration and covers the highlights of Prewitt's misfit existence during the Great Depression. Jones's opening sequence therefore contains all the components of the historical film as it had evolved in Hollywood since the 1930s: flashback, voice-over, text and document inserts.[21] The montage covering Prewitt's youth and early army experiences was an extraordinarily lengthy fifteen pages, ending with Prewitt's arrival in Schofield. But Jones's use of these old historical signifiers had an innovative edge; Prewitt was not a successful, famous man like Abraham Lincoln (*Young Mr. Lincoln*, 1939) or Charles Foster Kane (*Citizen Kane*, 1941). He was, like Anna Seghers's George Heisler, a Depression-era "forgotten man." Jones named his hero Robert E. Lee Prewitt for a reason. He may have been just as proud of the army as his namesake, but Prewitt is no privileged West Point graduate from Virginia, destined to become one of America's great war heroes. Prewitt is a twentieth-century rebel who had grown up in a depressed southern mining community. The police killed both his father and uncle in labor riots after the First World War, and he watched as his mother died of tuberculosis. He left home as a kid to ride the rails in search of work, and was raped by an older man. He joined the army in 1936 because he had nowhere else to go. Prewitt wasn't a literary exception; many young men joined the army to avoid unemployment and starvation.[22]

When Zinnemann was assigned to direct the film later in 1952, he read Jones's old script and notes and was deeply interested in Prewitt's Depression-era backstory. As he noted to Buddy Adler and Daniel Taradash, who had replaced Jones as screenwriter, "If at all possible, reference should be made to Prew's childhood—the fact that he was from Harlan County, Kentucky, that he grew up in the Depression—bummed all over the country and finally got into the Army because 'he wasn't ready to starve yet.'"[23] Zinnemann, like Jones, saw *From Here to Eternity* as history rather than pure fiction, a critical look at America in transition, and a story about people who were not part of the traditional war narrative.

Circumventing Censorship

While much of the extant scholarly criticism about *From Here to Eternity* focuses on the film industry's alleged accommodation of the military, ironically, from early in production, Jones was censoring his own material. In his script, Karen Holmes becomes "the Captain's younger sister" rather than the officer's adulterous wife. He also transformed the incompetent Captain Holmes in the novel into a good guy who pressures Warden to "lay off" his hazing of Prewitt. In this early version, a Japanese Zero pilot kills Prewitt rather than American soldiers from another unit, thereby absolving the American army of any blame for his death. Major Thompson, the head of the stockade, eventually busts "Fatso" Judson for killing Maggio, so the army looks better on all fronts. Jones did not remain a screenwriter for long, and Buddy Adler quickly hired Daniel Taradash to adapt the novel. Taradash, while still focusing on Prewitt's hazing by his company commander, built up a multistoried narrative that gave screen time to Warden, Maggio, and Holmes—and especially the two women in Jones's novel, Karen and Lorene.

Jones never documented his feelings about this script, but there is evidence that Sylvan Simon, the associate producer with whom Jones had most contact, may have been pressuring him to make Holmes more sympathetic in order to obtain army cooperation on locations. Many Columbia executives worried whether army resistance to the novel would make the project "unfilmable." Although Hollywood's own self-censoring body, the Production Code Administration, and the Catholic Legion of Decency, were losing credibility and would shortly receive the twin blasts of *From Here to Eternity* and *The Moon is Blue* (a 1953 film which focuses on premarital sex), the military and its employer, the federal government, enjoyed almost unbounded power in the 1950s. California in particular had grown fat with war contracts and these military-industrial links grew during the Cold War.[24] Since Roosevelt's death the film industry had faced an increasingly unfriendly government in Washington, and the repercussions of the Paramount antitrust decision (1948) and the HUAC hearings were still being felt. Within this political context, Columbia's anxiety about adapting Jones's critical appraisal of the army is understandable.

In a letter to Harry Cohn, Ray Bell, the studio's Washington representative, estimated that there would be four major sources of trouble if the studio tried to release *From Here to Eternity*: military trouble, state censorship, religious outrage, and political pressure: "From the Pentagon point of view the army personnel are most unfavorably shown."²⁵ Bell continued: "Corruption, incompetence, goldbricking, and preoccupation with sex and gambling seem to be the army's sole concerns. I do know that there exists in Washington a feeling against this book because, according to an officer who volunteered information, 'the book portrays a rotten and corrupt army, it propagandizes against officers and the tradition of the service, and it could be a demoralizing influence at a time when this country's trying to build a big army, draft eighteen year olds and win the confidence of parents and Congress.'" The war in Korea was not popular, and as he saw it, *From Here to Eternity* could only make things worse by antagonizing the armed forces. Other executives said that "this story must be pro-army" and that the anti-officer rhetoric needed to be cut.²⁶ Others advised Cohn to "wave the flag more."²⁷

Columbia had invited a range of military and studio executives to comment on the book, and Colonel Frank Dorn, the army's deputy chief of information, was particularly concerned with the screen presentation of Angelo Maggio, the working-class Italian American who voices some of Jones's toughest criticism of the military and heroic incompetents like General George Armstrong Custer. Dorn advised Columbia to portray Maggio as "a parasite on society" because he failed to fit in with the army.²⁸ Colonel Clair Towne of the motion picture section of the Defense Department's Office of Public Information was equally against Maggio, but he also disliked the cynical Warden and individualistic Prewitt. Towne thought that he had a solution, though: "By making it clear that while Warden, Prewitt, and others might dislike their officers, this dislike stems from the realization that they, as individuals, do not have the stuff to become officers . . . the officers might be placed in a better light."²⁹ In effect, the army was working hard to label any of the ethnic or critical components as aberrant and to rewrite Jones's working-class social history, where traditionally marginalized "voiceless" men and women could not speak.³⁰

Initially, Cohn had accepted that the studio would need some form of cooperation from the army, but it was not because he wanted them to look good during the Korean War or patch studio relations with the Washington establishment. Studio records reveal that at first their main interest was in acquiring Pearl Harbor footage to use in the film's climactic scenes,³¹ but things became less intense when it was realized that Fox Movietone cameraman Al Brick had supplied most of the famous footage of the Japanese air force bombing Pearl Harbor while he was shooting locations for the feature film, *To the Shores of Tripoli* (1942) on the morning of December 7.[32] Military photographs and footage of the attack had been declassified in 1942, and Gregg Toland's reconstructions for the documentary *December 7th* (1943) would supply any other needs of *From Here to Eternity*'s filmmakers. But locations were important, not simply to satisfy Zinnemann's particular demands for a "documentary" look at the military operations at Schofield, Hickam, and Pearl Harbor or because the exoticism and spectacle of the Hawaii shoot would potentially lure audiences away from their small screens at home. Cohn, Adler, and Zinnemann also realized that a studio set would undercut the credibility of *From Here to Eternity*'s critique of the prewar army.

Cohn agreed to hold the conferences and be genial, but he, Adler, Taradash, and later Zinnemann gave nothing away in the interests of military censorship. As Cohn wrote to Jones, explaining why they were rejecting the author's expurgated script, "Have we not changed certain characters in order to pacify the army and thus lost the quality and theme which you tried to put forth in your novel? I feel that the implications in the novel officer laxity and improper use of authority were so astonishing that it opened the eyes of all who read it. If in making the movie we eliminate this entirely, then we have bastardized the book and cleaned it up to present it for screen purposes without integrity. It is my candid opinion that we do not have to lose this idea."[33] However, they got temporary "approval" using Jones's conservative script, while Cohn kept Taradash's rewrites quiet for a year.

Taradash's revised script of February 1952 took a long time to get grudging army approval and even then the studio resisted their demands to eliminate the suggestion of Karen's other affairs, tone down the bordello atmosphere of the "New Congress Club," cut Maggio's descriptions of beatings in the stockade, and make Holmes "a more positive character who exerts an influence for good on Prewitt."[34] The army evidently liked Jones's idea to have Prewitt killed by a Japanese Zero pilot, but as Adler and Taradash revealed to Zinnemann, "this, we felt, was a typical Hollywood ending and had absolutely no meaning at all."[35] Taradash's only concession, documented in correspondence, was to have army brass dismiss the incompetent Holmes rather than promoting him, as in the novel. According to Adler and Taradash, the army had tried to skew things further in the conferences by suggesting: "Captain Holmes could be portrayed as being on the spot and likely to be relieved," hence, necessitating his pushing Prewitt to fight on the boxing team. This option did two things to exonerate the army system: it suggested that the army was already planning to get rid of an incompetent officer and also gave some excuse to Holmes for mistreating Prewitt. When Adler and Taradash relayed the suggestion to Zinnemann, he scrawled a large "NO" in the margins.[36] Although in general he liked Taradash's work, his script notes to Adler and Taradash begin, "I miss the basic feeling of a peace-time, professional army. I believe that we must show the peace-time professional soldier as an outcast in an antagonistic world of civilians."[37] He also felt that the caustic and cynical Warden of Jones's novel "has lost much of his bite and aggressiveness." Privately, upon reading Taradash's first draft in August 1952, he wrote, "There is no indignation in this script. The quality of anger is gone. The temperature has cooled off—from boiling point to comfortably warm."[38] As he took charge in the late summer of 1952, he vowed to change things.

Adaptation and Resistance

Taradash understood the importance of Prewitt as the ultimate outsider, yet one who would paradoxically represent old-fashioned American values. From the outset, Taradash had planned Prewitt's entrance at Schofield as the credits rolled. "His figure, tiny and far away at first, gets bigger as the CREDIT TITLES continue, and he comes closer and closer to camera. After the CREDIT TITLES end, SUPERIMPOSED over shot is the legend: 'Schofield Barracks, Hawaii, 1941—Six months before Pearl Harbor.'"[39] But Zinnemann made Prewitt's character even more explicit from the outset, using Taradash's setup as a starting point. As Prewitt (Montgomery Clift) walks slowly and deliberately toward the camera (with Alex North's quiet blues in the background), in the immediate foreground, a platoon of soldiers marches straight across the road past Prewitt, shouting their drill, and briefly cuts him from the audience's view. The army marches in another direction, and to another musical beat. Prewitt doesn't miss a step, but continues on his way, a different way from the platoon, as always (fig. 40). Zinnemann had used a similar introduction for Robert Ryan's avenging GI in *Act of Violence*. As he tries to cross the street, intent on finding the CO who betrayed his unit during the war (and who has since become a successful businessman in his community), Ryan's character "has to step back because a few old guys were walking past him carrying the American flag as if they owned it."[40] Such visual ironies amused Zinnemann. He also pursued the contrast in his extreme long shots of the company drilling followed by close-ups of Prewitt enduring the treatment, possibly inspired by a magazine photograph

FIG. 40 Private Robert E. Lee Prewitt (Montgomery Clift) walking in a different direction, *From Here to Eternity*, 1953, Columbia Pictures.

FIG. 41 On the set of *From Here to Eternity*: Rehearsing with his two misfits, Montgomery Clift and Frank Sinatra (Maggio), 1952, AMPAS.

of a review at Schofield Barracks captioned: "Human within the anonymity of the military machine."[41]

In his opening sequence, Montgomery Clift's face betrays no emotion; he is smart, spare, "deceptively slim," and as Jones had envisaged, the very picture of a soldier. Clift was Jones's pick for Prewitt when they met through mutual friend Norman Mailer in New York ("I've always felt, he'd probably make a better Prewitt than just about any body else I can think of"), and Zinnemann agreed enthusiastically.[42] Over the years he and Clift had developed a close friendship which enabled Clift's frequent improvisations and suggestions to coexist with Zinnemann's determination to camera cut and shoot as little footage as possible to avoid studio interference in the editing room. With Sinatra, the production's other "misfit," they formed a strong working relationship (fig. 41).[43]

Although Taradash's script had cut Jones's rougher tone, the communist musings of Jack Malloy and Angelo Maggio, and Warden's tougher outbursts against army goldbricking, it contained a lot of material Zinnemann liked, including Maggio's snide comment to Prewitt about the company, delivered in the first few pages, "This is the army, they can give it to General Custer," and also Prewitt's quiet confrontation with Sergeant Warden: "If a man don't go his own way, he's nothing."[44] At which point Warden lectures him, "Maybe back in the days of the pioneers a man could go his own way. But not in our time, kid. Today you have to play ball."[45] Zinnemann liked this dialogue, believing that it reinforced Prewitt's "innate dignity . . . Throwback to an earlier race of Americans that has been lost."[46] However, he felt that as the script continued, "there is a confusion as to what the picture is trying to prove about Prew from the time of the killing of Fatso. We lose the original idea of Prew's character leading him directly into the Stockade, and from there to certain doom—the tragic idea of 'one's character is one's destiny.'"[47]

Zinnemann's vision was not confined to the events of Pearl Harbor and the Second World War. He heavily underlined passages in his copy of Jones's novel where the Depression is credited with causing Prewitt to enlist.[48] Zinnemann also underlined an unusual passage in which Jones, via Prewitt, speculates on the untold histories "written" in the scars on a soldier's body: "Each one had its own history and memory, like a chapter in a book. And when a man died they buried them all with him and then nobody could ever read his histories and his stories and his memories that had been written down on the book of his body."[49] Prewitt is a work of living history: "Robert E. Lee Prewitt, a history of the US in one volume, from the year 1919 to the year 1941, uncompleted, compiled and edited by We the People." Jones recognized the tenuousness of the historical trace left by the ordinary soldier, but Zinnemann, though intrigued, never pushed Taradash to include this section in his script.

Taradash did retain some aspects of Jones's critical comments on the frontier myth and its relevance to the 1930s army. In the novel, Prewitt and Warden's different attitudes toward the army are based on the conflict between the traditional, nineteenth-century frontier discourse and a more skeptical view of America's international, twentieth-century frontiers. Prewitt had been drawn to the army by stories told by his Uncle John, who had briefly served during the Spanish-American War. Later, Jones explicitly links Prewitt's desire to join the army to the old nineteenth-century frontier myth and a desire to be an active participant in history. According to Jones, farming—associated with 1920s agricultural depression, southern tenant poverty, stasis, and anonymity—is the antithesis of American romanticism. Although Prewitt is convinced that Frederick Jackson Turner's agrarian ideal kills the American spirit, the army "impressed him with the sense of seeing history made," since it carries on the "noble" frontier tradition.[50] So he moves out of the South and heads west, as did millions of Americans during the Great Depression.

The frontier no longer exists: Prewitt wins no new territory, but he does follow in the footsteps of many pioneers by forming a relationship in Hawaii with a "native" Asian woman, whom he later discards. Like the pioneers and their historians, from George Bancroft to Frederick Jackson Turner and Theodore Roosevelt, Prewitt forgets this mixed-race union in order to pursue dreams of individual achievement. But even though he doggedly hangs on to the idea of the frontier past, others remind him that it is only a myth.[51] The old frontier has vanished and been reimagined as a Pacific empire. Prewitt and his company exist on its edges. Upward mobility is confined to a small salary on a thirty-year tread. Though Prewitt may dream of red brick houses with oak trees on a stateside barracks, for Lorene this isn't enough. For her and most other people on the islands, the soldiers are not heroes, but the dregs of a poor subclass. To a certain extent, Jones attributes the prevailing public romanticism of the army to the dominance of a class-based officer culture: "It is hard to be romantic about the cavalry when you have to curry your own horse, and it is hard to be adventurous about the uniform when you have to polish your own boots. And this explains why officers, who care about such menial tasks, are capable of such exciting memoirs of war."[52] These memories and their establishment derived discourse would later become the foundation for historical interpretations of US conquest and development.

Both the novel and film undercut these myths of progress and development with Warden and Maggio's stinging perspectives on officers like Holmes. They believe there is no essential difference between nineteenth- and twentieth-century army life. Class clashes are not defined by historical change, and there is no such thing as nostalgia or historical progress; the army has always been a grim place for the common solider and a haven for the fascist bully. Zinnemann liked Maggio's sharply delineated maverick character as a counterpart to Prewitt. Maggio had merged with Jack Malloy's role in the novel. Zinnemann penciled in the margins of his script notes, "Maggio = Red," and in one equation illuminates his thoughts about Maggio's hazing by others in power, and his death in the stockade at the hands of Fatso Judson.[53] He also wrote, "Maggio should be a very funny and very touching figure, perhaps along the lines of a Chaplin character."[54] Zinnemann had not forgotten his experience with *High Noon*, nor the professional fates of friends Foreman and Crosby, and even Chaplin himself.

In subsequent interviews, Zinnemann revealed not one but two aspects of *From Here to Eternity* had been affected by army pressure. Captain Holmes's court martial was seen as a way of redeeming army discipline. The other condition for army cooperation was that none of Maggio's "treatment" inside the stockade was shown. Yet in not showing the "gruesome details" of the stockade,[55] Zinnemann added yet another layer of complexity to his treatment of oppression and resistance. Via Taradash's script, Zinnemann not only located Maggio's political critique of capitalist machines like the army, but also the reason for his murder behind the closed doors of the stockade. In a world obsessed with the perfect image of a soldier, *Maggio talks back*. His final words to Prewitt and Warden are oral testimonies of his abuse and his continued resistance inside the stockade. It was neither the first nor the last time that Zinnemann's heroes would resist the system through oral testimony; significantly, when Prewitt first plays the bugle in Choy's, Taradash described him as playing "in overwhelming, uncontrollable protest" (fig. 42).[56] But in eschewing the more crude images of sadistic abuse within America's military prisons, Zinnemann also makes a connection between the way Spain and Germany and indeed the rest of Europe purged its Republican and communist dissidents from the army, politics, and public life. Certainly army officials had been uneasy with the stockade sequence and its connections with the worst abuses of German fascism. As Colonel Frank Dorn wrote to Columbia Pictures, "The entire stockade business sounds like a Nazi concentration camp."[57] There were equally uncomfortable connections to Franco's fascist government. After all, the US Army had formed a very powerful alliance with Franco in 1953, giving economic and military aid to the dictatorship in exchange for the construction of several military bases on Spanish soil.[58] Was the Scofield stockade the equivalent of Spain's Ventas prison? Were Americans now engaged in their own "fascist" purge of the left in Hollywood and in Washington?

But Zinnemann explored this idea still further. In his script notes for Adler and Taradash, he wrote, "There is a brief . . . which seems to me to be one of the most important elements in the book. It is a scene between Prew and Maureen, a girl in the whorehouse. Maureen voices one of the main themes of the book: 'You've got to remember that it ain't nobody's

FIG. 42 Music and protest, with Montgomery Clift, AMPAS.

fault. It's the system. Nobody's to blame.' This theme applies especially to Captain Holmes and to Fatso. The author seems to imply that people like Captain Holmes and Fatso are not so much to blame as individuals, because they are part of a system which forces them to function in a certain way. They are links in a chain of pressure which extends far above them. The only remedy, according to Maureen, is to get drunk and forget it all. And Prew's concluding observation is: '*No wonder there's so many goddamned alcoholics in this goddamned Twentieth Century*' [Zinnemann's emphasis]. I realize that we cannot use this element in the script because the Army would undoubtedly object." Zinnemann was right; this scene would have provided a wide-ranging, ideological basis for all of the repression of the individual in modern society—and the impossibility of combating the pressure of an evil "system." Yet looking at this suggestion in another way suggests further links between the American social system and European fascism. By blaming the system of power and not the individual men responsible for heinous acts against other human beings, one uses an argument which absolves not only American fascists like Holmes and Judson, but also German war criminals after the Second World War who claimed they were only obeying military orders. This is why, in his script notes, Zinnemann would comment that one of his major jobs as director was to tackle the sentiment "It ain't anybody's fault. It's the system. Nobody is to blame.' Weaken this point by handling of individuals."[59]

Zinnemann was not the only filmmaker thinking along these lines. In 1953, Billy Wilder was making *Stalag 17* with William Holden, a film about American POWs in a Nazi camp during the Second World War. Holden plays a streetwise, wheeler-dealer card sharp who has more cigarettes than he should. When it emerges that there may be a Nazi informer in the hut, the rest of the Americans immediately gang up on Holden and beat him to a pulp. Their treatment of their fellow prisoner is worse than the Nazi treatment of the Allied prisoners. Eventually the real culprit is unmasked: a homegrown, blond, non-urban type who seems the perfect American guy. Earlier in his career, Wilder had explored the notion that foreign repression was not so foreign after all when he made *Foreign Affair* with Marlene Dietrich and Jean Arthur. Arthur's blond, clean martinet senator creates a political atmosphere any Nazi would envy.

In his script notes and letters to Adler and Cohn, Zinnemann reveals his constant interest in not losing the critique of Jones's original work and in combating the forces of censorship.[60] Yet late in production he began to worry that perhaps Americans' capacity for self-critique might backfire on an international stage. As he wrote Harry Cohn, "In countries such as France, Italy, Germany, Austria, and India, this film would diminish respect for the United States and for the American Army at a time when we can ill afford it. It could conceivably help to tip the balance of major political decisions such as the EDC. As to Germany, soldiering even today is looked upon by the average German with awe and respect. I think we would be damaging ourselves tremendously in the eyes of the Germans by showing this picture. . . . Paul [Lazarus] told me of the idea of a foreword which would state, without apologizing, that our film deals with the pre-war army. I believe that this kind of foreword is urgently necessary wherever the picture is shown outside of the United States."[61] Ironically, Zinnemann's willingness to accept the suggestion of a foreword was playing right into the army's own desire to impose a "rollup statement at the end of the film" which would state "the conditions portrayed in this picture were the conditions of *one* company, due to the inefficiency of *one* company commander during the pre Pearl Harbor days. It would be desirable to emphasize that these conditions *do not* and *cannot* exist today."[62] These text forewords and epilogues were strange reminders of the Production Code's strictures for gangster films of the 1930s, which historicized and, to a certain extent, heroized crime. But Zinnemann's suggestion for a foreword applied only to international versions of the film—especially Germany, where he wanted to avoid any equation of Americans with Nazis. At home, he felt, Americans were politically tough enough for self-examination. Upon the film's international release, several British papers, including the *Observer* and the *Sunday Times*, wondered why a film studio would be so critical of its own institutions, yet one British reporter came back with a sound rejoinder: "The Americans tell the world through this film that their nation is strong enough to criticize itself with merciless realism. Could there be better propaganda than that? I wish they could learn the same lesson in Moscow."[63] Zinnemann need not have worried; German reviews were equally admiring of a country's ability for self-critique.[64]

Repressions and Revelations: Sexuality and Gender

From Here to Eternity had an even more uncomfortable dimension to its stockade scenes. Homosexuality was a strong and often repressive undercurrent in Jones's novel.[65] Prewitt is raped by an older man as a young boy; his gay "top-kick" in the Bugle Corps replaces Prewitt, the real bugler, with his young lover as first bugler, thereby precipitating Prewitt's move to the infantry. And he and Maggio, like many other broke common soldiers, go out with gay men who will pay for their drinks and meals on the islands. Although there is no suggestion that Sergeant "Fatso" Judson is gay in the novel, Taradash and Zinnemann's scripting and filming of his relationship with Maggio has all the indications of sexual abuse, and therefore reintroduces the fear of homosexuality in the 1930s military that the rest of the script had to repress for obvious reasons of censorship. Frank Sinatra's Maggio was an Academy Award-winning tour-de-force, a performance of a man literally and figuratively punching above his weight. Sinatra is skinny, short, expressive, and quick; Ernest Borgnine's Judson is fat, muscular, tall, slow, and grim. Judson attacks Maggio on a personal level, calling him a wop and a "little Mussolini" (ironic, given Borgnine's own strong resemblance to Il Duce on both a physical and performance level). While at Choy's bar, Judson kisses Maggio's picture of his sister and whispers dirty comments into Prewitt's ear, causing the usually mild-mannered Prewitt to nearly fight Judson. This is pushing the physical and visual line of sexual abuse. But later, when Maggio is hauled in front of Judson on his way to the stockade, Taradash makes Judson's brutal mastery of Maggio explicitly sexual.[66] As Maggio approaches his desk, "music is rising in a fearful crescendo." It stops when Judson stands. As the camera reveals Judson, he smiles and says, "Tough monkey." With his eyes never leaving Maggio, "his hand gropes on the desk." "Hard sister," he grins at Maggio. Then the "camera moves in to close shot of Fatso's hand as it finds and tightens around the billy. The music sweeps up." Maggio's look of fear at

FIG. 43 American fascists and sexual ambivalence: Sgt. Judson (Ernest Borgnine) with Maggio, Columbia Pictures.

the phallic billy club is undeniable. Here, Zinnemann filmed Taradash's script almost word for word (fig. 43).

Prewitt kills Judson late one night near Hotel Street, when the two are off duty, and, like so many other noncoms, dressed in civvies. Prewitt invites Judson up an alley off Hotel Street to "talk." Judson goes with him, smiling away, but it is not the kind of encounter he was perhaps expecting.[67] Zinnemann does something very unusual with Taradash's clearly described attack. It is carried out in almost complete darkness with only the harsh street lighting seen through the alley, and shows only their two bodies heaving in the shadows. There is ambiguity in just exactly when and where Prewitt knifes Judson, and the encounter is not about clear-cut mastery and cold revenge. We see only shadows, and both men stagger from exhaustion on unsteady legs. This ambiguous "revenge" for Maggio's death is in a stark contrast with Judson's near-assault by Warden (Burt Lancaster) earlier in the film, carried out in uniform in bright electric light in a public bar (and with the heterosexual validation of the well-endowed barmaid and subject of Warden's attention, Rose). Here, Zinnemann gives further visual resonance to Taradash's subtext of fear and desire fueling men's relationships in the military. Yet Judson's actions did not attract obvious outrage from the military. In fact, few reviewers or military critics paid attention to Judson, ignoring the "other" problem by focusing on the "resistance" of Sinatra's Maggio and Clift's Prew (who was himself gay and "out" to Zinnemann and many of his friends in Hollywood). Yet Prewitt and Maggio's spiritual rape by the military establishment was at times mirrored with unsettling images of male sexual abuse and homophobia.

As with the criticism of the Western, it might be assumed that women play little to no role in Hollywood wartime melodramas. Again, this is not borne out by analyses of wartime resistance or combat films. For every *Story of GI Joe* (1945), there was a *So Proudly We Hail* (1944). For every *Casablanca* (1942), there was a *Joan of Paris* (1942). Women formed a significant portion of overseas forces in the European and Pacific theaters (350,000 American women served overseas), and operated in significantly larger numbers in the Resistance. *From Here to Eternity*'s women were slightly different. They weren't army nurses or WACS or secretaries. One was a wife of an officer and the other a prostitute.

As with *High Noon*, Zinnemann was committed to revising American genres traditionally associated with masculinity. Both Will Kane and Prewitt are unconventional heroes willing to fight alone against public opinion. They also cry (Prewitt in front of his entire barracks as he plays Taps for Maggio). But as with *High Noon*, Zinnemann focused on the stories of two women as integral to the main narrative. Jones wrote Lorene and Karen's stories into the original narrative, but overall, they represent a much smaller percentage of the novel than the film. When Cohn, Adler, and Taradash adapted the book for the screen, much of the "treatment," imprisonment, and homosexuality were expunged while the women's stories remained. Jones himself was aware enough of Hollywood's need for properties that appealed to female audiences and in his first drafts of the script, included the dual relationships. But Taradash bolstered the twin narratives so that Lorene and Karen were even more prominent. One Columbia script reader, after looking at Taradash's first estimating script, commented, "I have heard *From Here to Eternity* described as a man's story. I think it is going to prove to be, in the picture version at least, a woman's story also . . . I think that the women of the movie audience are going to understand Karen and Alma, and sympathize with them deeply."[68]

Taradash's major contribution to the script was to arrange the structure as a series of personal histories revealed directly by each of the characters in long speeches. Women had roughly half of these personal narratives. While Lorene trades life stories with Prewitt in Mrs. Kipfer's "parlor" (his about Dixie Wells; hers about being jilted by her rich boyfriend and becoming a prostitute), Karen's revelations to Warden were the centerpiece of their post-kiss beach scenes. While we get almost no information about Sergeant Warden's past, Taradash had planned a painful personal account of Karen's marriage, betrayal, and miscarriage. But after reading this, Zinnemann wrote, "Karen is the weakest character in the script. She is very unsavory somehow. Her entire relation with Warden is very unconvincing, and the resolution of their affair is very weak. *Why does she live with Holmes after what he has done to her, hating him as she does?* [Zinnemann's emphasis] Why does she sleep with other men?" Taradash responded with easily one of the longest speeches in the script, in which Karen tells Warden about her husband's adultery, drunkenness, and responsibility for the death of their son and her postpartum hysterectomy. When Warden attempts to stop her narrative, she talks right over him, describing the labor she endured, completely alone: "And of course, one more thing, no more children. Do you know what that means? You're not a woman. The meaning of it is gone. You're a gutted shell . . . Yes, I went out with men after that. And if I'd ever found one that could turn a hair of my head, I'd have left Dana flat. You can see that, can't you?"[69] Zinnemann was never one to like long speeches, and was known for cutting script dialogue down while shooting, even encouraging his actors to make their own cuts during rehearsal.[70] Cohn, for one, was happy to let Zinnemann lower the script's word count, but Zinnemann slashed little of the horrifying content of Karen's speech. Zinnemann wanted to replace the dialogue with longer, silent shots of the main characters facing their various entrapments. While the two romances temporarily offer the four protagonists some happiness, Zinnemann wrote, "I believe it is very important not to play either one of the love stories as an *idyllic romance* at any time. There must always be a sense of constraint in the scenes. A constraint imposed by the outside world, the same as it is in the book."[71] At no point did he want to lose sight of them as marginal, lonely people in crushing social and professional systems.

There was an equally frank representation of Lorene/Alma's life on Hotel Street. Even the culture of Hotel Street prostitution, which Taradash semi-disguised as a "private club," was easily translatable to critics.[72] Film publicity in the press book emphasized Lorene's commodified sexuality ("Sure I'm nice to you. We're nice to all the boys"), and in a *New York Post* interview with Archer Winsten, actress Donna Reed mused on her role, "How would I have made all that money in two years, enough to buy a house back home, join the country club, become respectable. I couldn't make that much just being a dance hostess. No, I suppose it wouldn't make much sense unless you were a prostitute."[73] But *From Here to Eternity* was not remarkable just for its frank discussion of female sexuality in the 1950s; it was a startling picture of the honored American military that helped to win "the good war." The book and

FIG. 44 Women's history and Pearl Harbor myths: Lorene (Donna Reed) with Karen (Deborah Kerr) en route to the states, Columbia Pictures.

film's representations of the army's longstanding exploitation of women added a new historical dimension to the popular understanding of the recent national past.

Not without irony, Taradash and Zinnemann decided that Lorene should have the last word in *From Here to Eternity*—not the heroic Warden or any of the high-ranking officers who survive the Japanese attack. *From Here to Eternity* is a series of untold narratives excised by establishment history, related by people who have literally been pushed to the edges of American's empire. But even these personal histories begin to be corrupted by the myth-making projects of Pearl Harbor. The events of December 7th unleash a rabid historical consciousness. Within minutes of the bombing, Hawaiian civilians are calling the event "history."[74] On their way home, Lorene and Georgette meet a professor who is already planning a book about the attack. As soon as the new draftees begin arriving, Washington pressure groups begin to close down the Hotel Street brothels, wiping the peacetime army experience from the islands. But Lorene's final personal narrative is the most sustained example of reconstructing the past in the aftermath of the attack. Lorene's life is a series of stories she tells others to frame her past and future. Though Lorene finally falls in love with Prewitt, she refuses to marry an ordinary soldier and become an average housewife. Once she has enough money, she tells Prewitt, she will refashion her identity in the states and become an upper-middle-class housewife: "Because when you're proper you're safe."[75] With Zinnemann's coaching, Donna Reed gave a chilling, unsmiling delivery, which contrasts sharply with Taradash's "impassioned" script direction.[76] The actress who so soon would become famous for playing the straight-arrow, happy housewife on television (*The Donna Reed Show*, 1958–66) showed the other side of American domestic life on screen. Soon after Prewitt is killed, she begins to "fix" her official story in the same way Warden manages the infantry company's records while Holmes is out with his hatcheck girls. On board a ship taking them back to the States, Lorene tells Karen Holmes that her "fiancé" was killed during the Japanese bombing of Hickam Field. According to her, Prewitt was a bomber pilot and awarded the Silver Star for bravery in action. Although Lorene retains Prewitt's southern heritage, she transforms the poor white cracker and common soldier into a fine gentleman and a pilot. The war has just started, and already the civilian population is joining the army in rewriting its history and in constructing a heroic image. Although Karen recognizes that Lorene's story is false, she does not challenge the myth (fig. 44).

At first, Taradash was not sure how he would script this final scene. He knew this was where he wanted the adaptation to finish, and Zinnemann thought it was a fabulous way of underscoring the way Americans rewrite their own history. Although Jones's novel ended with Warden going off on another binge after Karen's departure for the states, Jones was happy with Lorene ending the film. However, he wanted to preserve her absolute faith in her story: "In connection with the last scene between Karen and Alma, I've always had the idea that in the movie the scene might be done so that Alma was unknown to audience. Either with different hairdo and dark glasses, or done so her face was in darkness. So that the audience wouldn't know her until Karen did. Maybe this is taking unfair advantage of the audience, I don't know. But, you see, the result of making her say her piece hurriedly—as if she herself knew she was wrong (or lying, or guilty)—is to make her out in some subtle sense a sort of villain. And making her entirely cold-blooded and really unfeeling—as if she herself is even enjoying her role as tragedienne, and is not aware she is lying. Or is wrong—is to leave the audience with the odd, extended, up-in-the-air feeling and kind of awareness of all human frailty, that I tried so hard and so long to get into the end of the book. (I must have rewritten that last chapter 20 or 30 times.) If you can get that effect—life going on, people going on, Prew's death (so important to us and to audience) really nothing but a small ripple in a vast moving tide and current that stops and mourns for no man; really nothing, all this emotion, all this wasted energy—then you will have the absolutely right ending."[77]

From Here to Eternity's Revisionist Histories

The film's production, shooting, and publicity were driven largely by the multistoried narrative with its unconventional group of protagonists. Yet Lorene's final story is directly connected with *From Here to Eternity*'s positioning within the Hollywood war genre. Prew, Karen, Maggio, and Lorene's marginal prewar social histories were the focus of the narrative that nonetheless ends with one of the most evocative and famous national events of the twentieth century. As historian Emily Rosenberg points out, Pearl Harbor is, like Little Big Horn, one of those American military events which had massive media and mythological appeal.[78] The military believed that the images were "dangerous" for public morale, so published photographs were banned for three months, and not until December 1942 was *Life* allowed to print an extensive spread.[79] Pearl Harbor initiated the regeneration of America after the Great Depression, it was the impetus for national unity in the war against the Axis, and it became the main rhetorical site for national myth-making. It is the first event in the established history of the war, the "Good War," which regenerated the army's reputation and America's role in the wider world. What made *From Here to Eternity* radical was that the attack on Pearl Harbor was only the end of Prewitt's story. The real images of Pearl Harbor were in glimpses of the lives of Jones's protagonists, when things weren't so "heroic."

One of the intrinsic qualities of myth is its resistance to change, its ability to transcend history. The great irony about John Ford and Gregg Toland's Academy Award-winning documentary, *December 7th* (1943) is that this government commissioned film, with documentary inserts, voice-over narration, and "location" shots, had almost no real footage of the attack. Instead, Toland used re-enactments, miniatures, process photography, and rear projection to simulate a true account of Pearl Harbor.[80] In *From Here to Eternity*, Zinnemann challenges Pearl Harbor's mythic status on several levels. Although films made about the Pacific campaign began to "document" World War II events with more historical text toward the end of the 1940s (*Battleground*, 1949; *Sands of Iwo Jima*, 1949), it was not until 1953 and *From Here to Eternity* that Hollywood really looked at the war as a finite historical era. Perhaps it was due to America's involvement in another Pacific war—this time in Korea. But *From Here to Eternity* certainly did not supply the "Good War" alternative to the increasingly unpopular stalemate in Korea. Instead, the film makes military apathy and incompetence a feature of the Second World War's historical context. The many script versions begin with an intertitle, "June 1941," and Taradash introduces key scenes with a soldier reading a newspaper with headlines such as "Japs advance in China" and "Lou Gehrig Dies." Script readers had objected to the interjection of text in the film, but Zinnemann resisted efforts to remove it. When outlining the December 7th attack, Taradash's script notes, "Stock Shots Bombing Hickam Field, Wheeler Field and Pearl Harbor from *December 7th* and other available material." During the 1940s, newsreels and fictional films about the war used reconstructions and limited government and military combat footage (often not from Pearl Harbor). Even during the 1930s, Hollywood had borrowed footage from the military to makes films about World War I (*The World Moves On*, 1934; *The Roaring Twenties*, 1939). The World War II footage in war films of the 1940s was contemporaneous and largely interchangeable with the cinematography of the fictional Hollywood footage.

But in *From Here to Eternity* there is a definite visual contrast in the quality of the documentary and fictional cinematography. The 1953 shots of the fictional historical content are in clear, sharp black-and-white. The documentary footage is grainy, dark, and blurred, with abrupt cuts. Even the character of the sound is different. The engines, guns, and bombs in the documentary footage are almost deafening compared to the scenes of Sergeant Warden attempting to manage the chaos of Schofield Barracks after the attack. The footage acts like a historical artifact—something literally from the vaults of history. This is what the American stateside public saw in 1942 and at intervals in newsreels thereafter, but in 1953 it had aged visibly and did not fit with the pristine cinematography and modulated sound of the rest of the narrative.

This is hardly a case of seamless Hollywood fiction juxtaposed with the rough accuracy of documentary, a historical touch added to bolster a romantic fabrication of Hawaii in 1941. These contrasting forms of cinematography and sound represent equally contrasting historical views of Pearl Harbor. What Zinnemann shows Americans in 1953 also happened in 1941 Hawaii—the desperate, painful stories of Prewitt, Lorene, Maggio, and Karen. Taradash's script streamlined the 850-page novel and connected four of the protagonists to devastating personal stories: Karen's miscarriage and hysterectomy; Lorene's decision to become a "frontier" prostitute; Prewitt's accidental crippling of his best friend in a boxing match; and Maggio's death scene, in which he tells of repeated beatings in the stockade. These types of people never made the newspaper headlines;

they were not interviewed after Pearl Harbor. Their stories, related in the film as lengthy personal narratives, were lost to traditional history, which instead emphasized Japan's treachery and the horror of the attack. In contrast, the filmmakers retained and expanded the marginal narratives, making them central to the film. Critics took note of its unique job editing Jones's controversial novel, and credited Zinnemann with "an expert directorial achievement in maintaining these various involvements on equal and lucid levels."[81]

From Here to Eternity reuses much of the iconography of the old historical film—the opening intertitle indentifying the historical locale and period, the use of dates (such as the glimpse of the calendar reading December 7 on the wall beside Warden), the documentary footage and location shots, the contrasting personal narratives. Ironically, however, it lacks one of the hallmarks of the genre: a credited military advisor or endorsement. Although the army allowed Zinnemann to photograph army personnel around Schofield Barracks, it "did not authorize Columbia Pictures to include in the picture the fact that army cooperation had been given."[82] Zinnemann, however, realized that obtaining and displaying army approval in the credits would have compromised Jones's original critique. Instead, the film constructs a historical world that does not rely on the spurious endorsements of the establishment.

Together, Taradash and Zinnemann kept the hard edge of Jones's novel, which pleasantly surprised both Jones and the critics in August 1953, when the film was finally released. As Jones wrote to Zinnemann, "I want to tell you what a bang-up job I think you two guys have done—along with Buddy—in getting as much into the screenplay as you have. I had long expected—and been resigned too—a typically sentimentalized, crapped up movie of the book. It was a hell of a fine surprise to find it wasn't that."[83] Critic Jesse Zunser was one of many critics across the country who agreed: "There has, for example, been no attempt to make angels of the playful girls in the New Congress Club, to blunt the amorality of the seductive wife of Company G's commanding officer or hide his own amorous escapades away from home; or to soften the book's bitter indictment of the army's occasional brass-hat brutality and the enlisted man's helplessness against unofficially condoned khaki cruelty and sadism."[84] While Jones, the audiences, and the critics may have enjoyed the surprise, the armed forces did not. The navy banned the film from being shown to servicemen because "it was 'derogatory of a sister service' . . . and was a 'discredit to the armed services.'" That same source revealed that the army was "'so shocked' at the preview that it refused to let its name be used in a credit line at the start of the film. 'We felt the movie portrayed the military in the wrong light,' he said . . . The only officer shown was a sadist, and so were the non-coms.'"[85] It was neither the first nor the last time that Zinnemann's work would be censured by one establishment bent on protecting its history. But the film was one of the top grossers of the decade and netted Zinnemann his first directing Oscar. For a time, at least, the Hollywood establishment was on his side.

CHAPTER FIVE

Breaking the Silence of Women in the Resistance

"If I am not for myself, who will be for me? And if I am
only for myself, what am I? And if not now, when?"
—**Hillel**, quoted by Fred Zinnemann, 1973[1]

"The story is a conflict of conscience, the interior conflict of the woman; it just
happens to be set against a religious background ... SHE is the battleground.
—**Fred Zinnemann**, 1959[2]

Fred Zinnemann first read Kathryn Hulme's novel, *The Nun's Story* (1956), at the suggestion of Gary Cooper, who thought the book would make a strong film.[3] Cooper was a shrewd judge of the studio system. Since at least the 1920s, producers had depended heavily on the adaptation of women's fiction to attract their largest group of patrons.[4] This connection was so strong that by 1937, American cultural critic Gilbert Seldes suggested that the studios masculinize their films in an effort to win back male viewers. But as other film historians have pointed out, filmmakers like David O. Selznick, Jerry Wald, and Joseph Mankiewicz continued to appeal to the tastes of women.[5] The adaptation of historical fiction by or about women had generated some of the industry's most prestigious and successful films, among them *Show Boat* (1936), Selznick's own *Gone with the Wind* (1939), *Rebecca* (1940), and *Duel in the Sun* (1946), *Kitty Foyle* (1940), *Mrs. Miniver* (1942), and *Forever Amber* (1947). More recently, Zinnemann's own work had concentrated on the representation of women's experiences, from Pier Angeli's American debut as an Italian war bride in Brooklyn in *Teresa* (1951) to Julie Harris and Ethel Waters's partnership in *Member of the Wedding* (1952). Even Zinnemann's forays into traditionally masculine genres like the Western (*High Noon*) and war picture (*From Here to Eternity*) reached a broader spectrum of audiences due to the development of two substantial female roles. Many historical films about women had the (perhaps surprising) added appeal of controversy; far from being the frequently conservative and admiring biopics of their masculine counterparts, many women's films addressed titillating social issues of adultery and divorce, work and careers, and racial, class, and gender inequities.[6]

In some ways, Kathryn Hulme's novel was perfectly tailored to this kind of filmmaking. *The Nun's Story* is a fictionalized biography of UNRRA nurse Marie Louise Habets, whom Hulme met while doing relief work for displaced peoples in Europe during and after the Second World War. Both Hulme and Habets worked together at the DP camp at Wildflecken, Germany, between 1945 and 1947 and then at other IRO camps through 1952. Hulme's previous book about Wildflecken, her 1953 memoir *The Wild Place*, was, like Zinnemann's *Search*, a powerful document of the women who made UNRRA and later the IRO help so many displaced men, women, and children.[7] In it, Hulme had described the Belgian nurse's untiring work in the TB ward and efforts to help unwanted DPs find a place in America's confusing and often obstructive immigration scheme. "Lou" Habets returned with Hulme to the states and the two lived together in California while Hulme wrote *The Nun's Story*. Hulme's novel, advertised as "true in all essentials" in the numerous published editions, told of Habets's life prior to her work for the Belgian resistance and later for UNRRA. Renamed Gabrielle van der Mal (and again renamed "Sister Luke" by the church), she joins a Catholic religious order, practices medicine in the Congo, and eventually leaves the order during the war to join the Belgian resistance. Although Gabrielle/Sister Luke struggles for years to endure the strictures of the religious order, she reaches her breaking point over the Catholic Church's neutral stance during the Nazi occupation of Belgium. Therefore, an adaptation of *The Nun's Story* offered to producers and audiences not only the ever-popular women's biographical/historical film, but also the controversies of a nun leaving the church—and a nun leaving the church for anti-Nazi resistance work.

Arguably, by the mid 1950s, historical films about women were not as numerous as they had been a decade before.[8] There were many biopics or fictionalized biographies of female entertainers based on a variety of material (*Annie Get Your Gun*, 1950; *Sunset Boulevard*, 1950; *A Star Is Born*, 1954; *Love Me or Leave Me*, 1955; *Jeanne Eagels*, 1957; *Too Much, Too*

Soon, 1958), but most of these women were portrayed struggling in vain against a system bent on their own destruction. In a recent study of the Hollywood biopic, Dennis Bingham focuses on these 1950s films of female entertainers, arguing that their template of victimization and decline permeated all Hollywood attempts at women's biographies.[9] Though Bingham's formulation of the female biopic is rigid, it is true that by the 1950s, Hollywood's age of the heroic woman, embodied by the indomitable Scarlett O'Hara, was over.

Even postwar films about men—particularly those with a Second World War context—often portrayed an ambivalent attitude toward traditional formulations of individualism and achievement. Zinnemann's *Act of Violence*, *The Men*, and his most recent *A Hatful of Rain* (1957) all featured American war veterans struggling to cope with the aftermath of psychological dysfunction, disability, and addiction in the confines of noirish urban and suburban spaces. The American landscape, for better or worse, became the new battleground for former men at war. Yet these three films are set exclusively in America—creating a kind of representational amputation between the US and the wider worlds of Europe and the Pacific (*Hatful of Rain*'s hero, played by Don Murray, is a Korean war veteran). The films, particularly *A Hatful of Rain*, also lack any wartime flashbacks, unlike *The Man in the Gray Flannel Suit* (1956, directed by Nunnally Johnson and produced by Darryl F. Zanuck), in which Gregory Peck's postwar commuter is haunted by memories of the European war. In Zinnemann's war films, from Aline MacMahon's UNRRA official in *The Search* to Vanessa Redgrave's Resistance leader in *Julia* (1977), women often act as bridges between cultures and nations, working for distinctly international organizations and traveling easily from America to other borders in Europe. As Hulme's novel demonstrates, however, these women also belong to powerful organizations which determine the course of their lives. Few are capable of resisting these wider forces and of acting alone. While Zinnemann was reading *The Nun's Story*, Darryl F. Zanuck's production of *The Man in the Gray Flannel Suit* played in theaters and addressed these tensions directly, and many American men and women in the postwar era were experiencing the life of William Whyte's *Organization Man* (1956).[10] Gabrielle's struggle with the church certainly resonates with these contemporaneous conflicts between the "Organization Woman" and the corporation that demands her anonymity and obedience. As Zinnemann remarked several years after the film's release, "the individual against a huge organization, following her conscience" was something he was drawn to throughout his career.[11]

The historical dimension of *The Nun's Story* links the film to another development in postwar cinema: the Resistance biopic. While France led the way with the filmed memoirs of men in the Resistance (from Melville's *Silence de la mer* (1947) to Bresson's more recent *Un condamné à mort s'est échappé* (1956), based on the experiences of André Devigny), British filmmakers pioneered women's wartime narratives, particularly director-producer Herbert Wilcox and actress Anna Neagle, who filmed the lives of First and Second World War heroines Edith Cavell (*Nurse Edith Cavell*, 1939) and Odette Sansom Churchill (*Odette*, 1950). *Odette* would pave the way for *Carve Her Name with Pride* (1958), in many ways the apex of the British women's Resistance genre. While *Odette* and *Carve Her Name with Pride*'s Violette Szabo (Virginia McKenna) fought their own wars against sexism in the Allied military and against Nazi barbarism, Gabrielle's struggle against the church before and during the war was even more controversial. In making his first women's "biopic," Zinnemann created a film that resisted traditional historical and cinematic representations of women and heroism but nonetheless occasionally compromised. This chapter will look at Zinnemann's work on *The Nun's Story* as part of a wider discussion of women's historical films about the Resistance and their indebtedness to popular literature and oral history.

Early Resistance Heroines from Edith Cavell to Violette Szabo

Kathryn Hulme's historical novel outraged many in the Catholic Church in the United States and Europe.[12] It may not have been James Jones's *From Here to Eternity*, but Zinnemann was intrigued by *The Nun's Story*'s mixture of controversy and history. At the director's insistence, Jack Warner purchased the rights to the book for Warner Bros. for $200,000.[13] That very year, Warner had gambled successfully with another adaptation of a controversial "women's" novel, Edna Ferber's *Giant* (1956).[14] However, Martin Quigley of the Catholic Legion of Decency cautioned Warner that any adaptation of *The Nun's Story* must handle the heroine's abandonment of the church in a particular way. It must argue clearly that "the fault was hers—not that of the Order. The motion picture must give no different impression."[15] He wrote that the property would certainly give offense to Catholics, and "it could easily degenerate into a blackguarding of Strict Religious Orders, a representation of stoney-faced and, by implication, stoney-hearted Religious Superiors and a "forced labor" kind of convent life."[16] Although Quigley correctly judged the film's potential impact on contemporary Catholicism, the most controversial aspects of *The Nun's Story* were embedded in its historical context. Kathryn Hulme's Gabrielle van der Mal/Sister Luke was not just a harmless figure of fiction; she was based upon a real person, and Little-Brown's jacket publicity advertised the novel as "a true story." Even those who pointed out Hulme's departure from the strict facts of Lou Habets's life were obsessed with its historical connections.[17] Many reviews emphasized *The Nun's Story* as a fictionalized biography as if its biographical context added greater legitimacy to the political and religious controversy of the narrative.[18]

Martin Quigley's initial unease about the book and his comments about "the 'forced labor' of convent life" also hint at Hulme and later Zinnemann's most powerful critique of the church. In Gabrielle's (Audrey Hepburn) slow physical transformation from privileged Belgian schoolgirl to postulant and nun and in her growing feelings of isolation and even imprisonment, her experience parallels that of other women in wartime concentration camps like Ravensbrück, Mauthausen, and Dachau. Zinnemann had Hepburn study two films in preparation for her role: Renée Falconetti's performance in *The Passion of Joan of Arc* (1928) and François Leterrier's in *Un condamné à mort s'est échappé/ A Man Escaped* (the latter had just been released in the US as production began on *The Nun's Story*).[19] Hepburn's performance links the contexts of Dreyer and Bresson's films with *The Nun's Story*'s dual narratives of resistance and oppression within the church and Nazi-occupied Europe. It was a powerful combination. A nun's decision to abandon the church for any reason was potentially embarrassing to Catholic administrators if highly publicized, but Sister Luke's decision to abandon the church in order to pursue Resistance work was explosive, for it touched upon the church's neutrality and effective complicity with the Nazis.

Things were particularly divisive in Belgium throughout the 1950s because of the church's failure to publicly protest the treatment of Belgium's Jewish citizens during the war and the clergy's postwar support of King Leopold, whose relationship with the Nazis was a bit too close for Belgian patriots.[20] When Leopold attempted to regain the throne after the war, the Catholic Party was his most prominent advocate. However, many Catholic priests and nuns supported the Resistance. As historian Suzanne Vromen comments, "It was members of the lower clergy who filled the moral vacuum left by the Catholic Church hierarchy through its failure to speak out publicly against the persecution of Jews and to organize their protection."[21] During the 1950s, this issue was widely explored by historians and cultural critics and the release of Zinnemann's film widened the debate.[22] In fact, Guenter Lewy began writing his celebrated *The Catholic Church and Nazi Germany* (1964) in 1960, shortly after *The Nun's Story* dominated international theaters and headlines.[23]

Following initial conflicts over the public exclusion of communist resisters, in the 1950s wider European Resistance historiography followed the project of individual and national commemoration of militant masculine Resistance heroes fostered by Charles de Gaulle. Although by the end of the decade, studies of individual Resistance networks and a more nuanced comparative dimension had emerged in Resistance historiography, full-scale revisionism, consisting of re-evaluations of widespread collaboration in the church and lay populations, did not emerge until the 1960s, the fall of the de Gaulle government, the cooling of Cold War politics, and the release of Marcel Ophüls's *The Sorrow and the Pity*.[24] Before the revisionist historiography of Stanley Hoffman and Robert Paxton, mainstream work on wartime France was dominated by Robert Aron and Sisley Huddleston's sympathetic looks at Vichy.[25] However, during the 1950s, women's roles in the Resistance remained a significant presence in popular history. While film historian Ginette Vincendeau has argued "the contribution of women to the Resistance has been marginalized in the cinema,"[26] popular literature and several major British films addressed the voice of women in Resistance history and anticipated many of the future revisionist debates.

In the immediate aftermath of the war, several prominent résistantes, including Lucie Aubrac and Suzanne Wittek (the Belgian sister of escape line leader Dédé de Jongh), published memoirs of their work during the occupation, but by and large, men's memoirs contributed to the "official histories." Sometimes, as in the case of American OSS operator Virginia Hall, their deeds were suppressed in the interests of not blowing their postwar cover. Many others couldn't speak for themselves because they had been tortured and killed. Alliance chief Marie-Madeleine Fourcade notes that women made up 20 percent of her organization, but a high percentage of them were caught, deported, and killed. Not until after 1968, with the publication of Fourcade's official history of Alliance, did large numbers of résistantes publish their memoirs and histories of their struggle against Nazi Occupation. These memoirs would later influence Zinnemann's adaptation of *Julia*. But while mainstream Resistance historiography continued to emphasize Resistance leadership as a masculine enterprise, the popular press and the British film industry arguably kept the flame of female resistance to the Nazis alive. Women formed an important component of Hollywood's Resistance films from the 1940s; however, they were mostly fictional women who entered the organization by accident or because of their lover or husband's involvement (*Escape*, 1940; *Casablanca*, 1942; *Joan of Paris*, 1942; *Edge of Darkness*, 1943; *Paris Underground*, 1945).

In early 1939, RKO lured British producer-director Herbert Wilcox and actress Anna Neagle to make a biography of Edith Cavell, the famed Great War heroine and nurse. Cavell's was one of the best-known names in modern British war history, and was part of Neagle's growing repertoire of historical women. The actress had begun by playing actress-courtesans Nell Gwyn (1934) and Peg Wolfington (*Peg of Old Drury*, 1935) before starring as Queen Victoria in two major biopics (*Victoria the Great*, 1937; *Sixty Glorious Years*, 1938). Nurse Cavell, who stayed in occupied Belgium during the war to continue her work, was caught helping British airmen escape from the Germans (something which Gabrielle/Sister Luke does in both the novel and script). The German military authorities tried and shot her as a spy. She became an instant heroine, with the Belgian, French, and British governments quickly building prominent monuments and statues dedicated to her memory.[27]

Though women's biopics were popular during the 1930s, it was extremely rare for the female protagonist to die on-screen for reasons of public interest.[28] Only royals like Katharine Hepburn's Mary, Queen of Scots (1936) and Norma Shearer's Marie Antoinette (1938) had that privilege. Edith Cavell, however, was a working woman, and RKO's script by Michael Hogan focuses on her unique organization of other women drawn from across the Belgian nobility to the ranks of the working class. *Nurse Edith Cavell*'s portrait of female solidarity and resistance was especially dangerous to the German war effort. As the German officers debate whether or not to execute Cavell, one argues in the script, "the spectacle of Germany defied by a gang of women will do much more harm than a little calculated severity."[29] Cavell's heroism and resistance to "Teutonic despotism" became a rallying cry for those gearing up for the Second World War (the film was released September 1, 1939, in the US), and Neagle was nominated for another Academy Award. The film should certainly be seen in the context of Warner Bros.'s prewar anti-Nazi cycle, which included the notorious *Confessions of a Nazi Spy*.[30] But things were different where more recent Resistance heroines were concerned. There were huge information barriers between America and Europe during the war, and arguably any known résistante would have been incarcerated or murdered. Anonymity kept them safe. Nowhere was this made more obvious than in *Two Thousand Women* (Gainsborough, 1944), a British film by Frank Launder and Sidney Gilliat about "ordinary" Resistance women in a Nazi concentration camp in occupied France, their efforts to survive, and even escape.

During the 1950s, cinema began to historicize the experience of women in the Resistance. British popular cinema, allied with Pan mass-market paperbacks, capitalized on the phenomenon of the women who worked for SOE (Special Operations Executive) on overseas operations in France. Odette Sansom (later Churchill) and Violette Szabo were some of the most prominent and photogenic stories to get screen treatment. The stunningly beautiful Szabo was a remarkably good shot, and her alleged killing of dozens of Nazi troops with her Sten gun in the days after D-Day was said to have provoked the Nazi atrocity at Oradour-sur-Glane.[31] Film publicity explicitly linked her wartime exploits with the best of British men's sacrifices: "Among all the stories of bravery in World War II, none is braver, none more deeply moving than hers. And now, Daniel M. Angel and Lewis Gilbert, producer and director of *Reach for the Sky* [the biopic of RAF hero Douglas Bader], bring her tale of dauntless courage to the screen."[32] Like Cavell, Szabo was shot as a spy, but only after enduring months of agony in Ravensbrück. While a ghostly shot of Cavell's marble monument in London completes her 1939 biopic, there is no statue to Szabo. Instead, the film itself and title calls for her future historical recognition as a great war heroine.

These biopics of female agents bear serious comparison with Zinnemann's work on *The Nun's Story*. While the Second World War occupies only a quarter of Zinnemann's film, all three biopics, based on best-selling women's historical literature, address women's lives in which the protagonists supersede romantic attachments in the interests of patriotic, intellectual, or spiritual careers. Both Cavell and Sister Luke were nurses with deep patriotic drives to serve in wartime Belgium. Even more crucially, the lives of an SOE agent and nun involve careers that paradoxically keep them in a private, anonymous sphere. Their names and identities are changed, their families and children are abandoned, their own lives are unknown to the public. All are women operating in large organizations apart from society where men dominate the hierarchies. While *Odette* and especially *Carve Her Name with Pride* struggle with creating a means of historically representing a life hidden by undercover war work and obliterated by the Nazis, Zinnemann was also faced with the problem of visually and orally representing a woman's life in an organization where singularization and documentation inevitably put her at odds with the organization.

Odette and *Carve Her Name with Pride* both explore the issue of historical legitimization in a woman's biopic about a traditionally masculine event. In *Odette*, Herbert Wilcox took a traditionalist approach, hiring Odette's real former boss, Maurice Buckmaster, to introduce the film in a variant of the historical film "foreword" and to appear as himself in several key scenes. Buckmaster's authoritative voice controls the initial flashback which introduces the audience to Odette (Neagle) and then discusses her training and first mission. Odette's own voice-over never comments or directs the narrative. Interestingly, the account also uses a number of transcribed radio messages to facilitate understanding of Odette's work. The messages are seen in close-up, yet she never writes or dictates any of these war documents. However, at the end of the film, when she is reunited with SOE colleague and future husband Peter Churchill (Trevor Howard), the real Odette endorsed the film in a text epilogue drawn from Tickell's biography in which she dedicated the film to her deceased female colleagues in SOE (among them Violette Szabo).[33] Something similar occurs in director Lewis Gilbert's *Carve Her Name with Pride*, when a male voice-over introduces the normal prewar life of the heroine.[34] Later, when Szabo (played by Virginia McKenna) returns to France on her fatal second mission, she gives her contact radio operator her unique code: a poem authored by her deceased French husband. Her husband's words run through the film as a theme, and, in fact, the Gestapo torture Szabo in an unsuccessful attempt to extract this code. When her voice appears in a posthumous voice-over, it is to recite this poem. Szabo's own words and heroic personal code are arguably articulated in the film narrative and publicity, but the textual and verbal authentication of the film is transmitted through masculine voices and authored texts.

Unlike these two earlier British films, Zinnemann's project is not about writing women into cinematic narratives of traditionally masculine military courage. As he famously argued in an interview with Gene Phillips decades later, "There is an expression in German, 'zivil' courage, which refers to the courage an ordinary citizen can rise to of his own free will when under pressure, as opposed to the military courage of a soldier who is expected to be brave."[35] He understood how Gabrielle's story differed from more traditional biopics and war stories. The question of a woman's voice and her textual "trace" in history form a significant part of Zinnemann's work on *The Nun's Story*, and the film's alternative positioning of women in history can be seen in the negotiation over the opening voice-over. From the early stages of the production, screenwriter Robert Anderson (*Tea and Sympathy*, 1956; *Until They Sail*, 1957) resisted demonizing Sister Luke to placate the church and censors or typifying her as an average woman (thereby making her a heroic everywoman). Faced with the massive opposition of Catholic censors and advisors against the experience of this one woman, Anderson argued that an omniscient voice-over might channel some of the Catholic fears by singularizing her as a misfit. He wrote to Zinnemann, "I think it's imperative to have a spoken foreword, well phrased, to say something like 'there are dozens, perhaps hundreds of religious orders for women in the Catholic Church . . . This is the story of one nun in one order. It is indeed the story of an extraordinary nun, but one who cannot be called *typical* [Anderson's emphasis]. . . . What we shall see is merely the story of the interior struggle of and exterior adventures of an extraordinary woman—Sister Luke.'"[36]

Omniscient voice-overs were staples of historical films, and both Wilcox and Gilbert had used variants on their biopics of Odette and Violette Szabo; however, with a few exceptions, "omniscient" voice-overs connoted "male" non-diegetic voice-overs—aka the voice of History. Women's films—historical and contemporary—more often used flashbacks narrated by the female protagonist. Zinnemann persuaded Anderson to drop the "disclaimer" foreword. Instead, the two developed an opening narration by the head of the order, Mother Emmanuel, in which she creates the image of the perfect nun. As Gabrielle takes her last walk through the streets of Brussels, Emmanuel begins: "The Purpose of this Holy Order of Sisters shall be to promote the Glory of God and the sanctification of its members by the practice of the three vows of Poverty, Chastity, and Obedience . . . They will force themselves not to look at either the qualities or the faults of their superiors, but simply at the authority with which the Holy Church invests them, and to submit themselves to it in the spirit of faith."[37] It was a brilliant decision, and although as the production progressed they cut the length of the foreword, the decision remained to align the foreword—the traditional voice of history and authority—with the church and a woman's voice. Mother Emmanuel's final comment spoke directly about the need to accept and submit, rather than question, and Zinnemann then proceeded to structure the film as Sister Luke's resistance to this dominant voice.

Audrey Hepburn was deeply committed to Zinnemann and to the making of the film, and arguably, *The Nun's Story* is the most autobiographical of her work. One of the most popular stars of the 1950s, Hepburn's other major roles were fictitious contemporary young women like Princess Anne/Anya Smith (*Roman Holiday*, 1953), Sabrina Fairchild (*Sabrina*, 1954), and Jo Stockton (*Funny Face*, 1957). Although not her first historical film (she had made *War and Peace* in 1956), *The Nun's Story*'s material was part of her experience of the Second World War.[38] Hepburn's half-brother was sent to a labor camp, her uncle was shot by the Nazis, and she and her mother starved through the occupation of the Netherlands. Gabrielle's decision to leave the order to help the Resistance was a dream of Hepburn's own when she was a young girl, and eventually the youngster acted as a Resistance courier.[39] Hepburn formed a close relationship with Lou Habets prior to shooting, discussing many aspects of Habets's experience and the role of Sister Luke.[40] Throughout production she continued to write affectionate letters to both Hulme and Habets. Hepburn was definitely suspicious of the church.[41] While she knew Zinnemann was playing a close and conciliatory hand with the Catholic leaders to gain location access to the convents, she was carefully attuned to the "advisors" and their efforts to curb Sister Luke's narrative. She also didn't like the church's cowardly role in the Holocaust; after making *The Nun's Story*, she had originally intended to play Anne Frank in George Stevens's adaptation of the diary. She informed Zinnemann that her agent and Stevens were trying "to work out a schedule whereby Anne Frank could possibly be done before the Nun, but I can see no way of doing this without jeopardizing your and my preparations."[42] In the end, she gave up playing one heroine of Nazi oppression to play another.

Hepburn frankly saw Sister Luke as a heroine and a patriot. Certainly the Belgian Resistance was studded with heroic women, ranging from couriers and escape guides to the famed Comète escape line leader, Andrée "Dédé" de Jongh. In the 1950s, de Jongh's life story became the subject of a popular mass-market paperback by British masterspy Airey Neave, and was certainly as widely read as Hulme's novel.[43] Like Sister Luke, Dédé or "Little Cyclone" was deeply influenced by her father's example as a Resistance organizer, and, following the war, she even undertook nursing in the Congo.[44] Dédé's story was more conventionally heroic in that it involved incredible physical courage, her guiding hundreds of British fliers from Belgium through France and over the Pyrenees, Gestapo interrogations, and finally, internment at Ravensbrück. Yet it would remain unfilmed until the popular British television series *Secret Army* (1977–79), starring Jan Francis in the first season's Dédé-esque role.[45] Sister Luke's story involved an intellectual and spiritual resistance that was far more difficult to convey visually. Hepburn realized this and wrote to Zinnemann, "I am especially anxious because, as you remember, I am already so bothered by the fact that Sister Luke class herself a 'failure' at the end of our story. She is too intelligent to display what sounds to me like false humility. I still wish she could somehow express herself as having failed as a nun but that her hopes and faith have been re-born at the thought of being able to function as a free human being and consequently with more devotion than before. I still would like to feel the start of something new and strong at the end of the story instead of a sense of dejection and defeat on her part and a kind of artificial whitewashing of the Order." Hepburn saw real significance in Gabrielle's decision to abandon the church in order to pursue Resistance work. But she was aware of the controversies involved in suggesting such a connection. "Like you I do want the final solution to be fifty fifty," she assured him, "so that neither the nun nor the Order becomes a villain. I am now frankly worried that the church may have loaded the dice a little in order to lend their co-operation." Hepburn felt that the entire narrative of Sister Luke's struggle is "brought to a head by the war, at which time her great urge to help and comfort is constantly curtailed by the rigid rules of the Order."[46] Zinnemann assured her that "certainly there will be no artificial white-washing of the Order any more than there was in the book,"[47] and he secretly gloated that none of the major creative talent involved in the production were Roman Catholics who might "sentimentalize" the church.[48]

However, producer Henry Blanke may have worried that in negotiating with the church for background and research connections, Zinnemann was undergoing a process of "indoctrination."[49] It was true that while Anderson was content to write to Hulme and Habets to verify details, Zinnemann needed to see the ceremonies and therefore needed access at a certain level to church procedures. His sincere interest in the accuracy of visual detail may have been read by the church as "compliance" with their interests in glorifying the religious life and enabled the director to enter rarely filmed spaces, yet as Anderson acknowledged, he and Zinnemann were engaged "in a last minute last ditch fight on some points with the church."[50] In the summer of 1957, as the director and screenwriter worked on the script, Zinnemann met with US Catholic officials like Monsignor Devlin and Jack Vizzard. When they read early versions of the scripts, they objected to the Sister asking for Gabrielle's dowry ("too crude . . . counting money like any good cashier"), the postulants writing down their self-accusations ("too petty"), Mother Marcella suggesting that Sister Luke fail her medical examination to become a better nun, and scenes of physical discipline.[51] These scenes all underscored the fundamental financial arrangement upholding the orders, the repressiveness of the convent life, and hypocrisy of obtaining perfect obedience. They also tinkered with the wording of Sister Katherine's admonition of wartime neutrality, arguing that "keep neutral" was less contentious than saying it was better "not to take part in any underground activities." Zinnemann's solution to the censorship was simple. He noted on their list of demands: "omit from script, but shoot anyway."[52] Hepburn's and Blanke's worry that Fred Zinnemann would be "converted" by his contact with Catholic officials was unfounded. As he continued preparations for the film, he contacted agents in Hollywood about buying the popular Jewish legend, *The Dybbuk*, which had been produced as a play in the 1930s. From 1958 to 1984, Zinnemann made several attempts to produce the film, but was always stymied by executives reluctant to gamble on its story of Jewish persecution and thwarted love in nineteenth-century Russia. But as he wrote to agent Abe Lastfogel, "Confidentially, the ideal cast for this picture would be Audrey Hepburn and Montogomery Clift . . . I will not approach Monty until after I have had a reaction from Audrey."[53] Zinnemann saw his two star-crossed individualists recast as the ultimate Jewish lovers. It was an ambitious plan to make one of the core texts of Yiddish cinema available to mainstream audiences, but came to nothing.

Throughout the production, Zinnemann saw *The Nun's Story* as a modern biography whose central intellectual and spiritual dilemma was activated by the war. He pasted a photograph of Lou Habets, with the caption, "The Real Sister Luke," on the back cover of his copy of Hulme's book. As was his habit, Zinnemann heavily annotated the book, and he paid special attention to the May 28, 1940, dictum: "*The sisters,* wrote the Superior General, *are urged not to accept or read any of the clandestine newspapers of the underground which have already begun to appear in the provinces under German occupation.*"[54] And while Hulme linked the Resistance and the church in their practice of silence ("The underground is as sealed as the confessional, she thought. What I do from now on is between me and God alone"), Zinnemann also underlined sequences in which Sister Luke showed fury with other sisters' compliance with Nazi dictates.[55] Screenwriter Anderson included scenes from the novel in which Sister Luke sequestered a British flyer, noted Nazi persecution of Jews, and helped a British spy, and Zinnemann shot them. However, with the director's first cut of the film running over three hours, Zinnemann made the decision to cut all of these scenes in the interests of time.[56] Though Sister Luke's decision to abandon the church clearly comes as a result of the German occupation and murder of her father, the Resistance lost some of its key screen time in the interests of Hollywood production.

Oral History

Initially, Zinnemann felt Anderson's script showed "too much benevolence" and "not enough battlefield." He wanted Anderson to heighten the sense of the individual struggling against a "system more rigid and more ever present." The church was "not oppressive enough," though in fairness, Anderson knew that in order for Zinnemann to gain access to authentic locations in Europe and the Congo, he needed to soothe Catholic advisors with an easy script.[57] As drafts developed, the script focused more on the issues of witnessing and voice. Often the freedom of voice is set in opposition to the controlling conformity of text (the "Book"). As Sister Catherine (Mildred Dunnock) teaches her novices, she writes rules like "Interior Silence" and "Detachment" on the blackboard, things which Gabrielle will never master. The nuns must write all of their faults in a book, and this unique autobiography constitutes a document on the repression of self. When Gabrielle becomes Sister Luke and utters her vows before the Order, she is reading from a printed script (fig. 45). Her first voice-over, ironically, is heard when she accuses herself "of breaking the Grand Silence." As she becomes more and more committed to the Resistance, her voice-overs and spoken dialogue increase.

When Sister Luke famously refuses to fail an exam unless the motherhouse knows that it was done "to order," she explains, remembering the words of her father, "Courage needs witnesses."[58] She remembers the voice of her surgeon father, who would one day die helping the Resistance: "'Le courage a besoin des témoins,' he would say and discount all the bemedaled heroes to point out the unknown real one who had died alone, unseen, near the ground." This dictum underscores the distinction between the "recorded" wartime deeds of masculine heroes and the more marginal, often forgotten struggles of women like Gabriel (and later Julia). While traditional heroic biography and mainstream history ignore their

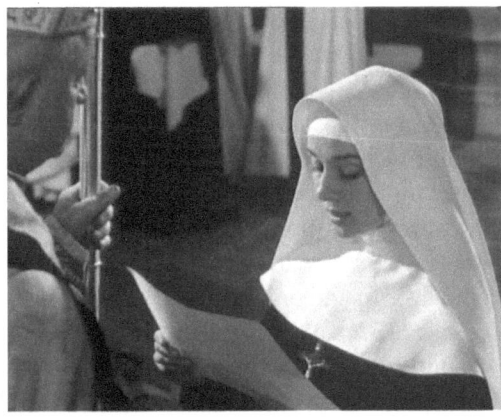

FIG. 45 Reading from a printed script: Audrey Hepburn as Gabrielle/Sister Luke, *The Nun's Story*, 1959, Warner Bros.

narratives, Zinnemann at least bears witness to their courage. Indeed, many of Zinnemann's historical films represent the lives of marginalized men and women. It is through voice and voice-over that Zinnemann recovers their historical importance, and Gabrielle's words become a kind of subversive oral history. For when Gabrielle refuses this pressure from her superiors, we begin to hear her voice as either an interior voice-over or aloud. If "interior silence" is the key to the law of the religious order, then Sister Luke's voice is the epitome of resistance.[59] In the scripts, her voice articulates her failure to conform and her essential difference from the other sisters. She agonizes, "Dear Lord, the more I try, the more imperfect I become" and "This I cannot do, O Lord."[60] It seems a woman's voice is a crime, and when she begins to speak internally she has broken inner silence and is on her way to complete rebellion. When the war comes, she makes a fateful decision to speak her resistance aloud: "Dear Lord, forgive me but I cannot obey anymore."[61] Something similar occurs in Bresson's adaptation of Resistance leader André Devigny's experiences, *Un condamné à mort s'est échappé*, in which the incarcerated hero must learn the "rules" of the new Nazi order before his escape. Bresson also uses Letterier's voice-over as a form of oral resistance against his captors as he documents his efforts to escape. Throughout much of the film, Letterier is silent, with downcast eyes, and an expressionless face. Hepburn evidently learned Zinnemann's lessons well and watched Bresson's film with care. One can detect an uncanny resemblance between the thin, ethereal bodies of Leterrier and Hepburn, their lowered, heavily lashed eyes, and quiet, yet rebellious interior voices. But while Leterrier's voice-over is traceable from early Resistance films such as Melville's *Silence de la mer*, voice-overs in Hollywood films were often women's voices, like Joan Fontaine's in *Rebecca* (1940) and Bette Davis's in *All This and Heaven Too* (1940) and *Now, Voyager* (1942). In different ways, the subjective female narration in these women's pictures invested the heroines with a certain amount of historical control and perspective over the material. In contrast, film historians Dana Polan and William Graebner have both linked voice-over narration in film noir to a postwar sense of claustrophobic personal disaster, and early Resistance films also used variations of the voice-over to add emotional intensity to personal tragedies, among them *Passage to Marseille* (1943) and Zinnemann's *The Seventh Cross*.[62]

But *The Seventh Cross*, like most of Hollywood's early wartime Resistance productions and France's postwar releases, was focused on the voices of men rather than those of women. As Zinnemann's career developed, he became more interested in women's subjectivity on screen and in the way women's narratives and perspectives were different from men. In making Hepburn model her performance on Leterrier's, Zinnemann was inverting and feminizing the genre of the Resistance film. Jean-Pierre Melville's *Silence de la mer* and *Léon Morin, prêtre* are also involved in this dialogue of Resistance on screen. Melville's first Resistance film was an adaptation of the work of Resistance hero Vercors (Paul Bruller). Spencer Tracy's performance as George in *The Seventh Cross* is rendered largely through his silent efforts to slip through the traps of the Gestapo and Nazi sympathizers, while French civilians' silent refusal to acknowledge the presence of Nazi occupiers is the major theme of Melville's adaptation. Melville's "compulsion to return to the Occupation and Resistance" has been described as both masculinist and politically conservative and Gaullist,[63] and *Léon Morin, prêtre*, released two years after *The Nun's Story*, stands in stark contrast to Zinnemann's work. *Léon Morin, prêtre* was, like *Nun*, adapted from the work of a female member of the anti-fascist Resistance, Beatrix Beck. But the book's female narrator and one of its protagonists, Barney (Emmanuelle Riva), though initially a communist and the widow of a Jew, plays no part in the Resistance.[64] Instead, it is the men who belong to the movement and return "to the woods." At first, Barney positions herself as a resister of the church (though Melville, unlike Hulme and Zinnemann, makes no allusion to the Catholic Church's complicity with fascism). However, the "flawless" priest (played by Jean-Paul Belmondo) overwhelms her with a flood of discourse and authoritative close-ups. At one point, when Barney attempts to parry his arguments about faith, he remarks that words are inadequate since God is "incommunicable." His perfection lies in silence and Barney's words cannot touch him. Compare Melville's heroic, Jew-aiding priest with Zinnemann's lonely and resistant Gabrielle, and Melville's film stands as a conservative reconstruction of the church's role in the war and success in silencing dissident women. Melville has in effect masculinized the historical and biographical conflicts of Zinnemann's film.

While Melville's film was lionized by critics at the Venice Film Festival, Zinnemann's preoccupation with Gabrielle's "voice" throughout the film represented a break with more conventional historical narratives of the Resistance and an alliance with more popular forms of women's resistance histories. As historian Paul Thompson points out, oral history is an especially politically subversive form of history, and early works of oral history in the twentieth century focused on lives and experiences marginalized by traditional forms of written history: the lives of slaves, the working class, women, minorities, and war testimonies.[65] "Oral history," he writes, "is a history built around people. It thrusts life into history itself and widens its scope. It allows heroes not just from the leaders, but from the unknown majority of the people . . . Equally, oral history offers a challenge to the accepted myths of history, to the authoritarian judgment inherent in its tradition. It provides a means for a radical transformation of the social meaning of history."[66] Several years later, Robert Rosenstone would argue something similar for films. Historical cinema, in many senses, is a partner in these kinds of historical enterprises, though few critics have explored the importance of the soundtrack to cinematic historical discourse. In *The Nun's Story*, Zinnemann's recovery of Gabrielle's voice represents not only the recovery of the individual's voice in the service of a corporation, but also the importance of women's history and histories of the Resistance.

The Controversy over Catholic Neutrality

Zinnemann was careful in historicizing the church's position on the war. In Anderson's script, the Mother Superior's voice is detached as she describes the havoc wrought by the Nazis: "The country's system of sluices has been put into operation, and certain main roads are already blown up to prevent the German advance." Zinnemann crossed out "the" and replaced it with "our" in order to maintain some connection with patriotism, but was undecided about the switch. But he did document "the set look of anger on Sister Luke's face" when the Mother Superior urges charity to one's enemies. The church's official position is clear, as Mother Catherine says: "The Sisters are urged not to take sides so that the orderly life of the Community is not disturbed, and so that our hospital work may go on without confusion."[67] Zinnemann had to fight to maintain these sequences; Catholic advisors were unhappy with the repressive language of the May 28, 1940, statement and its implications for the church as passive collaborator.[68] Zinnemann did show that being a nun and a member of the Resistance was not incompatible, for Sister Luke is introduced to the organization by Lisa (Diana Lambert), a lay student nurse who decides to become a nun. However, in eliminating Hulme's documentation of Sister Luke's Resistance activities while part of the church and effectively separating her two careers, the director articulated the church's failure to contest Nazi oppression.

Zinnemann's cinematic transformation of many of the initiation elements described within Hulme's novel had unexpected resonance with images of Nazi internment procedures and the Holocaust, made familiar in the work of Herbert Wilcox, Lewis Gilbert, and Robert Bresson. These images are initially unsettling due to their impact on Gabrielle's strong will; however, as time passes and war comes to Europe, the director's juxtaposition of the oppressors, the cloister, and the unseen camps makes the interior and exterior barriers between cloister and public life disappear. The cloister is dominated by closed or closing doors with grille fronts and long, slow processions of people passing through doors. As Gabrielle finally leaves the convent, she leaves the door open. When Gabrielle first accepts her number, 1072, upon entering the motherhouse, she is told that it formerly belonged to a dead nun of great courage.[69] This number effectively replaces Gabrielle's name; she will not be "Sister Luke" until many months later when she takes her vows. This is only Belgium in 1927, but the Catholic Church possesses an efficient identity-processing machine that was the envy of any organization—and would soon be adapted by the Nazis (fig. 46). This is also a place in which Gabrielle cannot speak with any sister or even look at another; when late for meals, she must even "beg" for food. At one point in the script, the novices are expected to give up trinkets when they enter the order. Gabrielle, with reluctance, gives up her gold pencil, but the scene is reminiscent of Nazis taking gold from Jews and other concentration camp prisoners before they are integrated within the system of the camp. Anderson's description is evocative: the basket "contains a pitiful collection of mementos which a girl would keep till the last moment, watches, small brooches, ribbon

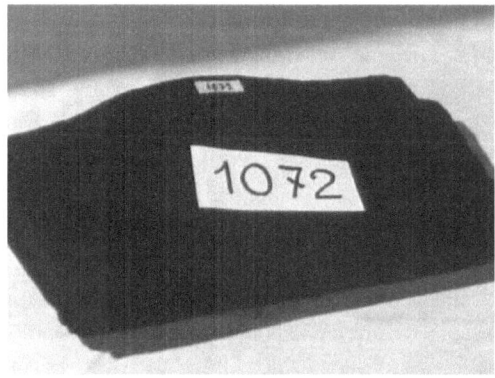

FIG. 46 Another uniform, another number: *The Nun's Story*, Warner Bros.

bows, rings, bracelets, gold berets, lace edged handkerchiefs, lockets, etc. The nun looks at her knowing she must have something. Everyone does."[70] This scene was so evocative that although part of the final script was shot, it was eventually cut. Instead, the only bit of the sequence that remains shows Gabriel clutching her father's gold pencil. We do not see her ever give this up, perhaps appropriately, since the pencil is both her one symbolic connection to the outside world she will one day rejoin and her means of "writing" her own story.

Anderson and Zinnemann were particularly drawn to the scenes in which older nuns cut Gabrielle's long hair as part of her transition from postulant to nun. In the novel, Hulme described Gabrielle's rather blasé attitude toward having her hair cut: "Gabrielle felt no emotion at the prospect of her head being clipped . . . To be shorn of your hair seemed to her not only the most logical of detachments . . . She had no curiosity about the actual operation."[71] Yet it is no simple haircutting scene; Hulme mentions the use of clippers as well as shears and heads now "as bare as a kneecap." Anderson was at pains to learn every detail; he saw it as a key scene in the film. As he wrote to Kathryn Hulme and Lou Habets, "I am concerned with the preparations immediately preceding vesture . . . Who says now go get your hair shorn . . . How do they go, in twos, sixes or what? It's done in the laundry you say . . . Since they have been wearing veils over their pony-tails up to this point, what are they given to put on their heads immediately after the clipping? Are they given the little draw-string cap then?"[72] Anderson's obsession with the scene begins early in his scripts. As Gabrielle bids goodbye to her sister Louise, Anderson writes, "Louise drawing her hand away from Gabrielle, tearfully looks at her, and straightens her hat, properly this time. When she has done this, her hand drops to touch Gabrielle's lovely hair, and the shaving and cropping come to her imagination."[73] It also fascinated Zinnemann, who wrote to his crew, "As a Postulant Gabrielle should still look her normal self. Her hair should be long so that we can dramatize the cutting during the Vesture."[74] Anderson would tinker with the scene, at pains to portray its latent horror and Gabrielle's efforts to project an image of acceptance. The shooting script surveys the scene: "Two nuns are finishing cutting two girls' hair. A few other novices including Gabrielle are waiting their turn and watching the proceedings with fascination, awe, and some misgivings. Gabrielle's defense is to look as much as possible to the floor, only now and then sneaking a look at her shorn sisters on the benches. One of the girls is finished, and the other girl on the bench looks at her and starts to laugh. The girl had born up well till now, but when the girl stars to laugh at her, she starts to cry. The nun, who is putting on her serre-tete holds her to her for a moment and comforts her.... The one who laughed is overcome with shame for her laughter, and she starts to cry too with her face in her hands. The nun lets her cry as she finishes her hair and puts the serre-tete on it. Gabrielle has now taken the place of the laughed-at novice, and behind her set smile might be running the phrase, 'All for Jesus.' The nun starts to cut her hair, as the locks fall into her lap . . . Gabrielle almost unconsciously touches the lock of hair and looks at it . . . The nun, without making a point of it, brushes it to the floor and continues. Gabrielle looks up at her with a quick smile as though to say 'I'm all right.'"[75] The hair-clipping evokes passionate shame and sadness among the women and in its postwar contexts is tied not only to images of centuries of female martyrdom (the hair was often shorn before immolation), but to the Holocaust and reprisals against alleged female collaborators (the Belgian reprisals against women were particularly fierce). But it also shows Gabrielle attempting to adjust her feelings to conform to the church's views, and is a strong indicator of her failure to submerge her personal conscience in the will of the church.

Zinnemann was aware of the potentially sensational aspects of cutting a major star's hair and forbade the press to take or publish photographs showing Hepburn having her hair removed.[76] The scene as shot is extremely violent, with Gabrielle somber and passive as the large clumsy scissors hack away at her long glossy hair. The shot shows the actress beneath the looming dark figure of the older nun, played by Hepburn's longtime hairdresser, Grazia de Rossi. She was given the part because only her skill with Hepburn's long wig could do the maximum damage to the hair without dislodging the wig (fig. 47).[77] The scene is immediately

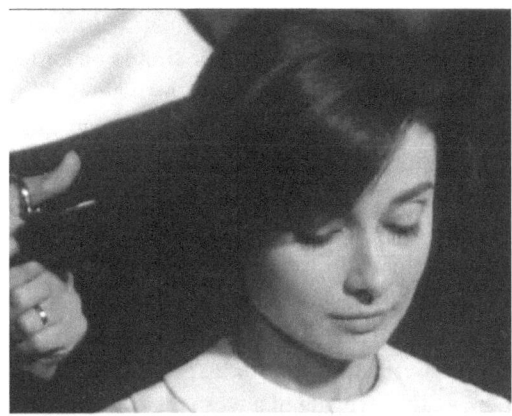

FIG. 47 The haircutting scene (Audrey Hepburn with Grazia de Rossi), Warner Bros.

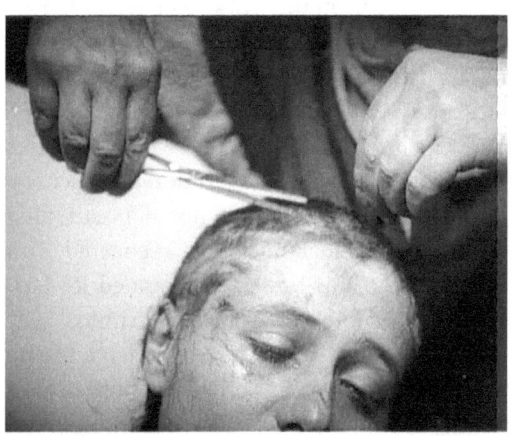

FIG. 48 Zinnemann's inspiration: Renée Falconetti in *Jeanne D'Arc* (1928), Société générale des films.

followed by the removal of Gabrielle's old postulant habit. She dons the white habit of a nun—or possibly of a martyr. Zinnemann and Hepburn rescreened not only Bresson's film, but also Carl Theodor Dreyer's *The Passion of Joan of Arc* (1928). Hepburn modeled her performance on Renée Falconetti's Joan for this sequence; indeed, Zinnemann set up the sequence and edited it like Dreyer, cutting from one off-center close-up to another and setting up a visual conflict between Gabrielle and the narrative space (fig. 48).[78] Hepburn's face in close-up, like Falconetti's, becomes the mechanism through which we view both submission—and later resistance—to the world around her.

For Gabrielle, it was a complete struggle from first to last that nearly wrecked her health, and Zinnemann wanted that struggle to show in Hepburn's face through a series of tight close-ups throughout the film. As he wrote to producer Henry Blanke: "1) As a Postulant Gabrielle should still look her normal self. Her hair should be long so that we can dramatize the cutting during the Vesture. 2) As a Novice she should look pale. Her skin should, if possible, have that translucent quality of alabaster or wax. It is very important that her lips should be as pale as the rest of her face! 3) She need not be quite so pale after the First Vows and throughout the Congo, but her lips should remain bloodless. 4) After her return from the Congo she should again look pale and a good deal older. 5) At certain times in the picture she should look a bit ill, especially when she is about to break down with TB and also at the time when she is over-tired and has to be put in a private room for a rest."[79] Like Falconetti, Gabrielle's face had to convey the struggle of a woman at odds with those in power, on trial, and locked away from the world. But in this haircutting sequence, Zinnemann may have had more contemporary martyrs in mind—and those unrecognized by the Catholic Church. For Hepburn's experience, occurring after 1945 and part of a historical film about the war, has another context Dreyer's film did not possess and is akin to that of women arriving and preparing for their incarceration at Auschwitz or Ravensbrück. No wonder that Zinnemann would not allow still photographers on the set.[80] Two years later, Gillo Pontecorvo reenacted Zinnemann's haircutting scene in *Kapo* (1961), in which condemned Jewish prisoner Susan Strasberg is transformed into a non-Jewish, "criminal" camp inmate by a sympathetic doctor. The sequence is heavily indebted to both Dreyer and Zinnemann's series of close-ups, but Strasberg's physical resemblance to Hepburn creates an even more powerful connection between the two films.

Franz Waxman, who allegedly loathed Catholicism, aided Zinnemann's "resistant" soundtrack by accompanying many of these sequences with ominous drumrolls, piercing isolated strings, and thunderous orchestrations (particularly during Gabrielle's haircut; with the scissors' first two cuts, Waxman also cut his score abruptly, so that the only sound we hear is the shearing). Waxman's impact was such that the director eventually had to ask Warner to cut some of his final score because, with the accompanying music, Waxman had made Gabrielle's renouncement of the church a joyous escape to freedom and had effectively eliminated Zinnemann's efforts to be objective in the final sequences.[81] With some reluctance, Warner agreed to remove the score and allow Gabrielle to exit without fanfare. Waxman was outraged and wrote letters to Steve Trilling complaining about Zinnemann's dictatorial behavior, and Zinnemann sent a chilling letter to Waxman, reminding him of his subordinate position in the production. Zinnemann may have been less sympathetic to Waxman because he had no control at Fox over the dubbing of Bernard Hermann's score for *A Hatful of Rain* (1957) or with Stanley Kramer over Dimitri Tiompkin's work on *The Men* (1950). He found the music obtrusive, and was particularly anxious that with *The Nun's Story*, a film he supervised completely from start to finish, non-diegetic music would be limited. Although Zinnemann would later indicate in interviews that the lack of music enabled viewers to make up their own minds about Gabrielle's decision, documents reveal that Zinnemann's primary concern at the end was "achieving a feeling of reality . . . to make the audience forget we were dealing with actresses, artificial sets, and motion picture extras" which non-diegetic "Hollywood" music often compromised.[82]

Did he want the silence of a Bresson film (he screened several in the course of the production, including *A Man Escaped* and *Diary of a Country Priest*) or of Dreyer's *Passion of Joan of Arc* in this final sequence? In his script, Anderson had planned only for the sound of gunfire in the distance. Zinnemann in the end opted for complete silence. The camera remains inside the cloister and does not accompany Gabrielle on her new life. It is immobile, focused on Gabrielle's retreating figure as she disappears into the distance before fade out. The image, with its many doorways, arches, and recessions, recalls the many Dutch Old Master paintings Zinnemann studied throughout production.[83] Like a fragment of the past, or an aged painting, its colors faded with time, Gabrielle disappears into the original lines, silently and without fanfare. If it was Zinnemann's idea of realism, it was both visually and aurally simple and richly layered with perspectives from Vermeer and Hobemma to Dreyer and Bresson.

Throughout his career, Zinnemann's interest in achieving "realism" meant that had a decided preference for black-and-white cinematography. *The Nun's Story* was only his second color film (*Oklahoma!*, 1955, was his first), and initially Zinnemann had hoped that Warner Bros. would allow him to film the first sequences in the Belgian convents in black-and-white, leaving the stunning color sequences for the locations in the Congo.[84] At one point, he even seemed willing to forego color entirely, and asked that friend and colleague from his *Redes* days, Manuel Figueroa, do the black-and-white cinematography.[85] When this proved unfeasible and Warner Bros. argued for a full color picture, he and Franz Planer struggled to find a dark cinematography that could adequately convey Gabrielle's struggle with the church. As he wrote Steve Trilling late in production, "In regard to brightness . . . It seemed to me that some of the Ceremonies by being printed too light lost some of the feeling of mysticism. Needless to say I feel that it is most important that the mysterious quality be maintained, especially in the first part of the picture . . . The second point is that all the scenes in the Belgian part of the picture, especially the Ceremonies in the Chapel and the Chapter Hall be printed in cold tones. The answer print has a warm golden glow in some of these scenes. To my mind this is quite wrong, because Franz Planer, Trauner and I were breaking our backs in order to maintain a cold, black and white feeling. The worst scenes in the answer print are, among others, the big speech of Edith Evans in the Chapter Hall, including the entrance of the postulants. It is almost sepia in tone and it gave me a terrific jolt when I saw it." Zinnemann's feelings about the cinematography again reflected the influence of Dreyer's *Passion of Joan of Arc*, particularly in his creation of tight close-ups with very little background distraction. As he continued to Trilling: "The third point is this: the scenes which we photographed as night effects were lit by Franz Planer with the idea that the background should fall off and be very sketchy, with very little detail—so that the audience's attention would be completely centered on the faces of the actors. Many of these scenes were printed for bright daylight—we see a great many details which are completely meaningless and which divert and scatter the audience's attention—such as bottles in laboratories etc.—while the actors' faces are pale and washed out, without any skin texture."[86]

Reception

In spite of its foreign locations in Europe and Africa, its lengthy production time, and cost ($3.5 million), *The Nun's Story*'s gross receipts more than reassured Steve Trilling and Jack Warner: an $11.5 million worldwide gross with a slightly higher take in Europe than America ($5.8 million foreign compared with $5.2 US gross).[87] Zinnemann's success in foreign markets ensured his continued attraction to an American film industry increasingly bent on maximizing foreign assets and audiences. Although Zinnemann may have worried that *The Nun's Story* would be received as a lurid exposé of the church, most reviewers and critics evaluated the film as a modern biography, a woman's picture, and a wartime film. Despite that it was only a fifth of the actual footage, critics focused on the war sequences as the definitive narrative event in Gabrielle's life. The *New York Times Magazine* wrote, "In *The Nun's Story*, she will be Sister Luke, who for 17 years was a nun in Belgium and the Belgian Congo before abandoning her calling to join the underground in World War II."[88] *Variety* was even more explicit: "In the end, when WW2 strikes, and her father is killed by the Germans, she knows she is not a true nun, at least of this Order. She cannot feel Christ-like love, she cannot turn the other cheek to the Nazis. With her superior's consent, she leaves the convent."[89] *Redbook* saw it as a biographical film, noting that "this picture is based on a fascinating true life story of a Belgian girl who became a nursing nun and then left the church during WWII."[90] The connection between Gabrielle's abandonment of the church and beginning of Resistance work was clear to critics. In fact, when Hulme's book was first received, critics saw Gabrielle's trip to the Congo as a "liberation" from the dreaded convent life: "How glad is the American to see this exceptional woman depart for the Congo, land of the great unfolding, after her seven lean years, narrow in the narrow-minded life of the convent. The day has come, the day of liberation from the small-mindedness of the convent, where life is measured in inches."[91] When the film was released, the contrast between the gray convent life in Belgium and the gorgeous Congo locations, not seen by filmgoers since Jack Cardiff's camerawork in John Huston's *The African Queen* (1951), was obvious. Zinnemann's original dream, to shoot the convent scenes in black-and-white and the "liberating" Congo sequences in Technicolor, turned out to be unnecessary. As the Protestant Motion Picture Council reviewed the film: "While this masterful production may be taken by many as a consideration of Roman Catholic religious orders and convent life, it is essentially the development of a girl's personality from repressed confinement to the finding of herself by free choice . . . World War II breaks out, she is involved in helping people escape, and before long, manifests the desire to be free herself."[92] This was not the kind of discourse the Catholic church had hoped for, but at least the filmmakers had heeded their advice on avoiding an affair between Fortunati (Peter Finch) and Sister Luke in the liberating Congo!

Zinnemann's close working relationships with actors and his unique sensitivity to their abilities and limitations had earned him a reputation as an "actor's director." He could capture Spencer Tracy's understated Hollywood brilliance, collaborate with Montgomery Clift on two of his most riveting performances, and even manage Method actors like Rod Steiger and Marlon Brando. From 1957–59, there were few actors who could match Audrey Hepburn's unique star quality, and while in recent years popular consciousness has focused on her body as a key to her fashion icon status, for Zinnemann, and indeed for cultural theorist Roland Barthes, Hepburn was all face.[93] But while Barthes had compared Hepburn's contemporary face, marked by present contexts, with classical Hollywood star Greta Garbo's timeless beauty, Zinnemann had seen a beautiful face that contained and defied Hepburn's violent experiences in the war. The fact is, she was marked by the past, and carried its European war legacy with her in her fragile and disease-weakened body, however much Hollywood and European fans would see her as an emblem of youthful modernity. Zinnemann's ability to see her role as Gabrielle van der Mal as a modern Joan of Arc, and to model her performance on Renée Falconetti's Joan and Letterier's Resistance hero, revealed the complexity of Zinnemann's cinematic eye. Hepburn's performance was remarkable. It earned her yet another Oscar nomination, and she would say of her full year of work for Zinnemann: "I gave more time, energy, and thought to this role than to any of my previous screen performances."[94]

She may not have played a traditional resister's role or endured a Nazi camp, but the shoot in the Congo was particularly damaging to her health, already severely impaired by anemia and long-term malnutrition during the Occupation. As Robert Anderson remarked succinctly, "She is a great actress and a great sport . . . went through Hell."[95] Unlike Falconetti, whom Dreyer forced to kneel for hours on painful stone floors, and whose expressions of pain were as much real as simulated, Hepburn created her role through a close and supportive relationship with Zinnemann which lasted the rest of their lives. Hepburn's personal resistance to Catholicism and her awareness of the church's role in occupied Belgium and Holland was given free rein in their lengthy improvisations at Cinecittà. As Hepburn remarked of her experience on Zinnemann's set, "Fred really does everything possible to help his actors, to create a mood, in ideal working conditions. With others—well, one's a good sport, but here, it's just not necessary."[96] Marie Louise Habets, Gabrielle, and Audrey Hepburn survived both the church and the war. Throughout her life in Hollywood, Europe, and later in Africa working for UNICEF, Hepburn would remain Zinnemann's heroine, deceptively delicate, as he remembered, "with a trace of iron in her jaw."

CHAPTER SIX
Aging Revolutionaries and the Loss of History

"I am by no means an opponent of tendentious programmatic poetry as such ... But I believe that the thesis must spring forth from the situations and action itself, without being explicitly displayed. I believe that there is no compulsion for the writer to put into the reader's hands the future historical resolution of the social conflicts he is depicting."
—**Frederick Engels to Minna Kautsky, 1885**[1]

"I think the era has passed when we can easily and flatly say this guy is a bastard and this guy is great."
—**Fred Zinnemann, 1964**[2]

After the grueling location work in Australia for *The Sundowners* (1960), Zinnemann became involved with Walter Mirisch's production of James Michener's *Hawaii* from 1961 to 1963. He eventually withdrew, finding this second Hawaiian film about European missionaries less interesting than *From Here to Eternity* and overburdened with a massive script and $15 million production cost.[3] While embroiled in the preproduction for *Hawaii*, he read former Archers screenwriter Emeric Pressburger's new novel, *Killing a Mouse on Sunday* (1961), and was excited by its resonances with the death of the Spanish anarchist leader, Francisco Sabaté, in 1960. Making this film would enable him to remain in Europe, and he signed with Columbia's Mike Frankovich. Pressburger's novel was set twenty years after the Spanish Civil War, and features fictional characters who largely avoid discussing their wartime pasts. As reviewer Daniel George noted rather dryly, Pressburger's novel views the war "at a safe distance."[4] This "safety" created a kind of moral and political relativism in the text that both intrigued and worried Zinnemann (as George continued, "Who was in the right we may never be able to decide").⁵ Yet, compared with the number of politically motivated Falangist and Loyalist historical novels printed about the war since the 1930s, Pressburger's work was unique.⁶

No successful Hollywood film had been made about the war since Sam Wood's adaptation of Ernest Hemingway's *For Whom the Bell Tolls* (1943),⁷ and when the Spanish government heard about Zinnemann's new film for Columbia, renamed, forebodingly at Renée Zinnemann's suggestion, *Behold a Pale Horse*, it panicked. When, under government pressure, the studio refused to cancel the project, the regime banned all Columbia films in Spain for several years. In advance publicity interviews, Zinnemann eschewed sensationalizing the topic. Yet his attitude toward the material engaged the political nature of documentary filmmaking during the Spanish Civil War era, and he drew attention to the fact that he hired the leftist Hungarian documentary filmmaker Jean Badal as director of photography. Zinnemann's claims for "simple" objectivity alarmed Franco's government more than a Hollywood treatment. Certainly Badal was a tendentious choice for cinematographer. Forced to leave Hungary for Paris after the 1956 uprising, Badal co-wrote, co-directed (with André Libik), and shot *Un homme dans l'inhumanité* (1958) about Hungarian premier Imre Nagy. In choosing Badal over a list of legendary Hollywood cinematographers (including Charles Clarke, William Daniels, and friend Joseph Ruttenberg), Zinnemann was making a very direct statement about his film's visual engagement with the idea of the individual versus the state.⁸ Yet, upon its release, some film critics began to claim that Zinnemann made "unsigned films"; others would argue over his lack of political commitment to a topic.⁹ His "documentary touch" and "objective vision" could be a two-edged critical sword, and nowhere were these issues thrown into more relief than in his work on the Spanish Civil War, an era in which many had to choose between being "politically ineffectual" or "poetically false."¹⁰

Zinnemann's decision to look at Spain "twenty years after" beholds a truly committed, but imperfect hero, Manuel Artigas (Gregory Peck), part D'Artagnan, part Francisco Sabaté. At the end of the film, when he dies after being shot by the Guardia Civil, the police ignore foreign press attention while the Spanish public remains largely indifferent to the revolutionary's death. Zinnemann's clash between different generations' attitudes toward the past makes the film one of his most complex. Critics expecting a traditional historical war film set in Spain had not been watching

Zinnemann's work with any attention. He did not make traditional war films with set combat, soldiers, and clear-cut ideologies. He made films about the resistance to fascism, and here, for his generation, he shows how true resistance, largely unnoticed by the public and condemned by the state, ages and dies.

Critical Histories of the Spanish Civil War

The fall of the Second Republic and the flight of nearly half a million Loyalists across the Pyrenees in February 1939 were overshadowed by the outbreak of the Second World War later that summer.[11] Many of the Spanish refugees interned in concentration camps in southern France would fight for the Resistance against the Nazis, hoping that after Hitler's fall, the Allies would turn their attention to Franco. But in 1945, the Allies did not like being reminded that one fascist dictatorship remained in Western Europe. Anti-fascist resistance continued in Spain, but was largely ignored by the United States and Western European governments responsible for reconstructing Franco as a bulwark against communism in Eastern Europe. In response to the Korean War, Franco made successful strategic overtures to the United States, and in 1953, he secured the construction of US military bases at Rota, Morón, Zaragoza, and Torrejón.[12] As the years passed, Spain's growing economy became more dependent upon American oil interests, while ex-Allies holidayed along the Spanish coast.

Through the Cold War and into the 1970s, European and American remembrance of Spain's Civil War was shaped by ambivalence and neglect. The American public's blasé attitude toward the conflict is illustrated in Zinnemann's *Julia*, when Lillian's wealthy "friend" Anne-Marie (Meryl Streep) expresses her bewilderment that any of her acquaintances would fight in Spain and "die a communist." But for many in Zinnemann's generation, the war polarized the European political spectrum and defined political commitment. In 1937, Arthur Koestler repudiated any writer who "pretends to be objective" in the face of the war's atrocities. When later in life, Loyalist supporter George Orwell looked back on the war and its influence upon his career, he recognized that when "I lacked a political purpose ... I wrote lifeless books."[13] As literary historian Gareth Thomas comments, in his writings about the war, "a lack of commitment is in itself a political stance: there is no such thing as neutrality. If you are not with the Republic, then you must be against it."[14] Neutrality was only another word for indifference, and arguably determined the fate of the Republic and other democratically elected governments in Europe during the 1930s. But commitment came at a historical price; competitive political propaganda among both government loyalists and fascist insurgents meant that a "truthful" representation of the war was almost impossible. Numerous international journalists and photographers, particularly those of the Loyalist persuasion like *New York Times* correspondent Herbert Matthews, argued passionately about the need for reliable reportage to declare its political bias openly without altering any facts.[15] But others were not so committed to facts, such as William Carney, Matthews's opposite number on the *Times* staff, who invented reports of insurgent successes. As media historian Philip Knightley has pointed out, no war to that point had more media coverage, nor more disputes over the reliability of its coverage, than the Spanish Civil War.[16] Matthews, in particular, was targeted by Catholic pressure groups in the United States, including a Catholic history professor, Joseph Thorning, who demanded his recall from Spain.

The war coincided with the height of the social documentary movement in the United States and Europe, when the photographic image's indexicality—or by another word, its objectivity—was harnessed to social reform.[17] The roots of the social documentary movement stretch back to the late nineteenth century, when flash photography enabled Jacob Riis to give immediacy to his studies of homeless urban children. Years later, Lewis Hine's images of child labor in American textile mills revealed similar horrors and would influence the work and philosophy of Zinnemann's colleague on *Redes*, Paul Strand. The photograph's intrinsic connection to its subject was said to guarantee its truth and silence any opponents of social reform. Yet over the past four decades, scholars such as John Tagg have argued that "the camera is never neutral," and that photographic truth or objectivity is an ideological fantasy encouraged by the state commissioning and exhibiting the photographs.[18] No photographic image can escape the ideological contexts of its own production or its reframing by captions, text, and voice-overs. Caroline Brothers and Anthony Aldgate have demonstrated how "documentary" images in journals and on screen were constructed to outrage and control public opinion about the war in Great Britain and France, and how one image could communicate to different publics with different textual overlays.[19] It is no accident that the most controversial image of modern photojournalism is Robert Capa's *Fallen Republican Soldier* (1937), which has been subject to extraordinary artistic and political praise and dismissed as a composed image and another example of Republican propaganda.[20] In the contemporaneous documentary *Spanish Earth*, director Joris Ivens and writers Ernest Hemingway, Archibald MacLeish, and Lillian Hellman use documentary narration to reinforce the film's denunciation of Franco and quash any ideological ambiguity in the images.

Yet there are obvious dangers in seeing images from the Spanish Civil War or the social documentary movement as cogs in an ideological wheel of state power; the significance of the origins of the movement lay in its renewed attention to technology and objectivity as tools for revisionist discourse. Resistance to grand narratives, whether it was America's "gospel of wealth" or Franco's holy crusade, animated the Left. Arguably, something similar occurred with new social historians such as Carl Becker, who believed that the practice of writing or making history was not confined to the historical "state" of the ivory tower, but could operate in daily life as a corrective to grand narratives and mainstream myths (recall that *The Spanish Earth*'s production company was named Contemporary Historians Inc.).[21] Obviously, these resistant counter-narratives could also function as ideologies as potentially repressive as the systems they opposed—unless they were intellectually flexible or fearless enough to train their critique upon themselves.

The Life and Times of Francisco Sabaté

Though for the most part, from 1939 resistance to Franco and the fascist government was forced outside Spain's borders, communist cadres, anarchists, Loyalist militants, Basque separatists, and other groups continued the fight. Nearly half a million survivors went into exile after the war, yet the pre-Occupation French government did not welcome the exiles. They were interned in overcrowded, disease-ridden concentration camps in southern France before being pressed into the war effort in 1940.[22] Many men, women, and children were deported back to Spain to face death and torture in prisons like Ventas. Those captured by the Nazis were put in German camps and forced to wear an S surrounded by a blue triangle, an obvious variant of the Jewish Star of David. Over 7,000 Spanish Loyalists would die in Nazi death camps.[23] Republican minister and activist Victoria Kent would compare her people's experience in France to the country's inhuman treatment of the French Jews during the Occupation.[24]

But a handful, like Francisco Sabaté, remained in France and made daring guerrilla raids throughout the 1940s and 1950s. As historian Paul Preston points out, the most significant factor determining the failure of exiled opposition was not Franco's successes but internal ideological divisions in the Socialist party, the PSOE, and their uneasy relations with the communists.[25] Sabaté and his brother José were libertarian anarchists opposed to the ideological infighting of both the socialists and communists, yet when the old anarchist party became the Movimiento Libertario Español (MLE) in early 1939, this created more factional rifts, indecision over an anti-fascist front, increased bureaucratic control, and infiltration by Francoists. Because Sabaté and others believed in continuing the anarchist resistance inside Spain—against party lines in Toulouse—the controlling faction lead by Federica Montseny refused financial help. Sabaté was forced to steal from banks and wealthy supporters of Franco to buy arms and supplies. This often led the Francoist press to portray him as a bandit rather than a resistance fighter.[26] After his assassination by the Guardia Civil in January 1960, MLE and PCE (Spanish Communist Party in Exile), stung by his criticism of both parties, refused to give him credit as a revolutionary fighter across three decades.[27] Ironically, it was the wider left-leaning European and American press which acknowledged Sabaté as an important figure of the Spanish resistance and first attracted Fred Zinnemann's attention.

The director was fascinated with Sabaté, and would later publicly acknowledge that Sabaté's life and death were the basis for his adaptation of Pressburger's Manuel Artigas (Gregory Peck), the aging Republican fighter, who in a final act of defiance, willingly walks into a Guardia trap.[28] But while Pressbuger was content to draw a mere sketch, Zinnemann was obsessed with the biographical details (fig. 49). He collected and annotated Sabaté's obituaries in the French and American press, heavily underlining *Time*'s obituary, which noted that "the 44-year-old Sabaté was a legend" betrayed by a colleague in France. According to *Time*, Sabaté had created "school of terrorism" for young men, but "stripped of his patriotic cause, the terrorist in time becomes a bandit." This would become a central interest of Zinnemann's, but he was equally drawn to the article's concluding remarks: "So astonishing were his exploits that Barcelonians finally concluded that Sabaté was a myth."[29] Ten years after the release of Zinnemann's *Behold a Pale Horse*, Sabaté's biographer Antonio Tellez observed the dearth of books on anti-fascist resistance in Spain, yet Zinnemann's film remained the one example of popular interest in Spanish anti-fascism.

FIG. 49 Researching *Behold a Pale Horse* (1964): Zinnemann's photograph of Francisco Sabaté, the model for Manuel Artigas, AMPAS.

Sabaté was one of the last original Spanish resisters. When he died in 1960, he had outlived the revolution and most of his colleagues. The anarchist party in Toulouse was more interested in obtaining legal recognition from the French government than in continuing the fight.[30] In 1951, the first stage of anti-fascist resistance came to an end with the symbolic withdrawal of communist armed groups inside Spain. Throughout the 1950s, Sabaté was increasingly alone and was even imprisoned by the French government for arms possession and alleged robbery. However, resistance, often symbolized by the exiles and guerrillas, did not die; instead, a new wave of opposition developed inside of Spain that continued after Franco's death and the assassination of Prime Minister Admiral Luis Carrero Blanco in 1973. As Paul Preston argues, "The battle for survival after the Civil War is very different from the activities of the prosperous lawyers and intellectuals who currently consider themselves to be at the forefront of the struggle."[31] The internal divisions and lethargy of the old movement in the 1950s and the contrast between obsolete heroism and contemporary Spain, would become central questions in Fred Zinnemann's film of the Spanish Civil War.

While Sabaté's heroic life and death attracted both Pressburger's and Zinnemann's attention, there were several other events which influenced

Zinnemann's decision to make a film about the aftermath of the war. In 1962, Spain was paralyzed by nationwide strikes opposing the Franco regime and it also witnessed the meeting of internal and political exiles at the Munich Congress. Zinnemann collected major press reports in 1962 on the political situation, and one *New York Times* article noted, "While the Opposition as it exists must operate in the shadows today, when General Franco is gone it will emerge and play an important role."[32] Spain had been modernizing since the 1950s and as its economy had grown, had become increasingly dependent on foreign sources of fuel. It also was exporting more of its consumer goods and produce to European countries. Spain was developing a practical New Left within Franco's government, and it largely developed from the economic realization that greater participation in the European economy would require a rethinking of their nationalist/fascist ideologies. Spain was in transition. Yet despite the new histories of the war appearing in the early 1960s which challenged the fiercely propagandistic "historiography" of the Franco regime, most notably the work of Herbert Southworth and Hugh Thomas, few of Spain's heroic resisters were attracting any public attention in the face of these policy changes.[33] Censorship affected Nationalists' writings from the 1930s until the press law reforms of 1966, and until 1967, no Republican novel was published in Spain.[34] Spanish filmmakers' preoccupation with the history and legacy of the war dates only from Franco's death and the release of Victor Erice's *Spirit of the Beehive* (1973), only becoming widespread from the 1990s.[35] The earliest Spanish films often use allegory, fantasy, and the perspectives of young children as a means of eluding censorship. When it appeared in mid-1964, *Behold a Pale Horse*'s documentary style and picture of contemporary Spain stood alone. As a major Columbia production, it was an obvious target for the Franco regime.

Hollywood and the Spanish Civil War

While *The Spanish Earth*'s Loyalist perspective was clear, in *Last Train From Madrid* (1937) and *Blockade* (1938), the only two major Hollywood feature films about the war released in wartime,[36] it is nearly impossible to decipher who is fighting on which side until well into the narratives. The words "Republican," "Loyalist," "fascist," or "communist" do not appear in the scripts or films, although Henry Fonda's character in *Blockade* does betray some Loyalist leanings. *Blockade* was picketed by Catholic pressure groups at Radio City Music Hall and later denied bookings for a second-run release on the West Coast. Historians have argued that PCA and political censorship of the film by right-wing elites not only barred producer Walter Wanger from creating a film which clearly delineated the conflict but also forbade generating any sympathy with the Loyalists. Only *Casablanca* (1942) would remember the war with honor. Part of hero Rick Blaine's (Humphrey Bogart) biography, as related by Captain Renault (Claude Rains), was that he "fought in Spain—on the Loyalist side," and the French captain suggests that principles must have been involved with the decision, since "the winning side would have paid much better." Rick only nods briefly, lost in thought. As film historian Robert Sklar notes, "It is a comment on the liberal political climate at Warner Bros. (or the disorder of *Casablanca*'s script development) that no questions seem to have been raised about making Rick a Spanish Civil War veteran."[37] But a year later, an adaptation of Ernest Hemingway's *For Whom the Bell Tolls* represented the first attempt to historicize the conflict with any seriousness. It also focused on a group of Loyalist mountain fighters, whose leader, Pilar (Katina Paxinou), is a staunch socialist and Republican.

However, some film and cultural historians have argued that *For Whom the Bell Tolls* is more travel romance than Civil War narrative, and that the wider historical debates about the war are completely submerged in the romance between American saboteur Robert Jordan (Gary Cooper) and Maria (Ingrid Bergman).[38] Ironically, Hemingway foregrounds Jordan's resistance to becoming entangled in the past as a means of heroic self-preservation. Early on, he refuses to contemplate the wider implications of the Republican attack, and instead concentrates on only his own role as an explosives expert: "He would not think about that. That was not his business. That was Golz's business. He had only one thing to do and that was what he should think about and he must think it out clearly and take everything as it came along, and not worry."[39] When he thinks about the past he stops himself because history, particularly in Spain, is dangerous. There was safety only in the present moment.

Jordan may resist thinking about the past out of fear of becoming "history" himself, but Pilar is truly fearless. Though traditionally war histories and films are dominated by the perspectives of men and male soldiers, it is Pilar who makes the ultimate decision of the group to fight in the Republican attack.[40] She also narrates the only substantial portion of Civil War history in the novel, telling an unwilling Jordan: "Furthermore, I like to talk. It is the only civilized thing we have."[41] She then tells of the public executions of fascists in her hometown and of the pillaging of the church. In Hemingway's novel, women tell the history of the war, and it is not heroic. While Maria tells of her rape in Valladolid at the hands of the Falangists, Pilar describes the Republicans entering the church and stabbing a priest to death with sickles. There is no sympathy for Catholicism in either the novel or film. While Pablo tells her that he is "disillusioned" because the priest he saw killed "died very badly," Pilar, who has no Christian superstitions, passes it off with a shrug.[42] Though Zinnemann's film would not give priority to Spanish women's resistance to fascism in *Behold a Pale Horse*, Manuel Artigas's Catholic-hating mother (Mildred Dunnock, reversing her role as nun Sister Catherine in Zinnemann's *Nun's Story*), is also named Pilar.[43] She, unlike her son, continued the fight inside Spain, ironically mirroring the experience of not only Spanish women after the war, but of French women fighting the Nazis during the Resistance.

Zinnemann may have seen other parallels between the Spanish refugee situation and the wider experience of the Second World War. During and after the war, the Nationalist government killed many men, women, and children. Still others were imprisoned, put in concentration camps, and their children sent to right-wing families in Argentina for adoption and indoctrination, or physically and sexually abused as wards of the church. In her study of female resisters in the Spanish Civil War, historian Shirley Magini notes a recurrent "theme in autobiographies of Spanish women in France": namely, that many Spanish women identified with Jews. Popular coverage of the 1939 "exodus" often compared the fleeing Loyalists to Jews and Franco to the Egyptian pharoah.[44] In her memoirs, MLE leader Federica Montseny writes, "They have condemned us to becoming the collective and reincarnated image of the errant Jew. Tossed from our homes, from our country, uprooted from our land, never again will we have a hearth, a mother country, or a place to rest."[45] Yet these Biblical associations had found new meaning in the context of the Nazis' removals of Jews in the Holocaust. Zinnemann's war pictures, though never focusing exclusively on the Jewish experience of the Holocaust, resonated with dispossession, resistance, and death. The Spanish Civil War was deeply tied to his generation's experience with fascism, nationalism, and conflict. As others have pointed out, however, there is a tendency in much exiled Republican and post-1960s revisionist historiography to focus upon and glamorize the foreign factors in the war: the war correspondents, the machinations of the Soviets, Nazis, and Italian fascists, the heroics of the Lincoln Brigade.[46] In consequence, the essential Spanishness of the war gets lost in wider debates about twentieth-century anti-fascism. Zinnemann was another of these outsiders with a broad interest in anti-fascist resistance, but arguably in *Pale Horse* he engages the issues of internal/external resistance, historical remembrance, and foreign influence.

Unconventional Resistance Heroes

Even in 1964, the Spanish Civil War was not an easy topic to negotiate, particularly in Hollywood, where Catholic pressure groups like the Legion of Decency still held sway over questions of censorship (The Legion's Cardinal Spellman was a close friend of Franco's). The origins of the anticommunist blacklist of the 1950s can be traced to the war's politicization of filmmakers. For Zinnemann, who was always drawn to the authenticity of location shoots, there were immediate and perhaps insurmountable problems about filming in Spain. Franco was still very much in power and still more than willing to shoot his political opponents.[47] Ironically, a film set in contemporary Spain had the potential to be as controversial as a film about insurgent and church atrocities during the Civil War. It could potentially undermine the regime's attempts to construct a more modern, even European economy and growing tourist industry. But Columbia, which had produced Zinnemann's adaptation of *From Here to Eternity* in 1953, was interested in the box-office potential of controversy.

Initially, Zinnemann asked Pressburger to draft the screenplay. Pressburger, the famed other half of Michael Powell's Archers production company (*Edge of the World*, 1937; *The Life and Death of Colonel Blimp*, 1942; *I Know Where I'm Going*, 1945; *The Red Shoes*, 1948) had ended his partnership with Powell and more or less turned away from filmmaking. But few screenwriters could resist the temptation of adapting their own work for the screen. Pressburger's novel concerns a young boy, Pablo, who meets aging guerilla fighter Manuel Artigas, exiled and living in the French town of Pau. Artigas no longer makes the daring raids against the Guardia Civil, and his archenemy, the Guardia Captain Viñolas, now spends his time with his mistress and worries whether his second-in-command (ironically named Zapater) will replace him as chief of police. When a Guardia informer posing as a friend tells Artigas of his mother's imminent death, he decides to visit her across the border in Spain. She dies before he can reach her, but she asks a young priest to warn her son that the Guardia will use her death as a trap to lure him across the border. Both the priest and a young boy and son of his former murdered associate warn Artigas, but the hero goes in spite of the risk, to shoot the traitor responsible for this trap and the death of the boy's father. Artigas kills the traitor but is subsequently shot by the Guardia Civil. The priest and Viñolas both speculate on why Artigas returns to his death, the priest entirely if erroneously convinced in his version of the story and the Guardia captain merely puzzled.

One of the more interesting characters in Pressburger's novel was the priest, Father Francisco. Too young to have fought in the war or to be involved in the church's collaboration with the Franco regime, he seems apart from his Order and resists telling the Guardia captain what Pilar Artigas has asked him to do for her son. Artigas was known as one of the Loyalist soldiers responsible for burning churches and killing nuns and priests, yet the young priest continues to help him. Different chapters in Pressburger's novel focus on the interior thoughts of his four main characters, Pablo, Artigas, Viñolas, and Father Francisco. Zinnemann underlined much of the chapter in which the priest describes his political impartiality. His father, he explains, took no sides in the war, but was shot by soldiers. Zinnemann underlined: "We never found out who the soldiers were, which army they belonged to . . . My mother said, 'I'm on no side, I'm against both sides . . . I don't want any help and as for my son, I have chosen a third side for him, the side of the Lord.'"[48] During the war, the church was fully on the insurgent side, even blessing the army as they went into battle and massacred civilians. They abetted the mass purges of Loyalist civilians and fighters, took newborn children away from imprisoned mothers, and physically and sexually abused thousands of children of dissidents taken in their care after the conflict. To speak of a third side is to invoke neutrality—to be, as others have argued, "against the Republic." Yet Zinnemann underscored and starred this passage in his copy of Pressburger's novel. Whether he wanted to partially redeem the reputation of the church through the faith of a pure young priest, to examine the modern church's role in the Franco regime, or to re-engage the concept of commitment and objectivity at its most controversial, is uncertain.[49]

Pressburger wrote his first draft over the summer of 1962, and in late October, Zinnemann began to pick it apart. He was most concerned with the depiction of Artigas. Zinnemann plainly saw him as both outlaw and hero, and did not want the young priest to take the moral high ground from Artigas. As he wrote, "Regarding the sentence 'The Priest's code of honor is so much higher than the bandits': I don't believe this. It seems to me that the whole point of the story is that the bandit's code of honor is just as high, according to his standards, as the priest's."[50] One of the things Zinnemann felt was lacking from Pressburger's novel and the first screenplay was historical context. This lack of context made the feud between Viñolas and Artigas seem almost trivial. Regardless of whether the narrative was set twenty years after the war, Zinnemann argued that "since the audience must be able to identify with Manuel, *they must understand the reason for his making the raids, and they must approve it.* Is the reason a continuing protest against oppression? Where and how will it be stated?" This was Zinnemann's major difficulty, for as he acknowledged, they were in the process of sending a Spanish translation of Pressburger's script to the Spanish government, in hopes that its appearance of political harmlessness would enable them to obtain permission to shoot locations in Spain. Zinnemann gambled that the Spanish officials would read only the surface story of the "bandit" killed by the Guardia captain. Zinnemann asked Pressburger: "It is of the greatest importance to delete dialog about the clergy and the police being brothers-in-arms. I think that this can only be implied, but never expressed."[51]

Zinnemann played a careful game with the few cards he possessed. By keeping direct accusations about the church out of the early screenplays shown to Spanish officials, Zinnemann hoped to obtain basic cooperation on the film production. He had done something similar in *From Here to Eternity* and more directly in *The Nun's Story*. The films' harshest criticism of the church was visual rather than textual, and therefore not seen by Catholic censors of pressure groups in the early stages of production.

But Zinnemann's enthusiasm for seeing Artigas as a resistance hero was unequivocal and he struggled with Pressburger to make him more accessible to American audiences. He and Paul Feyder had conducted extensive interviews with Francisco Sabaté's last surviving friends, and they told him many details of heroic escapes and killings of informers. According to the men, Sabaté "is a legend among all these people" and "at one time [1946] disarmed a Guardia Civil in a busy street in the middle of Barcelona in broad daylight." They told him stories about the chief of police of Barcelona, Quintela, who "apparently was mortally afraid of Sabaté, who had sworn to kill him, but was unsuccessful. Instead, he [Sabaté] killed the Chief of the Falange in Barcelona."[52] In another letter to Pressburger, Zinnemann wrote, "He is plainly an outlaw—but in the sense of the great legendary outlaws—like Billy the Kid, or Pancho Villa, or the Sicilian bandit, Salvatore Guiliano.... I feel that he has a strong relationship to some of the great characters in Hemingway's stories."[53] Zinnemann's close friend Gary Cooper, who played Robert Jordan in *For Whom the Bell Tolls*, had died of cancer in 1961, and was often in the director's thoughts. But Gregory Peck had also played Hemingway's Harry Street in *The Snows of Kilamanjaro* (1952) and headed Carl Foreman's *Guns of Navarone* (1961) the year before. With Cooper dead, Zinnemann clearly had Peck in mind for Artigas in late 1962, suggesting that the relationship between Artigas and Viñolas was "a little like Captain Ahab and Moby Dick."[54] He continued, "As to Manuel: I am almost convinced that there must be a deep personal reason why Manuel has been on the warpath for so long. Perhaps it is partly a vendetta for something which was done to his family during the Civil War (This doesn't need to be spelled out, only implied)." Yet Zinnemann's interest in a personal reason was one way of giving context to the political struggle in Spain. It wasn't enough that they both fought on opposite sides of the war and Artigas continued to resist the fascist regime. Zinnemann could potentially have been thinking of adding some more historical context to the narrative; Sabaté's brother José was assassinated by the Guardia in Barcelona in October 1949.

But when Pressburger sent a revised script, Zinnemann fired him. His action recalled his chilling treatment of close friend Peter Viertel on *The Search*. As he grew more interested in the project, he wanted complete control of the narrative, and hired screenwriter J. P. Miller (*The Young Savages*, 1961; *The Days of Wine and Roses*, 1962) at random. Miller's scenes and dialogue were brief and spare. He preserved the main lines of Pressburger's story, and emphasized the young boy Pablo's growing relationship with Artigas and its impact on regenerating Artigas's identity as a resistance leader. But Miller was uncomfortable with the historical background,[55] and even after the majority of the film was shot, Zinnemann still worried over the opening sequence. As Zinnemann wrote Miller: "The picture will be even stronger if the American audience understands clearly what the issues are right at the beginning. Therefore we propose to shoot an additional scene or two, in the form of a prologue, which would either precede or would be mixed in with the main title." There was no doubt whose side Zinnemann was on as he continued: "They should establish very clearly that the time is 1936 and that the place is Spain and a civil war is going on between a group of people in ragged civilian clothes, and another group in uniform, with good shining military equipment." The Loyalists would be represented by ordinary citizens fighting against the better equipped, insurgent military. Also, "a very clear basis should be established for the mutual hatred between Peck [Artigas] and Quinn

[Viñolas]." Zinnemann suggested shooting a scene in which a group of Loyalists, including Artigas, is ambushed by Viñolas. Viñolas executes Artigas's family in front of his house, and the Guardia leave a wounded Artigas for dead.[56] Including an insurgent atrocity would certainly have brought the most controversial legacies of the Civil War to the fore, and yet the historical reality and shock value of the purges could overshadow the contemporary drama.

Zinnemann continued to be nervous about the audience's lack of knowledge of the war: "The Audience does not know anything about the Civil War in Spain, much less about its aftermath, or about the fact that there are Spanish refugees living in France. The explanatory title which we planned only seemed to confuse them further."[57] He proposed about thirty seconds of stock war footage, interspersed with three short intertitles: "Spain 1939—The Civil War is Approaching its end," "The Defeated Side Crosses the border into France and is disarmed," and finally, "Twenty years later."

Miller responded, "My feeling is that 'the Civil War' can only mean the War Between the States to Americans and would—or could—lead to confusion."[58] Eventually, Zinnemann dropped the more expensive idea of shooting an involved atrocity prologue with Peck and Quinn, and developed a documentary foreword with footage.[59] Stock documentary footage of the war would blend seamlessly into a scene of a younger Artigas leaving Spain for France in 1939 with the Republican army. Artigas would turn back at the border, and his comrades in arms would have to force him to leave Spain. A man's voice-over would narrate the shots: "In 1939 a thousand years of history exploded in Spain. The forces of nationalism joined together against the forces of revolution. Soon, the whole world found itself involved in the passions of this struggle. The whole world looked toward Spain. Soon, it too would be a battleground."[60] Zinnemann and Badal used footage Frédéric Rossif collected for his 1963 documentary *Mourir à Madrid*. Taken from Gaumont, Pathé, Roman Karmen (Russian), and Movietone, the footage shows young boys training with guns in the cities, bombed and burned churches, and an insurgent air raid on Madrid and Barcelona.[61] There were no shots of General Franco or President Azaña; instead, the emphasis was on the destruction of the cities and the impact upon ordinary people. Badal's modern footage was shot with as grainy and high-contrast film stock as they possessed and is indistinguishable from the documentary footage. A long line of defeated troops crosses over the Pyrenees, Artigas (Peck) among them. The voice-over notes, "These were the men who lost—crossing the border into France—and exile."

But despite the construction of this prologue, Zinnemann was still planning additional dialogue in the main feature to reinforce Manuel Artigas's status as an historic resister. Following the US previews in early 1964, he wrote to Mike Frankovich at Columbia, arguing that Americans were still confused over Peck's character, and that he needed more historical context to show his heroism: "The new dialogue could establish easily the fact that Manuel is a great man in the eyes of Pedro and many of the Spanish exiles . . . In my opinion, the audience does not have any of the above information."[62] Ironically, this was Zinnemann's central dilemma: how to make an unconventional film about a defeated hero engaged in a long-term struggle largely forgotten by the rest of the world. In the film's opening sequences, as Pedro (Paolo Stoppa) accompanies young Pablo (Marietto Angelotti) across the Pyrenees to eventually meet Manuel, he tells Pablo of Manuel Artigas's great history as an anti-fascist. He even shows the boy old photographs. Yet when Pablo reaches Spanish Street in Pau and asks a group of young children to point out Artigas's address, they do not recognize his name, and when told, merely shrug, "All that was a long time ago." Zinnemann, like Pablo, had a largely apathetic audience to confront. The strength of *Behold a Pale Horse* lies in its internal awareness of these historical challenges. Zinnemann, like Manuel Artigas, had a reputation to defend.

Competing Resistance Narratives

The performances of stars Omar Sharif (Francisco), Anthony Quinn (Viñolas), and Gregory Peck broke with the personas established by their previous roles. Sharif, himself a Catholic, was, like Audrey Hepburn, sent to a monastery to prepare for his role. Peck had early in his career played a Soviet partisan in Jacques Tourneur's *Days of Glory* (RKO, 1944), and was able to embody both the desperate young partisan and aged, disappointed but not disillusioned Artigas. His long confrontation with Francisco is still compelling. Bluff, gruff, rigid, lonely, Peck refused to portray Artigas as disillusioned. Older, impoverished, and alone, he is a proud remnant of a once powerful force. In 1963, he was still fresh from his Academy Award-winning role as Atticus Finch in *To Kill a Mockingbird* (1962). In his notes, Zinnemann wanted Peck to distance himself from traditional "leading

FIG. 50 One of the army of shadows: Gregory Peck as Manuel Artigas, Columbia Pictures.

FIG. 51 The traitor in the crosshairs—*Behold a Pale Horse*'s final sequences are reminiscent of de Gaulle's near-assassination in *The Day of the Jackal*, Columbia Pictures.

man" conceptions and play "a character actor. A legend in limbo the way people talk about him . . . Enormous inner tension, preoccupied, introvert, until after decision is made. Then becomes extrovert."[63] In contrast, Quinn's Viñolas is charming, duplicitous, and willing to deceive wife, mistress, and church with empty promises and good humor. Yet Zinnemann wanted Quinn "de-glamorized." Peck's Artigas is interested in impressing no one—at first. Yet for Pablo, the son of one of his murdered comrades, he eventually spurns history and becomes the old Resistance hero, Manuel Artigas, one last time (fig. 50). Unlike Will Kane, he dies, but not before putting one of the movement's traitors in the crosshairs of his rifle (in a shot evocative of *The Day of the Jackal*) (fig. 51).

Quinn and Peck had recently starred together in Columbia's World War II Resistance box-office triumph, *The Guns of Navarone*. Playing a Greek colonel-turned-Resistance fighter and a New Zealand mountaineer-turned-intelligence operations captain, they made one of Hollywood's most memorable films about the European wartime resistance to fascism. Writer and producer Carl Foreman also boosted box office by creating two roles for female resisters Gia Scala and Irene Papas (which altered Alistair MacLean's original novel, but was a more historically accurate picture of the Resistance).[64] In deciding to shoot the film on location in Rhodes, Foreman and director J. Lee Thompson did wonders for the tourist industry in Greece.[65]

Unfortunately for Zinnemann, the Spanish Civil War, his almost exclusively male cast, and its setting in the mountains of Northern Spain (actually shot in Perpignon, Carcassonne, Toulouse, Tarbes, Narbonne, and Bayonne, with the interiors done at Studio St. Maurice in Vincennes) did not provide the same financial advantages. In *Guns of Navarone*, Nazis were easily identified enemies, and were dispatched in large numbers by Peck and Quinn's heroic protagonists. Something similar was happening on another Hollywood production shot at the same French studios Zinnemann used for his dubbing. John Frankenheimer was making *The Train* (1964) with Burt Lancaster, and Frankenheimer and Zinnemann used the same English-speaking French voices to dub their French and Spanish actors in English. Yet Frankenheimer's wartime resistance story represented a variation of the kind of hypermasculine glamour displayed in *Guns of Navarone*. Labiche (Lancaster), the longtime working-class Resistance hero, saves French culture and defeats Nazi barbarity with a cigarette, a bleak stare, and a machine gun. In contrast, while Artigas is heroic and Viñolas corrupt and unscrupulous, Artigas's heroism is portrayed more subtly. He has aged and has lost the battle with Franco. Viñolas receives medals for engineering Artigas's assassination, but does not pull the trigger. Throughout most of the film, Quinn's bluff charm masks his personal fear. His failure to capture Artigas means that his future position with the regime is uncertain. And in the final sequences after Artigas's assassination, ordinary Spaniards are seen to go about their business, oblivious to both the recent conflict and to the legacy of the war.

Resisting Franco and the Critics

Although he may never have practiced what he preached, Ernest Hemingway once argued that in representing the war, one must "write straight, honest prose," and that "anyone is cheating who takes politics as a way out."[66] Zinnemann, whose dislike of rhetoric and nationalist ideologies was deep, approached *Behold a Pale Horse* from a similar perspective. By the early 1960s, film journals in France and the United States had begun to take a "serious" interest in popular cinema, and in a series of interviews, Zinnemann spoke at length about his approach to filming *Behold a Pale Horse*.[67] While he emphasized the historical context and documentary philosophy, he downplayed the fact that it was adapted from Pressburger's novel.

Zinnemann acknowledged his attraction to making a film about the war's legacy twenty years after the fall of the Republic. Though often chided by critics for not "taking sides," his sympathies were quite obviously with Manuel. "Manuel is not a bandit, if you were to use the modern termology [sic] you would say he's a kind of Robin Hood . . . You could say it's a man who temporarily has lost his courage as a result of his wounds who is trying to reestablish himself and regain his self-respect." He wrote at length about his concept of resistance and how different contexts could be brought to bear on the war and its aftermath: "Last year in Saigon . . . nobody in the world knew really what was going on or why a man had to burn himself to death. Everybody said it must have been something very important for a person to decide to burn himself as a protest; it focused the attention of the world on it, and in some ways led to the downfall of the Diem regime of that time. This is only a general comparison—but in a sense Manuel's return to Spain and getting killed you might say is also a protest against what it is easy to answer, you can answer it yourself: it is a protest against oppression, against a police state . . . and this happens all the time, this is not fiction in that sense."[68]

Here, Zinnemann draws a parallel between the Franco regime, which the US supported as a bulwark against communism in Europe during the 1950s, with America's fear of communist power in Vietnam. It was a daring thing for a major Hollywood filmmaker to say in 1964 (four years before the bleak television coverage of the Tet Offensive turned public opinion against the war), but it expressed his disgust with America's economic and political support of Hitler's former fascist peer. But rather than merely criticizing the anti-communist ideologies in America which endorsed fascism as a bulwark of democracy, Zinnemann took a more inclusive swipe at all forms of political repression. He had hired Jean Badal as the cinematographer, who famously had "filmed the revolution" in Hungary and fled the communist tanks during the 1956 uprising.

While Zinnemann clearly indicted Franco and the fascist political legacy, his attitude toward Catholicism, particularly after 1961, is more complicated. Although he identified himself as a secular Jew throughout his life, his wife Renée was raised a Catholic, as was close friend Gary Cooper. As Cooper was slowly dying from cancer in early 1961, Zinnemann agreed to remarry Renée in a Catholic ceremony with Cooper as his best man. As Cooper's daughter Maria recalls, "The last time Poppa ever left the house in 1961 was to stand up with Fred at the wedding service . . . four weeks later he was buried from the same altar."[69] Zinnemann's personal commitments to his wife and friend aside, his own attitude toward Catholicism was more critical. He had done enough research on the church's involvement in the Holocaust to make him deeply cynical about religion. On the one hand, his visual treatment of the religious order in *The Nun's Story* revealed their oppressive authoritarianism and the limited place for women in the most rigid of patriarchal structures. Several years later, in his preparation for *A Man For All Seasons*, he planned to cast *Nun* star Audrey Hepburn as famed Catholic dissenter and martyr Thomas More's daughter before scheduling difficulties and Hepburn's advancing age forced him to recast. Yet while Gabrielle van der Mal, like Margaret More, was loyal to her famous father, she lacks Thomas More's commitment to the authority of the Catholic Church. As Zinnemann put it, the great question Thomas More faces in *A Man For All Seasons* was, "Is the state supreme, or is there a moral law above the laws which the state makes?" This resonates with *The Nun's Story*'s narrative of resistance, but a historically accurate, devoutly Catholic More—in effect, subordinate to the Catholic "state" in sixteenth-century Europe—does not. So Zinnemann's vision of More was even more secularized than Bolt's. As he observed during production, More should be "full of gaiety and of the joy of life."[70] He spent many sessions with Paul Scofield attempting to drive the saintliness out of him. It was quite a struggle, given that the actor's portrait of heroic seriousness was acquired through thousands of theatrical performances. On screen and without this scripted "isolation" from the church, Thomas and Henry (Shaw) are merely inverse twins, representatives of two warring but structurally similar absolute governing systems.

Zinnemann's representation of the modern church in *Behold a Pale Horse* makes the individual's resistance to oppressive fascist political and social structures starker. In opposing Franco and the fascists, Artigas was also opposing their chief ally, the church. The Catholic church's complicity in the Franco regime's murder and incarceration of hundreds of thousands of Loyalists and political dissidents and their families is well documented. Early in production, when Zinnemann had interviewed friends of Francisco Sabaté in Toulouse and Perpignon, he remembered: "All the Catalonians had a lot to say about the church. Among other things, they said that 'the priests blessed the soldiers and the guns of the executioners.' After the war the priests had absolute power in Barcelona. They had the power of execution. If a prisoner was to be liberated, they could revoke this. It was standard procedure in Barcelona in 1945 for the priest to ask the prisoner who was about to be liberated about the catechism. If the man did not know it, or would not talk about it, he damn well stayed in jail. Often the priests would suggest that certain men should be executed." They also told Zinnemann, "In Catalonia, very often priests in soutanes would finish off the wounded enemies with pistol shots." Zinnemann shows us none of this in *Behold a Pale Horse*.

However, by the late 1950s, according to historian Norman Cooper, the Spanish Catholic church had revised its close relationship with the fascists, arguably becoming "virtually a church in opposition."[71] Zinnemann pays heed to these shifting definitions of anti-fascist resistance. Artigas and Guardia Captain Viñolas are older men and epitomize their pasts. Of the two, Artigas is the hero who still remains true to his beliefs, aged and racked with self doubt and the ravages of time and the defeat of the Republic, he is still a man of "faith"—poor, chaste (he lives alone), but famously disobedient, he is oddly like the third member of Zinnemann's Spanish trinity, Father Francisco (Sharif), who leaves his party of brothers to deliver a warning to the guerilla leader. Sharif is young, a member of the new generation. As he tells Artigas, Francisco was only ten when the war broke out and unknown soldiers killed his father. Representative of this younger generation and not motivated by the ideological concerns of the past, Father Francisco can both resist collaborating with the corrupt police captain, Viñolas, and help the famous bandit who once pillaged their churches and killed priests.[72] Granted, allowing the church any ground as an objective third party in this conflict between the fascists and the opposition is morally untenable; yet, Father Francisco is part of that new generation. It is he who watches a triumphant Viñolas stride out of the police station amidst a blasé crowd who neither wave flags for Franco nor wipe their eyes for the dead Artigas. In a final close-up, Francisco's eyes, glistening with tears, mourn Artigas. Another assassination has taken place. Though his family never discovered which side killed his father, Father Francisco has witnessed another assassination where the Spanish spectators do not know or care about the victim.

Only the foreign journalists seem aware of the historical contexts. In a scene Zinnemann added to the script, actor Michael Lonsdale, in an early role as a French reporter, repeatedly tries to suggest a connection between the end of the war twenty years before and the continued defiance of Artigas. Viñolas, parodying Franco's consistent obliteration and fabrication of history, brushes off the questions and analysis of the "foreigners," but is privately puzzled why Artigas should continue to resist him and the regime after all this time. Some people, Zinnemann argues, do not forget.

This is how the Franco government interpreted the film. Although early in production, Zinnemann had attempted to negotiate for Spanish locations, his decision to send them a translated version of the script backfired. Mike Bell, who had worked with Zinnemann on *From Here to Eternity*, wrote to Mike Frankovich, using language straight out of *From Here to Eternity*: "After your departure we had heard that the Spanish government had been giving us the 'treatment.' Thus, while in Washington last week I called on Alonso De Toledo ... He said that apparently someone in the government had read *To Kill a Mouse on Sunday* and concluded that no picture could be made without having serious political implications ... De Toledo, however, concurred that any punitive action based on such a reaction was not fair. He therefore asked the Ambassador to write a letter emphasizing that his talks with you and Fred were friendly, and that no action of any kind should be taken until you were afforded an opportunity to discuss this matter as you had with him."[73] Almost as soon as the script reached government offices, the Spanish minister for entertainment imposed a blanket ban of the production and exhibition of all Columbia films inside of Spain for two years. Mike Frankovich was incensed by the ban, but told Zinnemann not to worry. At one point, Zinnemann wrote to the head offices at Columbia suggesting that Cardinal Spellman might do something for them since he was a personal friend of Franco. Nothing came of it.[74] Zinnemann was stunned, but in many press interviews, continued to claim that the story was "apolitical."[75] In the end, he was able to use this to his ironic advantage, proving that one side of the Pyrenees is very much like the other (there are no frontier checkpoints except in the opening historical prologue).[76] The crew shot mostly around Pau and Bayonne, using Toulouse as a base. But he hoped that the government would eventually reconsider the ban. It did not, and instead planned its own pro-Franco documentary to celebrate the twenty-fifth anniversary of the end of the war. *Franco: ese hombre* (1964), directed by José Luis Sáenz de Heredia, was an attempt to counteract Zinnemann's suspected attack on the Spanish leader, but had little distribution outside of Spain.

According to *Variety*, "It's understood that the main Spanish objection to the finished film is the depiction of the police chief as a man who has a mistress and takes bribes. The Guardia Civil, the national Spanish police, enjoys elite status in Spain and the government feels this film character played by Tony Quinn throws discredit on the entire organization. Zinnemann finds this objection rather parochial and today noted that many American films have shown that some of our police are not exactly saints without blackening the image of all American policemen."[77] After screening the rough cut, native Spaniard and Columbia executive Emilio López responded, "I have not found in its exciting story anything offensive or derogatory to Spain or to its political regime. As a clear-thinking Spaniard of constructive ideas, I can assure you that the screening of the film has impressed me deeply and that I have not at any moment felt offended nor ridiculed and, sincerely believe, that there will be no critic or spectator that can honestly say that the Spanish political system is attacked or that religious sentiments are offended ... The only deplorable thought is the million dollars we are losing without any possible compensation and not to know who can make up to us for the disturbances caused by the official hostility spread."[78]

But when nothing came of this, Columbia's front office retaliated and sent out a lot of publicity emphasizing Franco's fascist, undemocratic attitudes. According to *Variety*, "American film officials close to the international scene this week expressed incredulity with what one termed 'the dictatorial behavior of the Spanish government' in banning Columbia Pictures from that country."[79] The ban, issued by the Spanish minister for entertainment, extended for four months. *Variety* continued, "The film concerns a couple of individuals ... who had been on opposite sides during the Spanish Civil War. But it's said there's no partisanship either way and, in fact, nothing at all political in the basic story ... Yank observers say the sanction against Columbia is particularly peculiar because it comes at a time when Spain is seeking to become more of a member of the Western world, including NATO." One Columbia official called it "strangely undemocratic for a country which is seeking to join our civilized western world club." As Columbia front office man, George Thomas, Jr., wrote Zinnemann, "I think this is a very good story, putting the Spanish government on the defensive and following the lines we discussed in Paris." Zinnemann also publicly praised Columbia pictures for being so "courageous" in going ahead with production despite the ban.[80] With its financial back to the wall, Columbia momentarily became an anti-fascist corporation.

Critical responses to the film were almost as polarized as political reactions to the war. Most called the film a masterpiece, a "director's film" the equal of anything produced in Europe, but acknowledged that few mainstream spectators would understand it.[81] British critic John Russell Taylor would write that while some filmmakers impose their personality or style on films or develop personal themes which don't vary, "there is also a rare and often underestimated breed, whose films paradoxically mirror their maker's personality most clearly when he seems most determined to step out of the picture, to leave his subject-matter as far as possible to stand up for itself and speak to us in its own terms. Fred Zinnemann is one of these."[82] Other critics observed his less-than-simple formulation of modern heroism: "Few of Zinnemann's heroes and heroines have been outwardly and obviously heroic. They have shared the characteristic of a quiet demeanor that often masks an inner turmoil and a latent capacity to face the ultimate danger. They are people who rise to the occasion to put up the climactic fight for their own dignity and peace of mind."[83]

James Powers of the *Hollywood Reporter* noted: "Some spectators will find the film opaque and baffling. Some will find it frustrating, as Zinnemann takes a highly charged story and deliberately transposes it to a low key. . . . But Zinnemann, with his painstaking, iron-and-velvet command, keeps it human; drama not melodrama, a twentieth-century tragedy of non-heroic heroes. It may be the first film in anti-theatre terms."[84] *Entertainment* agreed, writing that Zinnemann focuses on "vital human issues" but "he never presents these issues in cut-and-dried, oversimplified form."[85] Yet despite the nuances, a majority of critics recognized that Artigas was another one of Zinnemann's resistance heroes. As the *Hollywood Reporter* noted: "The one-man fight against a corrupt and powerful adversary is an obvious losing battle, but the guerilla's last stand, he knows, can be effective."[86] *Newsweek* went further, drawing parallels between Artigas's lone fight against the fascist government and Zinnemann, who "refused to be pressured" by the Spanish government during production. In spite of its contemporary setting, "the old conflict is repeated and, as before, the organized, efficient Nationalist defeat the threadbare Loyalists. And again, there is a moral victory for the Loyalists (Peck all alone) can claim ... When Francisco Sabaté, the old Loyalist fighter, made his last—and fatal—raid into Spain in 1960, he earned the tribute, 'Muy Hombre'—a real man. *Behold a Pale Horse* is based, roughly, on Sabaté's last exploit. Zinnemann, Peck, and Quinn, for having done him well, deserve ours."[87]

But it was too complicated for many critics. Richard Schickel invoked *High Noon* and said that Zinnemann should have stuck to Westerns and clear-cut images of right and wrong.[88] Many European critics for right-leaning newspapers agreed. Despite Zinnemann's European background, some Hollywood critics felt that the film was too "depressing" and "complicated" to be a Hollywood product. Brendan Gill of the *New Yorker* wanted a standard "eyeball to eyeball" confrontation between Peck and Quinn, and, when he didn't get that Western motif, felt cheated.[89] Another Italian critic complained that "Zinnemann did not realize that you cannot remake *High Noon* with such different material. A Spanish anarchist has little in common with a cowboy." Others said the film "exhausted itself in antifascist polemics."[90] Once again, Zinnemann was pushing critical boundaries few wanted to rethink. Hollywood was simply not supposed to make politically engaged films about Europe—and certainly not a studio-era director a generation away from the "New Wave" embodied by Sidney Lumet, Martin Ritt, Alan J. Pakula, and Arthur Penn.

Like many "art films," *Behold a Pale Horse* lost money for Columbia: at least the $2.5 million of its production cost, and uncounted revenue from Spain's three-year ban on Columbia films.[91] It only grossed $900,000 in the US and Canada.[92] Zinnemann would later say of *Behold a Pale Horse*, "I suppose my basic mistake there was to suppose that the subject, with its background in the Spanish Civil War, would mean a lot to other people, that other people would know a lot about it, because it meant a lot to people of my generation. But of course one forgets that to people of yours it is history, something that happened virtually before you were born. I took too much on trust, and the film just did not get over."[93] Like Artigas, Zinnemann was an aging exile in a country that had long condoned Franco's fascism and its own variants. The new generation of supposedly engaged, New Wave film critics and audiences were like the children that Pablo encounters on Spanish Street, viewing the past with glazed eyes.

In one of the great ironies of his career, Zinnemann's next production, shot in Britain on a more economical budget of $2 million for Columbia's tolerant Mike Frankovich, was an adaptation of a successful theatrical costume drama, Robert Bolt's *A Man For All Seasons*. The historical contexts of sixteenth-century British political and religious life were even further removed from the memories of American and European audiences, but lacked the contemporary controversy of the Spanish Civil War. Audiences and critics responded to the colorful costume drama with its bravura performances by Paul Scofield, Robert Shaw, Orson Welles, Wendy Hiller, Leo McKern, and the debut of another Zinnemann discovery, John Hurt. John Box's production design, with its seasonal shots of the Thames, was inspired by Zinnemann's off-the-cuff viewing of a Yeats Country photo spread and the magnificent, well-known portraits of Holbein in Britain's National Portrait Gallery.[94] When the director persuaded Vanessa Redgrave to play Anne Boleyn opposite Shaw's Henry, he had her replay her famous seduction scene in *Morgan!* (1966). His famed long takes and "bull-in-the-arena" shots of Thomas More entering the court for his trial, famously copied by an admiring Martin Scorsese years later in *Raging Bull* (1980), were shots executed more for economy than artistic complexity, as Tim Zinnemann has pointed out.[95] It was, as the director recalled, a quick, happy production, where everything from locations to the usually fickle English weather fell into place. There were no disagreements over the script or fights over censorship. Zinnemann, still smarting from the critical and box-office failure of *Pale Horse*, was on his best behavior for Frankovich. *A Man for All Seasons* achieved the ideal harmonious production environment of old Hollywood's factory system. But a decade after he picked up his second Oscar for Best Director, Zinnemann would return to a world that was far less sumptuous, colorful, or comfortable than the historical costume drama: the world of his youth, America and Austria in the emerging fascism of the 1930s.

CHAPTER SEVEN
Resistant Women in Contested Frames

"For many years at Hull House I have at intervals detected in certain old people, when they spoke of their past experiences, a tendency toward an idealization, almost to a romanticism suggestive of the ardent dreams and groundless ambitions we have all observed in the young when they recklessly lay their plans for the future."
—Jane Addams, *The Long Road of Women's Memory* (1916)[1]

"I like your anger. . . . Don't you let anyone talk you out of it."
—Julia (Vanessa Redgrave) to Lillian (Jane Fonda), from Alvin Sargent's *Julia*, 1976[2]

In a corner of one of his pages of film notes on *Julia*, Fred Zinnemann wrote, "I am in a totally false position," and then circled it for emphasis. As it is part of a tapestry of sketches for camera set-ups, script jottings, commentary, and phone numbers written in several varieties of his handwriting, the small note is very difficult to see. There are thousands of pages of Zinnemann's production notes in his archive. But as with all of his films, every detail counts. When Zinnemann signed to direct *Julia* for Twentieth Century-Fox, he was nearing seventy. He had made ten films about the history of the European resistance to fascism, the Second World War, and its aftermath (*Forbidden Journey, The Seventh Cross, The Search, Act of Violence, The Men, Teresa, From Here to Eternity, The Nun's Story, Behold a Pale Horse,* and *Day of the Jackal*), and had planned at least half a dozen other projects around these themes (among them *Zapata, The Young Lions, Sabra, The First Circle, Gandhi, Man's Fate,* and *The Last Secret*). Adapted from the memoirs of screenwriter Lillian Hellman, *Julia*'s Resistance context was perfect material for the director. Its story of the friendship between Hellman and a childhood friend-turned-anti-fascist leader united the history of the Hollywood Left with the rise of fascism in Austria and France. Zinnemann had experienced both firsthand. With the collaboration of Vanessa Redgrave and Jane Fonda, *Julia* would also become one of the most important films made about women's history. There was one problem, however: Lillian Hellman's story was not true.

The Women Behind *Julia*

During the 1930s and 1940s Lillian Hellman was one of Hollywood's most prominent female screenwriters and she was one of the few playwrights to adapt her plays regularly and successfully for the screen (*These Three*, 1936; *The Little Foxes*, 1941). One of her last Hollywood efforts before being blacklisted, *The Searching Wind* (Dieterle, 1946), told the story of a American diplomat (Robert Young) who ignored the threat of fascism in the 1920s and 1930s in order to protect his career. Although her Hollywood career was effectively over after her HUAC testimony confirmed her brief membership in the Communist Party, she continued to be visible on Broadway throughout the 1960s. By the 1970s, Hellman had made a new career as a memoirist and became something of a Cold War revisionist icon. Her perspectives on women's liberation in the 1920s, golden-age Hollywood, American liberalism, and the anti-communist witch-hunts were constructed as critical correctives of the traditional historiography and did not go unchallenged by her contemporaries and colleagues.[3] But it was her story of childhood friend "Julia" which raised the most public controversy. In *Pentimento* (1973), Hellman remembers her best friend as a heroic maverick. Born to wealth and privilege, Julia spurns her family, attends Oxford and later medical school in Vienna, and becomes a committed socialist and anti-fascist leader. Though the two women's lives diverge, they keep in touch largely through letters. But while on a trip to Europe in the mid-thirties, Julia asks Hellman to bring some money across the German border for her anti-Nazi organization. Hellman, though terrified, agrees, and the friends meet once more before Julia's murder at the hands of the Gestapo some months later in Frankfurt. Hellman's memory of Julia comprised only one of several stories in *Pentimento*, but critics would focus on it almost to the exclusion of the other stories. Some even argued that she invented the courageous, anti-Nazi heroine and her connection with Hellman.[4] At present, all evidence strongly suggests that

FIG. 52 With Redgrave on the set at Oxford, AMPAS.

Hellman invented the friendship, but she patterned "Julia" after the lives of several real women.

Over the years, Hollywood films have been singled out for their failure to adhere to the standards of historical/textual accuracy; but what happens when the text itself is corrupt?[5] In *Julia*'s case, it is particularly important to recognize the consequences of Hellman's inaccuracies because her memoir and especially the film memorialize a great woman and a Resistance leader, and do so through the legitimization of oral history—a mode crucial for much of women's historiography and certainly to that of the Resistance.[6] Zinnemann was troubled by the problems with Hellman's memoirs and their relationship was totally severed by the end of the filmmaking. In an interview shortly before his death in 1997, Zinnemann would reveal for the first time that *"Julia* . . . was not true. Lillian Hellman . . . would portray herself in situations which were not true . . . My relations with her were very guarded and ended in pure hatred."[7] Yet the director's discomfort with Hellman's ambiguities enabled him to explore the very real struggle for historical legitimacy plaguing Hollywood cinema and, more particularly, women's history in film. Though Zinnemann's two directing Oscars were awarded for films with heroic men at the heart of the narratives (*From Here to Eternity* and *A Man For All Seasons*), and he was famed for introducing the actors Marlon Brando (*The Men*), Montgomery Clift (*The Search*), and Rod Steiger (*Teresa*) to the screen, he was equally drawn to stories about women. He spoke frequently about his respect for the work of Janet Leigh, Audrey Hepburn, Donna Reed, and Wendy Hiller, but Zinnemann's favorite actress was without doubt the woman who played Julia, Vanessa Redgrave. When film and stage work made her unavailable to play Margaret More in *A Man For All Seasons*, she worked for free as Anne Boleyn. She was his unrealized dream for May in *Man's Fate*, and at last, in 1976, they finally got the chance to work together at length (fig. 52).

But who is this woman who has half an hour of screen time, but is the focus of the narrative? Hellman's Julia is a combination of several anti-fascist and Resistance leaders, among them Virginia Hall, Marie-Madeleine Fourcade, and Muriel Gardiner.[8] Hall left her American university to study in Europe and became a consular official in the 1930s. She, like Julia, had a false leg, the result of a freak accident on a shooting holiday in Austria. Hall was one of the most successful MI6 and OSS agents during the Second World War and would eventually become part of the CIA. Fourcade, chief of the largest intelligence network in the French Resistance, used to carry false documents and money in the lining of her hat (as Lillian allegedly carried money for Julia), and, due to a childhood hip-dislocation, often walked with a pronounced limp (fig. 53).[9] This made her extremely vulnerable to Gestapo agents, and parallels Julia's comment to Lillian at their last meeting: "I can't last much longer in Europe; the crutches make me too noticeable." In addition, Foucade spent long years separated from her two children, who were eventually sent to Switzerland for their safety when the Nazis discovered their mother's identity as a high-ranking Resistance leader. Some of this anxiety is transferred to Lillian following Julia's death, when she embarks on a painful and abortive search for Julia's daughter Lily. But critics have overlooked these other sources and have instead concentrated attention on psychoanalyst, lecturer, and anti-fascist activist Gardiner, the only known American woman to have worked in the Austrian underground. Why was there so much outrage about an invented friendship between two famous American women? As Hellman biographer Carl Rollyson comments, though others were shocked and angry after reading *Pentimento*, Muriel Gardiner was "amazingly tolerant of what her friends took to be Hellman's plagiarism."[10] She did not rush to challenge Hellman publicly, and only published her memoirs in

FIG. 53 Marie-Madeleine Fourcade, ca. 1943, AP.

1983. Gardiner writes that for a long time, due to her need for privacy and her background as a psychoanalyst, she was "unable to write openly about many important aspects of my life."[11] Several years after the publication of the "Julia" memoir and the release of Zinnemann's film, however, she decided that she "would rather risk lack of modesty than questionable honesty." While compiling her memoirs, Gardiner asked the director of the archives of the Austrian Resistance whether there were other American women involved in the anti-Nazi underground. He and all of her surviving colleagues replied, "Only Mary," which was Gardiner's code name.[12] Her autobiography focuses on her underground work from 1934 to 1938, and though she describes almost daily aid to political fugitives from the Nazis, Gardiner scrupulously avoids portraying herself as a conventional hero. She presents the obvious dangers involved in procuring passports, hiding hunted men, women and children, and surviving police interrogations in straightforward, dispassionate, and carefully documented prose.

But while Hellman lacked Muriel Gardiner's understated approach to autobiography and her careful use of dates, the playwright's memories of Julia were supported with self-conscious endorsements of their honesty and historical relevance. Hellman even argued that Julia grounded the writer's sense of truth and history: "I think I have always known about my memory: I know when it is to be trusted and when some dream or fantasy entered on the life, and the dream, the need of dream, led to distortion of what happened. And so I knew early that the rampage angers of an only child were distorted nightmares of reality. But I trust absolutely what I remember about Julia."[13] Hellman claims that "Julia" is unknown to conventional histories of the war and Resistance, and styles herself as Julia's historical guardian. It is she who rescues Julia from obscurity. Hellman's memoir is interspersed with comments affirming her perfect remembrance of Julia's correspondence ("I still remember every word of that note"), and she constantly refers to cables, notes, and letters in her possession which document their relationship.[14] In interviews following the publication of *Pentimento*, Hellman reinforced this connection, claiming that although she did consult her archive of letters and material about Julia when finishing the memoir, it was not necessary: "Nothing on God's earth could have shaken my memory about her."[15]

Julia's story had unique historical appeal. Work on Eastern European and Austrian anti-fascist resistance was far less plentiful than the bibliographies of Western European and especially French resistance.[16] As Gardiner commented, histories of the Anschluss tend to portray the Austrian population as compliant and even enthusiastic fascists, completely ignoring the strong socialist base of anti-fascist protest in Vienna of which she was a part. In addition, mainstream Resistance histories and political remembrance of the era focus overwhelmingly on the work of men, despite women's participation and leadership in all aspects of Resistance work, from the running of Maquis and escape lines, to publishing tracts and fighting.[17] Despite a small cluster of mostly British films which consider Resistance women (Simone Signoret in Ealing's *Against the Wind*, 1950; *Odette*, 1950; *Carve Her Name with Pride*, 1958; *The Nun's Story*, 1959; Gia Scala and Irene Papas in Columbia's *Guns of Navarone*, 1961; Ingrid Pitt and Mary Ure in *Where Eagles Dare*, 1968), they are severely outnumbered by wartime blockbusters with all-male casts. To this day, historians of the French Resistance persist in the belief that no women led Resistance networks, blatantly ignoring the work of Fourcade, whose three thousand-strong intelligence network survived five years of Nazi occupation and the deaths and deportation of over four hundred of her workers.[18] Fourcade, at the time a single mother with young children, transmitted information to British intelligence and avoided the sabotage and costly political infighting of other French networks. Though the work of her agents, named after animals and nicknamed "Noah's Ark" by the Nazis, was arguably more extensive and important than that of any other intelligence network, the petite, elegant "Hedgehog" kept her identity so secret that the Germans failed to recognize her after two captures. Despite publishing her memoir in 1968 (which was translated into English in 1973), historians, ironically like Nazi interrogators, refused to believe women could be capable of such deception.[19]

Encouraged by the popular international success of Fourcade's memoir and the trend in women's history, other female leaders and workers published their memoirs during the 1970s; however, they were not incorporated into "official" histories.[20] Within the past ten years, academic historiography has begun to address the significance of women—many of them dedicated communists or socialists—in European resistance movements, particularly in France, Italy, Spain, and Russia.[21] However, most continue to either ignore the presence of women in the Resistance or underplay their participation.[22]

In her memoir, Hellman offers few concrete details about early Austrian resistance to fascism in the mid-1930s and admits she has "changed most of the names," thereby continuing to leave Julia in heroic obscurity.[23] Unlike Kathryn Hulme's relationship with Marie Louise Habets (Sister Luke), Hellman never publicly produced Julia or offered textual evidence of their friendship. Later, she defended her decision to conceal Julia's true identity by arguing there had been "previous threats from [Julia's] family," fears of privacy suits, and the belief that "there is no country in the world that pays honor to early anti-Nazis."[24] These were certainly shaky claims by the 1970s, given the number of histories and memoirs by both men and women. Women's historiography, particularly in Europe and the US, emerged as a powerful force in the 1970s. However, if by "early anti-Nazis" Hellman meant "communists," then she had a point. As Pieter Lagrou, Bob Moore, and other historians have noted, though communists often dominated ranks of Resistance workers throughout Europe, national governments worked to obliterate the memory of their participation in the wake of the Cold War.[25] Particularly in France, the history of the Resistance had to be completely reconstructed—democratized, nationalized, and de-communized.

However, Hellman's clumsy attempts at concealment, coupled with historical justifications and details, angered those who felt she was capitalizing on the real heroism of women like Gardiner, and, in linking herself with Julia's exploits, arrogating a Resistance profile to which she had no claim. Hellman's own documented political interests during the 1930s were far more focused on defenses of Stalinist Russia than attacks on Nazi anti-Semitism and political repression.²⁶ During the Broadway run of *The Little Foxes*, actress Tallulah Bankhead planned a benefit performance for Finnish war relief, but Hellman refused to participate, even though the Soviet invasion of Finland was enabled by Stalin's pact with Hitler (it is worth pointing out that the communists' claims to be the party of the Resistance are not valid between August 23, 1939, when the non-aggression pact was signed, and June 22, 1941, when Germany invaded the Soviet Union). Shortly after the publication of Gardiner's autobiography, writer Samuel McCracken examined Hellman's historical data in detail and found in every case that Hellman provided names, dates, and explanations for her involvement with Julia, she had lied.²⁷ Her name was not on steamer or train passenger lists, there were no records of Hellman's signature on medical or death certificates (as an American expatriate, Julia's death would have been reported), and Hellman had never shown anyone the letters, cables, and notes from Julia quoted in the memoir. Gardiner also reveals that Americans abroad had no trouble in moving money from bank to bank during the thirties—even after the Anschluss.²⁸ The real problem was moving quantities of passports across borders. The elaborate ruse Hellman describes, in which she is asked to carry $50,000 for Julia's anti-fascist group, was completely unnecessary given the financial and political contexts of 1930s Europe.

But as film historian Bernard Dick reasons, Hellman was a Hollywood playwright, not a journalist, historian of the Resistance, or feminist biographer.²⁹ "Julia" is a memoir and is not organized chronologically in a traditional autobiographical/historical format; Hellman self-consciously moves from one memory of the 1930s to childhood memories of Julia in the 1910s. Hellman even begins *Pentimento* by likening her past to an Old Master painting which has deteriorated and flaked away, revealing different images: "Old paint on canvas, as it ages, sometimes becomes transparent. When that happens it is possible, in some pictures, to see the original lines: a tree will show through a woman's dress, a child makes way for a dog, a boat is no longer in an open sea. That is called pentimento, because the painter 'repented,' changed his mind. Perhaps it would be well to say that the old conception, replaced by a later choice, is a way of seeing and then seeing again."³⁰ According to Hellman, the image of memory is of a creative work by the author, a canvas (or Old Master painting—Hellman was never modest) in which the artist changes her mind and makes creative choices to change the overall impression. Rather than enduring and resisting creative transformation, Hellman describes her past as something essentially visual, constructed by herself, and subject to fundamental change.

However, despite Hellman's description of mutable images and memories, she mixes visual terms and phrases like "transparent" and "see the original lines" which cue the reader to the writer's objective vision—a trace, rather than a transformation. This tension between the reflective and transformative elements of the visual representation of the past is central to Hellman's story. Hellman's perspective is arguably similar to Hayden White's in the landmark *Metahistory* (also published in 1973), in which he argues that the style and structures of historiography and fiction are essentially the same.[31] Yet in both her memoirs and in interviews, Hellman contained her mutable, almost postmodern idea of personal memory within the empirical demands of history. In the "Julia" chapter, the author uses the structures and discourse of historiography (dates, references to letters, telegrams, and notes, references to other known historical personages, discussions of wider historical and political contexts, remarks on history, memory, and objectivity) to bolster her own personal connection to anti-fascism and a heroic woman. In interviews, Hellman stated that any dramatic elements or idiosyncratic narration were subject to the facts of her own life: "The structure was difficult because I did not want to alter the facts."[32]

Assuming that Hellman's connections with Julia and the anti-fascist movement are false, Hellman used both the structures of historiography and even fiction for personal aggrandizement. Are the creative consequences really as unimportant as film historians like Bernard Dick claim? Zinnemann was certainly angry with her until his death, and Alvin Sargent, who adapted her work, has acknowledged Hellman's flagrant disrespect for the truth. Postmodern appropriations of relativism, the construction of memory, and the fluidity of identity wither against the continuing need for historical truth—particularly in the realm of anti-fascist, anti-Nazi, and Holocaust historiography. Even White was to recant some of his postmodern discourse when opponents argued that his brand of hyper-relativism sanctioned Holocaust denial.[33] Resistance histories and memoirs are chronicles of those who opposed the Nazis' campaign of lies and racial propaganda, the falsification and destruction of documents, and the murder of those with dangerous memories. Additionally, the accuracy of personal memory becomes even more precious because, as H. R. Kedward explains, "it was clearly in the nature of Resistance activity to avoid all paper records which might fall into the wrong hands."[34] Some of the most dramatic events in Fourcade's memoir describe her burning and even eating incriminating documents, and, at the end of the war, recovering beloved colleague Léon Faye's hidden papers from the stones of Sonnenburg prison.[35] Memory and the preservation of precious words become moral testaments. Therefore, there was a moral and ideological obligation to old-fashioned empiricism and truth, particularly when writing about those who have allegedly been marginalized in the historical records. As historian Thomas Haskell writes, "one of the principal anchors of the twentieth-century mind" was public knowledge and moral outrage for the rise and impact of Nazi Germany; historical relativism and moral relativism were entwined, and that however tempting historical relativism was to writers in the postmodern age, "we know that we cannot permit that anchor to break loose."[36]

Women's history has suffered similar distortions and silencing at the hands of male academics and historians. Ironically, women's widespread exclusion from the American historical "profession" dates from when scientific history and devotion to positivism undercut women's previous historical strongholds in popular social and cultural histories and pedagogy. As a result, historian Julie Des Jardins argues, "As marginal figures to the historical profession, many represented the pasts of Americans marginalized by race, class, ethnicity, or gender in ways that scholars have little acknowledged."[37] Hellman used this historical strategy to great effect in "Julia," claiming that a variety of forces thwarted the publication of her friend's true and unique heroism. One could argue that in creating her elliptical, non-chronological, and fragmentary narrative of Julia, Hellman was not merely remembering, but constructing an alternate form of biography for a classic subaltern. She resisted molding Julia's story into a traditional "great woman" narrative because it followed the conventions of masculine biography.[38] Tempting though it may be to credit Hellman with creating a "feminine" alternative to masculine memoir and biography, this assumes that accuracy, chronology, and objectivity are masculine qualities. After all, Hellman's greatest critics in the *Julia* controversy were women—historians and journalists Mary McCarthy and Martha Gellhorn—writers who valued and demanded accuracy and historical honesty throughout their careers, particularly when chronicling the anti-fascist and liberal struggles of the twentieth century.[39] Indeed, one of the great ideological ironies of women's historiography is that though the turn toward "scientific" history temporarily removed women from the universities and the profession, it is through careful research and objective discourse that the gender inequities in the American system become apparent and subject to change (i.e., formerly unknown Resistance heroines such as Muriel Gardiner earn the public recognition they deserve). As Nancy Cott and Elizabeth Pleck point out, "To unearth the lives of the 'anonymous,' traditional historical sources . . . would not serve. Historians had to seek more popular sources, such as folktales, work songs, and oral histories."[40] Likewise, Kedward would argue to reconsider formerly marginal areas and figures of the Resistance "by removing the masks and giving names to the anonymous," essentially by naming names, something that Hellman had been unable to do in another context decades before.[41]

Constructing *Julia*

The historical unease about *Julia* did not become widespread until well after the film's release in October 1977. *Julia* was adapted by Alvin Sargent (*Paper Moon*, 1973), shot, and marketed as a "true" or historical film about two courageous women, and supplemented the life of one of its most famous screenwriters with appearances by other recognizable historical figures Dashiell Hammett (Jason Robards), Dorothy Parker (Rosemary Murphy), and Alan Campbell (Hal Holbrook). Young Fox producer Richard Roth encouraged Sargent's unusual non-chronological construction of Hellman's memoirs, and the production gained momentum as first Jane Fonda and then Vanessa Redgrave agreed to star. Initially Sydney Pollack was approached to direct, possibly due to his success with *The Way We Were* (1973), which touched upon Hellman's 1930s political activism and the Hollywood blacklist.[42] He dropped out and recommended Zinnemann. Zinnemann, who had been toying with the idea of making Joseph Wiseman's *The Secret Policeman* with Fox, read Sargent's script and accepted enthusiastically.[43] The choice of director and the two female leads also created reassuring historical press. Like Zinnemann, Vanessa Redgrave (Julia) specialized in historical or period films.[44] A significant part of her career was spent playing courageous but doomed nonconformists Anne Boleyn (*A Man for All Seasons*, 1966), Isadora Duncan (*Isadora*, 1968), Sylvia Pankhurst (*Oh! What a Lovely War*, 1969), and Mary Stuart (*Mary, Queen of Scots*, 1971).

Though less known for performances in biopics or other forms of historical cinema, Jane Fonda's (Hellman) connection with *Julia* enhanced the film's status as an important work of Hollywood history on more than one level. According to publicity releases, Fonda, who was associated with the project long before either Zinnemann or Redgrave, agreed to star in *Julia* "without seeing a script and was most supportive during the period of putting it all together."[45] Fonda claimed she responded to her role more than any other because of the "truth" inherent to the film. It represented the lives of thinking women and after playing a succession of limited romantic roles which emphasized female dependence on men, Fonda said, "I don't want to do films that are dishonest."[46] Fonda's own left-wing politics were well known to the public, and during *Julia*'s pre- and postproduction periods, she and the press successfully linked her history as an anti-Vietnam War protestor with Hellman's career as a witch-hunted communist in the 1940s and 1950s. Journalist Mary Rourke commented, "In some obvious ways, Fonda's life parallels Hellman's. Hellman saw the ruination of her blacklisted literary friends during the McCarthy era ... [while Fonda] was gray-listed in the early '70s for her radical antiwar activities." Fonda said, "Being gray-listed was extremely harmful. I thought of giving up movies."[47] The studio carefully underscored these parallels when Fonda was asked to introduce Hellman at the Academy Awards in the spring of 1977.[48] The following year, Fonda was nominated for Best Actress for her role as Hellman, but lost to Diane Keaton's Annie Hall.

By the late 1960s, Redgrave was as committed to her political work as her acting, and she became particularly close with Simone Signoret, who had starred as a tough Resistance fighter in *Against the Wind* and *Armée des ombres* (1969).[49] Redgrave and Fonda knew each other well before starring together in *Julia*, having corresponded about their political work in the early 1970s. In a curious parallel with the film narrative, in which Julia names her daughter Lily after Lillian Hellman, Fonda named her daughter Vanessa after Redgrave. Redgrave's interests had expanded from nuclear disarmament and protests against the Vietnam War to support of the Palestinian cause in Israel (she lived with a Palestinian family in Paris while they shot *Julia*),[50] and this was more difficult for Hollywood's Jewish community to swallow than Fonda's antiwar past. Later, Redgrave's Academy Award acceptance speech compared the Jewish American protesters who picketed her nomination to "gangsters" opposing free speech and human rights. When Redgrave implied that Jewish people no longer automatically held the moral high ground in their dispute with the Palestinians, it angered many in Hollywood and arguably curtailed her film career. Sargent's script also makes connections between women's activism in the 1930s and 1970s. At one point, during their last meeting in Berlin, Hellman explodes, "Why does it have to be like this?" "Are you still as angry as you used to be?" asks Julia. "Yes," replies Lillian, with a grim smile, "I try not to be, but there you are." "I like your anger," Julia says steadily. "Don't you let anyone talk you out of it." The two actresses could have been talking about either the 1930s or their own lives in the 1970s.

But more than feminism and radical politics linked Fonda, Hellman, and *Julia*. In returning to Twentieth Century-Fox, Fonda was returning to the studio which made her father, Henry Fonda, a star. During the latter half of the 1930s, he became one of Hollywood's most popular and critically respected stars, largely by performing in American historical productions for studio head Darryl F. Zanuck (*The Farmer Takes a Wife*, 1935; *Way Down East*, 1935; *Jesse James*, 1939; *The Story of Alexander Graham Bell*, 1939; *Drums Along the Mohawk*, 1939; *Young Mr. Lincoln*, 1939). Like his daughter, Henry Fonda was committed to the political Left and will always be identified by his role as Tom Joad in John Ford's adaptation of John Steinbeck's *The Grapes of Wrath* (1940). Fonda would later work for Zinnemann for free in 1951, narrating a documentary short to benefit the Los Angeles Orthopedic Hospital. *Benjy* would go on to win an Oscar for Best Documentary. But while her father made traditional American heroes such as Abraham Lincoln human and reassuringly flawed, in making *Julia*, Jane Fonda was historicizing her father's era and creating a new generation of left-wing, twentieth-century American heroines who were successful on their own terms. Thanks to Hellman, Sargent, and Zinnemann, *Julia*'s protagonists and film style would differ fundamentally from traditional Hollywood historical epics which, even by the early 1970s, still lionized individualism and courageous public lives in a chronological and progressively styled format (*Patton*, 1970; *Dillinger*, 1973; *Serpico*, 1973).

It would therefore be wrong to view *Julia* as a feminist version of the "Great Man" biopics made famous by Jane Fonda's father—or even Orson Welles and Herman Mankiewicz's definitive revisionist biopic, *Citizen Kane* (1941). *Julia* was built upon a much more ambiguous historical presence of women in Hollywood. Julia does not crave traditional success or approbation from elites, and though Lillian is more ambivalent about fame and the sable coats she can purchase with her royalties, she abandons everything to help Julia and later look for her lost daughter. Charles Foster Kane belongs to the establishment. He is an international political figure who rubs shoulders with Hitler and Mussolini. While Julia is born to this establishment, she abandons the American social and political system and its ideological hypocrisy to fight against everything Charles Foster Kane stands for in the 1930s. She is not Colin Wilson's "Outsider," but rather the child of progressive reformer Jane Addams (like Muriel Gardiner, a native of Chicago). While newspaper inserts avidly document the life and death of media mogul Charles Foster Kane, Julia avoids documentation. Zinnemann and editor Walter Murch did not insert shots of her letters to Lillian. When she dies, only a secret network claims to remember her. And while Kane's manipulation of his wife Susan's stage career parallels Bingham and other scholars' view of the dominant Hollywood actress/performer-as-victim biopic (*Love Me or Leave Me*, 1955), in *Julia*, Hellman authors her own career on Hollywood and Broadway as screenwriter and playwright. Yet as Rosebud and the real shadow of media mogul William Randolph Hearst sit uncomfortably at the heart of *Citizen Kane*,[51] so too Julia's identity would thwart and inspire Sargent and Zinnemann.

Nevertheless, from its early stages, the production developed as a conventional heroic biopic, with Hellman functioning as both reverently transcribed source and protagonist. It is tempting to read *Julia* as a variation of George Custen's conventional argument about studio-era Hollywood's "construction of public history," in which biopics supported mainstream, politically innocuous ideologies.[52] One could argue that Twentieth Century-Fox eagerly repackaged the Stalinist Hellman as a charming, anti-fascist hero-worshipper, fulfilling the industry's need to defuse the political controversies of the 1930s and McCarthy era and to regenerate a historical genre with Hollywood luminaries as its protagonists. Hiring Zinnemann was part of the strategy; the director of the anti-McCarthy Western *High Noon* (abetted by Carl Foreman's interviews in the 1960s and early 1970s) combined aspects of Hellman's political persuasion with a career-long reputation for honesty. Hellman's "Julia" was advertised as Twentieth Century-Fox's one unimpeachable source. Studio press releases introduced the film as "a true account of events in the author's life. Set in 1937 Europe, against a background of the rise of Nazism and military unrest, the plot deals with a profound friendship and a lone fight against fascism." Julia was identified only as "Lillian Hellman's closest school friend" who became a major activist in the anti-fascist movements.[53] Executives at Fox, Alan Ladd, Jr., and Jay Kantor, probed no deeper. Trade reviews and posters even added a subtitle to Hellman's original: "Julia: Based on a true story."[54]

In film historian Arthur Knight's interview with Sargent, Knight commented on the dual nature of the "literary and real" characters, and

FIG. 54 Zinnemann at work on the script, 1976, AMPAS.

Sargent replied that in this case he had to "saturate" himself with period research to properly adapt Hellman's memoirs. Yet he also commented on his most difficult task: "I knew I had to be careful that Julia didn't take over the movie."[55] Julia may have been only a "memory," but Sargent wanted to keep most of the narrative focused on Hellman. The screenwriter emphasized how carefully he adapted Hellman's work and that he went to the additional trouble to consult her personally. Yet he did not amplify Julia's historical presence in the film. The writer had begun to suspect Hellman's story about Julia was partially fictional.[56]

Zinnemann and his research team were equally aware of the problems with Julia's identity and compiled surveys of the Austrian anti-fascist movement, even going so far as to xerox pages from *In the Twilight of Socialism*, written by Gardiner's second husband and leader of the Social Democrats in exile, Joseph Buttinger,[57] and collecting oral testimony from Professor Maria Jahoda (former assistant to the central committee of the Revolutionary Socialist Party or Austria's Social Democrats) about the then barely known activities of Gardiner. Research records describe Gardiner as "a rich American woman 'Mary,' a divorcee, who did immense work for the Party, gave a lot of money . . . Her real name was Muriel Gardiner." It went on: "'Mary' . . . had lived in Vienna since 1927. She had been a pupil of Freud's . . . She made her flats available for illegal meetings, came into contact with all the groups and factions and gave help and money to those in need." Zinnemann noted all of this, underlining the passages which connected Gardiner most strongly to Julia (fig. 54).[58]

Zinnemann, who grew up in Vienna, may have noted and been intrigued by the parallels between Gardiner and Julia. It may also have bothered him; by the end of filming, the former friends weren't speaking and he was scrawling comments about his "impossible position."[59] Zinnemann had arranged a special screening of the film for her in the late spring which she refused to attend and about which she complained at great length: "I am bewildered by all the attempted arrangements. I was first given one date on which I could see the picture in a projection room. (The print 'had to be returned to London' the next day.) I protested this rather command-like performance and received no answer for two weeks. I was then given a New Haven date which, because of my eye trouble, I cannot manage. So on, so forth. It is obvious that I am not wanted at any performance."[60] Zinnemann drafted a bland letter to her, but in an unsent copy, he wrote, "You are a severe rectal pain, I'm sorry to say."[61] But they hadn't seen eye-to-eye over the script. Ironically, Hellman's thoughts on Sargent's final script of *Julia*, which had Zinnemann's input, were that the production paid too little attention to old-fashioned historical details. She wrote to Zinnemann: "There are times when I had trouble understanding what period it was and why. But O.K. if it seems clear to other people who have not read the story. *But this is not a work of fiction and certain laws have to be followed for that reason*" [author's emphasis].[62] Hellman evidently believed the film was part of Hollywood's long-established historical genre and wanted more dates and newspaper inserts. But she also wanted more historical contextualization of Julia and less of herself. "Your major difficulty to me is the treatment of Lillian as the leading character ... my role was passive. And nobody and nothing can change that unless you write a fictional and different story." Hellman wanted more scenes of Julia and her career in Europe; she believed that as things stood, her political convictions and the history of the fascist takeover of Austria were too superficial: "It is absolutely necessary to have some indication of why Julia is living in the working class section of Vienna."

Vanessa Redgrave shared some of these thoughts, arguing that the second draft of the script had removed some of Julia's original historical specificity. Zinnemann agreed to "sharpen" some of the scenes from Julia's childhood and later at Oxford, but worried that too much discussion of Julia's political convictions would "turn out to be a full-blown soap box speech." He also commented, "I wanted Julia to be an active anti-fascist, but NOT an active anti-capitalist. I said that Vanessa would have to accept this and agree to it without reservation, otherwise I didn't see how she could be in the film."[63] But in an interview, Redgrave persisted, "I would think Julia was a member of the Communist Party but in our script you wouldn't see it. Insofar as you can tell from the material, Julia was a serious political fighter. But we don't know what she was doing. I know there's more to the story."[64] To a certain extent, Redgrave was right; in the scripts and film, Lillian questions Julia about her Oxford reading habits. While Julia lists Engels, Hegel, and Einstein, Marx is suspiciously absent from the discussion. Furthermore, Redgrave (possibly disingenuously) said she did not see why Hellman's former communist politics (and the assumed politics of Julia) had to be bowdlerized for a 1970s audience, but for the studio, retouching Hellman's political identity was paramount. Redgrave herself was a political dynamo, and in addition to her commitment to the Palestinian cause, handed out Marxist pamphlets to guests at their location hotels in Britain.[65] Zinnemann's long-term concerns were about making Julia too real, and he may also have felt that the film was political enough with Hellman's name attached. Lillian's empty-headed New York friends Anne-Marie (Meryl Streep) and Sammy (Julian Glover) stumble over the words "anti-fascist" and "socialist" in their descriptions of Julia; here, Zinnemann pinpointed Americans' inability to articulate the political Left. Yet Zinnemann's dislike of Hellman led him to a playful visual identification of Lillian: throughout the film he dressed his loudmouthed communist heroine in red sweaters, blouses, and evening gowns.[66]

Most film critics would agree with Hellman and Redgrave, wishing there had been more scenes between the two women and more of a historical indication of Julia's career and influence.[67] Sargent was questioned about these omissions, and used fidelity to Hellman's original material as his excuse. Others, as yet unaware of Hellman's historical peccadilloes but unwilling to respect her as an unimpeachable historical source, poked fun at the script's devoted transcription of her work. One critic wrote that Sargent "has relied heavily on Hellman's book to the degree of having the characters mouth verbatim dialog from it," and Andrew Sarris jeered at the idea of Hellman's memoirs being a "sacred text."[68] But Zinnemann's resistance to adding more historical context to Julia's character may have represented his own anxieties about the veracity of the source material. Though Hellman speaks of Julia's letters and frequently alludes to the text in *Pentimento*, there are no shots of Julia's handwriting or her actual

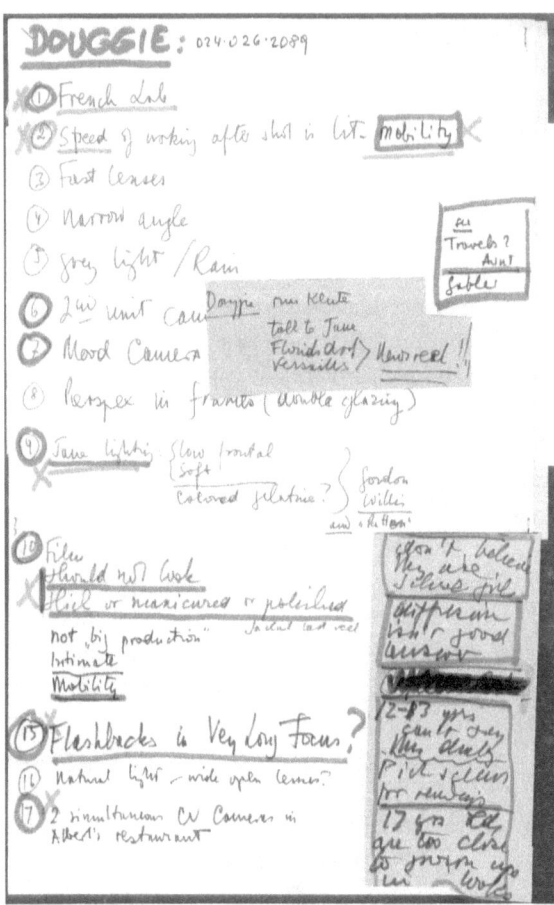

FIG. 55 Zinnemann's notes to Douglas Slocombe, 1976, AMPAS.

FIG. 56 Zinnemann with editor Walter Murch, 1976, AMPAS.

documents in the film. Only the sound of her voice survives in Hellman's memory on screen. If the director did suspect that his renowned memoirist and collaborator was a fake, it must have been worrying. But few were to know of these basic conflicts facing Zinnemann as a historical filmmaker.

In London, he spent weeks poring over research findings and script drafts, sharpening and justifying Sargent's breathtaking and complex leaps in voice, time, and place.[69] He and Douglas Slocombe developed a visual style that deliberately turned away from the grittier "realism" associated with the post-studio era. Zinnemann wrote to Slocombe that he was anxious to avoid making *Julia* seem "slick or manicured or polished" because it was based on one woman's shifting memories of another woman (fig. 55).[70] He wanted the cinematography to match the language, or, to paraphrase Hayden White, the form to match the content. Slocombe would use the gauzes for the lens and lighting he remembered from his start in films in the 1930s.[71] Zinnemann's notes and production documents confirm he was moving away from a positivist approach to women's history and toward a postmodern style curiously linked to the traditions of old Hollywood followed and reconfigured in part by Welles, Mankiewicz, and Toland. Even setting aside his worries about Hellman, it was difficult work, but a visit from old friend Floyd Crosby that summer lifted his spirits. He clowned for the camera while on location in Norfolk and the Lake District. He and Slocombe worked well together and shooting proceeded without a hitch. Later, he would spend weeks working through the complex editing sequences with his young editor, Walter Murch (fig. 56).

Revisioning Women's History

Although much of Zinnemann's layered sound cues and editing sequences (faithfully adapted from Sargent's scripts and mixed by Murch) resonate with the work of Chris Marker, Luis Buñuel, and especially with the 1930s fascist and wartime contexts of Bernardo Bertolucci's *The Conformist* (1974) and Alain Resnais's *Hiroshima, Mon Amour* (1959) and *Stavisky* (1974), *Julia* also entwines many of the themes from studio-era Hollywood's historical women's pictures, from complicated women's voiceovers (*All This and Heaven Too* and *Kitty Foyle*, both 1940; *The Great Man's Lady*, 1942) to the image of the protagonist in defiance of convention (*A Woman Rebels*, 1937; *Gone with the Wind*, 1939; *Saratoga Trunk*,

1946; *Desirée*, 1953) to the conflicting demands of fame and friendship (*The Sisters*, 1938; *The Great Lie*, 1941; *All About Eve*, 1950). Many critics, regardless of whether they endorsed the film, viewed *Julia* as a self-conscious throwback to studio-era filmmaking. Some highlighted the film's ties to the 1940s women's genre, others noted the obvious connection with Hellman and Zinnemann (both active in that period), and others identified the cinematography, lavish sets, and period polish with old Hollywood glamour (something both Resnais and Roman Polanski evoked in *Stavisky* and *Chinatown*, 1974).[72] Yet critics missed the fact that in returning to the 1930s and its accompanying Hollywood look, *Julia* was returning to a period where women were far more historically prominent, most memorably in the work of Greta Garbo (*Camille*, 1937), Joan Crawford (*The Gorgeous Hussy*, 1936), Bette Davis (*The Private Lives of Elizabeth and Essex*, 1939), Ginger Rogers (*Magnificent Doll*, 1945), and Irene Dunne (*I Remember Mama*, 1948).

Many of the old Hollywood connections were difficult to miss—after all, the opening image is of the Twentieth Century-Fox logo in grainy black-and-white. But the logo is not accompanied by the famous trumpet fanfare; instead, a single drum beats as the credits begin. Jane Fonda's voice-over as Lillian begins the film with Hellman's original introduction to *Pentimento*: "Old paint on canvas, as it ages, sometimes becomes transparent...."[73] Besides affirming its faithful adaptation of Hellman's memoirs and introducing the narrative's underlying conflict between the accuracy of history and the creative work of the writer, *Julia*'s opening recalls the tradition in studio-era history films of introducing the narrative with either a text foreword or a voice-over. While forewords often established a conventional historical period, they were also capable of highlighting a historical question or, like Zinnemann's *Seventh Cross*, underscoring the film's project to rescue an event or person from obscurity or infamy.[74] Occasionally, as in *Citizen Kane*, authoritative textual and oral narration was revealed for its own portentous inadequacies and even inaccuracies. Indeed, knowing what one does about Zinnemann's attitude toward Hellman, his version of "seeing through the original lines" acquires new meaning and irony.

But the opening sequence is remarkable for other reasons, too. *Julia*'s foreword is narrated by a woman's voice. It introduces not only the film's central questions about authorship and memory, but of history and women's role in writing it. Most importantly, Hellman's voice-over doesn't merely introduce the film like a perfunctory historical gloss; it is sustained throughout the narrative. "Classical" Hollywood cinema has long been criticized for its inability to invest female characters with visual agency and power. Over the past forty years, psychoanalytic and feminist film studies have explored the range of Hollywood's male gaze and its punishment, both through narrative and visual means, of the transgressive woman.[75] Yet in foregrounding contemporary thrillers and melodramas of Alfred Hitchcock and Douglas Sirk, scholars have often ignored the preponderance of women's historical films in the studio era and the degree to which these female protagonists articulated a memorable and often critical voice. In mainstream historiography, the link between women's history and oral history is clear.[76] A fair share of research has already uncovered the importance of women's historical fiction to prestige Hollywood cinema, yet it reinforces the paradox of women's cinematic history: while the female protagonists dominate the narratives, motivate camera movement, and change major currents in history, very often they are based on works of fiction.[77]

Standard biopics often rely on projected text and document inserts to inject traditional historical prestige and position the subject as a "Great Man" of history. Zinnemann made some of these short films for MGM in the 1930s, including *One Against the World* (1939) and *A Way in the Wilderness* (1940). But beginning in the 1940s, women's voice-overs act in counterpoint to traditional historical discourse. The voice-over both situates the protagonists in a broader social milieu and personalizes lives of ordinary women often marginalized in standard historical narratives.[78] The voice-over also links the women's historical genre to oral history—a mode of social and cultural history that is deeply tied to *Julia*'s subjects of women's historiography and Resistance historiography.[79] While at least since the nineteenth century, men's historical achievements, particularly in the revered genres of diplomatic and political history, have been measured in the importance of extant documents, the historical traces of women's lives have been more difficult to assess. Oral history is equally essential to chronicles of the Resistance. Since women were so central to all levels of Resistance activity—and were particularly "invisible" as couriers and guides—many left no trace of their roles in any historical record. The interviews conducted by Margaret Rossiter and Margaret Collins Weitz in the 1970s and 1980s only recovered a fraction of these lost heroic lives. But the voices of the survivors acquired a human credibility that no written document could equal. Over the years, however, mainstream historians have often regarded oral history as a poor second to textual

[222]   Resistant Women in Contested Frames

FIG. 57 *Julia* (1977): Separation of word and image, Twentieth Century-Fox.

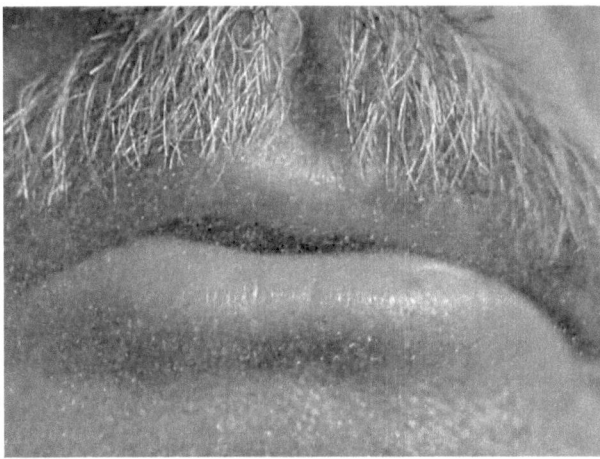

FIG. 58 Kane's lips as he utters the ambiguous "Rosebud," RKO Pictures.

sources. It was populist, ambiguous, and often contradicted conventional chronologies and narratives. Its lack of textual antecedents also made it susceptible to charges of fiction and invention, something not new to criticism of women's history and historical films. Hellman's "memoirs" were particularly controversial with journalists and historians who saw any inventions as personal affronts to the "accuracy" of Resistance history.

Although Zinnemann followed Sargent's original decision to begin with Hellman's older voice defining "pentimento" and the changing nature of memory and intention, the director wanted to emphasize the shadowy boundaries between history and memory even more. Hellman (Fonda) first appears with her back to the camera. She is fishing in a dory at dusk, in a long shot. Hellman's outline is visible, but the details are obscured in the dark. She may be the author of this unusual dual biography, but from the outset, Zinnemann projected Hellman's and his own self-reflective distance from the narrative.[80] Voice and image are separated (i.e., we do not see Hellman speaking the foreword or even see her face). Sound cues drift across images; the cry of a gull is echoed by the menacing scream of a train engine at night. Again, Hellman's voice returns, "I am old now, and I want to remember what was there for me once, and what is there for me now. . . ." In Zinnemann's shots, there is no historical unity between the sound (word) and the image (our visual documentation of those words); we see her eyes, but not her lips. The gap between "the original lines" and what lies beneath is glaring (fig. 57). This disjunction between word and image, history and myth, oral history and visual history, is something that *Citizen Kane* explores in an elaborate juxtaposition between the journalistic bombast of the *News on the March* narrator and the ambiguity of Kane's voice—particularly when he speaks "Rosebud" (fig. 58). But while Kane's biopic relies on the contrast between reportage of his very public life and private memories of his friends and colleagues, *Julia* explores the memory of a life in the absence of traditional textual documentation. This is arguably Zinnemann's point: Lillian is the hollow Hollywood celebrity, the well-known woman, the (screen)writer, and the embodiment of historical distortion. While she is obsessed with going to Paris and seeing the Eiffel Tower, Julia's political life and the reality of French fascism darkens these upbeat, deliberately kitschy images of the "swell town." Julia is the other side of the "great woman," not known to contemporary history, or only imperfectly. She keeps no written historical records. She is one of the "army of shadows," as Fourcade once put it, "that army . . . who shifted and succeeded one another and changed places like images in a film, fading and being replaced by others to ensure continuity."[81]

Sargent's script makes extensive use of Hellman's non-chronological, fragmentary sequences in *Pentimento*. However, while Hellman's narrative contains one large flashback narrating the outline of Julia's life in chronological order (roughly 1905–36), from the outset, Sargent splintered Hellman's memories and the chronology, creating a complex interplay between Hellman's life in the 1930s and her memories of Julia.[82] This choice curiously mirrors Herman Mankiewicz and Orson Welles's decision to insert multiple and contradictory flashbacks of Kane throughout the contemporary hunt for "Rosebud."[83] Hellman's creative life in 1934, when she was in the midst of constructing *The Children's Hour*, triggers memories of her childhood and young adulthood with Julia in New York. Zinnemann pushed Hellman's attitudes toward the past still further, accentuating the narrative's refusal to follow a traditional, chronological format in which

FIG. 59 Divided Hammett (Jason Robards) and Hellman (Jane Fonda), Twentieth Century-Fox.

image and sound work in sync to support and authenticate the truth of the recorded events. The form of traditional (masculine) biography and biopics would not work for the content of women's history, so Sargent and Zinnemann simply shattered it.

While Gregg Toland's famous long shots, deep-focus photography, and use of shadows often represent Kane's isolation from wife Susan and friend Leland and the antihero's own elusive personality, Douglas Slocombe's camera is frequently deliberately placed too close to his protagonists. This distances Hellman and Hammett in their shot-reverse shots while establishing a need for closeness to Julia, a closeness which paradoxically separates Hellman and Julia in the frame. Zinnemann heightens Hellman's resentment of Hammett's literary reputation and dictatorial attitudes by rarely shooting them in a two-shot. Instead, he follows a distinct shot-reverse shot format, in both long shots and close-ups, which accentuates their personal separateness. When Hammett (Jason Robards) chides Hellman to "give up" writing because "nobody will miss you," Zinnemann shoots her in the dark alone. Even the fire on the beach provides her with little warmth or clarity as she hunches over her drink. Though Hammett's dislike of her first effort on *The Children's Hour* spurs her to rewrite the play, she writes her second, like everything else, alone. Hammett does not help her. He is at the margins of the frame when she types at night, not daring to approach her. She talks to herself on the beach alone and does not speak to others. Alone at work and recalling her relationship with Julia, she becomes content and even confident (Zinnemann's sequences with Hellman throwing her old typewriter out the window and sighing with pleasure over the new model are one of the film's many creative treats). However, when Hammett finally approves the second draft, calling it "the best thing that's been written in a long time," Zinnemann refuses to unite them in a single shot. Her confidence wavers: "Are you sure?" she asks. Wooden spars and piling separate them (fig. 59). Shot-reverse shot sequences dominate their exchanges.

This sequence is in stark contrast to the fireside chats she had with Julia at the latter's Park Avenue mansion. In two sequences, one when they are teenagers and the other several years later, a fire warms their room as they create an alternating story together. Zinnemann shoots them both in close two-shots (figs. 60–61). Even when Lillian (Susan Jones) cannot understand a French quotation of Julia's, Zinnemann keeps them in two-shot. There is love, companionship, and a shared creative power between these two young women. Young Julia is a perfect muse for the older Hellman, with actress Lisa Pelikan recalling the Pre-Raphaelite beauty of the paintings of Edward Burne-Jones and Dante Gabriel Rossetti. The older Lillian comments on these sequences: "I think I have always known about my memory . . . But I trust absolutely what I remember about Julia" and later, "I cannot say now that I had ever used the words gentle or strong or delicate, but I did think that night that it was the most beautiful face I had ever seen." While both Sargent and Murch believed the film replicated Zinnemann's attitude toward Julia and Hellman's material ("The narration here challenges the audience to find Vanessa to be perfect, which I think may be an impossible goal"), Zinnemann was quick to explain.[84] The director's visualization of Julia via Lillian's narration is ironic. That face is seen through a nostalgic haze. Slocombe used special filters on his lenses when shooting the two young girls and later Fonda and Redgrave together precisely because he wanted to emphasize Hellman's nostalgia—even historical fantasy. While Lillian's scenes with Hammett have a cold clarity, the shots of Lillian and Julia together are misty, glowing, and blurred. Though Zinnemann had great respect for Sargent and Murch's opinions, he was less gentle with producer Richard Roth's criticism of this sequence, writing: "Thank you for the notes you sent me from Paris. I have read them carefully. We have made a few of the changes which you and I discussed while you were here. I think that the rest should wait until after the previews, so that we can get a clear indication from the audience as to what changes are really necessary."[85] In a move reminiscent of his power struggles over *The Search* and *Behold a Pale Horse*, he later banned Roth from

[226]   Resistant Women in Contested Frames

FIG. 60 United women: young Lillian (Susan Jones) and young Julia (Lisa Pelikan), Twentieth Century-Fox.

FIG. 61 Keeping Lillian and Julia together in a shot (Jane Fonda and Vanessa Redgrave), Twentieth Century-Fox.

the locations in Europe and persuaded Fox to credit Julien Derode (*Day of the Jackal, Behold a Pale Horse*) as executive producer.

Zinnemann's close shots of Julia reveal his and Hellman's need to establish her historical presence. And as much as *The Children's Hour* and her years with Hammett are matters of recorded literary history, for Hellman, it is the memory of Julia which allegedly gives Hellman the confidence to remember the past with personal accuracy. Hellman's

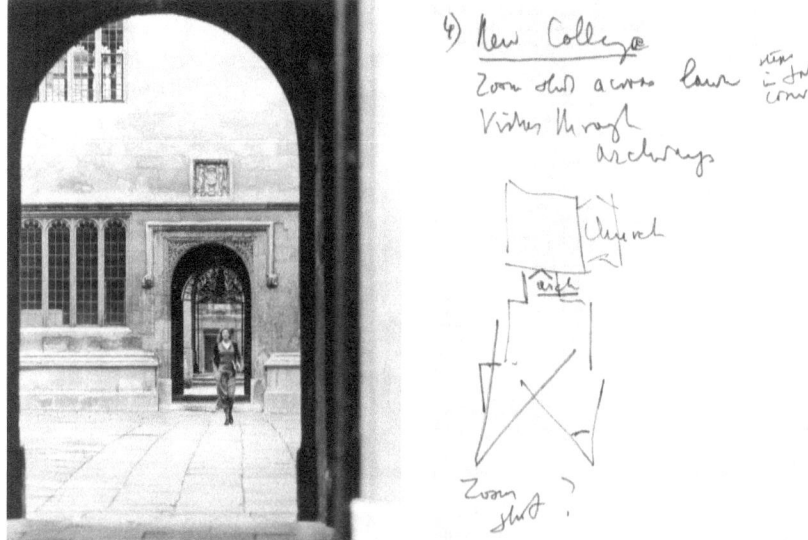

FIGS. 62–63 Zinnemann's notes for the Julia-Oxford sequence, 1976, AMPAS.

memories of Julia at Oxford accentuate the latter's connection to the past, but it is a past which Zinnemann deliberately over-frames. The director chose to shoot Redgrave framed in a succession of Oxford doorways, and as she approaches, her perfect beauty and grace and power seem to rival the architecture (figs. 62–64). She walks closer and closer to the waiting camera, which remains stationary even when Redgrave's luminous eyes threaten to swallow up the screen.[86] Sargent disliked the over-determined close-up as "too obviously a gimmick" and wrote to Zinnemann asking it to be cut. Zinnemann politely ignored him, dwelling on the structure of her approach to the camera in many sketches and notes.[87] As she pauses in the final doorway, Zinnemann and Murch's slow dissolve makes her "framed" image look like a superimposed photograph in the Oxford landscape, giving the sequence a constructed look, like a recent photograph superimposed on another, older photograph.[88] When Julia later attacks fascism for the first time in the February 1934 riots, Zinnemann replicates the shot of the woman moving through an old corridor, replacing the process of nostalgia with that of heroism (fig. 65). Hellman, after all, wasn't the only one to construct or reframe "heroic" Resistance history.

Through many of these memories, the director struggles, like Lillian, to keep the two women together in one frame. The camera moves swiftly, but only to keep the pair in a two-shot aboard the boat that will take Julia

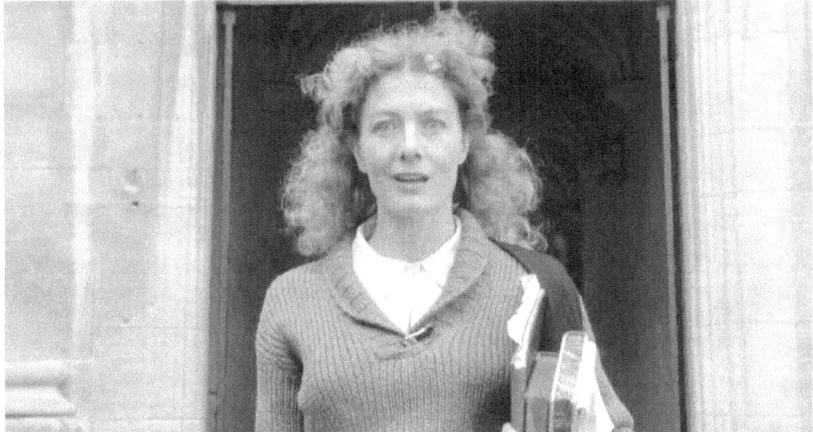

FIG. 64 "There are women who reach a perfect time of life": The St. John's corridor with Julia (Vanessa Redgrave), Twentieth Century-Fox.

FIG. 65 Resistance and repetition Julia (Redgrave) defends Jewish medical students in Vienna, 1934, Twentieth Century-Fox.

to Britain and Oxford. Later, as Lillian tells of her gradual understanding about Julia's warnings about fascism, the camera pulls into a crane shot, following the two as they cross the quad to Julia's rooms. Yet, paradoxically, we cannot hear what Julia says and what Lillian says she now understands. There isn't even an illusion of historical unity between evidence and interpretation. The historical voice has obliterated Julia's original voice. Georges

Delerue's distorted strings are already sounding like air-raid sirens as the camera travels up the architecture of St. John's Chapel.

But Zinnemann pushes the idea of historical translation further in *Julia*. When they are children, Lillian cannot comprehend Julia's dislike of Cairo and her wealthy family's refusal to help the poor, and later Julia's enthusiasm for Vienna's Floridsdorf district in the 1920s. Young Lillian (Susan Jones) wants to know about Paris, and later Zinnemann's postcard-like establishing shots and folksy accordion music jar with the roar of fascist crowds and black-and-white images of Vienna and Nuremberg. Hellman also reveals that she cannot understand the threat of Hitler despite Julia's early warnings. When she visits Julia in a Vienna hospital, Julia tries to communicate silently with her hands that Lillian must go and seek someone; Lillian replies despondently, "I don't know what you mean." Zinnemann follows this scene with a silent shot of the two sailing in upstate New York. Again, we cannot hear their words. When Hellman returns to consciousness, Julia has disappeared. A note related in voice-over makes nothing clearer to Lillian. As Hellman wrote in *Pentimento*, Julia's note included the phrase, "Something else is needed," which she realized only later related to their school days when they were translating Latin and missed a word.[89]

History, regardless of whether it is written or filmed, involves tricky editing and attempts at authenticity. Unlike the neat chronology and careful presentation of the 1930s masculine biopics, nothing is perfect or polished in this narrative. It, like Hellman's *Children's Hour* or Thompson's search in *Citizen Kane*, is mostly a work in progress. *Julia*'s refusal to unfold in chronological order, to separate time and space into distinct sequences, to invest the narrator with omniscience, are all choices which break down traditional boundaries between history, fiction, and memoir. While other historical films produced in Hollywood have certainly used flashbacks (*The Pawnbroker*, 1964), ironic voice-overs (*Badlands*, 1973), sound bridges (*The Nun's Story*, 1959), self-reflexivity (*Kitty Foyle*, 1940; *Dillinger*), and documentary inserts and newsreels (*The Godfather*, 1972), no other film equals the breadth of *Julia*'s historical innovations—with, arguably, the exception of *Citizen Kane*. Yet the stakes are higher for revisionist women's history and its narratives of resistance to traditional "heroic" ideals and methods for adapting and valorizing their lives. Zinnemann went further, casting his film loose from the corrupted text of Hellman's "biographical" Resistance tale, blurring his focus, muting

FIGS. 66–67 Death scenes of *Julia* and *Hamlet*, Twentieth Century-Fox.

dialogue, separating sound and image. Late in the film, the Nazis' attack on Julia and her death are juxtaposed with Lillian's bored response at a Moscow performance of *Hamlet*. As the assassin drives the knife through Julia's body, applause erupts, waking a sleepy Hellman (figs. 66–67).[90] For Zinnemann, Hellman's Julia, her heroic life and death, and "History" itself are staged events like *Hamlet* or *The Children's Hour*. He spent more time with Murch perfecting the sound and film editing for this sequence and for Julia's walk in the St. John's quad than any other part of the film. These were moments when the filmmakers foregrounded the constructed nature of the image and narrative, moments when the form became as revolutionary as its female protagonists.

Women's Audiences

Zinnemann may have worried that a historical film about a little-known member of the Austrian resistance would raise little interest with American viewers. His last Resistance film made for a Hollywood studio, *Behold a Pale Horse*, had failed in part because the American public had forgotten about the Spanish Civil War.[91] However, *Julia* emerged in a somewhat more positive social context. Zinnemann's exploration of women's memory and voice-overs was part of a growing historical interest in oral history and feminism. Though oral histories had long been a staple of Resistance historiography and Holocaust survivor accounts, by the late 1970s, historians and cultural critics began to discuss the historiographic consequences of joining oral history with women's history.[92] Sherna Berger Gluck's oral history of American suffragettes was received with great acclaim in 1976, but it was her classic article, "What's So Special About Women? Women's Oral History," that focused the debate.[93] As Gluck summarized: "Women's oral history, then, is a feminist encounter, even if the interviewee is not herself a feminist. It is the creation of a new type of material on women; it is the validation of women's experiences; it is the communication among women of different generations; it is the discovery of our own roots and the development of a continuity which has been denied us in traditional historical accounts."[94]

Julia also emerged in a year Hollywood critics called "The Year of the Woman."[95] While *The Goodbye Girl, Annie Hall, An Unmarried Woman*, and *Three Women* played in theaters across the country, the public awaited the first National Women's Conference in November, the first and only sponsored by the federal government. Part of the United Nations' creation of an International Day of Women's Rights (March 8) and a celebration of "International Women's Year," the conference addressed issues in childcare, financial and educational inequities, and human rights. As Fonda commented during production, "The old female roles have been done away with, but the financiers of movies—those men who run the multinational corporations—can't figure out which new female stereotypes are bankable."[96] *Julia* was a risk for Twentieth Century-Fox.

Within this widespread atmosphere of intellectual and social expectation, *Julia* emerged as a hugely popular film.[97] Some American critics would argue that "*Julia* does for women what Lean's *Lawrence of Arabia* and Zinnemann's own *A Man For All Seasons* did for men."[98] British critics, many of them women, loved *Julia*. As Valerie Jenkins wrote in the *London Evening Standard*, "Women, on screen as in life, have long been accorded secondary roles as wives, mothers, lovers, daughters. Now they are finding a new identity as people who act rather than react, and do rather than get done by."[99] Another critic predicted that the film would fundamentally change women's representation on screen: "The cinema screen has always been a predominantly male preserve, where women are sometimes invited for decoration and variety, like a gentleman's club. All this may change with *Julia*. It is tipped to sweep the Oscars later this year and cut a new path for the role of women in films."[100]

Zinnemann's complex narrative structure and interplay of sound bridges and non-chronological flashbacks were potentially confusing for mass audiences, but the director approached the film as both a development of themes in his Resistance works and an alternate form of narration for women's history.[101] He handled Hellman's reliability with care: "I wanted the story to be valid whether the people it concerns existed or whether they did not. . . . The prime attraction of *Julia* for me was the way in which it treated American attitudes toward fascism."[102] His post-production audience research contributed yet another facet to women's film history. In a series of unique interviews with the New Haven preview audience, the production staff probed dozens of women's reactions to the film.[103] Many highlighted *Julia*'s flashbacks, voice-overs, and complex narration, and some of the interviewed female spectators were surprised that women actually participated in the Resistance let alone to have lead a réseau. But most of those women loved the film for precisely these reasons. Kate Sonderegger was delighted that finally there was "a strong woman's film" based upon real women's lives.[104] A number of women, like Leslie Blake, were fans of Hellman and read women's fiction and history regularly, but even women who had just come to the film on the spur of the moment, like Olympia Delaci, responded to the material and its complex presentation: "I liked . . . the way that the war was seen through a woman's eyes and not like movies through the man's eyes as in John Wayne pictures on the battlefield. This role showed two women's roles during World War Two." While Wayne's *They Were Expendable* (1945), *Sands of Iwo Jima* (1949), and *The Longest Day* (1962) might be one way of entering the historical world of the Second World War, *Julia*'s focus on women's history and alternatives to traditional military heroism broadened their understanding of the era. Jill Greengrove went further, arguing that knowing that Julia and Hellman were real women living through this era changed people's overall perspective on the film. It was not a conventional suspense narrative or war film, and while others might find its pace and complex narration confusing or "irrelevant as a piece of fiction," its historical complexity "gave it depth, meaning." *Julia*'s unique material and narrative structure encouraged not only alternate understandings of the resistance to the Nazis and women's history, but also a different way of viewing Hollywood cinema.

While audiences and many small-time reviewers loved *Julia*, major American film critics Vincent Canby, Andrew Sarris, Pauline Kael, and Molly Haskell (Sarris's wife) disliked it.[105] Popular auteurism, championed by Sarris since the late 1960s, had always snubbed Zinnemann's work. But Sarris also loathed Hellman and what he perceived to be the recent Hollywood project to heroize her; Haskell and Kael resented Hellman and the film's canonization of Julia. Though the revelations about Hellman's historical inventions were in the future, Canby poked fun at the "conventional" soft-focus flashbacks of Julia and complained that the film was "an illusive narrative fragment in desperate need of further amplification," little realizing that Julia's shadowy, ambiguous historical presence evoked a central problem in rendering the history of women by traditional means. Its fragmentary oral history couldn't trumpet the great success/backstory of more conventional biopics; it amplified only what was marginalized, undocumented, and historically "imperfect." Even more than Canby and Sarris, Haskell and Kael resented Hellman's simplistic and often fragmented memories. Haskell wrote, "Who can believe in the idealized portrait of a Madonna of the Left that Hellman paints?" Kael, a longtime defender of *Citizen Kane*'s co-screenwriter, Herman Mankiewicz, and the film's status as a Hollywood biopic, almost perversely ignored *Julia*'s script innovations and meditations on women's history and memory. Haskell, whose book *From Reverence to Rape* (1977) lambasted Hollywood's alleged stereotyped portrayal of women, also resisted the film's obvious appeal as a prestige film about two American women and the way important women have been lost to the historical record. For some, *Julia* would be an abstruse fragment—a frustrating enigma which fell short of being the impressive but simply structured historical biopics that *A Man For All Seasons* and *Lawrence of Arabia* were, and lacked the complexity and critical accolades of *Citizen Kane*. For others, its portrait of female heroism was too impressive to be credible. To a certain extent, this was true: Hellman, who had made a career of not naming names, was eventually discredited by her former public virtue.

But had Hellman written truthfully about Muriel Gardiner or Virginia Hall or Marie-Madeleine Fourcade, would Twentieth Century-Fox

FIG. 68 Muse and agent of history, and for Zinnemann, a woman who looked "like no one else": Julia (Redgrave) in Berlin, Twentieth Century-Fox.

have filmed the property as a major historical film? Would Muriel Gardiner's life have been an "appropriate" and "believable" historical subject for Haskell and Kael? Would the lives of truly heroic women always be too unbelievable for film critics? Biopics of resistance heroines, such as *Odette* or *Carve Her Name With Pride*, can be counted on the fingers of one hand. Virginia McKenna's Violette Szabo carries and uses a sten gun, and is eventually lined up and shot with two female compatriots, yet the stark biography included an invented romance with her CO (Paul Scofield) and emphasized her status as an SOE underling in a man's world. Even today, *Black Book* (2006), *Women of the Shadows* (2008), and *Blessed is the Match* (2009) focus on women as sexual pawns or minor martyrs. Zinnemann, as always, pursued a nuanced visual manifestation of the Resistance hero/heroine. Julia's ultimate significance may lie in Redgrave's portrayal. Zinnemann was fascinated with Redgrave, and believed that she, like Spencer Tracy, was one of the greatest actors of all-time. A woman "who looks like no one else," Redgrave's Julia spurns expensive clothes, mirrors, makeup, and men as romantic partners. Instead, the leading man, Maximillian Schell, portrays her gentle, slightly awkward courier, Mr. Johann, and she employs as many women as men in her réseau (actresses Dora Doll and Elisabeth Mortensen act as Fonda's anonymous, principal guardians on the train to Berlin). If we want to truly see women like Julia, then, like Redgrave in her final scenes with Fonda, we have to look steadily without blinking (fig. 68).

In the early 1970s, several prominent feminist historians had written that traditional explorations of women's history heroizing the individual did so because they resembled men in their public achievements.[106] They argued, to paraphrase Julia, that something else was needed. The exploration of formerly unknown women needed a new examination of sources, and possibly a new form of historiography. In *The Long Road of Women's Memory* (1916), Jane Addams looks at the pasts of poor immigrant women and focuses on the impact a spurious tale has on prompting the revelation of women's stories which otherwise would have been lost to posterity. Regardless of accuracy, Addams believed, memory and oral testimony were key in both "interpreting and appeasing life for the individual, and ... activity as a selective agency for social reorganization."[107]

Zinnemann's films envelop many such paradoxes—visual, oral, textual, historical, interpretive. Because he was so engrossed with discovering and analyzing these different dimensions in his production notes, and so articulate in documenting his questions and solutions, we have perhaps the most complete archival picture of a filmmakers' mind. Some might view Zinnemann's archive at the Library of the Academy of Motion Picture Arts and Sciences as a variant of Charles Foster Kane's eclectic warehouse, and Julia, his resistant "Rosebud"—an element of fakery or gimmickry with which to construct a story.[108] Yet the recovery of Julia's past, like histories of many anti-fascist resisters and filmmakers, involves both creation and historical recreation, confrontations with realism and mythology, and a re-evaluation of traditional critical interpretations of Hollywood film genres and auteur theories.

More than any other filmmaker of his generation, Fred Zinnemann exuded the visual acuity and intellectual combativeness to dramatize a uniquely twentieth-century struggle against fascism and collective control of the individual. Unlike his mentor Robert Flaherty, Zinnemann chose to remain in the Hollywood system, but had the toughness and endurance to gradually wrench total creative power over his productions from an industry intent on streamlining costs and avoiding ideological controversy. Unlike many members of the Directors Guild (Frank Capra and his auteurist autobiography, *The Name Above the Title*, spring to mind in this regard), Zinnemann believed that films were essentially collaborative efforts. He was enormously respectful of the talents of many cinematographers, writers, and production designers, but he had little tolerance for producers. Paradoxically, however, when anyone got in his way, whether it was old friend Peter Viertel, Lazar Wechsler, Stanley Kramer, Franz Waxman, Oscar Hammerstein, Emeric Pressburger, Paul Scofield, Lillian Hellman, Richard Roth, or MGM itself, his letters and memos could be

FIG. 69 He enjoyed his isolation at times..., AMPAS.

FIG. 70 Zinnemann alone, 1976, AMPAS.

chillingly formal. His drafted responses were even more brief and devastating, but he had the good sense not to send many. In the course of his career, though, there were casualties—projects he pursued in some cases for decades (*The Dybbuk*, 1958–84; *The Last Secret*, 1977–80), only to be forced to abandon them due to the studios' lack of interest.[109] Yet when an opportunity arose for him to join forces with the likes of William Wyler, John Huston, and Billy Wilder, perhaps guaranteeing him more financial backing from production companies, he politely refused, determined to go his own way, much as Robert E. Lee Prewitt, Gabrielle van der Mal, or Julia would have done.[110] He outlasted the studio system that gave him his start, and survived alone.

Throughout his career, Zinnemann was as careful to maintain control of his films' post-release reputations as he was on the set. He could be as dismissive with critics as with colleagues and friends. Yet "a Fred Zinnemann film" retains an identity beyond traditional definitions of national and international filmmaking, commercial and independent cinema, and fictional and historical narratives. Zinnemann was aware that his "complicated" films had antagonized mainstream critics, conservative politicians, and censors, and had even lost touch with younger generations of filmmakers and audiences. A man with very real personal demons, he also cultivated this image of isolation throughout his career (figs. 69–70). As he remarked late in life, "The whole trend of thinking has gone in a direction which isn't the way I look at life or the kind of pictures I make. People like more films with entertainment values; maybe my pictures are more like lectures."[111] His attempts to acquaint new generations of filmgoers about the evils of fascism, the history of the Spanish Civil War, or the Nazis were sometimes deeply frustrating. But, as he would shrug, "I was never too worried about what people thought." He was, however, quite meticulous about preserving what *he* thought throughout a lifetime of filmmaking. From the pages in his archive as much as on screen, Fred Zinnemann embodies a visual, textual, and intellectual resistance unequaled in his own generation.

NOTES

Introduction

1. Chaim Potok and David Rudkin, *The Dybbuk*, 2 July 1984, D111, folder 975, box 73, FZ Papers, Academy of Motion Picture Arts and Sciences Library (hereafter AMPAS).
2. André Malraux, *Man's Fate* (1933; repr., London: Penguin, 2009), 235.
3. Of the more than forty books on Alfred Hitchcock, see Donald Spoto, *The Dark Side of Genius: The Life of Alfred Hitchcock* (Boston: Little, Brown, 1983) and Leonard Leff, *Hitchcock with Selznick* (New York: Weidenfeld & Nicholson, 1987). Of the more than thirty books on John Ford, see particularly Tag Gallagher, *John Ford: The Man and His Films* (Berkeley: University of California Press, 1986). Of the more than forty books on Orson Welles, see James Naremore, *The Magic World of Orson Welles* (New York: Oxford University Press, 1978) and Clinton Heylin, *Despite the System: Orson Welles Versus the Hollywood Studios* (Chicago: Chicago Review Press, 2005). Of the twenty books on John Huston, see Gaylyn Studlar and David Desser, eds., *Reflections in a Male Eye: John Huston and the American Experience* (Washington: Smithsonian Institution Press, 1993) and Stephen Cooper, ed., *Perspectives on John Huston* (New York: G. K. Hall, 1994). There are four books on Zinnemann, one his autobiography (Fred Zinnemann, *An Autobiography* [London: Bloomsbury, 1992]), one a compilation of interviews (Gabriel Miller, ed., *Fred Zinnemann Interviews* [Jackson: University of Mississippi Press, 2005]), and two critical studies, which, although introducing a variety of perspectives on many of his key films, rely primarily on interpretive rather than archival evidence (Arthur Nolletti, Jr., ed., *Films of Fred Zinnemann: Critical Perspectives* [Albany: State University of New York Press, 1993]); Neil Sinyard, *Fred Zinnemann: Films of Character and Conscience* [Jefferson, NC: McFarland & Co., 2003]).
4. Tim Durrant to FZ, 14 May 1952, box 33, folder 428, FZ Papers, AMPAS; William H. Wells to FZ, 10 December 1952, box 33, folder 428, FZ Papers, AMPAS.
5. See, for example, Jane Morris, "The Zinnemanns: An International Family," *Parents' Magazine* (January 1951), 32–33, box 111, folder 10, FZ Papers, AMPAS, and *The Nun's Story*, Souvenir Program (1959), 16 pp., 13, Premier Leicester Square Theater, London, WB Archive, USC.
6. "Zinnemann's *Pale Horse* Is a Film Masterpiece," *Hollywood Reporter*, 14 August 1964, 3.
7. Andrew Sarris, *The American Cinema: Directors and Directions, 1929–1968* (New York: E. P. Dutton, 1968), 169; Sinyard, passim; Noletti, 1.

8. FZ with James Silke, quoted in Miller, 21.

9. Ibid., 14–15. For auteurist studies of Hawks, see Peter Bogdanovich, *The Cinema of Howard Hawks* (New York: MoMA, 1962); Robin Wood, *Howard Hawks* (Garden City, NY: Doubleday, 1968); Jim Hillier and Peter Wollen, eds., *Howard Hawks, American Artist* (London: BFI Publishing, 1996); Jean-Michel Durafour, *Hawks, cinéaste du retrait* (Villeneuve d'Ascq: Presses universitaires du septentrion, 2007).

10. James Silke, "Zinnemann: True or False," *Cinema* 2, no. 1 (February 1964): 15–19.

11. FZ to Carson McCullers, 3 April 1952 and 26 May 1952, box 48, folder 634, FZ Papers, AMPAS.

12. Fred Zinnemann, *An Autobiography* (London: Bloomsbury, 1992), 223.

13. George Zinnemann to FZ, 11 January 1945, box 1, 2004 add-ins, FZ Papers, AMPAS.

14. FZ, interview for *Politiken*, Sunday, 19 February 1978, translated transcript, box 39, folder 515, FZ Papers, AMPAS. For more on the *Dybbuk*, see J. Hoberman, *Bridge of Light: Yiddish Film Between Two Worlds* (Hanover, NH: Dartmouth College Press, 2010), 55–57, 277–84. For years, Zinnemann listed his place of birth as Vienna, Austria, but he only grew up there after his parents moved from Poland, the true country of his birth.

15. See Brook, *Driven to Darkness, Jewish Émigré Directors and the Rise of Film Noir* (New Brunswick, NJ: Rutgers University Press, 2010).

16. See *Carlotta and Maximilian* (1973–74) files, FZ Papers, BFI.

17. Though the adaptation of Robert Bolt's historical play about Thomas More and Henry VIII lies outside the boundaries of World War II, anti-fascist resistance, and the US's Cold War purges, Zinnemann would consciously link Paul Scofield's performance as More with that of Spencer Tracy's German communist resister in *The Seventh Cross*, Audrey Hepburn's Belgian nun-turned-Resistance worker in *The Nun's Story*, and Vanessa Redgrave's anti-fascist leader in *Julia* across many interviews from the 1950s until his death in 1997.

18. Paul Scofield to FZ, 10 July 1968, box 87, folder 1154, FZ Papers, AMPAS.

19. See FZ's *Autobiography* (1992) for an account of this "non film." John Russell Taylor also comments that *Man's Fate* may seem "a strange choice, one would think, for an American-financed film considering that some of its most heroic characters are early followers of Chairman Mao. But no doubt the company knows that if anyone can be relied on to play fair with everyone it is Fred Zinnemann, a master in the delicate art of suggesting without compromise both the advantages and the disadvantages of the other fellow's point of view" (Taylor, "Film Director who likes to let his subject speak for itself," *Times* [18 March 1967], 7.

20. FZ quoted in Paul R. Michaud, "The Lone Wolf and the Jackal," 1972, reprinted in Miller, 31–36.

21. See André Malraux's own *Anti-Memoirs* (1964) and Guy Penaud, *André Malraux et la Resistance* (Paris: Faniac, 1986). See also R. Batchelor, "André Malraux and the Concept of Revolt," *Modern Languages Review* 67, no. 4 (October 1972): 799–809;

Walter Langlois, "Anarchism, Action, and Malraux," *Twentieth-Century Literature* 24 (autumn 1978): 272–89.

22. While Malraux was allegedly blasé about his lies regarding his participation in the revolution, Lillian Hellman, who clamed a similar role in Resistance activities, continued to insist on the authenticity of her account.

23. Malraux (1933), 91.

24. Zinnemann was proud of his association with this film, but dismissed any creative impact on the material: "The sum total of my contribution was to carry the camera around and to stay out of trouble," he said (Zinnemann, 1992: 16).

25. Ibid., 24.

26. See box 42, Robert J. Flaherty Papers, Columbia University, New York.

27. See Richard Barsam, *The Vision of Robert Flaherty: The Artist as Myth and Filmmaker* (Bloomington: Indiana University Press, 1988), 52, and Zinnemann, "Remembering Robert Flaherty," *Action* (May-June 1976): 25–27.

28. For instance, Vincent Deveau, "Honoring the Artistry of Fred Zinnemann," *DGA News* 19, no. 3 (June-July 1994): 18–24; Brian Neve, "A Past Master of His Craft," *Cineaste* 23, no. 1 (1997): 15–19.

29. Zinnemann (1992), 54. Although only the best directors seem to have been fired from productions (von Stroheim, MGM; Hawks, Samuel Goldwyn), suspended directors were even rarer.

30. FZ quoted in Paul R. Michaud, "The Lone Wolf and the Jackal," 1972, reprinted in Miller, 36.

31. See Barsam, 96, Arthur Calder-Marshall, *The Innocent Eye: The Life of Robert J. Flaherty* (New York: Harcourt, Brace and World, 1963), passim, and William T. Murphy, *Robert Flaherty: A Guide to References and Resources* (Boston: G. K. Hall & Co., 1978), 14–16. See also David Flaherty, "Serpents in Eden," *Asia* (October 1925), 858–69, 895–98, and Newton Rowe, *Samoa Under the Sailing Gods* (London: Putnam, 1930), 108, 181–82.

32. For Zinnemann's efforts to keep the final sequence silent, see Franz Waxman to FZ, 2 October 1958 and FZ to Franz Waxman, 2 October 1958, *The Nun's Story*, memos and correspondence, WB Archive, University of Southern California (hereafter USC).

33. FZ to Silke, quoted in Miller, 9.

34. Bob Moore, ed., *Resistance in Western Europe* (New York: Berg, 2000), passim.

35. Pieter Lagrou, *The Legacy of Nazi Occupation: Patriotic Memory and National Recovery in Western Europe, 1945–1965* (Cambridge: Cambridge University Press, 2000), 222–24.

36. Ibid., 224.

37. Margaret Collins Weitz, *Sisters in the Resistance: How Women Fought to Free France, 1940–1945* (New York: Wiley, 1995).

38. Weitz, 7–11, 305. For the classic masculine perspectives on the Resistance, see Alban Vistel, *Héritage spirituel de la Résistance* (Lyons: Lug, 1955); Henri Michel, *Bibliographie critique de la Résistance* (Paris: Institut Pedagogique National, 1964); Lagrou, 38–47.

39. Ginette Vincendeau, *Jean-Pierre Melville: An American in Paris* (London: BFI, 2005), 49–98.

40. Vincent Brook has pointed out that Zinnemann's *Act of Violence* uses the classic oppositional style of film noir to deconstruct the American public's ideal of a war hero. See Brook, *Driven to Darkness: Jewish Émigré Directors and the Rise of Film Noir* (New Brunswick, NJ: Rutgers University Press, 2009), 207–10. See also Wheeler Winston Dixon, "*Act of Violence* (1949) and the Early Films of Fred Zinnemann," in *The Films of Fred Zinnemann: Critical Perspectives*, ed. Nolletti, 52.

41. Although many of these disagreements are dealt with in subsequent chapters, Paul Scofield's case is instructive. Shortly after *A Man For All Seasons*, he gave an interview in which he praised John Frankenheimer's work with actors, but regarding Zinnemann, "Scofield was not sure how good he really is with actors. . . . 'Perhaps you remember the scene that I had with Susannah York on the beach, which is the real crux of the action of ideas, when the daughter comes to her father and seems to oppose him as an intellectual equal, using her wits that he had helped form, against him. Now Susannah York was marvelous, but she did that scene at first all supplicating and feminine, not as an equal, which was the way I knew Robert Bolt had intended it. So I went to Zinnemann and said that I thought that she should be told this and all he said was, 'I can't do that' and would not be involved. I had to suggest the idea to her myself and I think it worked out quite well.'" Scofield apologized for the interview, but Zinnemann's friendship cooled (Tom Hutchinson, "Scofield," *Arts Guardian*, 4 August 1971, 8; PS to FZ, August 8. 1971; both box 108, folder 17, FZ Papers, AMPAS).

Chapter One

1. Fred Zinnemann, with Gordon Gow, 1976, reprinted in Miller, 58.
2. Zinnemann (1992), 17.
3. Ibid., 27.
4. Ibid., 39.
5. *Redes* was funded by the Secretaría de Educación Pública (SEP) as the first in a series of educational films designed to give cultural legitimacy to the new Mexican government which had done away with land peonage. See William Alexander, *Film on the Left: American Documentary Film From 1931 to 1942* (Princeton, NJ: Princeton University Press, 1981): 67–81.
6. James Krippner, *Paul Strand in Mexico* (New York: Aperture, 2010), 70, 93–94. See also Joel Eisinger, *Trace & Transformation: American Criticism of Photography in the Modernist Period* (1995; repr., Albuquerque: University of New Mexico Press, 1999), 56–59.
7. Zinnemann (1992), 36–37.
8. Smyth (2006), passim.

9. He nonetheless prepared meticulously, annotating every page of his script with camera set ups and notes. Marsha Hunt, by then a veteran star of six years, remembered she had never seen any director prepare so carefully (interview, 3 April 2012).

10. FZ to Jack Chertok, 8 August 1941, box 1, item 15, FZ Papers, BFI, London.

11. Walter Wanger's Spanish Civil War drama, *Blockade!* (1937), was so ideologically ambiguous that many critics could not distinguish between the insurgents and Loyalists: "Lawson . . . disguises the warring factions" and "the Hays Office advised radical alterations in the original script to avoid offense to foreign powers. Fact is, that the strength and power of a film of this type reside in offensiveness and partisanship," "*Blockade!*," *Variety*, 31 December 1937.

12. Through Berman, Zinnemann became friends with Tracy and Hepburn, both well-known Hollywood liberals. The relationship soured on the set of *The Old Man and the Sea* (1958), when Zinnemann was fired for, among other things, implying that Tracy was too out-of-shape to play Hemingway's hero.

13. For more on the political context of *The Seventh Cross*, see Jan-Christopher Horak, "The Other Germany in Zinnemann's *The Seventh Cross* (1943)," in *German Film and Literature*, ed. Eric Rentschler (London: Routledge, 1986), 117–31.

14. Deutsch would later go on to adapt *National Velvet* (1945), *Kim* (1950), and *King Solomon's Mines* (1951).

15. Anna Seghers, *The Seventh Cross* (1942; repr., Boston: David R. Godine, 2004), esp. 5–6, 22, 31, 36–37, 163, 186–88, 295, 394–95.

16. Helen Deutsch, 26 April 1943, first pink script, folder 683, MGM Script Collection, AMPAS; Helen Deutsch, 10 April 1944, narration, folder 814, FZ Papers, AMPAS.

17. Anna Seghers to FZ, 3 September 1945, box 60, folder 819, FZ Papers, AMPAS. See also Leonard Quart, "There Were Good Germans: Fred Zinnemann's *The Seventh Cross* (1944)," in *The Films of Fred Zinnemann*, ed. Arthur Nolletti, Jr. (Albany: State University of New York Press, 1999), 73.

18. Smyth (2006).

19. Dana Polan, *Power and Paranoia: History, Narrative and the American Cinema, 1940–1950* (New York: Columbia University Press, 1986) and William Graebner, *The Age of Doubt: American Thought and Culture in the 1940s* (New York: Waveland Press, 1991).

20. Margaret Collins Weitz, *Sisters in the Resistance* (New York: John Wiley, 1995), 11.

21. Helen Deutsch, 10 April 1944, narration, box 60, folder 814, was an expansion of a more abbreviated version dating from MGM Script Collection, Helen Deutsch, 22 October 1943, complete script. Helen Deutsch, 26 April 1943, first pink script, folder 683, 4 June 1943, inserted version has earlier version of full narration. Evidently this was a trial version and as drafts increased and Zinnemann got involved with production, expanded in length.

22. Some reviewers of the film argued that Hollywood had dissolved Seghers's political energy (*Time*, 18 September 1944), yet Seghers herself argued that she had deliberately written a fairly non-political novel in order to breach the American market.

23. Alexander Stephan, "Ein Exilroman als Bestseller," in *Exitforschung: Ein Internationales Jahrbuch* 3 (1985): 239–47.

24. Frank Whitbeck, Trailer of *The Seventh Cross*, 4 May 1944, 4 pp., box 60, folder 816, FZ Papers, AMPAS, with note, "Freddie: never show trailer scripts to directors—but you are Zinnemann. F [Whitbeck]."

25. FZ to Pandro Berman, 28 July 1943, box 60, folder 820, FZ Papers, AMPAS.

26. Ibid.

27. FZ, storyboard sketches, box 61, folder 825, FZ Papers, AMPAS.

28. FZ, "Notes for Revision Attached to Script," 3 June 1943, 6 July 1943, 4 pp., MGM Script Collection, folder 684, AMPAS.

29. See Anthony Williams, "Resistance and Opposition Amongst Germans," in *Resistance in Europe: 1939–1945*, eds. Stephen Hawes and Ralph White (Harmondsworth: Penguin Books, 1976), 135–69; Eve Rosenhaft, *Beating the Fascists? The German Communists and Political Violence* (Cambridge: Cambridge University Press, 1983); Conan Fischer, *The German Communists and the Rise of Nazism* (London: Palgrave, 1991); for more general studies of German resistance, see Francis Nicosia and Lawrence Stokes, eds., *Germans Against Nazism: Nonconformity, Opposition and Resistance in the Third Reich* (Oxford: Oxford University Press, 1990); Klemens von Klemperer, *German Resistance Against Hitler: The Search For Allies Abroad, 1938–45* (Oxford: Clarendon Press, 1994); Michael Thomsett, *The German Opposition to Hitler: The Resistance, the Underground, Assassination Plots 1938–45* (Jefferson, NC: McFarland & Co., 1997).

30. As a director of shorts, Zinnemann often conceived his shots in a series of thumbnail sketches. His sketches for *The Seventh Cross* are the most extensive extant sketches for any of his features, and testify to his interest in using repeated off-center close-ups, canted angles, and rhythmic cutting (see box 60, folder 825, FZ Papers, AMPAS).

31. FZ, "Notes for Revision Attached to Script," 3 June 1943, 6 July 1943, 4 pp., MGM Script Collection, folder 684, AMPAS.

32. FZ, notes, annotated script, 22 October 1943, 108, box 60, folder 811, FZ Papers, AMPAS.

33. FZ to Michael Buckley, quoted in Miller, 86. See also Zinnemann (1992), 52.

34. George Character Outline, 2 pp., box 60, folder 820, FZ Papers, AMPAS.

35. FZ to Pandro Berman, 28 July 1943, box 60, folder 820, FZ Papers, AMPAS.

36. Annotated script, 81.

37. FZ, annotations on 22 October 1943 script, 115, "from a long distance—at other end of room, very LS," box 6, folder 811, FZ Papers, AMPAS.

38. Ibid., annotations, opposite 114.

39. Helen Deutsch, 22 October 1943, complete script, 139–42, with FZ's notes, MGM Script Collection, AMPAS.

40. Helen Deutsch, 10 April 1944, narration, folder box 60, 814, FZ Papers, AMPAS.

41. FZ, Memo to Natalie Angel, 21 August 1943, box 60, folder 820, FZ Papers, AMPAS.

42. Hunt and Leigh: interviews with the author; Hepburn: Robert F. Hawkins, "Seen on the Italian Screen Scene: Nun's Story Unfolds Behind Closed Doors," 12 April 1958, unmarked press clipping, box 50, folder 698, FZ Papers, AMPAS; Redgrave: Redgrave (1992).

43. FZ to Natalie Angel, 21 August 1943, box 60, folder 820, FZ Papers, AMPAS.

44. FZ, notes, undated, 8 pp., 7, box 60, folder 820, FZ Papers, AMPAS.

45. Though the idea of German resistance has gained wider acceptance, during the first few decades following the war, historians largely focused on issues of collective guilt (see Peter Hoffman, *The History of the German Resistance, 1933–1945* [McGill: Queen's University Press, 1996]).

46. FZ to Pandro Berman, 22 July 1943, production notes, box 60, folder 820, FZ Papers, AMPAS.

47. George Zinnemann to FZ, 12 Sept 1944, box 1, 2004 add-ins, FZ Papers, AMPAS.

48. Howard Barnes, *New York Herald Tribune*, 29 September 1944. See also *New York Journal-American*, 29 September 1944, and *Los Angeles Herald*, 29 September 1944.

49. Crowther, *New York Times*, 1 October 1944.

50. On Hollywood's anti-fascist/anti-Nazi films, see Michael Birdwell, *Celluloid Soldiers* (New York: New York University Press, 1999) and Clayton R. Koppes and Gregory Black, *Hollywood Goes to War: How Politics, Profits and Propaganda Shaped World War II Movies* (New York: Free Press, 1987); on the blacklist and early investigations of Hollywood, see Larry Ceplair, *Inquisition in Hollywood: Politics in the Film Community, 1930–1960* (Garden City, NY: Doubleday, 1980) and Victor Navasky, *Naming Names* (New York: Viking, 1980).

51. FZ to Arthur Loew, 7 September 1949, and Loew to FZ, 9 September 1949, box 64, folder 891, FZ Papers, AMPAS.

52. See correspondence, box 60, folder 819, with General Rudolph Puchlinger and Charles Pati of MGM, 28 October–16 December 1954, FZ Papers, AMPAS. Although several retrospectives of Zinnemann's work appeared in the late 1950s, *The Seventh Cross* was not shown.

53. "Profile: André Malraux: The Veteran," *New Statesman*, 1 November 1968, 578, box 88, folder 1167, FZ Papers, AMPAS.

54. Peter Elnnon, "Private Revolutionary, Public Bourgeois," *Manchester Guardian*, 29 July 1969. See Malraux, *Anti-Memoirs* (1964; repr., New York: Holt, Rinehart, Winston, 1968) for his ambiguous understanding of fiction, myth, and history. For more recent assessments, see Isabelle de Courtivron, "The Other Malraux in Indochina," *Biography* 12, no. 1 (winter 1989): 29–42.

55. FZ to Carlo Ponti, 25 May 1967, box 83, folder 1116, FZ Papers, AMPAS.

56. FZ to Ponti, 4 January 1967, box 88, folder 1169, ibid.

57. Jean Cau, *Man's Fate*, treatment, 19 August 1966; 42 pp., box 83, folder 1114, FZ Papers, AMPAS; John McGrath, "Man's Fate: Notes on Outline of Action," 8 March 1967, box 83, folder 1116, FZ Papers, AMPAS.

58. Blue note in FZ's handwriting, "Cau vs. Bolt: persuade Bolt," box 88, folder 1167, FZ Papers, AMPAS.

59. Robert Bolt to FZ, 16 October 1966; 3 pp. letter to Bolt from FZ says he cannot direct a non-Indian actor as Gandhi, 18 October 1966, both box 79, folder 1051, FZ Papers, AMPAS.

60. Undated fragment of letter, Han Suyin (hereafter HS), to Russell Thacher, box 88, folder 1169, FZ Papers, AMPAS.

61. HS to FZ, 26 March 1968, 3pp, 2, box 95, folder 1240, FZ Papers, AMPAS.

62. HS to FZ, 16 September 1969, box 95, folder 1240, FZ Papers, AMPAS.

63. HS, *Man's Fate*, first draft script, 17 May 1968, box 85, folder 1130, FZ Papers, AMPAS.

64. FZ annotations, *Man's Fate*, final script, 8 December 1968, back of p. 16, box 86, folder 1137, FZ Papers, AMPAS.

65. HS, *Man's Fate*, final script, 8 December 1968, not in blue, back of p. 1.

66. Zinnemann notes, Hotel Merlin Berhad stationery, Kuala Lumpur, Sept 8, 1968, box 94, folder 1233, FZ Papers, AMPAS. See also green notes, "Kyo group wants to improve the human condition. Explain what means Human condition," box 94, folder 1231, FZ Papers, AMPAS.

67. FZ, script notes, undated, box 94, folder 1231, FZ Papers, AMPAS.

68. HS, *Man's Fate*, first treatment, 31 January 1968, 12, box 83, folder 1118, FZ Papers, AMPAS.

69. FZ to Russell Thacher, 20 June 1967; he met with Malraux on June 15, 3pp., 2, box 88, folder 1169, FZ Papers, AMPAS.

70. FZ to Russ Thacher, 18 November 1967, box 95, folder 1240, FZ Papers, AMPAS.

71. HS to FZ, 16 February 1968, box 95, folder 1240, FZ Papers, AMPAS.

72. FZ notes on Hotel Merlin Berhad stationery, Kuala Lumpur, 8 September 1968, box 98, folder 1233, FZ Papers, AMPAS.

73. FZ, script notes, box 94, folder 1233, FZ Papers, AMPAS.

74. Roger Davis to FZ, 24 May 1968, box 88, folder 1170, FZ Papers, AMPAS.

75. FZ to William Macomber, Assistant Secretary of State for Congressional Relations, 22 January 1968, box 88, folder 1170, FZ Papers, AMPAS.

76. André Malraux to Huang Chen, China's ambassador in France, 27 March 1968, box 89, folder 1174, FZ Papers.

77. HS to FZ, 8 August 1968, box 95, folder 1240, FZ Papers.

78. HS to FZ, 16 September 1969, box 95, folder 1240, FZ Papers.

79. For full budgetary breakdown, see production budget, 27 October 1969, starting date 24 November 1969, finishing 1 May 1970, box 87, folder 1150, FZ Papers, AMPAS.

80. "Fate Steps in on Fred Zinnemann," *Daily Mirror*, 24 November 1969, 15; "No Borehamwood Sale; MGM Ends *Fate*," *Variety*, 25 November 1969.

81. FZ to André Malraux, 10 December 1969, box 89, folder 1174, FZ Papers, AMPAS.

82. "*A Man for All Seasons* Gets Four Oscars," *Times*, 12 April 1967; Leo Armati, "Oscars Scoop For Britain," *Evening Standard*, 11 April 1967; Nadine Edwards, "Is Oscar

Becoming a British Subject?," *Hollywood Citizen-News-Valley Times*, 11 April 11 1967, 13, AA section.

83. De Gaulle's first veto came on 14 January 1963 and the debate continued until his death. See Nesta Roberts, "Emphatic No by de Gaulle," *Manchester Guardian*, 28 November 1967; "Nation: Once More de Gaulle v. Britain," *Time*, 28 February 1969. Britain finally obtained membership in the EEC in January 1973 ("Just a Normal Winter's Day in Dover," *Times*, 2 January 1973).

84. "Fred Zinnemann, Edward Fox, and *Day of the Jackal*," *International Herald Tribune*, 5–6 August 1972; "*The Day of the Jackal*," *Independent Film Journal* 71, no. 13 (28 May 1973).

85. "Caveat for the General," *Time*, 23 August 1971.

86. For more histories of the OAS, see Vincent Quivy, *Les Soldats perdus: Des anciens de L'OAS racontent* (Paris: Seuil, 2003); Alexander Harrison, et al., *Le défi à de Gaulle: L'OAS et la contre-révolution en Algérie 1954–1962* (Paris: Harmattan, 2008); Jean-Bernard Ramon, *L'OAS et ses appuis internationaix: Alliés, influences et manipulations extérieures* (Paris: Atelier Folfer, 2009); Jean-Pax Mefret, Jusqu'au bout de l'Algérie francaise: Bastien-Thiry (Paris: Pygmalion, 2007). See also Louis Vallon, *L'Anti de Gaulle* (Paris: Seuil, 1969).

87. Régis Debray, *Charles de Gaulle: Futurist of the Nation* (London: Verso, 1994), vii. For more on the centrality of fascism in French political life, see Zeev Sternhell, *Neither Right Nor Left: Fascist Ideology in France* (Berkeley: University of California Press, 1986); Pierre Milza, *Fascisme francais passé et present* (Paris: Flammarion, 1987); Robert Soury, *French Fascism: The First Wave, 1924–1933* (New Haven: Yale University Press, 1986) and *French Fascism: The Second Wave, 1933–1939* (New Haven: Yale University Press, 1999); Ernst Nolte, *Three Faces of Fascism: Action francaise, Italian Fascism, and National Socialism* (London: Weidenfeld & Nicholson, 1965).

88. Frederick Forsyth, "Experimental lay-out of a possible format for the first ten minutes of the film," January 1971, 2–4, box 4, folder 49, FZ Papers, AMPAS.

89. Kenneth Ross, *The Day of the Jackal*, July through October 1971, box 5, folder 55, FZ Papers, AMPAS.

90. FZ to Sid Payne, 20 March 1973, box 13, folder 149, FZ Papers, AMPAS.

91. First uttered by Labor MP George Wigg in 1949, alleging that it was Winston Churchill's attitude to all foreigners. This was an odd allegation, given that Churchill was half-American (*Hansard*, House of Commons, Fifth Series, vol. 467, col. 2845).

92. Frederick Forsyth, "Experimental lay-out of a possible format for the first ten minutes of the film," January 1971, 10, box 4, folder 49, FZ Papers, AMPAS.

93. In his editing notes, Zinnemann mentions Robert Walker's (Bruno) performance in *Strangers on a Train* (1950) as a key to the Jackal's genial menace.

94. "Edward Fox is the Jackal," *CinemaTV Today*, 11 March 1972, 1, 7; Ken Eastaugh, "Better than Bond, More Crafty than Callan," *Sun*, 10 April 1972; Penelope Gilliatt, *The Day of the Jackal*, *New Yorker*, 2 June 1973, 66–67, Carole Cass, "Anti de Gaulle Plot on Film," *Richmond Times Dispatch*, 20 May 1973; Cecil Wilson, "The

Day the Fox Triumphed as the Jackal," *Daily Mail*, 15 June 1973; Bridget Byrne, "*The Day of the Jackal*: The Hunter and the Hunted," *Los Angeles Herald-Examiner*, 18 May 1973, B4.

95. Frederick Forsyth, "Experimental lay-out of a possible format for the first ten minutes of the film," January 1971, 12, box 4, folder 49, FZ Papers, AMPAS; Kenneth Ross, *The Day of the Jackal*, July through October 1971, 9, 17, box 5, folder 55, FZ Papers, AMPAS.

96. Zinnemann added the sequence of Lebel at home with his pigeons, soiled trousers, and the sneers from the Elysée Palace officials (see Forsyth script which does not include this: Forsyth, first draft treatment, 19 May 1971, box 4, folder 52, FZ Papers, AMPAS).

97. Box 4, folder 50, novel uncorrected proof copy—annotated. FZ copy, note on cover, "provisional date 8thJune 1971," "FZ. Feb 1971 LA," in pencil, 81–82.

98. See opposite 159, insert photograph, *The Day of the Jackal*, director's script, box 7, folder 71, FZ Papers, AMPAS.

99. *Day of the Jackal* script, p. 160, insert unmarked French news clipping, box 7, folder 71, FZ Papers, AMPAS.

100. Ibid., 30–31.

101. Julien Derode to FZ, 18 June 1971, box 12, folder 119, FZ Papers, AMPAS.

102. Julien Derode to David Deutsch, 7 July 1971, box 13, folder 149, FZ Papers, AMPAS.

103. See Worldwide Box Office Figures, 21 November 1973, box 8, folder 81, FZ Papers, AMPAS.

104. Claude Garson, "Chacal," *L'Aurore*, 17 September 1973; R. B. "Chacal," *Le Point*, no. 51 (10 September 1973): 75; Francoise Roubicek, "Chacal . . . objectif de Gaulle," *Presse-Ocean*, 12 November 1973.

105. FZ to Julien Derode, 4 April 1973, box 12, folder 119, FZ Papers, AMPAS.

106. Murf, "*The Day of the Jackal*," *Variety*, 2 May 1973, 6.

107. According to *Variety*, *The Day of the Jackal* grossed a respectable $8.53 million in the U.S. (*Variety Annual*, 9 January 1974).

108. FZ, notes on uncorrected proof of novel, 50–51, 147–48, 155, 158. See also box 12, folder 126, FZ Papers, AMPAS, for more editing notes. Grid notes at base of green page: "clocks, 1:20, 3:20, 3:40, 3.58, 3:59."

109. FZ, "First Outline Treatment for Factual Principles of *Jackal*," Forsyth, January 1971, Paris, 10 pp., 1, box 4, folder 48, FZ Papers, AMPAS.

110. Murf, "*The Day of the Jackal*," *Variety*, 2 May 1973, 6.

111. Ken Eastaugh, "Better than Bond, More Crafty than Callan," *Sun*, 10 April 1972, 1.

112. FZ, large editing notebook, cutting notes, 1 December 1972, box 12, folder 127, FZ Papers, AMPAS.

113. David Sterritt, "*Day of the Jackal*: Screen Chiller," *Christian Science Monitor*, 1 June 1973, 9. See also Louise Sweeney, "Fred Zinnemann: Profile," *Christian Science Monitor*, 22 June 1973, 9.

Chapter Two

1. Albert Camus, *Letters to a German Friend*, in *Resistance, Rebellion, and Death* (London: Hamish Hamilton, 1964), 16.

2. FZ, interview for *Politiken*, Sunday, 19 February 1978, translated transcript, box 39, folder 515, FZ Papers, AMPAS.

3. Zinnemann (1992), 54.

4. Jeannette Robbins, "Personal Inquiry Department of the American Jewish Joint Distribution Committee Inc. to FZ," 2 November 1945; Gilson Blake, Assistant Chief Special Project Unit, Department of State, to FZ, 26 November 1945, Correspondence 1945, folder 119, FZ Papers, AMPAS. FZ's repeated, failed efforts to join the OSS are also documented in his archive.

5. FZ documented his parents' fates with Yad Vashem, 4–5 August 1984, Shoah Database of Victims' Names, http://www.yadvashem.org/.

6. Dorothy Macardle, *Children of Europe: A Study of Children of Liberated Countries, Their War-Time Experiences, Their Reactions, and Their Needs—with a Note on Germany* (1949; repr., Boston: Beacon Press, 1951), 292.

7. Pieter Lagrou, *The Legacy of Nazi Occupation* (Cambridge: Cambridge University Press, 2000), 81–82; Michael Marrus, *The Unwanted: European Refugees in the Twentieth Century* (Oxford: Oxford University Press, 1985), 296–345.

8. Statistics, 20 January 1947, UNRRA research, folder 800, FZ Papers, AMPAS.

9. Mark Wyman, *DP. Europe's Displaced Persons, 1945– 1951* (1989; repr., Ithaca: Cornell University Press, 1998), 131–55, 201–204.

10. Macardle, 231, 305.

11. Wyman, 93. See also Tara Zahra, *Reconstructing Europe's Families after World War II* (Cambridge: Harvard University Press, 2011).

12. Macardle, 296.

13. "War Crimes: 'It was only 2,000,000,'" *Time*, 14 April 1947, clipping, box 58, folder 796, FZ Papers.

14. "Lidice Women Face Accused As Trial Opens," 27 March (1946), AP clipping, box 58, folder 796, FZ Papers. For contemporaneous responses, see Edna St. Vincent Millay, *The Murder of Lidice* (New York: Harper & Bros., 1942) and especially Zena Irma Trinka, *A Little Village Called Lidice: Story of the Return of the Women and Children of Lidice* (Lidgerwood, ND: International Book Publishers, 1947); *Lidice* (London: George Allen & Unwin, 1944); for histories, see J. F. N. Bradley, *Lidice, Sacrificial Village* (London: Ballantine Books, 1972); Ivan Ciganek, *Lidice* (Prague: Orbis Press Agency, 1982); Eduard Stehlík, *Lidice: The Story of a Czech Village*, trans. Petr Kurfürst (Prague: Kejrová, 2004).

15. Macardle, 234–35.

16. Ruth S. Fede, "Children at Lindenfels Center Recall Nazi Horror," unmarked press clipping, box 58, folder 796, FZ Papers, AMPAS.

17. Unmarked German press clipping, Nurnberg, 14 April, UP, folder 796, FZ Papers, AMPAS.

18. I. A. R. Wylie, "Returning Europe's Kidnapped Children," *Ladies' Home Journal*, October 1946, 22–23, 254–57; Wyman, 88.

19. Macardle, 301–303.

20. Wyman, 186–90. Thirty-nine other countries contributed to the funding of the UNRRA camps. By 1947, when the IRO took over, only fifteen nations were willing to feed the DPs (Kathryn Hulme, *The Wild Place* [London: F. Muller, 1954], 143).

21. Hulme (1954), 159.

22. Thérèse Bonney, *Europe's Children: 1939–1943* (New York: Thérèse Bonney, 1944).

23. Jacob Riis, *How the Other Half Lives* (1890; repr., London: Penguin, 1997); Kate Sampsell-Willmann and Alan Trachtenberg, *Lewis Hine as Social Critic* (Jackson: University Press of Mississippi, 2009).

24. Bosley Crowther, "From The War's Fringe: *Marie-Louise* (1945)," *New York Times*, 13 November 1945.

25. Lazar Wechsler (hereafter LW) to FZ, 13 September 1946, box 57, folder 779; LW to FZ, 7 October 1946, box 57, folder 779, FZ Papers, AMPAS.

26. Gerd Gemunden, "In the Ruins of Berlin: A Foreign Affair," in *German Postwar Films*, eds. Wilfried Wilms and William Rasch (London: Palgrave Macmillan, 2008), 112–13.

27. Wilder, 40.

28. FZ to LW, 12 July 1946; LW to FZ, 19 July 1946, all box 57, folder 779, FZ Papers.

29. Peter Viertel (hereafter PV) to FZ, 12 December 1946, p. 2, ibid.

30. Arthur Loew to LW, 21 October 1946, and LW to FZ, 23 October 1946, box 57, folder 779, FZ Papers.

31. Tim Zinnemann, interview with the author, 10 June 2010.

32. PV to FZ, 12 December 1946, box 57, folder 779, FZ Papers. Brian C. Etheridge has also examined this part of *The Search*'s production history, but argues, unlike me, that Zinnemann's eventual rejection of Viertel's script was effectively an ideological capitulation to anti-communist, pro-American, cold war consensus (see Brian C. Etheridge, "In Search of Germans: Contested Germany in the Production of *The Search*," *Journal of Popular Film and Television* 34, no. 1 [April 2006]: 34–45).

33. PV to FZ, 12 December 1946, ibid.

34. Atina Grossman, *Jews, Germans, and Allies: Close Encounters in Occupied Germany* (Princeton: Princeton University Press, 2007), 32–41.

35. Grossman, 38; Bourke-White, *Dear Fatherland, Rest Quietly: A Report on the Collapse of Hitler's 'Thousand Years'* (1946), 5.

36. On deprivations of German children, see Grossman, 30–31; Macardle, 285–92; Victor Gollancz, *In Darkest Germany* (London: Victor Gollancz, 1947); on the Harrison Report, see Wyman, 131–37; Grossman, 138–39. Hulme writes at length about the army's callous treatment of Polish DPs in Wildflecken, 1954: 100–104.

37. *Report of Earl Harrison*, Department of State *Bulletin* 13 (30 September 1945): 456–63 (reprinted *New York Times*, 30 September 1945); Grossman, 139. See also Hulme, 163.

38. PV, Outline, 19 November 1946, box 57, folder 768, FZ Papers, AMPAS. Viertel acknowledges that director Leopold Lindtberg (*Marie-Louise*) also had a hand in developing the early stages of the child story, PV to FZ, 12 December 1946, FZ Papers, AMPAS.

39. PV to LW, 22 June 1946, 4pp, box 57, folder 779, FZ Papers, AMPAS. Though Tara Zahra (2011) has argued Czechoslovakia's predominantly Catholic populace made it a comfortable, non-Jewish state in which the postwar West could imagine the rebuilt Europe, Viertel and Zinnemann were also drawn to the unique multi-ethnic makeup of the prewar Czech state and its democratic constitution. See also Camus, 16.

40. PV, Outline, 8, ibid.

41. PV to LW, 22 June 1946, ibid.

42. Vroman, 88–89.

43. Marc Silberman, "What's New? Allegorical Representations of Renewal in DEFA's Youth Films, 1946–1949," in *German Postwar Films*, eds. Wilms and Rasch (London: Palgrave Macmillan, 2008), 93–108.

44. FZ may have been thinking of Robert Lynen's work in connection with his plans for a resistance epic. The young Lynen became a prominent member of the Alliance network led by Marie Madeleine Fourcade, was captured and interned by the Gestapo before being shot in Karlsruhe, April 1, 1944.

45. PV to FZ, 12 December 1946, p. 2, box 57, folder 779, FZ Papers, AMPAS.

46. FZ to PV, 2 December 1946, box 57, folder 779, *The Search*, FZ Papers, AMPAS.

47. Ibid.

48. See Billy Wilder, "The Wilder Memorandum," in *The Americanization of Germany, 1945–1949* ed. Ralph Willett (London: Routledge, 1989), 40–44, and Gerd Gemunden, "In the Ruins of Berlin: *A Foreign Affair*," in *German Postwar Films*, eds. Wilms and Rasch (London: Palgrave Macmillan, 2008), 109–124.

49. LW to FZ, 19 November 1946, box 57, folder 779, FZ Papers, AMPAS.

50. PV to FZ, 25 November 1946, ibid.

51. Bonney evidently had to get FZ in Germany by saying he was a documentarian, and "US correspondent—Praesens Film." See HHQ Command, 26 March 1947, signed by Flo Nicholson, box 57, folder 780, FZ Papers, AMPAS.

52. Therese Bonney, "Report Re: Film: War and Children to Information Control Division," Berlin, 18 December 1946, 2 pp., box 57, folder 779, FZ Papers, AMPAS.

53. William Wells to Richard Mokler, 30 December 1946, box 57, folder 779, FZ Papers, AMPAS. Zinnemann was actually born in Poland, but throughout his life identified himself as Viennese, where he grew up with his younger brother George and other Zinnemann and Feiwel relatives.

54. "Religion: Come and Follow Me . . . ," *Time*, 15 December 1947, 31–32, on Albert Schweitzer, box 58, folder 796, FZ Papers, AMPAS.

55. FZ to Arthur Loew, 18 February 1947, box 57, folder 779, FZ Papers, AMPAS.

56. FZ, interviews and transcribed oral testimonies (1947), box 59, folder 801, FZ Papers, AMPAS.

57. "Eye-Witness Account of a German Action," in Sambor, Poland, April 1943, 17 pp, typed, box 58, folder 795, FZ Papers, AMPAS.

58. Annotations on *Search* script, box 57, folder 770, FZ Papers, AMPAS.

59. UNRRA Report, 2 June 1946, box 59, folder 801, FZ Papers, AMPAS.

60. Macardle, 270.

61. See Robert Shandley, *Rubble Films: German Cinema in the Shadow of the Third Reich* (Philadelphia: Temple University Press, 2001) and Marc Silberman, 94–98.

62. Constantin Parvelescu, "The Continent in Ruins and Its Redeeming Orphans: Géza Radványi and Béla Balázs's *Somewhere in Europe* and the Rebuilding of the Post-War Polis," *Central Europe* 10, no. 1 (May 2012): 55–76.

63. FZ to LW, 2 December 1946, box 57, folder 779, FZ Papers, AMPAS.

64. Ibid.

65. PV to FZ, December 1946, box 57, folder 779, ibid.

66. "Fred Zinnemann Talking with Gene Phillips" (1973) reprinted in Miller, ed., 43.

67. PV to FZ, 12 December 1946, box 57, folder 779, FZ Papers, AMPAS.

68. FZ to Arthur Loew, 18 February 1947, box 57, folder 780, FZ Papers, AMPAS.

69. FZ to Abe Lastfogel, 24 January 1947, ibid.

70. *Variety*, 12 March 1947.

71. FZ to PV, 3 April 1947, 4 pp., FZ Papers, AMPAS.

72. FZ to William Wells, 5 April 1947, 2 pp., ibid.

73. Lazar Wechsler's son David, whose subsequent novel about a Swiss war orphans' home became the basis of *The Village* (Praesens, 1953), was credited as a co-writer, but existing production material hardly mentions him, and the producer always referred to it as "Mr. Schweizer's script."

74. FZ to LW, 11 March 1947, box 57, folder 780, FZ Papers.

75. FZ to LW, Davos, 4 March 1947, 4 pp., ibid.

76. FZ to Gene Phillips (1973), reprinted in Miller, 43.

77. The text was typed up separately for commentary (typescript of voice-over narration, 14 January 1948, 3pp, box 57, folder 771, FZ Papers, AMPAS).

78. Schweizer, et al., *The Search* (1947), Incomplete Script, "Additional Pages," box 57, folder 770, FZ Papers.

79. Paul Thompson, *Oral History* (Oxford: Oxford University Press, 1978).

80. Paul Jarrico was later hired to edit the opening voice-overs and dialogue, but the exposition was largely unchanged (Paul Jarrico, 16 January 1948, box 57, folder 772).

81. Schweizer, et al., *The Search*, Incomplete Script (1947), 1–4, box 57, folder 770, FZ Papers.

82. Schweizer, et al., *The Search* (1947), 82, box 16, folder 4, Montgomery Clift Papers, New York Library for the Performing Arts.

83. Eileen Blackey (UNRRA Child Welfare Chief, Paris) to FZ, undated, box 57, folder 779, FZ Papers.

84. Mutual Undertaking Between UNRRA and Praesens Films, 4 June 1947, box 57, folder 779, FZ Papers.

85. Schweizer, et al., *The Search*, Incomplete Script (1947), Incomplete Script, 12, box 57, folder 770, FZ Papers.

86. Dialogue and cutting continuity, 16 February 1948, 212pp, 11, box 59, folder 807, FZ Papers, AMPAS.

87. De Sica's first postwar neorealist film depicts the treatment of Italian children all boys) convicted of petty crimes. Starring child actors, the film is set mainly inside a juvenile prison. Unlike *The Search*, there is no international presence (only American GIs) and the narrative focuses entirely on Italy's postwar "problem."

88. *UNRRA Newsletter*, no. 6, September 1945, box 59, folder 800, FZ Papers; Macardle, 234.

89. Schweizer, et al., *The Search*, Incomplete script (1947), 18, box 57, folder 770, FZ Papers.

90. The educated classes of Czechoslovakia, particularly those in Prague and Brno, were specifically targeted throughout the occupation, with vicious raids on the universities in November 1939 (Macardle, 40–42).

91. Schweizer, et al., *The Search*, Incomplete screenplay (1947), 28, box 57, folder 770, FZ Papers, AMPAS.

92. Schweizer, et al., *The European Children* (1947), 126, box 16, folder 4, Montgomery Clift Collection, New York Library for the Performing Arts.

93. Ibid., 124, 154.

94. Ibid., 184, see FZ and Schweizer's notes on necessity of camera following Karel and imitating his movements.

95. Eileen Blackey, "Children Have Forgotten the Czech Language," *UNRRA Newsletter*, no. 9 (December 1945), 9 pp., box 59, folder 800, FZ Papers.

96. Ibid.

97. Grossmann, 331–32, 183–84.

98. Macardle, 297, 301. In 1943, it was estimated that 40 million European children were starving.

99. FZ, "Notes on Interview with John Troniak," Regensburg, box 59, folder 801, FZ Papers, AMPAS.

100. FZ, Annotations, Excerpts from Report of John Troniak, 3 December 1946, box 59, folder 801, FZ Papers, AMPAS.

101. Macardle, 58–59.

102. Jewish Agency for Palestine Child and Youth Immigration Bureau records, box 58, folder 795, FZ Papers, AMPAS.

103. Allan Zullo and Mara Bovsun, *Survivors: True Stories of Children in the Holocaust* (New York: Scholastic, 2004), 46, 82, 180.

104. Zinnemann (1992), 8.

105. Wechsler to FZ, 30 June 1947, 2 pp., box 57, folder 780, FZ Papers, AMPAS.

106. Paul Jarrico, "Re-Actions to Second Treatment, 10 June 1947, ibid.

107. LW to Jarrico, 30 June 1947; LW, comments on Jarrico's script, 30 June 1947, 2 pp., box 57, folder 780, ibid; LW to FZ, 2 July 1947, box 57, folder 782, ibid.

108. FZ to LW, 2 July 1947, box 57, folder 782, ibid.

109. For instance, LW to FZ, 5 August 1947, box 57, folder 782; FZ to Wechsler, 8 August 1947, box 57, folder 782, ibid.

110. FZ to LW, 8 August 1947, box 57, folder 782, ibid.

111. LW, "Notes on Mr. Zinnemann's alteration to the dialog," 4 pp., 17 September 1947; Wechsler to FZ, 5 August 1947, both box 57, folder 782, FZ Papers, AMPAS.

112. LW to Montgomery Clift, 1 September 1947, and LW, "Re: Mr. Clift's Suggestions," 8 September 1947, 3 pp., both box 57, folder 782, ibid.

113. Montgomery Clift to FZ, undated, box 102, folder 41, FZ Papers, AMPAS. Shortly after making *The Search*, he approached Irwin Shaw with the idea of filming *The Young Lions* as an independent production with Clift and Marlon Brando. Shaw's price was too high and eventually Twentieth Century-Fox made the film in 1958 (see *Young Lions*, Correspondence, box 95, folder 1322, FZ Papers, AMPAS).

114. FZ to Floyd Hendrickson (MGM), 12 September 1947, box 57, folder 782, FZ Papers, AMPAS.

115. TZ, interview with the author, June 2010.

116. See "Treatment by Richard Schweizer" (May 1947), 19, box 16, folder 1, Montgomery Clift Papers, New York Library for the Performing Arts.

117. Hulme (1954), 131, 170–71, 191.

118. Ivan Jandl to FZ, letters, box 58, folder 790, FZ Papers; see also FZ to Margaret Herrick, 18 August 1949, box 57, folder 782, FZ Papers, AMPAS.

119. The decision in favor of the government ended the studios' abilities to block book films and maintain a vertically integrated production, distribution, and exhibition system. Costs went up, and studios were forced to make films abroad where access to frozen assets enabled the system to continue in some measure. Nevertheless, fewer and fewer films were made following the decision.

120. Unmarked newspaper advertisement for *The Search*, 4 March 1948, box 57, folder 775, FZ Papers, AMPAS: "In 23 years MGM has produced only seven pictures abroad": *Ben-Hur* (1925), *White Shadows in the South Seas* (1928), *Trader Horn* (1931), *A Yank at Oxford* (1938), *The Citadel* (1938), *Goodbye, Mr. Chips* (1939), and *The Search*.

121. Ibid.

122. Post-Academy Award publicity does feature the faces of Clift, Corey, MacMahon, Novotna, and Jandl.

123. Unmarked photograph, *Life* (1948), box 57, folder 775, FZ Papers, AMPAS.

124. Circular, Manila, UNAC Drive Closing Benefit Premiere of film 17 August 1948, unmarked clipping, ibid.

125. Anon., "Hollywood Looks at Waifs in Germany," *New York PM*, 10–11, ibid.

126. Jean Benoit-Levy, Executive Director UN Film Board to staff of Department of Public Information, 3 May 1948, ibid.

127. Thomas Pryor, "Epic of Europe's Lost Children: History of *The Search*," *New York Times*, 14 March 1948, box 57, folder 776, FZ Papers, AMPAS.

128. The Story of *The Search* by Fred Zinnemann in *Screenwriter* 4, no. 2 (August 1948): 12–13, 30.

129. Bosley Crowther, "*The Search*," *New York Times*, 24 March 1948, box 57, folder 776, FZ Papers.

130. "*The Search* No. 2 on 1948 Ten Best List," *Film Daily*, 2 December 1948; Archer Winsten, "Movies," unmarked press clipping; Alton Cook, "*The Search*," *New York World-Telegram*, 30 December 1948, 8; all clippings box 57, folder 776, FZ Papers, AMPAS.

131. John Beaufort, "*The Search* Puts Accent on Realism: Movie Delves into Plight of DPs and Reaffirms Faith in Humanity," *Christian Science Monitor*, 26 July 1948; Anon., "*The Search*," *Box Office*, 9 October 1948; "*The Search*," *Kansas City (MO) Star*, 21 November 1948; "The New Pictures: *The Search*," *Time*, 29 March 1948; Anon., "A Noble Purpose in *The Search*," *Life*, 5 April 1948; Thomas Prior, "Epic of Europe's Lost Children," *New York Times*, 14 March 1948; all clippings box 57, folder 775, FZ Papers, AMPAS.

132. Jay Carmody, "New Film Directors Climb to Top-Flight Positions," *Washington Star*, 31 August 1948, clipping, box 57, folder 776, FZ Papers, AMPAS.

133. FZ, *Sabra*, notebook D, "Jerusalem," box 96, folder 1260, FZ Papers, AMPAS.

134. FZ, foreword and script notes, undated, box 96, folder 1261, FZ Papers, AMPAS.

135. FZ, *Sabra*, notebook A, "Start through Galil," 1, unproduced films, box 96, folder 1260, FZ Papers, AMPAS: "[T]he Arab farmer who doesn't know any better, deep down needs the same thing as the Jew: progress, human dignity as an individual, a minimum standard of living, land, a clean house, education. But over 2,000 years he has been so oppressed that he has forgotten his needs."

136. Thorold Dickinson to FZ, 5 August 1958, box 98, folder 1294, FZ Papers, AMPAS.

137. See box 98, folder 1294 and 1295, FZ Papers, AMPAS. See especially Luther Burdick, "The Terrorists," treatment for "UN Peace-Keeping Observer Corps, Kashmir—Film Project," 1964–65, 89 pp. FZ's annotations indicate he saw either Robert Mitchum or Peter Finch as a possibility for the UN peacekeeper who gets Muslim and Hindu extremists to work together.

138. Thorold Dickinson to FZ, 5 August 1958, box 98, folder 1294, FZ Papers, AMPAS.

139. FZ to Thorold Dickinson, 22 August 1958, FZ Papers, AMPAS.

140. See Silberman and Gemunden.

Chapter Three

1. FZ to Frank Thompson, 15 January 1954, box 1, item 15, FZ Papers, BFI, London.

2. Malraux (1933), 211.

3. FZ, copy contract with Stanley Kramer Productions, 8 February 1951, $60,000 per picture and 5 percent of profits, box 33, folder 427, FZ Papers, AMPAS.

4. FZ (1992), 85.

5. *High Noon* eventually cost $786,600. Cooper was paid $100,000, with Zinnemann getting just under $75,000 and 5 percent of the profits (folder 429, FZ Papers, AMPAS).

6. FZ (1992), 96.

7. See Sarris, *The American Cinema: Directors and Directions, 1929–1968* (New York: E. P. Dutton, 1968); James Silke, "Zinnemann: True or False," *Cinema* 2, no. 1 (February 1964), 15–19, 15.

8. See Robert Warshow, "Movie Chronicle: The Westerner," in *The Immediate Experience* (New York: Athenaeum, 1970), 135–54, 149. Warshow cites *The Ox-Bow Incident* (1943), *The Gunfighter* (1950), *High Noon*, and *Shane* (1953) as the major "violators" of the genre.

9. On genre, see Rick Altman, *Film/Genre* (London: BFI, 2000) and Janet Staiger, "Hybrid or Inbred: The Purity Hypothesis and Hollywood Genre History," *Film Criticism* 22, no. 1 (fall 1997), 5–20. For *High Noon*'s critical reputation in cinema studies, see Jeremy Byman, *Showdown at High Noon: Witchhunts, Critics, and the End of the Western* (Lanham, MD: Scarecrow Press, 2004).

10. See *Time* (19 January 1953): 96, which notes *Variety*'s list of top 10 box-office giants of 1952. *High Noon* is eighth at $3.4 million, ahead of *Singin' in the Rain* ($3.3 million).

11. Phillip Drummond, *High Noon* (London: BFI, 1997), 66.

12. André Bazin, "The Evolution of the Western" [1955], in *What is Cinema? Volume II*, trans. Hugh Gray (Berkeley: University of California Press, 1971), 152.

13. For a summary of *High Noon*'s mutable critical reputation, see Richard Combs, "Retrospective: *High Noon*," in *The Western Reader*, ed. Jim Kitses and Gregg Rickman (New York: Limelight, 1998), 167–72, and Byman, passim.

14. Zinnemann (1992), 108.

15. Crosby was FZ's choice to do the cinematography for *From Here to Eternity*, and though he appears in the prep off-camera shots of the crew, Columbia replaced him with the more innocuous Burnett Guffey by the time shooting began (*From Here to Eternity*, off camera stills, FZ Papers, AMPAS). Crosby later went to work for Roger Corman.

16. Zinnemann spoke out against Cecil B. DeMille's attempted coup of the liberal Joseph Mankiewicz at the Directors Guild and was appalled at the treatment Crosby received, but could do little else. Given his association with communists Paul Strand and Anna Seghers and many other far left-leaning people in Hollywood, it is curious that Zinnemann was not attacked, but no evidence exists suggesting he was under investigation by the committee. Kenneth L. Geist's biography of Joseph Mankiewics includes director H. C. Potter's account of Zinnemann appearing before an American Legion committee to clear his name of any communist taint, but incorrectly says that Zinnemann was blacklisted for two years (Kenneth Geist, *Pictures Will Talk* [New York: Scribners, 1978], 188).

17. FZ (1992), 18.

18. See Sarris (1968); Jim Kitses's *Horizons West* (London: BFI, 2004) virtually ignores Zinnemann's film except as an influence on other directors.

19. French, 43.

20. Will Wright, *Six-Guns and Society* (Berkeley: University of California Press, 1970), 57. Bazin also singles Wyler out in a list of Western film directors, stating Wyler's "gift seemed to be for anything but this genre," (Bazin, *What is Cinema? Volume II*, trans. Hugh Gray [Berkeley: University of California Press, 1971], 149).

21. Bosley Crowther, "*Rancho Notorious*," *New York Times*, 15 May 1952.

22. Florence Jacobowitz, "The Dietrich Westerns," in *The Movie Book of the Western*, eds. Ian Cameron and Douglas Pye (London: Studio Vista, 1996), 88–98.

23. Yet Ford's famous comment at a Directors Guild meeting in which Cecil B. DeMille planned to oust left-leaning chair Joseph Mankiewicz, "I'm John Ford. I make Westerns," was uttered in a Cold War context. It is during the Cold War that the Western "code" and its authors are defined.

24. Stephen J. Whitfield, *The Cultures of the Cold War* rev. ed. (Johns Hopkins University Press, 1996), 146.

25. FZ, in Paul R. Michaud, "The Lone Wolf and the Jackal," (1972), reprinted in Miller, 34.

26. Prince, "Historical Perspective and the Realist Aesthetic in *High Noon* (1952)," in *The Films of Fred Zinnemann: Critical Perspectives*, ed. Nolletti (Albany: State University Press of New York, 1999), 84

27. One of the few books FZ brought to America from his native Vienna was a copy of May's *Der Schatz im Silbersee* (1891). May's *Winnetou* series (1893) went through countless editions in Europe and was the major cultural source on the frontier experience, but has been more or less ignored in mainstream American literary and historical analysis of the West (see Tassilo Schneider, "Finding a New Heimat in the Wild West: Karl May and the German Western in the 1960s," in *Back in the Saddle Again*, eds. Roberta Pearson and Edward Buscombe [London: BFI, 1998]), 141–59 and Lutz Koepnick, "Unsettling America: German Westerns and Modernity," *Modernism/modernity* 2, no. 3 (September 1995): 1–22.

28. This is also André Bazin's point in "The Evolution of the Western," 152.

29. Michael Coyne, *The Crowded Prairie: American National Identity in the Hollywood Western* (London: I. B. Taurus, 1997), 1–2, 68–69.

30. See Philip French, *Westerns* (London: Secker & Warburg, 1977), 65–67; Bazin, "The Evolution of the Western," 149–57; Daniel Doniol-Valcroze, "Un homme marche dans la trahison," *Cahiers du cinéma* III, no. 16 (October 1952), 58–60.

31. John M. Cunningham, "The Tin Star," *Colliers*, 6 December 1947.

32. See Carl Foreman, *High Noon*, shooting script, Foreman Papers, BFI; Foreman, "Anatomy of a Classic," transcripts of four lectures at AFI, Los Angeles, 1976, Foreman Papers, BFI.

33. Drummond, 31–36. See also FZ (1992), 99–100; Donald Spoto, *Stanley Kramer* (New York: Putnam, 1978), 98–100; and Stanley Kramer with Thomas Coffey, *It's a Mad, Mad, Mad, Mad World: A Life in Hollywood* (New York: Harcourt, 1997).

34. Drummond, 19.

35. See FZ's annotated shooting script, *High Noon*, pages variously dated 30 July–7 August 1951, box 33, folder 420, FZ Papers, AMPAS.

36. See also the captions for Stanley Kramer Productions' production stills, which note that FZ is "new to six guns" (Stanley Kramer Collection 161, box 6, UCLA). Kramer's shooting script is all but unmarked and displays no evidence that the producer was involved in reconceiving the editing and structure (Stanley Kramer Collection 161, box 6 UCLA).

37. Tim Zinnemann, interview with the author, 30 March 2011.

38. Crowther, "Western Legend," *New York Times*, 5 August 1952, X. Mainstream American critics would continue to name *High Noon* as one of the all-time best Westerns, despite increasing "professional" and academic criticism (see "Shock Around the Clock," *Time*, 9 September 1957, 58).

39. "Fred Zinnemann Talking to Gene Phillips," 44.

40. See Edward Buscombe, "Inventing Monument Valley," *The Western Reader*, 114–30. While Buscombe also sees Tim O'Sullivan and W. H. Jackson's photographs as part of this grand tradition, he ignores the starkness of the photographic images and the very different qualities of the landscapes and close shots which influenced FZ and Crosby.

41. "A Guide of Virginia City: The cover of the 'pot of gold' and silver," copyright 1941 by Gerry Gould, box 33, folder 422, FZ Papers, AMPAS.

42. *High Noon* annotated shooting script, FZ Papers, AMPAS, inserted yellow sheet notes.

43. *High Noon* annotated shooting script, FZ Papers, AMPAS, esp. 5, 11, 12, 15, 21, 25, 32, 42, 47, 48, 84, 92.

44. Howard Thompson, "Directed by Zinnemann," *New York Times* (25 January 1953).

45. Otis Guernsey, Jr., "The Elusive Art of a Hollywood Director," *New York Herald Tribune*, 25 January 1953, section 4, 1.

46. *High Noon*, annotated shooting script, p. 21, FZ notes, "Simplify? Down to earth?," FZ Papers, AMPAS.

47. Zinnemann (1992), 50.

48. Frederick Jackson Turner, "The Significance of the Frontier in American History," in *Rereading Frederick Jackson Turner*, ed. John Mack Faragher (1893; repr., New York: Henry Holt, 1995), 31–60, 39. Gilles Deleuze's discussion of the Western and the movement image also enforces this sense of the long shot as the definitive element. See Marcia Landy, "The Hollywood Western, the Movement-Image, and Making History," in J. E. Smyth, ed., *Hollywood and the American Historical Film* (London: Palgrave Macmillan, 2012).

49. See, especially, p. 97 of the annotated shooting script.

50. For example, *The Vanishing American*, 1925; *Cimarron*, 1931; *Laughing Boy*, 1934; *Annie Oakley*, 1935; *Robin Hood of El Dorado*, 1937; *Destry Rides Again*, 1939; *Drums Along the Mohawk*, 1939; *Arizona*, 1940; *Belle Starr*, 1941; *Duel in the Sun*, 1946; *Rancho Notorious*, 1950.

51. For a sample of critic Bosley Crowther's contempt for Westerns which step outside too many boundaries, see Crowther, "*Duel in the Sun:* Selznick's Lavish Western That Stars Jennifer Jones, Gregory Peck, Opens at Loew's Theatres," *New York Times*, May 8, 1947.

52. Julie Des Jardins, *Women and the Historical Profession in America* (Chapel Hill: University of North Carolina Press, 2003), 101–17.

53. Smyth, *Edna Ferber's Hollywood: American Fictions of Gender, Race, and History* (Austin: University of Texas Press, 2009), 114–27, 191–200.

54. Ibid., 223.

55. See Foreman, *High Noon* script, in *Film Scripts Two*, eds. P. Garrett, O. B. Hardison, Jr., and Jane R. Gelfman (New York: Meredith, 1971). Foreman's feminism would recur again when he scripted *Guns of Navarone* (1961), replacing two of the original all-male cast with female resistance fighters, played by Gia Scala and Irene Papas.

56. Joanna E. Rapf, "Myth, Ideology, and Feminism in *High Noon*," *Journal of Popular Culture* 23, no. 4 (spring 1990): 75–80; Gwendolyn Audrey Foster, "Women in *High Noon*: A Metanarrative of Difference," *Film Criticism* 18, no. 1 (spring-fall 1994): 72–81.

57. Floyd Crosby to FZ, 8 February 1978, box 108, folder 42, FZ Papers, AMPAS.

58. Anne M. Butler, "Selling the Popular Myth," in *The Oxford History of the American West*, eds. Clyde Milner II, Carol A. O'Connor, and Martha A. Sandweiss (Oxford: Oxford University Press, 1994), 793–94.

59. Matthew J. Costello, "Rewriting *High Noon*," in *Hollywood's West*, eds. Rollins and O'Connor (Lexington: University Press of Kentucky, 2005), 175–197, 180. Costello argues that Zinnemann's portrait of community responsibility is undermined by subsequent films in which "the retreat into privacy . . . becomes virtuous" (184). See also Whitfield, *The Culture of the Cold War*, 2nd ed. (Johns Hopkins University Press, 1996).

60. Molly Haskell, *From Reverence to Rape: The Treatment of Women in Movies* (1977; repr., Chicago: University of Chicago Press, 1987), 271.

61. French, 67.

62. See Dee Brown, *The Gentle Tamers* (New York: Putnam, 1958); Susan Armitage and Elizabeth Jameson, eds., *Women's West* (Norman: University of Oklahoma Press, 1987); Kenneth L. Holmes, ed., *Covered Wagon Women: Diaries and Letters from the Western Trails* (Lincoln: University of Nebraska Press, 1995); Glenda Riley and Richard W. Etulain, eds., *By Grit and Grace: Eleven Women Who Shaped the American West* (Golden, CO: Fulcrum, 1997).

63. J. B. Frantz and J. E. Choate, *The American Cowboy: The Myth and the Reality* (Norman: University of Oklahoma Press, 1955).

64. Coyne, 34, 42.

65. "A Discussion with the Audience of the 1970 Chicago Film Festival," in *Focus on Howard Hawks*, ed. Joseph McBride (Englewood Cliffs, NJ: Prentice-Hall, 1972): 15–16. John Wayne's attack on the film as "the most un-American thing I've ever seen in my whole life," was part of a May 1971 *Playboy* interview with Richard Warren Lewis.

66. James Silke, "Zinnemann Talks Back," reprinted in Miller, 11.

67. "Fred Zinnemann Talking to Gene Phillips," in Miller, 44.

68. Andrew Sarris, "The World of Howard Hawks" (1962), in *Focus on Howard Hawks*, ed. McBride, 58.

69. Zinnemann (1992), 24.

70. Tim Durrant to FZ, 14 May 1952, Correspondence, box 33, folder 428, FZ Papers, AMPAS. Friend Robert Surtees also wrote FZ after seeing *High Noon* that he "wired Eisenhower allow Chaplin's return," undated telegram, box 33, folder 428, FZ Papers, AMPAS.

71. William H. Wells to FZ, 10 December 1952, box 33, folder 428, FZ Papers, AMPAS.

72. Drummond 38. See also Comb's erroneous claims, 168–69.

73. Eldridge (2006), 96–97; see also *Product Digest Section*, 3 May 1952 (*High Noon* "introduces several elements not ordinarily found in Westerns") and Herblock cartoon, circa 1954, box 33, folder 426, FZ Papers, AMPAS.

74. Jesse Zunser, "*High Noon*," *Cue*, 26 July 1952, 26.

75. Bosley Crowther, "*High Noon*, A Western of Rare Achievement," *New York Times*, 26 July 1952.

76. Ibid. See also Hollis Alpert, "*High Noon*," *Saturday Review of Literature*, 5 July 1952, 29–30.

77. Bosley Crowther, "The Oscar Awards: Showmanship Rather Than Artistry Reigned at the Academy Affair," *New York Times*, 29 March 1953; Otis Guernsey, Jr., "Oscar's Getting Stodgy," *New York Herald Tribune*, 29 March 1953.

78. Harry Schein, "The Olympian Cowboy," *American Scholar* 24, no. 3 (September 1955): 309–20.

79. Richard Slotkin, *Gunfighter Nation: The Myth of the Frontier in Twentieth-century America* (Norman: University of Oklahoma Press), 392–96.

80. Matthew J. Costello, "Rewriting *High Noon*," in *Hollywood's West*, eds. Rollins and O'Connor (Lexington: University Press of Kentucky, 2005), 175–197.

81. Suzanne Clark, *Cold Warriors: Manliness of Trial in the Rhetoric of the West* (Carbondale: Southern Illinois University Press, 2000), 26.

82. Clipping, *Kinematograph Weekly*, May 1952, box 33, folder 426, FZ Papers, AMPAS.

83. See Drummond, 80; Hector Arce, *Gary Cooper, An Intimate Biography* (New York: William Morrow & Co., 1979) and Larry Swindell, *The Last Hero: A Biography of Gary Cooper* (New York: Doubleday, 1970).

84. Shortly before his death, Crosby would write to FZ, "Fred, the happiest and most productive days of my life were the 30 days we spent making *High Noon*," 17 August 1984, box 108, folder 42, FZ Papers, AMPAS.

85. FZ (1992), 100.

86. Clipping, *Movie Life Magazine*, June 1952, box 33, folder 426, FZ Papers, AMPAS.

87. FZ was asked to direct *The Sun Also Rises* by Fox in 1956–57, but eventually backed out when scheduling threatened to interfere with *The Nun's Story*. FZ's greatest interest was in casting Brett (it was he who wanted Gardner) and resisted efforts to cast

Jennifer Jones in the role (*The Man in the Gray Flannel Suit*, Production Files [1956], DOS Papers, Harry Ransom Center, University of Texas, Austin).

88. See FZ's discussion of the famous Directors Guild Meeting, in which DeMille sneered at many of the "foreign" names on the letter opposing his planned oath of loyalty (FZ to Vincent Deveau, quoted in Miller, 141). See also Simon Louvish, *Cecil B. DeMille and the Golden Calf* (London: Faber & Faber, 2007); and on Hawks, see Lauren Bacall, *By Myself* (New York: Knopf, 1979).

89. FZ (1992), 108. Zinnemann would continue to approach the Western from different angles, not only in his musical, *Oklahoma!* (1955), but in his unrealized plan to film Custer's famous defeat at Little Big Horn from the Sioux point of view (1965).

90. Maria Cooper Janis, *Gary Cooper Off-Camera: A Daughter Remembers* (New York: Harry N. Abrams, 1999), 154.

91. In a European surrealist moment undermined by Stanley Kramer, FZ had originally planned the last clock shot—above Kane's head as he writes his will—to have no face (annotated FZ script, 94).

92. FZ to Vincent Deveau, in Miller, 143.

Chapter Four

1. Jerry Wald to FZ, 23 July 1953, box 28, folder 346, FZ Papers, AMPAS.

2. FZ, annotations in James Jones, *From Here to Eternity* (New York: Scribners, 1951), 47, box 27, folder 333, FZ Papers, AMPAS.

3. GZ to FZ, VMail nd (1944), 2004 add-ons, FZ Papers, AMPAS.

4. FZ to Vincent Deveau, quoted in Miller, 141.

5. MC to FZ, 29 April 1953, box 27, folder 340, FZ Papers, AMPAS.

6. Frederick Lewis Allen, *Only Yesterday: An Informal History of the 1920s* (New York: Harper & Bros., 1931) and *Since Yesterday: The 1930s in America* (New York: Harper & Bros., 1940); Bell Irvin Wiley, *The Life of Johnny Reb, Common Soldier of the Confederacy* (Garden City, NY: Doubleday, 1943) and *The Life of Billy Yank, Common Soldier of the Union* (Indianapolis: Bobbs-Merrill, 1952). For more discussion of Jones's novel and the film as revisionist history, see Smyth, "James Jones, Columbia Pictures, and the Historical Confrontations of *From Here to Eternity*, in *Why We Fought: America's Wars in Film and History*, eds. Peter C. Rollins and John E. O'Connor (Lexington: University Press of Kentucky, 2008), 283–302.

7. James R. Giles, *James Jones* (Boston: Twayne, 1981); Frank MacShane, *Into Eternity: The Life of James Jones, American Writer* (Boston: Houghton Mifflin, 1985).

8. Jane Hendler, *Best-Sellers and Their Film Adaptations in Postwar America* (New York: Peter Lang, 2001), 30; Rebecca Bell-Metereau, "1953: Movies and Our Secret Lives," in *American Cinema in the 1950s: Themes and Variations*, ed. Murray Pomerance (New Brunswick, NJ: Rutgers University Press, 2005), 89–110, 92.

9. Peter Biskind, *Seeing Is Believing* (London: Pluto Books, 1983), 222; Lawrence Suid, *Guts and Glory: Great American War Movies* (Reading, MA: Addison-Wesley, 1978), 117–29.

10. Lawrence H. Suid, "Zinnemann on Working with the Military in *From Here to Eternity*," in Miller, 47–54.

11. Whitfield, 63.

12. Schallert, "*From Here to Eternity* Blasts Viewers with Atomic Power," *Los Angeles Times* (1 October 1953): B11. See also "Movie Version of Army Novel Opens," *New York Herald Tribune*, 2 August 1953, section 4, and A. H. Weiler, "*From Here to Eternity* Bows at Capitol With Huge Cast, Five Starring Roles," *New York Times*, 6 August 1953.

13. Ibid.

14. Malloy was cut from Taradash's script early on, not necessarily because he was a communist, but in the frequently documented interests of Cohn and Adler to keep the 800-page story under two hours on screen.

15. Leslie Dennis, *The Coming of American Fascism* (New York: Harper & Bros., 1936); and on the opposing side, Raymond G. Swing, *Forerunners of American Fascism* (New York: J. Messner, 1935); Dwight MacDonald, *Fascism and the American Scene* (New York: Pioneer Publishers, 1938); Earl Browder, *A Political Program of Native American Fascism* (New York: New Century Publishers, 1945); Eugene Dennis, *Fascist Danger and How to Combat It* (New York: New Century Publishers, 1948); Leland V. Bell, *In Hitler's Shadow, The Anatomy of American Nazism* (Port Washington, NY: Kennikat Press, 1973). See also Stanley G. Payne, *History of Fascism* (Madison: University of Wisconsin Press, 1995).

16. See, for example, Suzanne Clark, 37–38, 51–52.

17. See Diane Johnson, *Dashiell Hammet: A Life* (New York: Random House, 1983), 276–77; Brook, 95–96, 209.

18. Burroughs Mitchell to James Jones, 26 April 1950, box 36, folder 538; Jones to Mitchell, December 1950, box 36, folder 537, Jones Papers, Beinecke Rare Book and Manuscript Library, Yale University (hereafter Jones Papers).

19. *New York Times*, 6 March 1951.

20. James Jones, *From Here to Eternity*, Preliminary Treatment, 16 May 1951, 3–18 box 36, folders 340–41, Jones Papers.

21. See Smyth (2006).

22. MacShane, 38; Jones, 367.

23. FZ, "Notes on *From Here to Eternity*," 30 September 1952, 8 pp., 6, box 28, folder 360, FZ Papers, AMPAS.

24. Richard White, *It's Your Misfortune and None of My Own: A History of the American West* (Norman: University of Oklahoma Press, 1991); Gerald Nash, *World War II and the West* (Lincoln: University of Nebraska Press, 1990).

25. Raymond Bell to Harry Cohn, 13 March 1951, box 36, folder 342, Jones Papers.

26. "Report on *From Here to Eternity*," 20 March 1951, box 36, folder 342, Jones Papers.

27. E. P. Hogan, "Notes on *From Here to Eternity*," 22 March 1951, box 36, folder 342, Jones Papers.

28. Frank Dorn to Columbia Pictures, 31 March 1951, box 36, folder 342, Jones Papers, and Comments and References, Department of Defense Files, RG 33, entry 141, box 705, National Archives, College Park, MD.

29. Clair Towne, Undated Comments on *From Here to Eternity*, box 36, folder 342, Jones Papers.

30. James Jones, *From Here to Eternity* (New York: Scribners, 1951), 130.

31. Dorn to Columbia; *From Here to Eternity* Conference Notes, 13 March 1951, box 36, folder 345, Jones Papers; Clair Towne, Memo for Chief of Information, Department of Army, 2 April 1953, Department of Defense Files.

32. Thomas Doherty, *Projections of War: Hollywood, American Culture, and World War II* (New York: Columbia University Press, 1999), 231–32.

33. Harry Cohn to James Jones, 29 June 1951, box 36, folder 342, Jones Papers.

34. Daniel Taradash, *From Here to Eternity*, revised final script, 24 February 1952, FZ Papers; Clair Towne to Ray Bell, 21 January 1953, Dept. of Defense Files; Towne, Memo for Chief of Information, Department of Army, 11 February 1953, Department of Defense Files; Hogan; Buddy Adler, "Opinion of the Requested Changes on the part of the Department of Defense to Col. Dorn," January 1953, Department of Defense Files.

35. "Comments and Constructive Suggestions for Columbia Pictures Screen Treatment of FHTE," 9 pp. plus 1 p. rec. Sent to FZ—lightly annotated, 3, box 28, folder 358, FZ Papers, AMPAS.

36. Ibid., 5–6.

37. FZ, "Notes on *From Here to Eternity*," 30 September 1952, 10 pp., 6, box 28, folder 360, FZ Papers, AMPAS.

38. Ibid., white note attached to back of notes.

39. Daniel Taradash, *From Here to Eternity*, 1st estimating script, 17 December 1952, Columbia production no. 1271, Montgomery Clift Papers, Series III, subseries II, box 11, folder 1, New York Library for the Performing Arts (hereafter Clift Papers).

40. Zinnemann, interview with Arthur Nolletti, Jr., in Miller, 117.

41. Unmarked magazine clipping, folder 362, FZ Papers, AMPAS.

42. James Jones to Ned Brown, 29 April 1952, box 36, folder 342, Jones Papers.

43. The then-"washed-up" Sinatra's efforts to convince Cohn to hire him have become part of the film's lore.

44. Scripts indicate that this terse wording was Clift's idea. In the December 1952, script, a reworking of Taradash's first attempt, Clift has written this dialogue and crossed out what is printed: "I know where I stand. I don't believe that's the only way a man can get along. A man's got to go his own way. If he don't he's nothing. . . ." (11).

45. Taradash, *From Here to Eternity*, December 1952, 12, Clift Papers.

46. FZ, "Further Notes on FHTE," 23 October 1952, 2 pp., box 28, folder 360, FZ Papers, AMPAS.

47. FZ, "Further Notes on FHTE," 23 October 1952, 2 pp., box 28, folder 360, FZ Papers, AMPAS.

48. FZ, *From Here to Eternity* (New York: Scribners, 1951), marginalia on personal copy of book, 7, 676, 854–55, AMPAS.

49. Ibid., 696.

50. Ibid., 17.

51. Ibid., 11.

52. Ibid., 79.

53. On the back page of notes he writes: "Maggio = Red." 5 pp. undated in pen and pencil; "Notes on *From Here to Eternity* (Odds and Ends)," 25 October 1952, box 28, folder 360, FZ Papers, AMPAS.

54. FZ, "Notes on FHTE," 30 September 1952, p 9, box 28, folder 360, FZ Papers, AMPAS.

55. Miller, 49.

56. Taradash, first version *FHTE*, 1st estimating script, 17 December 1951, 72, Columbia production no. 1271, Series III, subseries II, box 11, folder 1, Clift Papers.

57. Frank Dorn to Columbia Pictures, 31 March 1951, box 36, folder 342, Jones Papers, and Comments and References, Department of Defense Files, RG 33, entry 141, box 705, National Archives, College Park, MD.

58. Paul Preston, *The Politics of Revenge* (London: Unwin Hyman, 1990), 30.

59. FZ, handwritten script notes, undated, box 28, folder 360, FZ Papers, AMPAS.

60. FZ to Harry Cohn, undated, box 28, folder 360, FZ Papers: "I don't want to commit myself until I'm sure that this can be a *good picture* . . . Censorship may kill us."

61. Neve, in Miller, 153.

62. "Comments and Constructive Suggestions for Columbia Pictures Screen Treatment of FHTE," 9 pp. plus 1 p. rec. Sent to FZ, lightly annotated, 5, box 28, folder 358, Zinnemann Papers, AMPAS.

63. Unmarked press clipping, box 28, folder 341, FZ Papers, AMPAS.

64. V. Hausmann, "*Verdammt in alle Ewigkeit*," *Weser-Kurier* (3 March 1954); Manes Kadow, "*Verdammt in alle Ewigkeit*," *Frankfurter Neue Preise* (24 February 1954); "Soldaten ohne Glorie," *Hamburg Morgenpost* (5 February 1954), all box 28, folder 342, FZ Papers, AMPAS.

65. Allan Bérubé's *Coming Out Under Fire: The History of Gay Men and Women in World War II* (New York: Free Press, 1990) gives a more positive context for gay culture in the armed forces during the war. See Amy Lawrence, *The Passion of Montgomery Clift* (Berkeley: University of California Press, 2010), 152–73 for a different analysis.

66. Taradash, *From Here to Eternity*, December 1952, 93–95, Clift Papers.

67. Taradash, *From Here to Eternity*, 23 February 1953 script, 131, Clift Papers.

68. J. Crow, "Notes on First Estimating Draft," annotated by FZ, 23 December 1952, 5 pp., 2, box 28, folder 358, FZ Papers, AMPAS.

69. Taradash, *From Here to Eternity*, First Estimating Script, 17 December 1952, 58, Series III, subseries II, box 11, folder 1, Clift Papers.

70. See, for example, the director's discussion of *The Sundowners* (Noletti, in Miller, 132) and *A Man For All Seasons* (*Action*, in Miller, 29).

71. FZ, "Notes on *From Here to Eternity*," 30 September 1952, p. 4, box 28, folder 360, FZ Papers, AMPAS.

72. Jesse Zunser, "*From Here to Eternity*," *Cue*, 8 August 1953, 16

73. Archer Winsten, *New York Post*, 2 August 1953, box 28, folder 344, FZ Papers, AMPAS.

74. Jones (1951), 763.

75. Taradash, *From Here to Eternity*, First Estimating Script, 17 December 1952, 103, series III, subseries II, box 11, folder 1, Clift Papers.

76. Ibid.

77. Post Script, undated letter from Jones to Adler pasted in 23 Feb 1953 script, folder 337, FZ Papers, AMPAS.

78. Emily Rosenberg, *A Date Which Will Live: Pearl Harbor in American Memory* (Durham, NC: Duke University Press, 2003).

79. The first public pictures of the attack appeared in the February 1942 edition of *Life* ("Pictures of the Nation's Worst Naval Disaster Show Pearl Harbor Hell," 30–35). See also "Pearl Harbor Damage Revealed," *Life* (December 1942): 31–37.

80. James M. Skinner, "*December 7*: Filmic Myth Masquerading as Historical Fact," *Journal of Military History* 55, no. 4 (1991): 507–16.

81. Weiler (1953).

82. Rear Admiral Lewis S. Parks to Raymond Bell, May 1954, Department of Defense Files.

83. James Jones to FZ, 25 January 1953, folder 346, FZ Papers, AMPAS.

84. Zunser (1953), 16.

85. "Navy Bans two Films: *Moon* and *Eternity*," reprint from *Daily News Los Angeles*, 29 August 1953. Chief of Naval Operations Admiral Stark denounced *December 7th* for implying naval incompetence, leading to its heavy censorship (nearly fifty minutes were cut). The original version was unvailable to the public until 1991 (Dawn Sova, Forbidden Films [New York: Checkmark Books, 2001], 93–94).

Chapter Five

1. FZ, interview with Gene Phillips (1973), reprinted in Miller, 45.

2. FZ to Philip K. Scheuer, "Devotion to Book Told by Director; Zinnemann Spends Two Years Filming, Cutting *Nun's Story*," *Los Angeles Times*, 13 April 1959.

3. FZ (1992), 155; Kathryn Hulme, *The Nun's Story* (Boston: Little, Brown, 1956).

4. Smyth (2009), passim.

5. Robert Sklar, *Movie-Made America* (1975; repr., New York: Vintage, 1994), 178; Gilbert Seldes, *The Movies Come From America* (New York, 1937).

6. Compare Custen's assessment of the male biopic's conservative hagiography to women's films in the studio era (George Custen, *Biopics: How Hollywood Constructed Public History* [New Brunswick, NJ: Rutgers University Press, 1992]); J. E. Smyth,

"Classical Hollywood and the Filmic Writing of Interracial History, 1931–1939," in *Mixed Race Hollywood*, eds. Mary Beltran and Camilla Fojas [New York: New York University Press, 2008]), 2–36.

7. Kathryn Hulme, *The Wild Place* (1953; repr., London: Frederick Muller, 1954).

8. There was a decline in historical films overall during the war, with a resurgence of historical war films and biopics of men in the 1950s. For more on Hollywood's historical interests during the 1950s, see David Eldridge, *Hollywood's History Films* (London: I. B. Taurus, 2006).

9. Bingham, *Whose Lives Are They Anyway? The Biopic as Contemporary Film Genre* (New Brunswick, NJ: Rutgers University Press, 2010).

10. See Smyth, "The Organization Woman Behind *The Man in the Gray Flannel Suit*," *Camera Obscura* 27:1 (fall 2012), 80.

11. FZ to Gordon Gow, quoted in Miller, 59.

12. Charles Hugo Doyle, "*The Nun's Story*: Trash or Treasure?" *Oratory*, July-August 1957, 5–11; "Reactions to *The Nun's Story*," *America*, 26 January 1957, 482–83; Sister Dolores Burgard, "Sister Luke Had No Vocation," *Catholic World*, April 1957, 40–50; David Price, "*The Nun's Story*," *Ave Maria*, 8 September 1956, 23; Sister May Hestor, "*The Nun's Story*," *Books on Trial*, October 1956, 74; Dan Herr, "Stop Pushing!" *Books on Trial*, November 1956, 140, 152. See also Harold C. Gardiner's "Enchanting Revolutionary," *America*, 15 September 1956, 568–69, for another view.

13. R. J. Obringer to Jack Warner, 7 March 1958, *The Nun's Story* Correspondence, folder 1 of 2, WBA.

14. Edna Ferber's expose of white Texans' racism in *Giant*, filmed in 1956, was the number three box-office grosser of 1956 behind *The Ten Commandments* and *Around the World in 80 Days*.

15. Martin Quigley to Jack Warner, 3 June 1957, box 54, folder 726, FZ Papers, AMPAS. See also Archbishop of Los Angeles to Henry Blanke, 27 August 1957, box 16, folder 399, Hulme Papers, in which he states the Belgian Church "did not favor the story being screened."

16. Ibid.

17. Edward Weeks, "The Nun's Story," *Atlantic Monthly*; E. J. Vandenbussche, "Gabrielle in Wonderland," Linie Brussels (12 April 1957), 12 pp.

18. Kathryn Hulme, "The Real Sister Luke," *American Weekly*, 30 December 1956, 6–7; JWG, "*The Nun's Story*: A Magnificent Failure," *Prairie (Muenster, Saskatchewan) Messenger*, 12 September 1957, box 51, folder 698, FZ Papers, AMPAS.

19. Henry Blanke to Harry Mayer, 24 July 1957, Steve Trilling Correspondence, *The Nun's Story*, WBA.

20. Vromen, 101. See also Pieter Lagrou, *The Legacy of Nazi Occupation* (Cambridge: Cambridge University Press, 2000), 47–58, 221–226.

21. Vromen, 132–33.

22. L. H. Lehmann, *Vatican Policy in the Second World War* (New York: Agora Press, 1946); A. Manhattan, *The Catholic Church Against the Twentieth Century* (London:

Watts, 1950). For more recent studies, see Michael Phelps, *The Catholic Church and the Holocaust, 1930–1965* (Bloomington: Indiana University Press, 2001); Daniel Jonah Goldhagen, *A Moral Reckoning: The Role of the Catholic Church in the Holocaust and Its Unfinished Duty of Repair* (New York: Knopf, 2002).

23. Guenter Lewy, *The Catholic Church and Nazi Germany* (New York: McGraw-Hill, 1964). See review, Dennis Killeen, *Western Political Quarterly* 18, no. 2 (June 1965): 406–08.

24. *European Resistance Movements 1939–1945: First International Conference on the History of the Resistance Movements held at Liege-Bruxelles-Breendonk 14–17 September 1958* (London: Pergamon, 1960). The second such conference was held in Milan in 1960.

25. Robert Aron, *The Vichy Regime* (1954; repr., New York: Macmillan, 1958); Sisley Huddleston, *France: The Tragic Years, 1939–1947* (New York: Devin Adair, 1955). See also the formerly pro-Wehrmacht perspective by Henry de Montherlant, *Textes sous une occupation, 1940–1944* (Paris: Gallimard, 1953).

26. Ginette Vincendeau, *Jean-Pierre Melville: An American in Paris* (London: BFI, 2003), 88.

27. See William Thomson Hill, *The Martyrdom of Nurse Cavell* (London: Hutchinson & Co., 1915); Helen Judson, *Edith Cavell* (New York: Macmillan, 1941); Tammy Proctor, "'Patriotism is Not Enough': Women, Citizenship, and the First World War," *Journal of Women's History* 17, no. 2 (summer 2005): 169–76; Sue Malvern, "'For King and Country': Frampton's *Edith Cavell* (1915–1920) and the Writing of Gender in Memorials to the Great War," in *Sculpture and Pursuit of the Modern Ideal in Britain, 1880–1930*, ed. David Getsy (Aldershot: Ashgate, 2004).

28. Fictional women's melodramas are the exception, when the death or sacrifice is connected to personal rather than public interest (see, for example, *Christopher Strong*, 1933; *Camille*, 1937; *Wurthering Heights*, 1939; or *Dark Victory*, 1939).

29. Michael Hogan, *Nurse Edith Cavell*, shooting script, 12 May 1939, 123 pp., 93, S6512, BFI, London.

30. See Michael Birdwell, *Celluloid Soldiers* (New York: New York University Press, 1998).

31. R. J. Minney, *Carve Her Name with Pride* (London: Pan, 1958), 148–49. See also Jerrard Tickell's *Odette: Story of a British Agent* (London: Chapman & Hall, 1949), which went through several editions throughout the 1950s.

32. *Carve Her Name With Pride*, "World Premiere to Aid the Special Forces Fund and the Special Forces Benevolent Fund at Leicester Square Theatre, 20 February 1958," synopsis, BFI, Special Collections.

33. See Tickell, "Epilogue."

34. Lewis Gilbert and Vernon Harris, *Carve Her Name With Pride*, Post-Production Script, 13 March 1958, S13981, BFI.

35. Gene D. Phillips, "Fred Zinnemann: An Interview," *Journal of Popular Film and Television* 7, no. 1 (June 1978): 57–66.

36. Robert Anderson, notes on script, undated, box 54, folder 726, FZ Papers, AMPAS.

37. Robert Anderson, *The Nun's Story*, shooting script, 20 December 1957, box 50, folder 669 (page is dated 10-4-58), 1, FZ Papers, AMPAS.

38. Hepburn starred as Natasha in *War and Peace* (1956).

39. Lesley Garner, "Lesley Garner Meets the Legendary Actress as She Prepares For This Week's UNICEF Gala Performance," *Sunday Telegraph*, 26 May 1991. See also Charles Higham, *Audrey* (New York: Macmillan, 1984), 11–22, on her family's war experience. Hepburn gave interviews to *Dance* (1951) and *American Weekly* (May 1958), where she discussed her Resistance work.

40. FZ to Steve Trilling, 4 October 1957, notes Habets was working with them since September 11 on preparation, wardrobe, and with Hepburn (hereafter AH) three times a week, Steve Trilling Correspondence, *The Nun's Story*, WBA.

41. In his autobiography, FZ points out that Anderson was a Protestant and AH a Christian Scientist (1992: 163), perhaps accounting for their slightly "resistant" attitudes.

42. AH to FZ, 16 July 1957, box 52, folder 701, FZ Papers, AMPAS.

43. Group Captain Douglas Bader, foreword to *Little Cyclone*, by Airey Neave (London: Hodder & Stoughton, 1954; London: Panther, 1957).

44. Ibid., 160.

45. Andy Priestner, *The Complete Secret Army* (London: Classic TV, 2006).

46. AH to FZ, 19 November 1957, box 52, folder 701, FZ Papers, AMPAS.

47. FZ to AH, 4 December 1957, box 52, folder 701, FZ Papers, AMPAS.

48. Zinnemann (1992), 163.

49. Henry Blanke to Lou Habets, 3 December 1957, p. 2, box 16, folder 399, Kathryn Hulme Papers, Beinecke Rare Book and Manuscript Library, Yale University (hereafter Hulme Papers).

50. Robert Anderson to Kathryn Hulme and Lou Habets, 1 July 1958, box 16, folder 388, Hulme Papers.

51. Notes of conference with Monsignor Devlin 27 August 1957, with Jack Vizzard, Henry Blanke, FZ, and Finlay McDermid; Notes from Devlin on First Draft of *Nun's Story*," p. 3 of 4, both box 54, folder 726, FZ Papers, AMPAS.

52. FZ annotations on Jack Vizzard's notes on new draft, 3 September 1957, box 54, folder 726, FZ Papers, AMPAS.

53. FZ to Abe Lastfogel, 3 October 1958, folder 985, FZ Papers, AMPAS.

54. The following notations are taken from FZ's personal copy of the book (Boston: Little, Brown, 1956), 284, box 49, folder 668, FZ Papers, AMPAS.

55. Hulme (1956), 201, 305, box 49, folder 668, FZ Papers, AMPAS.

56. Ibid., 292–308. See Anderson script, 133, scenes 270–282 out, box 53, folder 669, FZ Papers, AMPAS and Jack Warner to Russell Downing, 23 January 1959 notes that he saw earlier version in Rome "when it was 1 hour 20 minutes longer," Warner File 2953, Jack Warner Collection, WBA.

57. FZ, pink script notes, 7 August 1957, base first page of these typed and annotated notes, box 54, folder 726, Zinnemann Papers, AMPAS.

58. Hulme, *The Nun's Story* (London: Pan [film edition], 1960), 67. Anderson, script, 20 December 1957–18 January 1958, 52, box 50, folder 669, FZ Papers, AMPAS.

59. Anderson, script 20 Decemer 1957–18 January 1958, 10, box 50, folder 669, FZ Papers, AMPAS.

60. Ibid., pages dated 13 January 1958, 38, 53.

61. Ibid., 133.

62. See Dana Polan, *Power and Paranoia: History, Narrative and the American Cinema, 1940–1950* (New York: Columbia University Press, 1986) and William Graebner, *The Age of Doubt: American Thought and Culture in the 1940s* (New York: Waveland Press, 1991).

63. See Vincendeau (92) and Noël Burch and Geneviève Sellier, *Drôle de guerre des sexes du cinema francais* (Paris: Nathan, 1996), 224, which says *Silence de la mer* is misogynist.

64. Beatrix Beck, *Léon Morin, Prêtre* (Paris: Gallimard, 1952). The book won the prestigious Goncourt prize.

65. Paul Thompson, *The Voice of the Past: Oral History* (Oxford: Oxford University Press, 1978), 54–55, 87.

66. Ibid., 18.

67. Hulme (1956), 131.

68. 28 August notes of conference with Monsignor Devlin, 27 August 1957, with FZ, Finlay McDermid, Blane, Vizzard. See p. 3, "page 15: Monsignor Devlin objected to the phrasing of the May 28 bulletin and suggested the instructions to the Nuns should be "Not to take part in any underground activities" or alternatively, "to try to maintain a neutral position," box 54, folder 726, FZ Papers, AMPAS.

69. Pan edition, 11–12.

70. Anderson, script, 20 December 1957, box 50, folder 669, page dated 13 January 1958, 30a–31, FZ Papers, AMPAS.

71. Pan edition, 29.

72. Robert Anderson to Kathryn Hulme and Lou Habets, 11 April 1957, box 16, folder 388, Hulme Papers.

73. Robert Anderson, *The Nun's Story*, shooting script, 20 December 1957, 5, box 50, folder 669, FZ Papers, AMPAS.

74. FZ to Robert Anderson, 28 December 1957, attached to final script, *The Nun's Story*, shooting script, 20 December 1957, 29, box 50, folder 669, FZ Papers, AMPAS.

75. Robert Anderson, *The Nun's Story*, shooting script, 20 December 1957, 29, box 50, folder 669, FZ Papers, AMPAS.

76. FZ, memo, 1 July 1958, folder 703, FZ Papers, AMPAS.

77. Zinnemann (1992), 166.

78. Henry Blanke to Harry Mayer, 24 July 1957, Steve Trilling Correspondence, *The Nun's Story*, WBA. Arthur Nolletti points out that Hepburn's face is individualized by a series of painterly close-ups (128–29), but ironically, this technique "singularlizes" Sister Luke, making her commitment to the rule still more tenuous (Arthur Nolletti, Jr.,

"Spirituality and Style in *The Nun's Story*," in *The Films of Fred Zinnemann*, ed. Nolletti [State University Press of New York, 1999], 119–38).). "Jeanne d'Arc: Indirect Light!!," folder 728, notepads 10 of Normandie stationery. See also Sean Desilets, "The Rhetoric of Passion," *Camera Obscura* 53, no. 2 (2003): 57–91. Zinnemann would remember seeing Dreyer's film for the first time as "one of the greatest film experiences of my life" (Interview, *Politiken*, 1978).

79. FZ, office letter to Blanke and Mussetta, 28 December 1957, "Make-up and Continuity for Audrey Hepburn," enclosed in Anderson shooting script, FZ Papers, AMPAS.

80. FZ, notes, notepads 10 of Normandie stationery, "Audrey 1) makeup 2) See *Jeanne D'Arc* (Planer, Piero, HB)," box 54, folder 728, and notes, "Figure out haircut scene," box 54, folder 729, FZ Papers, AMPAS.

81. FZ (1992), 169.

82. FW to FZ, memo, 2 October 1958 and FZ to FW, 2 October 1958, 3pp, Steve Trilling Correspondence, WBA.

83. "Material on Dutch and Flemish Paintings Sent to Fred Zinnemann for *The Nun's Story*," 1 July 1957, Research, *The Nun's Story*, WBA. The work of Hobbema is the closest match to this recessed landscape.

84. "Expects Hierarchy Approval for Filmed *Nun's Story*," *Variety*, 10 July 1957, 3.

85. Walter MacEwan to Trilling notes FZ wants Figueroa, "a friend of his," to do cinematography: "As you know, Figueroa is famous for black and white, and Zinnemann appears to be reconciled to forgetting color," 1 April 1957, Steve Trilling correspondence, *The Nun's Story*, WBA.

86. FZ to Steve Trilling, 20 March 1959, box 52, folder 712, FZ Papers, AMPAS.

87. Abe Weiss to FZ, 22 March 1965, distribution statement by WB for period ending 2 January 1965, box 52, folder 709 (financial), FZ Papers, AMPAS. Zinnemann (1992), 171.

88. "Two Movies, Two Audrey Hepburns," *New York Times Magazine*, 23 November 1958, 62–63.

89. Powr, *Variety*, 6 May 1959, 6.

90. Typed *Redbook* review July 1959, box 53, folder 718, FZ Papers, AMPAS.

91. E. J. Vandenbussche, "Gabriel in Wonderland," Linie Brussels, 12 April 1957, box 53, folder 718, FZ Papers, AMPAS.

92. "Reviews and Ratings of Current Films by the Protestant Motion Picture Council, June 1959, unmarked press clipping, *The Nun's Story*, box 53, folder 718, FZ Papers, AMPAS.

93. Roland Barthes, "The Face of Garbo," in *Mythologies* (1957; repr., London: Vintage, 1993): 56–57.

94. *The Nun's Story*, program, p. 4 of 16, Publicity, WBA.

95. Robert Anderson to Kathryn Hulme and Lou Habets, 1 July 1958, box 16, folder 388, Hulme Papers.

96. Robert F. Hawkins, "Seen on the Italian Screen Scene: *Nun's Story* Unfolds Behind Closed Doors," 12 April 1958, unmarked press clipping, box 50, folder 698, FZ Papers, AMPAS.

Notes [271]

Chapter Six

1. Frederich Engels to Minna Kautsky, 26 November 1885, quoted in Gareth Thomas, *The Novel of the Spanish Civil War (1936–1975)* (Cambridge: Cambridge University Press, 1990).

2. Silke, "Zinnemann Talks Back," reprinted in Miller, 15.

3. See, for example, FZ to Abe Lastfogel, 7 July 1963, box 31, folder 393, FZ Papers, AMPAS.

4. Emeric Pressburger, *Killing a Mouse on Sunday* (London: Collins, 1961).

5. Ibid., dust jacket review.

6. See Gareth Thomas, *The Novel of the Spanish Civil War (1936–1975)* (Cambridge: Cambridge University Press, 1990), passim.

7. *Confidential Agent* (Warner Bros., 1945), with Charles Boyer and Lauren Bacall, and *The Angel Wore Red* (MGM, 1960), starring Dirk Bogarde and Ava Gardner, were critical and box-office disappointments, and unlike *Behold a Pale Horse*, did not deal with the thorny issue of Spanish resistance to Franco and its persistence into the 1960s.

8. Fred Zinnemann, "Cameraman Availability," undated, box 2, folder 29, FZ Papers, AMPAS. It would be completely erroneous to argue that Badal's flight from Soviet controlled Hungary was a political inverse of the communist battle against the fascists in Spain during the war. Spanish anarchists and indeed many Spanish communist fought lengthy battles against the Soviet control of the military and government.

9. James R. Silke, "Zinnemann Talks Back," *Cinema* 2, no. 4 (October-November 1964), 20–22, 30, reprinted in Miller, 9–25. See also Zinnemann, "Revelations."

10. Louis MacNeice, quoted in Thomas (1990), 27.

11. "Spaniards Flee to France in Greatest Mass Exodus of Modern Times," *Life* 6, no. 8 (20 February 1939).

12. As Paul Preston points out, this event coincided with the US-lead initiative to bring Spain into UNESCO and the Concordat with the Vatican; Preston, *The Politics of Revenge: Fascism and the Military in Spain* (London: Unwin Hyman, 1990), 30. See also David Gilmore, *The Transformation of Spain: From Franco to Constitutional Monarchy* (London: Quartet, 1985), 44–45, 85.

13. George Orwell, "Why I Write," in *Collected Essays* (London, 1961), 426; Koestler, *Spanish Testament* (London, 1937), 177.

14. Thomas (1990), 24.

15. Phillip Knightley, *The First Casualty: From the Crimea to the Falklands: The War Correspondent as Hero, Propagandist, and Mythmaker* (London: Book Club Edition, 1975), 199–200.

16. Ibid., 197–214.

17. William Stott, *Documentary Expression and Thirties America* (New York: Oxford University Press, 1973); Alan Sekula, "Dismantling Modernism, Reinventing Documentary: Notes on the Politics of Representation," in *Photography/Politics: One*, eds. T. Dennet and J. Spence (London: Photography Workshop, 1979).

18. John Tagg, *The Burden of Representation: Essays on Photographies and Histories* (London: Macmillan, 1988), 64.

19. Anthony Aldgate, *Cinema and History: British Newsreels and the Spanish Civil War* (London: Scholar Press, 1979); Caroline Brothers, *War and Photography: A Cultural History* (London: Routledge, 1997).

20. Knightley, 210–12; Brothers, 178–85.

21. Carl Becker, *Everyman His Own Historian* (New York: F. S. Crofts, 1935).

22. Eduardo Pons Prades, *Republicanos españoles en la Segunda Guerra Mundial* (Madrid: La Esfera de los Libros, 2003), 35; Antonio Soriano, *Exodos: historia oral del exilio republicano en Francia* (Barcelona: Crítica, 1989), 42; Paul Preston, "The Anti-Francoist Opposition: The Long March to Unity," in *Spain in Crisis: The Evolution and Decline of the Franco Regime*, ed. Paul Preston (Hassocks, Sussex: Harvester Press, 1976), 129.

23. Soriano, 42.

24. Victoria Kent, *Cuatro años en París* (Buenos Aires: Sur, 1947).

25. Preston (1976), 129.

26. Antonio Téllez, *Sabaté: Guerilla Extraordinaire* (London, 1974), 115–17; Preston, 142.

27. Tellez, 178–83.

28. Zinnemann, "Revelations," *Films and Filmmaking* (September 1964), 5–6; Tellez, 13.

29. "Anarchist's End," *Time*, January 6, 1960; see also "Guerrilla Leader Killed by Spanish Police," *New York Times*, January 6, 1960, and "Francisco Sabaté," *Newsweek*, 18 January 1960, 28, 30.

30. Preston (1976), 130.

31. Ibid., 127.

32. "Franco's Control Firm; But Meeting of Foes in Munch and the Labor Unrest Revel There is Discontent With the Regime," *New York Times*, 17 June 1962, section B, box 3, folder 33, FZ Papers, AMPAS.

33. See Preston, "The Spanish Civil War and the Historians," 2–6; Herbert Southworth, *El mito de la cruzada de Franco* (Paris: 1963); Hugh Thomas, *The Spanish Civil War* (London, 1961). Dionisio Ridruejo's attack on Franco, *Escrito en España*, also appeared in 1962.

34. Thomas, 15.

35. Notable films include *El espiritu de la colmena* (1973), *Las largas vacaciones del 36* (1976), *La colmena* (1982), *Belle Epoque* (1992), *Land and Freedom* (UK, 1995), *Libertarias* (1996), *A Time for Defiance* (1998), *The Devil's Backbone* (2001), *Soldiers of Salamis* (2003), and *Pan's Labyrinth* (2006). See Mercedes Maroto Camino, *Film, Memory, and the Legacy of the Spanish Civil War: Resistance and Guerilla 1936–2010* (London: Palgrave, 2011).

36. See Christopher Robé, "The Good Fight: The Spanish Civil War and US Left Film Criticism," *Framework: The Journal of Cinema and Media* 51, no. 1 (spring

2010): 79–107; John Whiteclay Chambers II, "The Movies and the Antiwar Debate in America, 1930–1941," *Film and History* 36, no. 1 (Fall 2006): 44–57; Larry Ceplair, "The Politics of Compromise in Hollywood: A Case Study," *Cineaste* 8, no.4 (1982): 2–7. For contemporary coverage of *Blockade*, see Winchell Taylor, "Secret Movie Censors," *Nation* 124 (9 July 1938), 38–40.

37. Robert Sklar, *City Boys: Cagney, Bogart, Garfield* (Princeton: Princeton University Press, 1992), 146.

38. Caroline Brothers, *War and Photography* (London: Routledge, 1997), 189 and Geneviete Ostyn, "Pour qui sonne le glas: L'Espagne: non; Les Etats-Unis: oui," *Revue Belge du cinéma*, no. 17 (autumn 1986): 43.

39. Ernest Hemingway, *For Whom the Bell Tolls* (New York: Scribners, 1941), 12. Hemingway's novel was criticized by some Republican novelists for its lack of historical authenticity, but Hemingway's emphasis on women's heroism in the war may have been the real source of their criticism. See Arturo Barea, "Not Spain But Hemingway," *Horizon* (May 1941): 350–61 and F. Ayala, "La excentricidad hispana," *Histrionismo y representación* (Buenos Aires, 1944).

40. Hemingway, 53–54.

41. Ibid., 96–127.

42. Ibid., 123.

43. Brothers, 76–98; Maria Marmo Mullaney, *Revolutionary Women: Gender and the Socialist Revolution* (New York: Praeger, 1983); Mangini, 67–94.

44. See *Life* (1939).

45. Magini, 155–74; Federica Monseny, *El éxodo, pasión y muerte de los españoles en el exilio* (Barcelona: Galba Ediciones, 1977), 31–32.

46. See, for example, Preston's critique (Preston, 1984: 6).

47. "Julian Garcia Grimau Executed By Firing Squad," *Los Angeles Times*, 21 April 1963, clipping, FZ Papers, AMPAS.

48. Pressburger, 143.

49. Zinnemann would obviously continue to speculate on these issues in another widely different historical context in *A Man For All Seasons* (1966).

50. FZ to Emeric Pressburger, 26 October 1962, box 2, folder 25, FZ Papers, AMPAS.

51. Ibid.

52. Paul Feyder and FZ with Six Revolutionaries at Centro Espano, "Report on Trips to Perpignan and Toulouse" (8–9 June 1963), 13 pp., box 3, folder 34, research, Zinnemann Papers, AMPAS.

53. FZ to Emeric Pressbuger, 29 October 1962, box 2, folder 25, FZ Papers, AMPAS.

54. Peck played Captain Ahab in John Huston's *Moby Dick* in 1956.

55. J. P. Miller, *Behold a Pale Horse*, box 1, folder 10, first estimating draft, 3 May 1963 to 22 February 1964, FZ Papers, AMPAS.

56. FZ to J. P. Miller, 1 February 1964, box 2, folder 25, FZ Papers, AMPAS.

57. FZ to J. P. Miller, 10 February 1964, box 2, folder 25, FZ Papers, AMPAS.

58. J. P. Miller to FZ, 15 February 1964, box 2, folder 25, FZ Papers, AMPAS.

59. For more on the mix of documentary and fictional elements in Spanish Civil War films, see Linda C. Ehrlich, "*Behold a Pale Horse*: Zinnemann and the Spanish Civil War," in Nolletti, 139–155.

60. Script Changes, 18 and 22 February 1964, box 2, folder 12, FZ Papers, AMPAS.

61. "Mourir à Madrid," 3 pp., box 2, folder 29, FZ Papers, AMPAS.

62. FZ to Mike Frankovich, 30 May 1964, box 2, folder 25, FZ Papers, AMPAS.

63. FZ, handwritten production notes, box 3, folder 27, FZ Papers, AMPAS.

64. See, for example, Thomas Wiseman, "For Grant the Guns Are Not Enough—So a Naval Novel Gets a Romantic Feminine Lead," *Glasgow Evening Citizen*, 2 June 1958, 6.

65. "A Plan of Public Relations and Promotional Activity Covering Pre-Production, Production, Production and Pre-Release Phases of Carl Foreman's Production of *The Guns of Navarone*," 54 pp. item 35, *The Guns of Navarone*, Carl Foreman Collection, BFI; George Weller, "Tourists Follow the Film Stars," *Philadelphia Inquirer* (29 April 1960), clipping, item 102, American book, 1959–60, *The Guns of Navarone*, Carl Foreman Collection, BFI.

66. Quoted in Thomas, 24–25.

67. Zinnemann, "Revelations," *Films and Filmmaking*, September 1964, 5–6.

68. Ibid.

69. Janis, 98.

70. See Zinnemann's notes, box 43, folder 567, and box 47, folder 630, FZ Papers, AMPAS.

71. Norman Cooper, "The Church: From Crusade to Christianity," in Preston (1976), 48–81.

72. He also shares Francisco Sabaté's first name.

73. Mike Bell to Mike Frankovich, 27 February 1963, box 2, folder 25, FZ Papers, AMPAS.

74. A. Schneider to FZ, 25 September 1963, box 2, folder 25, FZ Papers, AMPAS.

75. "Saga of a Tired Spanish Loyalist," *Daily Variety*, 10 July 1963.

76. FZ, "Shooting Continuity," 24 February 1964, box 2, folder 29, FZ Papers, AMPAS: "Emphasize the fact that landscape looks exactly the same on both sides of the barrier."

77. "Columbia Beyond *Pale* in Spain," *Variety*, 11 August 1964.

78. Emilio López to M. Rothman of Columbia, 8 December 1963, box 2, folder 25, FZ Papers, AMPAS.

79. "Spanish Displeasure over filming of *Pale Horse* Results in Total Ban on Col. Films, Shooting Affected," *Variety*, 4 September 1963, 3.

80. "Columbia Backing of *Pale Horse* Was Courageous, Zinnemann Says," *Motion Picture Daily*, 11 August 1964.

81. Dale, "*Behold a Pale Horse*," *Variety*, 7 August 1964; William Johnson, "*Behold a Pale Horse*," *Film Quarterly* (winter 1964–65): 46–50, 47; *Cue*, 15 August 1964.

82. John Russell Taylor, "Film Director Who Likes To Let His Subject Speak For Itself," *Times*, 18 March 1967, 7. See also William Johnson, "*Behold a Pale Horse*."

83. Oscar Barnes, "Zinnemann's Concept of the Hero," *New York Herald Tribune*, 9 August 1964.

84. "Zinnemann's *Pale Horse* is a Film Masterpiece," *Hollywood Reporter*, 14 August 1964, 3.

85. William Johnson, "Zinnemann Pictures a Modern Dilemma," *Entertainment*, 30 September 1964, 28.

86. "*Behold a Pale Horse*," *Hollywood Reporter*, 7 August 1964.

87. "Muy Hombre," *Newsweek* (24 August 1964).

88. Richard Schickel, "*Behold a Pale Horse*," *Life*, 21 August 1964.

89. Bernard Gill, "Instructive Blunders," *New Yorker*, August 29, 1964.

90. *Il Giorno*, Milan (28 November 1964), press clipping, box 2, folder 20, FZ Papers, AMPAS.

91. According to *Variety*, the "box-office flop" cost Columbia Pictures $2,500,000 through the loss of Spanish markets ("*Pale Horse* Lost Firm 2,500,000," *Variety*, 26 January 1966).

92. *Variety Annual*, 6 January 1965.

93. John Russell Taylor, "Film Director who likes to let his subject speak for itself," *Times*, 18 March 1967, 7.

94. "Yeats' Country," *Weekly Telegraph*, no. 23 (26 February 1966), 19–23, box 46, folder 607, FZ Papers.

95. Tim Zinnemann, interviews with author, 2010, 2011.

Chapter Seven

1. Jane Addams, *The Long Road of Women's Memory* (Urbana: University of Illinois Press, 2002).

2. Sargent, *Julia*, Second Draft, 4 June 1976, incorporating revisions 24 June, 7, 21 and 29 July, 11 and 25 August, and 1 September 1976, box 35, folder 443, 103–105, FZ Papers, AMPAS.

3. Lillian Hellman, *Three: An Unfinished Woman, Pentimento, Scoundrel Time* (Boston: Little, Brown, 1979). Diana Trilling, *We Must March My Darlings: A Critical Decade* (New York: Harcourt Brace Jovanovich, 1977); Martha Gellhorn, "On Apocryphism," *Paris Review* 23, no. 79 (spring 1981): 280–301.

4. Carl Rollyson, *Lillian Hellman: Her Legend and Her Legacy* (New York: St. Martin's Press, 1988): 503–28. See also Justus Reid Weiner, "Lillian Hellman: The Fiction of Autobiography," *Gender Issues* 21, no. 1 (2003): 78–83.

5. Robert Sklar, "Historical Films: Scofflaws and the Historical Cop," *Reviews in American History* 25, no. 2 (June 1997): 346–50.

6. H. R. Kedward, *In Search of the Maquis* (Oxford: Clarendon, 1993) and Margaret Collins Weitz, *Sisters in Resistance* (New York: Wiley, 1995).

7. Zinnemann (1997), 19.

8. Muriel Gardiner, *Code-Name "Mary"* (New Haven: Yale University Press, 1980). See also Samuel McCracken, "*Julia* and Other Fictions By Lillian Hellman," *Commentary*, June 1984, 35–43; Michael Davie, "The Life and Lies of Lillian Hellman," *Observer*, 26 October 1986, 64. For the most recent biography of Gardiner, see Sheila Isenberg, *Her War* (London: Palgrave Macmillan, 2010). For a summary of Hall's remarkable experiences, see Margaret Rossiter, *Women in the Resistance* (New York: Praeger, 1986), 189–98. See also transcribed interview with Professor Maria Jahoda collated by Tom Pevsner, 19 May 1976, 1–3, with notations by FZ, *Julia*, research (Vienna), box 40, folder 525, FZ Papers, AMPAS.

9. Marie-Madeleine Fourcade, *L'Arche de Noé* (Paris: Fayard, 1968); *Noah's Ark*, with introduction by Commander Kenneth Cohen (London: Unwin, 1973); Fourcade, *Noah's Ark* (New York: E. P. Dutton, 1974, 53; Rossiter, 126. See Hellman, *Pentimento*, 432.

10. Carl Rollyson, 515. Among Gardiner's friends, historian J. C. Furnas and poet Stephen Spender identified her as Julia. Her second husband Joseph Buttinger documented some of her work in *In the Twilight of Socialism*, but even in the 1970s she was not widely known as a celebrity of the anti-Nazi resistance.

11. Gardiner, xvi.

12. Gardiner, xv.

13. Hellman, *Pentimento*, 412.

14. Hellman, "Julia," in *Pentimento*, 411, 407, 418, 421, 443.

15. Christine Doudna, "A Still Unfinished Woman: A Conversation with Lillian Hellman," *Rolling Stone*, 24 February 1977, 53.

16. Bob Moore, ed., *Resistance in Western Europe* (London: Berg, 2000), 11. Moore's introduction gives a useful overview of "Resistance" historiography. Charlie Jeffrey's *Social Democracy in the Austrian Provinces, 1918–1934: Beyond Red Vienna* (London: Leicester University Press, 1996) is the only major study of Austria in the 1930s; see Fritz Molden, *Fires in the Night: Sacrifices and Significance of the Austrian Resistance* (New York: Westview Press, 1989). For Czechoslovakia, see Peter Demetz, *Prague in Danger: The Years of Occupation, 1939–1945* (New York: Farrar, Straus and Giroux, 2008).

17. Margaret Collins Weitz, *Sisters in the Resistance* (New York: Wiley, 1995).

18. Fourcade, 9–12, 15–16, 362–71; Rossiter, 129.

19. Suzanne Vromen, *Hidden Children of the Holocaust* (Oxford: Oxford University Press, 2008), 116–17.

20. Marie-Madeleine Fourcade, *L'Arche de Noé* (Paris: Fayard, 1968). See also Brigitte Friang, *Regarde-toi qui meurs* (Paris: Lafront, 1970); Jeanne Bohec, *La Plastiquese a bicyclette* (Paris: Mercure de France, 1975); Suzanne Bidault, *Souvenirs de guerre et de l'occupation* (Paris: Le Table Ronde, 1973); Anne-Marguerite Dumilieu, *Moi, une cobaye* (Paris: SEFA, 1975).

21. Kazimiera Jean Cottam, *Women in War and Resistance: Selected Biographies of Soviet Women* (New Military Publishers, 2006); Ingrid Strobl, *Partisanas: Women in the Armed Resistance to Fascism* (Edinburgh: AK Press, 2008); Frank McDonough, *Sophie*

Scholl, *The Real Story of the Woman Who Defied Hitler* (London: The History Press, 2009).

22. See, for example, Olivier Wieviorka, "France," in Moore, 125–55.

23. Hellman, "Julia," in *Pentimento*, 401.

24. Hellman, 449, 452.

25. Moore (2000), 2; Lagrou (2000), 2, 67–68, 211, 220–21, 231–4.

26. Rollyson, passim.

27. Samuel McCracken, "Julia and Other Fictions By Lillian Hellman," *Commentary*, June 1984, 35–43.

28. Gardiner, 90, 101.

29. Bernard F. Dick, *Hellman in Hollywood* (Rutherford: Fairleigh Dickinson Press, 1982), 156–57, 162.

30. Hellman, introduction to *Pentimento*, 309.

31. This position would become more pronounced in White's 1978 *Tropics of Discourse*. Frederic Jameson has also identified 1973 as the year of the "postmodern" nostalgia film, indicative of the inability of the present generation to position itself within a traditional historical trajectory or relationship.

32. Doudna, 53.

33. White, "Historical Emplotment and the Problem of Truth," in *Probing the Limits of Representations: Nazism and the 'Final Solution,'* ed. Saul Friedlander (Cambridge: Harvard University Press, 1992), 37–53.

34. H. R. Kedward, *Resistance in Vichy France* (Oxford; Oxford University Press, 1978), vi–vii.

35. Fourcade, 166, 168, 369–71.

36. Thomas Haskell, "Deterministic Implications of Intellectual History," in *New Directions*, eds. Higham and Conkin, 138–39, 145; "The Curious Persistence of Rights Talk in the 'Age of Interpretation,'" *JAH* 74 (1987): 984–1012; see also Peter Novick, *That Noble Dream: The 'Objectivity Question' and the American Historical Profession* (Cambridge: Cambridge University Press, 1988), 625–28.

37. Julie Des Jardins, *Women and the Historical Enterprise in America* (Chapel Hill: University of North Carolina Press, 2003), 7.

38. See Ann D. Gordon, Mari Jo Buhle, and Nancy E. Schrom's critique of traditional women's history in "Women in American Society: A Historical Contribution," *Radical America* 5, no. 4 (1971): 3–36.

39. For more on Gellhorn and McCarthy's criticism of Hellman, see Rollyson, passim.

40. Cott and Pleck, eds., *A Heritage of Her Own: Toward a New Social History of American Women* (New York: Simon & Schuster, 1979), 10.

41. H. R. Kedward, *In Search of the Maquis* (Oxford: Clarendon Press,) 231.

42. Barbra Streisand bears more than a passing physical resemblance to Hellman in this film.

43. See *The Day Before Sunrise*, box 70, folder 946, FZ Papers, AMPAS.

44. Joe Baltake, "A Tale of Two Women," *New York Daily News*, 12 October 1977, box 37, folder 476, FZ Papers, AMPAS.

45. "Production notes," *Julia*, Press Kit and Production Information, box 38, file 504, p. 2, FZ Papers, AMPAS.

46. Susan Smith, "Julia: The Hellman Connection," *W*, 7–14 January 1977, 19. See also Judith Weinraub, "Two Feisty Feminists Filming Hellman's *Pentimento*," *New York Times*, 31 October 1976, 17, in which she again asserts the truth of *Julia*.

47. Mary Rourke, "Jane and Vanessa and Lillian and *Julia*," *W*, 30 September-October 7, 1977, 10.

48. Stephen Schiff, "Two Women: In Defense of *Julia*," *Boston Phoenix*, 18 October 1977, III, 5, 8.

49. Redgrave, *An Autobiography* (1991; repr., London: Arrow, 1992), 143–46.

50. Redgrave (1992), 153, 193.

51. Mankiewicz and Welles were even sued by Ferdinand Lundberg over the alleged similarities between their portrait of Kane/Hearst and Lundberg's biography of Hearst, published in 1936. See Smyth (2006), especially chapter 11, and Pauline Kael, "Raising Kane," in *Raising Kane and Other Essays* (1971; repr., London: Marion Boyars, 1996), 159–266; Morris Dickstein, "The Last Film of the 1930s: Nothing Fails Like Success," in *Perspectives on* Citizen Kane, ed. Ronald Gottesman (New York: G. K. Hall, 1996), 82–93.

52. George Custen, *Bio/pics: How Hollywood Constructed Public History* (New Brunswick, NJ: Rutgers University Press, 1992).

53. Bob Dingilian, "Fred Zinnemann Directs Fonda and Redgrave," *Julia*, Press Kit, AMPAS, 2.

54. *Julia* (Twentieth Century-Fox), trade ad, *Los Angeles Times*, 16 October 1977, AMPAS.

55. Arthur Knight with Alvin Sargent, "Writing the Screenplay for *Julia*," Press Kit, 2–3, AMPAS.

56. AS, interviews with author, April-June 2012.

57. *Julia*, research—Vienna, box 40, folder 525, FZ Papers, AMPAS.

58. Transcribed interview with Professor Maria Jahoda collated by Tom Pevsner, 19 May 1976, 1–3, with notations by FZ, *Julia*, Research (Vienna), box 40, folder 525, FZ Papers, AMPAS.

59. FZ to Lillian Hellman (hereafter LH), June 1977 and FZ to LH (undated), both box 38, folder 491, Zinnemann Papers, AMPAS. Zinnemann's autobiography (1992) also acknowledges that Gardiner was the likely model for Julia (222).

60. LH to FZ, 20 June 1977, box 1, FZ Papers, BFI.

61. FZ, draft of letter, June 1977, box 1, FZ Papers, BFI.

62. LH to FZ, undated, 4 pp., *Julia*, box 38, folder 491, FZ Papers, AMPAS.

63. FZ, memorandum of meeting between Vanessa Redgrave, FZ, and Alvin Sargent on 8 July 1976, box 39, folder 519, FZ Papers, AMPAS.

64. Mary Blume, "A Friendship For All Seasons," *Los Angeles Times*, 26 December 1976, 48.

65. Linda Ayton, interview with the author, July 2010. See also FZ's notes, where he says they have a "gentleman's agreement" for her to "refrain from political activity damaging to film," undated, box 40, folder 542, FZ Papers, AMPAS.

66. Lillian (Jane Fonda) wears a red blouse, lipstick, and nail polish in her meeting with Julia in Vienna (1934); she wears a red dress to Sardi's for the opening of *A Children's Hour*; and again wears red when she meets Mr. Johann (Maximillian Schell) and decides to help Julia's réseau. Zinnemann's relationship with Fonda was noticeably cooler than with Redgrave. He would refer to her as "Fonda" in correspondence, and in a letter to his agent, went out of his way not to say he enjoyed working with her.

67. Clyde Gilmour, "Julia Lingers Hauntingly But Its Script Is Flawed," 8 October 1977, unmarked Toronto paper, box 37, folder 476, FZ Papers, AMPAS.

68. MD, *Julia*, October 1977: 169; Andrew Sarris, "Good Intentions Are Not Enough," *Village Voice*, 10 October 1977, 47.

69. As Zinnemann wrote on Alvin Sargent's first draft, "I would like this scrambled continuity if it were clearer . . . Interesting . . . But time sequences garbled and confusing, unless INTENTION of Al Sargent is clarified." Sargent sometimes had as many as four time jumps on a page, and Zinnemann's main goal was to maintain the disjunctive narration while clarifying its purpose to the overall story. He also substantially developed the intellectual connection between the two women. See *Julia*, first draft screenplay, annotated by FZ, "working script," January 1976, 20, box 34, folder 439, FZ Papers, AMPAS.

70. FZ, notes to Douglas Slocombe, undated, box 40, folder 542, FZ Papers, AMPAS.

71. Nevertheless, film historians are so invested in viewing Zinnemann as a kind of grim realist they cannot see the differences between the crisper, black-and-white cinematography of *The Men* (1950) and *Julia*'s glowing, even blurred sequences. Although Stephen Prince did not use any archival material or Zinnemann's notes, the contrast in cinematographic styles is undeniable (Prince, "'Do You Understand?': History and Memory in *Julia*," in *The Films of Fred Zinnemann: Critical Perspectives*, ed. Nolletti [Albany: State University Press of New York, 1999], 187–97).

72. See Baltake (*New York Daily News*) 10, 12, 77; Schiff; Crist; Sarris; Tom Dowling, "The Trouble with *Julia* is Lillian," *Washington Star*, 12 October 1977, section C, C5.

73. Sargent's original first draft script and all subsequent scripts begin with Hellman's voice-over. See box 34, folder 438, FZ Papers, AMPAS.

74. For more discussion of the historical foreword, see Smyth (2006).

75. Laura Mulvey, "Visual Pleasure and Narrative Cinema," *Screen* 16, no. 3 (1975): 6–18; Mulvey, "Afterthoughts on 'Visual Pleasure and Narrative Cinema,' Inspired by *Duel in the Sun*," *Framework* 15/16/17 (summer 1981): 12–15; Diane Waldman, "At last I can tell it to someone! Feminine Point of View and Subjectivity in the Gothic Romance Films of the 1940s," *Cinema Journal* 23, no. 2 (1983): 29–40; Molly Haskell, *From Reverence to Rape: The Treatment of Women in the Movies* (New York: Penguin, 1974); Mary Ann Doane, *The Desire to Desire* (Bloomington: Indiana University Press, 1987); Tania Modleski, *The Women Who Knew Too Much: Hitchcock and Feminist Theory* (London: Routledge, 1988).

76. Weitz, 15.

77. For more on American historical fiction and the representation of racial minorities and women, see Smyth, *Edna Ferber's Hollywood* (Austin: University of Texas Press, 2009) and Camilla Fojas and Mary Beltran, eds., *Mixed Race Hollywood* (New York: New York University Press, 2007).

78. A cluster of major Hollywood films—among them *All This and Heaven Too* (1940), *Kitty Foyle* (1940), *So Proudly We Hail* (1943), *Since You Went Away* (1944), *I Remember Mama* (1948), *A Letter to Three Wives* (1949), *Cheaper by the Dozen* (1949), *All About Eve* (1950), *Belles on Their Toes* (1950), *To Kill a Mockingbird* (1962)—employ the woman's voice as a structuring historical device throughout the entire narrative, rather than as just an introductory historical gloss.

79. Weitz, 14–17.

80. Dick, 140–45. For another view, see Stephen Prince, "'Do You Understand?': History and Memory in *Julia*," in *The Films of Fred Zinnemann: Critical Perspectives*, ed. Arthur Nolletti (Albany: State University of New York Press, 1999), 187–97.

81. Fourcade, 16.

82. See first, revised, and final drafts of scripts, FZ Papers, AMPAS.

83. For more on the development of *Citizen Kane*'s scripts, see Carringer.

84. Walter Murch, Editing Notes, annotated by FZ, undated 12pp, box 38, folder 487, FZ Papers, AMPAS.

85. FZ to RR, May 1977, folder 527, FZ Papers, AMPAS.

86. AS to FZ, 12 May 1977, box 40, folder 528, FZ Papers, AMPAS.

87. FZ, handwritten notes to editing notes, p. 3, box 38, folder 487, FZ Papers, AMPAS.

88. Zinnemann's inspiration for the recessed colonnades very likely comes from a number of research photographs he ordered of the Bodleian stacks.

89. Hellman, 427–28.

90. Zinnemann's editing notes reveal how carefully he planned the intercut death sequences. While the original script had not interwoven the two deaths, Zinnemann's notes mapped each cut (see Moscow Theatre notes, box 38, folder 487, FZ Papers, AMPAS).

91. FZ to Miller, 1 February 1964, box 2, folder 25, FZ Papers, AMPAS. See also Kate Cameron, "*Pale Horse* Spain Drama," *New York Daily News*, 9 August 1964, section 2.

92. *Les femmes dans la résistance. Actes du colloque tenu à l'initiative de l'Union des Femmes Françaises, Paris, 22 et 23 novembre, 1975* (Paris: Rocher, 1977). See also Paul Thompson's massive *The Voice of the Past: Oral History* (1978).

93. Sherna Berger Gluck, "What's So Special About Women? Women's Oral History," *Frontiers: A Journal of Women's Studies* 2, no. 2 (summer 1977): 3–17. See also *From Parlor to Prison: Five American Suffragettes Talk About Their Lives* (New York: Vintage, 1976). John A. Neuenschwander's *Oral History as a Teaching Approach* was also published that year.

94. Gluck (1977), 5.

95. Richard Cuskelly, "Richard Roth and *Julia*," *New York Herald-Examiner*, 13 March 1977.

96. Judith Weinraub, "Two Feisty Feminists Filming Hellman's *Pentimento*," *New York Times*, 31 October 1976, section 2, 17.

97. According to *Variety*, *Julia* grossed more than $20.7 million in the US (*Variety Annual*, 6 January 1979).

98. Joe Baltake, "A Tale of Two Women," *New York Daily News*, 12 October 1977, AMPAS clipping file.

99. Valerie Jenkins, "*Julia*: A Tale of Two Women," *London Evening Standard*, 26 January 1978, 17.

100. Nicholas Wapshott, "Woman's Hour," *Scotsman (Edinburgh)*, 27 January 1978, clipping, box 37, folder 474, FZ Papers, AMPAS.

101. See, for example, the French press kit, box 38, folder 505, FZ Papers, AMPAS.

102. John Higgins, "Fred Zinnemann's Search for *Julia*," 18 January 1978, 13, unmarked press clipping, box 37, folder 474, FZ Papers, AMPAS.

103. Viewers originally expected to see Woody Allen's *Annie Hall*.

104. All reports, box 39, folder 506, Comment Cards, New Haven preview, 7 and 11 July 1977, FZ Papers, AMPAS.

105. For previews, see box 39, folder 506, 507, FZ Papers, AMPAS. See Vincent Canby, *New York Times*, 3 October 1977; Sarris, "Good Intentions are Not Enough"; Haskell, *Village Voice*, October 1977; Kael, *New Yorker*, October 1977.

106. Ann D. Gordon, Mari Jo Buhle, and Nancy E. Shrom, "Women in American Society: An Historical Contribution," *Radical America* 5, no. 4 (July-August 1971): 3–66.

107. Jane Addams, *The Long Road of Women's Memory* (Urbana: University of Illinois Press, 2002), 5.

108. This was Welles's famous snap remark about Mankiewicz's creation of the Rosebud plot device which initiates the "search" for Kane's true nature.

109. During the production of *Julia*, Zinnemann became interested in Nicholas Bethell's *The Last Secret*, a history of the British Army's repatriation of thousands of Russian Cossacks and partisans after Yalta. The refugees were all doomed to extermination or internment by Stalin. Christopher Hampton's script was finished and elaborate production plans made when Alan Ladd, Jr.'s Highland Films refused finance, largely due to the expensive locations involved (see box 79, folder 1058, box 80, folder 1073, FZ Papers, AMPAS). After attempting a script rewrite with *Secret Army*'s John Brason in 1980 (box 80, folder 1068), the deal again fell through and Zinnemann made an adaptation of the fictional *Five Days One Summer* (1982), which was not a commercial success.

110. FZ to JH, 18 December 1953, box 118, folder 1484, John Huston Papers, AMPAS. FZ was approached by Huston to join him in working for Mirisch Productions and United Artists. In refusing, FZ promised to keep his decision confidential.

111. Leo Verswijver, *Movies Were Always Magical* (Jefferson, NC: McFarland & Co., 2003), 228–42.

BIBLIOGRAPHY

Archival Sources

Montgomery Clift Papers, New York Library for the Performing Arts, Lincoln Center, New York, NY.
Department of Defense Files, National Archives, College Park, MD.
David Flaherty Papers, Butler Library, Columbia University, New York, NY.
Robert J. Flaherty Papers, Butler Library, Columbia University, New York, NY.
Carl Foreman Papers, British Film Institute, London, United Kingdom.
Kathryn Hulme Papers, Beinecke Library, Yale University, New Haven, CT.
James Jones Papers, Beinecke Library, Yale University, New Haven, CT.
Stanley Kramer Papers, UCLA Special Collections, Los Angeles, CA.
Joseph Levine Papers, Mugar Memorial Library, Boston University, Boston, MA.
MGM/Paramount Script Collection, Academy of Motion Picture Arts and Sciences Library, Beverly Hills, CA.
Rosemary Murphy Papers, Mugar Memorial Library, Boston University, Boston, MA.
Anna Neagle Papers, British Film Institute, London, United Kingdom.
Gregory Peck Papers, Academy of Motion Picture Arts and Sciences Library, Beverly Hills, CA.
Production Code Administration Files, MPPDA, Academy of Motion Picture Arts and Sciences Library, Beverly Hills, CA.
David O. Selznick Papers, Harry Ransom Center, University of Texas. Austin, TX.
George Stevens Papers, Academy of Motion Picture Arts and Sciences Library, Beverly Hills, CA.
Twentieth Century-Fox Collection, University of Southern California, Los Angeles, CA.
Jack Warner Papers, Warner Bros. Archive, University of Southern California, Los Angeles, CA.
Warner Bros. Studios. Archive, University of Southern California, Los Angeles, CA.
Billy Wilder Papers, Academy of Motion Picture Arts and Sciences Library, Beverly Hills, CA.
William Wyler Papers, Academy of Motion Picture Arts and Sciences Library, Beverly Hills, CA.
Fred Zinnemann Papers, Academy of Motion Picture Arts and Sciences Library, Beverly Hills, CA.

Fred Zinnemann 35mm and 16mm Film Collection, Pickford Center for Motion Picture Study, Los Angeles, CA.
Fred Zinnemann Papers, British Film Institute, London, United Kingdom.

Interviews with Author

Lynda Ayton, July 2010.
Marsha Hunt, March 2002; April 2012.
Maria Cooper Janis, February–April 2012.
Janet Leigh, March 2002.
Virginia McKenna, July–August 2011.
Walter Mirisch, May 2012.
Walter Murch, January–March 2012.
Richard Roth, May 2013.
Alvin Sargent, February 2012.
Tim Zinnemann, 2010–2012.

Primary Sources

Addams, Jane. *The Long Road of Women's Memory*. 1916. Urbana: University of Illinois Press, 2002.
Allen, Frederick Lewis. *Only Yesterday: An Informal History of the 1920s*. New York: Harper & Bros., 1931.
———. *Since Yesterday: The 1930s in America*. New York: Harper & Bros., 1940.
Alpert, Hollis. "*High Noon*." *Saturday Review of Literature*, 5 July 1952, 29–30.
"Anarchist's End." *Time*, 6 January 1960.
Aub, Max. *Campo del moro*. Mexico: Ediciones Joaquín Mortiz, 1963.
Aubrac, Lucie. *La Résistance, naissance et organization*. Paris: Lang, 1945.
A. W. "*From Here to Eternity* Bows at Capitol With Huge Cast, Five Starring Roles." *New York Times*, 6 August 1953.
Ayala, Francisco. "La excentricidad hispana." In *Histrionismo y representación*. Buenos Aires, 1944.
Bach, Julian, Jr. *America's Germany: An Account of the Occupation*. New York: Random House, 1946.
Baltake, Joe. "A Tale of Two Women." *New York Daily News*, 12 October 1977.
Barea, Arturo. "Not Spain But Hemingway." *Horizon*, May 1941, 350–61.
Barnes, Howard. "*The Seventh Cross*." *New York Herald Tribune*, 29 September 1944.
Barnes, Oscar. "Zinnemann's Concept of the Hero." *New York Herald Tribune*, 9 August 1964.

Barthes, Roland. "The Face of Garbo." In *Mythologies*. 1957. London: Vintage, 1993, 56–57.
Beaufort, John. "*The Search* Puts Accent on Realism: Movie Delves into Plight of DPs and Reaffirms Faith in Humanity." *Christian Science Monitor*, 26 July 1948.
Beck, Beatrix. *Léon Morin, prêtre*. Paris: Gallimard, 1952.
Becker, Carl. *Everyman His Own Historian: Essays on History and Politics*. New York: F. S. Crofts & Co., 1935.
"Behold a Pale Horse." *Hollywood Reporter* (7 August 1964).
Bertrand, Simone. *Mille visages, un seul combat: Les femmes dans la résistance*. Paris: Français Réunis, 1965.
Bidault, Suzanne. *Souvenirs de guerre et d'occupation*. Paris: La Table Ronde, 1973.
Blackey, Eileen. "Children Have Forgotten the Czech Language." *UNRRA Newsletter*, no. 9 (December 1945), 9.
"*Blockade!*" *Variety*, 31 December 1937.
Blume, Mary. "A Friendship For All Seasons." *Los Angeles Times*, 26 December 1976, 48.
Bohec, Jeanne. *La plastiqueuse à bicyclette*. Paris: Merceure de France, 1975.
Bolt, Robert. *A Man for All Seasons*. London: William Heinemann, 1962.
Bonney, Thérèse. *Europe's Children*. New York: Thérèse Bonney, 1942.
Browder, Earl. *A Political Program of Native American Fascism*. New York: New Century Publishers, 1945.
Buckmaster, Maurice. *They Fought Alone: The Story of British Agents in France*. New York: W. W. Norton, 1958.
Burgard, Sister Dolores. "Sister Luke Had No Vocation." *Catholic World*, April 1957, 40–50.
Byrne, Bridget. "*The Day of the Jackal*: The Hunter and the Hunted." *Los Angeles Herald-Examiner*, 18 May 1973, B4.
Camus, Albert. *Resistance, Rebellion, and Death*. London: Hamish Hamilton, 1964.
Carmody, Jay. "New Film Directors Climb to Top-Flight Positions." *Washington Star*, 31 August 1948.
Cass, Carole. "Anti de Gaulle Plot on Film." *Richmond Times Dispatch*, 20 May 1973.
"Columbia Backing of *Pale Horse* Was Courageous, Zinnemann Says." *Motion Picture Daily* (11 August 1964).
"Columbia Beyond *Pale* in Spain." *Variety* (11 August 1964).
Crowther, Bosley. "*The Seventh Cross*." *New York Times*, 1 October 1944.
———. "From The War's Fringe: *Marie-Louise* (1945)." *New York Times*, 13 November 1945.
———. "*The Search*." *New York Times*, 24 March 1948.
———. "*High Noon*, A Western of Rare Achievement." *New York Times*, 26 July 1952.
———. "Western Legend." *New York Times*, 5 August 1952.
———. "The Oscar Awards: Showmanship Rather Than Artistry Reigned at the Academy Affair." *New York Times*, 29 March 1953.

Cunningham, John M. "The Tin Star." *Colliers*, 6 December 1947.
Cuskelly, Richard. "Richard Roth and *Julia*." *New York Herald-Examiner*, 13 March 1977.
The Dark Side of the Moon. London: Faber and Faber, 1946.
"*The Day of the Jackal*." *Independent Film Journal* 71, no. 13 (28 May 1973).
Dennis, Eugene. *Fascist Danger and How to Combat It*. New York: New Century Publishers, 1948.
Dennis, Leslie. *The Coming of American Fascism*. New York: Harper & Bros., 1936.
Doudna, Christine. "A Still Unfinished Woman: A Conversation with Lillian Hellman." *Rolling Stone*, 24 February 1977, 53.
Dowling, Tom. "The Trouble with *Julia* is Lillian." *Washington Star*, 12 October 1977.
Doyle, Charles Hugo. "*The Nun's Story*: Trash or Treasure?" *Oratory*, July–August 1957, 5–11.
Dumilieu, Anne-Marguerite. *Moi, une cobaye*. Paris: SEFA, 1975.
Eastaugh, Ken. "Better than Bond, More Crafty than Callan." *Sun*, 10 April 1972.
"Edward Fox Is the Jackal." *CinemaTV Today*, 11 March 1972, 1, 7.
Edwards, Nadine. "Is Oscar Becoming a British Subject?" *Hollywood Citizen-News-Valley Times*, 11 April 1967, 13, AA section.
Elnnon, Peter. "Private Revolutionary, Public Bourgeois." *Manchester Guardian*, 29 July 1969.
"Expects Hierarchy Approval for Filmed *Nun's Story*." *Variety*, 10 July 1957, 3.
"Fate Steps in on Fred Zinnemann." *Daily Mirror*, 24 November 1969, 15.
Flaherty, David. "Serpents in Eden." *Asia*, October 1925, 858–69, 895–98.
Forsyth, Frederick. *The Day of the Jackal*. New York: Viking, 1970.
Fourcade, Marie-Madeleine. *Noah's Ark: A Memoir of Struggle and Resistance*. 1968. New York: E. P. Dutton, 1974.
"Francisco Sabaté." *Newsweek*, 18 January 1960, 28, 30.
"Fred Zinnemann, Edward Fox, and *Day of the Jackal*." *International Herald Tribune*, 5–6 August 1972.
Friedman, Paul. "Can Freedom Be Taught?" *Journal of Social Casework* 29, no. 7 (July 1948): 247–55.
———. "The Road Back for the DPs." *Commentary* 6, no. 6 (December 1948): 502–10.
Friedman, Ina. *The Other Victims: First-Person Stories of Non-Jews Persecuted by the Nazis*. New York: Sandpiper, 1995.
"From Here to Eternity." *New York Times*, 6 March 1951.
"From Here to Eternity." *Los Angeles Times*, 2 August 1953.
Gardiner, Harold C. "Enchanting Revolutionary." *America*, 15 September 1956, 568–69.
Gardiner, Muriel. *Code Name "Mary"*. New Haven: Yale University Press, 1981.
Garner, Lesley. "Lesley Garner Meets the Legendary Actress as She Prepares for This Week's UNICEF Gala Performance." *Sunday Telegraph*, 26 May 1991.
Gazzo, Michael Vincente. *A Hatful of Rain*. New York: Random House, 1956.
Gellhorn, Martha. "On Apocryphism." *Paris Review* 23, no. 79 (spring 1981): 280–301.

Gilliatt, Penelope. "*The Day of the Jackal.*" *New Yorker*, 2 June 1973, 66–67.
Gironella, José María. *Los cipreses creen en Díos*. Barcelona: Planeta, 1955.
———. *Un millón de muertos*. Barcelona: Planeta, 1961.
Gollancz, Victor. *In Darkest Germany*. Hinsdale, IL: Henry Regnery, 1947.
"Guerrilla Leader Killed by Spanish Police." *New York Times*, 6 January 1960.
Guernsey, Otis, Jr. "Oscar's Getting Stodgy." *New York Herald Tribune*, 29 March 1953.
———. "The Elusive Art of a Hollywood Director." *New York Herald Tribune*, 25 January 1953, section 4, 1.
Harrison, Earl G. *Report*. Department of State Bulletin, 30 September 1945, no. 13, 456–63 (reprinted in Dinnerstein, app. B 291–305).
———. "The Last Hundred Thousand." *Survey Graphic*, December 1945, 469–73.
Hast, Henry. *Films in Review* 4, no. 2 (February 1953): 88.
Hellman, Lillian. *Three: An Unfinished Woman, Pentimento, Scoundrel Time*. Boston: Little, Brown, 1979.
Hemingway, Ernest. *For Whom the Bell Tolls*. New York: Scribners, 1941.
Herr, Dan. "Stop Pushing!" *Books on Trial*, November 1956, 140, 152.
Hestor, Sister May. "*The Nun's Story*." *Books on Trial*, October 1956, 74.
"High Noon." *Sight and Sound* 22, no. 1 (July 1952): 17+.
Hill, William Thomson. *The Martyrdom of Nurse Cavell*. London: Hutchinson & Co., 1915.
Holmes, Kenneth L., ed. *Covered Wagon Women: Diaries and Letters from the Western Trails*. Lincoln: University of Nebraska Press, 1995.
Hulme, Kathryn. *The Wild Place*. Boston: Little, Brown, 1953.
———. *The Nun's Story*. Boston: Little, Brown, 1956.
———. "The Real Sister Luke." *American Weekly*, 30 December 1956, 6–7.
Ibárruri, Dolores. *They Shall Not Pass: The Autobiography of La Pasionaria*. New York: International Publishers, 1966.
Janis, Maria Cooper. *Gary Cooper Off-Camera: A Daughter Remembers*. New York: Harry N. Abrams, 1999.
Johnson, William. "Zinnemann Pictures a Modern Dilemma." *Entertainment*, 30 September 1964, 28.
———. "*Behold a Pale Horse*." *Film Quarterly* (winter 1964–65): 46–50.
Jones, James. *From Here to Eternity*. New York: Scribners, 1951.
———. *World War II*. New York: Grosset & Dunlap, 1975.
Kent, Victoria. *Cuatro años en Paris*. Buenos Aires: Sur, 1947.
Knauth, Percy. *Germany in Defeat*. New York: Knopf, 1946.
Koestler, Arthur. *Spanish Testament*. London: Victor Gollancz, 1937.
Kramer, Stanley, with Thomas Coffey. *It's a Mad, Mad, Mad, Mad World: A Life in Hollywood*. New York: Harcourt, 1997.
Lehman, L. H. *Vatican Policy in the Second World War*. New York: Agora Press, 1946.
Levin, Meyer. *In Search: An Autobiography*. New York: Horizon Press, 1950.

Lewis, Richard Warren. Interview with John Wayne. *Playboy* (May 1971), 1–19.
Lichten, Hans. *"Collaboration": Phantom und Wirklichkeit*. Offenbach: Bollwek-Verlag, 1948.
Macardle, Dorothy. *Children of Europe—A Study of the Children of Liberated Countries: Their War-Time Experiences, Their Reactions, and Their Needs, with a Note on Germany*. Boston: Beacon Press, 1951.
MacDonald, Dwight. *Fascism and the American Scene*. New York: Pioneer Publishers, 1938.
MacDonald, Elizabeth. *Undercover Girl*. New York: Macmillan, 1947.
Malraux, André. *Man's Fate*. 1933. London: Penguin, 2009.
———. *Anti-Memoirs*. 1964. New York: Holt, Rinehart, Winston, 1968.
A Man for All Seasons, Program. Columbia Pictures Corp., 1966.
Manhattan, A. *The Catholic Church Against the Twentieth Century*. London: Watts, 1950.
McBride, Joseph, and Howard Hawks. "A Discussion with the Audience of the 1970 Chicago Film Festival." In *Focus on Howard Hawks*, edited by Joseph McBride, 15–16. Englewood Cliffs, NJ: Prentice-Hall, 1972.
McCullers, Carson. *The Member of the Wedding*. 1946. New York: Penguin, 1962.
Michaelson Annette, et al., ed. *Drawing into Film: Directors' Drawings. Catalog of Exhibition at Pace Gallery, New York, 26 March–23 April 1993*. New York: The Pace Gallery, 1993.
Miller, Gabriel, ed. *Fred Zinnemann Interviews*. Jackson: University Press of Mississippi, 2004.
Minney, Rubeign James. *Carve Her Name With Pride*. London: Collins, 1956.
Montseny, Federica. *El éxodo, pasión y muerte de los españoles en el exilio*. Barcelona: Galba Ediciones, 1977.
Morris, Jane. "The Zinnemanns: An International Family." *Parents' Magazine* (January 1951), 32–33.
"Movie Version of Army Novel Opens." *New York Herald Tribune*, 2 August 1953, section 4.
Murf. "*The Day of the Jackal*." *Variety*, 2 May 1973, 6.
"Muy Hombre." *Newsweek*, 24 August 1964.
Neave, Airey. *Little Cyclone*. 1954. Foreword by Group Captain Douglas Bader. London: Panther, 1957.
"No Borehamwood Sale; M-G-M Ends *Fate*." *Variety*, 25 November 1969.
"*The Nun's Story*." *Films and Filming* 6, no. 3 (December 1959): 7.
"The Old Dependables." *Film Quarterly* 3, no. 1 (October 1959): 14.
Orwell, George. *Collected Essays*. London: Secker & Warburg, 1961.
"*Pale Horse* Lost Firm 2,500,000." *Variety*, 26 January 1966.
Papanek, Ernst. "They Are Not Expendable: The Homeless and Refugee Children of Germany." *Social Service Review* 20, no. 3 (September 1946): 312–19.
Pettiss, Susan T., with Lynne Taylor. *After the Shooting Stopped: The Story of an UNRRA Welfare Worker in Germany, 1945–1947*. Victoria, BC: Trafford Press, 2004.

Phillips, Gene D. "Fred Zinnemann: An Interview." *Journal of Popular Film and Television* 7, no. 1 (June 1978): 57–66.
Politiken. 19 February 1978.
Popkin, Zelda. "Europe's Children." *Ladies' Home Journal*, August 1946, 168, 170–71.
Powr. "*The Nun's Story*." *Variety*, 6 May 1959, 6
Pressburger, Emeric. *Killing a Mouse on Sunday*. London: Collins, 1961.
Price, David. "*The Nun's Story*." *Ave Maria*, 8 September 1956, 23.
Prior, Thomas. "Epic of Europe's Lost Children: History of *The Search*." *New York Times*, 14 March 1948.
Radio Times 216, no. 2807 (7 August 1977): 9–10.
Redgrave, Vanessa. *An Autobiography*. 1991. London: Arrow, 1992.
Reid, John Howard. "A Man for All Movies: The Films of Fred Zinnemann." *Film and Filming* 13.8 (May 1967): 5–11.
Ridruejo, Dionisio. *Escrito en España*. Buenos Aires: Editorial Losada, 1962.
Riis, Jacob. *How the Other Half Lives*. 1890. London: Penguin, 1997.
Rosenheimer, Arthur [Arthur Knight pseud.] "They Make Documentaries: Number One: Robert Flaherty." *Film News* 7, no. 6 (April 1946): 1–23.
Rourke, Mary. "Jane and Vanessa and Lillian and *Julia*." *W*, 30 September–October 7, 1977, 10.
"Saga of a Tired Spanish Loyalist." *Daily Variety*, 10 July 1963.
Sarris, Andrew. "Good Intentions Are Not Enough." *Village Voice*, 10 October 1977, 47.
Sartre, Jean-Paul. "Presentations des tempes modernes." In *Situations II*. Paris: Gallimard, 1948.
Schallert, Edwin. "*From Here to Eternity* Blasts Viewers with Atomic Power." *Los Angeles Times*, 1 October 1953, B11.
Schein, Harry. "The Olympian Cowboy." *American Scholar* 24, no. 3 (September 1955): 309–20.
Scheuer, Philip K. "Devotion to Book Told by Director; Zinnemann Spends Two Years Filming, Cutting *Nun's Story*." *Los Angeles Times*, 13 April 1959.
Schickel, Richard. "*Behold a Pale Horse*." *Life*, 21 August 1964.
Schiff, Stephen. "Two Women: In Defense of *Julia*." *Boston Phoenix*, 18 October 1977, III, 5, 8.
Seghers, Anna. *The Seventh Cross*. Boston: Little, Brown, 1942.
"*The Seventh Cross*." *New York Journal-American*, 29 September 1944.
"*The Seventh Cross*." *Los Angeles Herald*, 29 September 1944.
Silke, James R. "Zinnemann: True or False." *Cinema* 2, no. 1 (February 1964): 15–19.
———. "Zinnemann Talks Back." *Cinema* 2, no. 3 (October-November 1964): 20–22, 30. In *Fred Zinnemann Interviews*, edited by Gabriel Miller, 9–25. Jackson: University of Mississippi Press, 2005.
Smith, Susan. "*Julia*: The Hellman Connection." *W*, 7–14 January 1977, 19.
"Spaniards Flee to France in Greatest Mass Exodus of Modern Times." *Life*, 20 February 1939.

Sterritt, David. "*Day of the Jackal*: Screen Chiller." *Christian Science Monitor*, 1 June 1973, 9.
Sweeney, Louie. "Fred Zinnemann: Profile." *Christian Science Monitor*, 22 June 1973, 9.
Swing, Raymond G. *Forerunners of American Fascism*. New York: J. Messner, 1935.
Tannehill, Evelyne. *Abandoned and Forgotten: An Orphan Girl's Tale of Survival in World War II*. New York: Wheatmark, 2007.
Taylor, John Russell. "Film Director who likes to let his subject speak for itself." *Times*, 18 March 1967, Arts, 7.
Taylor, Winchell. "Secret Movie Censors." *Nation* 124 (9 July 1938), 38–40.
Terrenoire, Elisabeth. *Combattantes sans uniforme: les femmes dans la résistance*. Paris: Bloud et Gay, 1946.
Thompson, Howard. "Directed by Zinnemann." *New York Times*, 25 January 1953.
Ticknell, Jerrard. *Odette: Story of a British Agent*. London: Chapman & Hall, 1949.
Trilling, Diana. *We Must March My Darlings: A Critical Decade*. New York: Harcourt Brace Jovanovich, 1977.
Trinka, Zena Irma. *A Little Village Called Lidice: Story of the Return of the Women and Children of Lidice*. Lidgerwood, ND: International Book Publishers, 1947.
Turner, Frederick Jackson. "The Significance of the Frontier in American History." 1893. In *Rereading Frederick Jackson Turner*, edited by John Mack Faragher. New York: Henry Holt, 1995.
"Two Movies, Two Audrey Hepburns." *New York Times Magazine*, 23 November 1958, 62–63.
Vandenbussche, E. J. "Gabrielle in Wonderland." *Linie Brussels*, 12 April 1957.
Verswijver, Leo. *Movies Were Always Magical*. Jefferson, NC: McFarland & Co., 2003.
Viertel, Salka. *The Kindness of Strangers*. New York: Holt, Rinehart, and Winston, 1969.
"War Crimes: 'It was only 2,000,000.'" *Time*, 14 April 1947.
Weinraub, Judith. "Two Feisty Feminists Filming Hellman's *Pentimento*." *New York Times*, 31 October 1976, 17.
Wilder, Billy. "The Wilder Memorandum." In *The Americanization of Germany, 1945–1949*, edited by Ralph Willett, 40–44. London: Routledge, 1989.
Wilson, Cecil. "The Day the Fox Triumphed as the Jackal." *Daily Mail*, 15 June 1973.
Wittek, Suzanne. *Comète, histoire d'une ligne d'évasion*. Brussels: M. Thomas, 1948.
Woodbridge, George. *UNRRA: The History of the United Nations Relief and Rehabilitation Administration*. 3 vols. New York: Columbia University Press, 1950.
Wylie, I. A. R. "Returning Europe's Kidnapped Children." *Ladies' Home Journal*, October 1946, 22–23, 254–57.
Zinnemann, Fred. *An Autobiography*. New York: Scribners, 1992.
———. "The Story of *The Search* by Fred Zinnemann." *Screenwriter* 4, no. 2 (August 1948): 12–13, 30.
———. "Different Perspective." *Sight and Sound* 17.67 (Autumn 1948): 113.
———. "Remembering Robert Flaherty." *Action* (May-June 1976): 25–27.
———. "Revelations." *Films and Filming* 10, no. 12 (September 1964): 5–6.

"Zinnemann's *Pale Horse* is a Film Masterpiece." *Hollywood Reporter*, 14 August 1964, 3.
Zullo, Allan, and Mara Bovsun, eds. *Survivors: True Stories of Children in the Holocaust*. New York: Scholastic, 2004.
Zunser, Jesse. "High Noon." *Cue*, 26 July 1952, 26.
———. "From Here to Eternity." *Cue*, 8 August 1953, 16.

Secondary Sources

Aldgate, Anthony. *Cinema and History: British Newsreels and the Spanish Civil War*. London: Scholar, 1979.
Alexander, William. *Film on the Left: American Documentary Film From 1931 to 1942*. Princeton, NJ: Princeton University Press, 1981.
Altman, Rick. *Film/Genre*. London: BFI, 2000.
Anderson, Benedict. *Imagined Communities: Reflections on the Origins and Spread of Nationalism*. London: Verso, 1991.
Archibald, David. *The War That Won't Die: The Spanish Civil War in Cinema*. Manchester: Manchester University Press, 2012.
Arendt, Hannah. *The Origins of Totalitarianism*. 1951. New York: Harcourt, Brace, Jovanovich, 1973.
Armitage, Susan, and Elizabeth Jameson, eds. *Women's West*. Norman: University of Oklahoma Press, 1987.
Aron, Robert. *Histoire de Vichy, 1940–1944*. 1954. New York: Macmillan, 1958.
Bailey, Beth, and David Farber. *The First Strange Place: Race and Sex in World War II Hawaii*. Baltimore: Johns Hopkins University Press, 1992.
Barsam, Richard. *The Vision of Robert Flaherty: The Artist as Myth and Filmmaker*. Bloomington: Indiana University Press, 1988.
Batchelor, R. "André Malraux and the Concept of Revolt." *Modern Languages Review* 67, no. 4 (October 1972): 799–809.
Bazin, André. "The Evolution of the Western." 1955. In *What is Cinema? Volume II*, translated by Hugh Gray. Berkeley: University of California Press, 1971.
Bell, Leland V. *In Hitler's Shadow, The Anatomy of American Nazism*. Port Washington, NY: Kennikat Press, 1973.
Bell-Metereau, Rebecca. "1953: Movies and Our Secret Lives." In *American Cinema in the 1950s: Themes and Variations*, edited by Murray Pomerance, 89–110. New Brunswick, NJ: Rutgers University Press, 2005.
Bérubé, Allan. *Coming Out Under Fire: The History of Gay Men and Women in World War II*. New York: Free Press, 1990.
Bingham, Dennis. *Whose Lives Are They Anyway? The Biopic as Contemporary Film Genre*. New Brunswick, NJ: Rutgers University Press, 2010.
Birdwell, Michael E. *Celluloid Soldiers: The Warner Bros. Campaign Against Nazism*. New York: New York University Press, 1999.

Biskind, Peter. *Seeing Is Believing*. London: Pluto Books, 1983.
Bradley, J. F. N. *Lidice, Sacrificial Village*. London: Ballantine Books, 1972.
Brook, Vincent. *Driven to Darkness: Jewish Émigré Filmmakers and the Rise of Film Noir*. New Brunswick, NJ: Rutgers University Press, 2009.
Brothers, Caroline. *War and Photography: A Cultural History*. New York: Routledge, 1997.
Brown, Dee. *The Gentle Tamers*. New York: Putnam, 1958.
Burch, Noël, and Geneviève Sellier. *Drôle de guerre des sexes du cinéma francais*. Paris: Nathan, 1996.
Buscombe, Ed. "Inventing Monument Valley." In *The Western Reader*, edited by Jim Kitses and Gregg Rickman, 114–30. New York: Limelight, 1998.
Byman, Jeremy. *Showdown at High Noon: Witchhunts, Critics, and the End of the Western*. Lanham, MD: Scarecrow Press, 2004.
Calder-Marshall, Arthur. *The Innocent Eye: The Life of Robert J. Flaherty*. New York: Harcourt, Brace and World, 1963.
Camino, Mercedes Maroto. *Film, Memory, and the Legacy of the Spanish Civil War: Resistance and Guerilla 1936–2010*. London: Palgrave, 2011.
Camparros-Lera, J. M. "Cinematic Contextual History of *High Noon*." *Film-Historia* VI, 1 (1996), 37–61.
Carringer, Robert. *The Making of Citizen Kane*. Berkeley: University of California Press, 1985.
Casper, Drew. *Postwar Hollywood*. London: Wiley-Blackwell, 2007.
Ceplair, Larry. "The Politics of Compromise in Hollywood: A Case Study." *Cineaste* 8, no. 4 (1982): 2–7.
———. *Inquisition in Hollywood: Politics in the Film Community, 1930–1960*. Garden City, NY: Doubleday, 1980.
———. *Under the Shadow of War: Fascism, Antifascism, and Marxists*. New York: Columbia University Press, 1987.
Chambers, John Whiteclay. "The Movies and the Antiwar Debate in America, 1930–1941." *Film and History* 36, no. 1 (fall 2006): 44–57.
Chatel, Nicole. *Des femmes dans la Résistance*. Paris: Juilliard, 1982.
Choate, J. B., and J. E. Frantz. *The American Cowboy: The Myth and the Reality*. Norman: University of Oklahoma Press, 1955.
Clark, Suzanne. *Cold Warriors: Manliness of Trial in the Rhetoric of the West*. Carbondale: Southern Illinois University Press, 2000.
Clarke, David. "German Martyrs: Images of Christianity and Resistance to National Socialism in German Cinema." In *Screening War*, edited by Paul Cook and Marc Silberman, 36–55. Rochester, NY: Camden House, 2010.
Combs, Richard. "Retrospective: *High Noon*." In *The Western Reader*, edited by Jim Kitses and Gregg Rickman, 167–72. New York: Limelight, 1998.
Cook, Pam. *Screening the Past: Memory and Nostalgia in Cinema*. London: Routledge, 2004.

Cook, Paul, and Marc Silberman, eds. *Screening War: Perspectives on German Suffering.* Rochester, NY: Camden House, 2010.
Cooper, Norman. "The Church: From Crusade to Christianity." In *Spain in Crisis*, edited by Paul Preston, 48–81. Hassocks, Sussex: The Harvester Press, Ltd., 1976.
Costello, Matthew J. "Rewriting *High Noon*." In *Hollywood's West*, edited by Peter C. Rollins and John E. O'Connor, 175–197. Lexington: University Press of Kentucky, 2005.
Cott, Nancy, and Elizabeth Pleck, eds. *A Heritage of Her Own: Toward a New Social History of American Women.* New York: Simon & Schuster, 1979.
Cottam, Kazimiera Jean. *Women in War and Resistance: Selected Biographies of Soviet Women.* Nepean, Canada: New Military Publishing, 2006.
Courtivron, Isabelle de. "The Other Malraux in Indochina." *Biography* 12, no. 1 (winter 1989): 29–42.
Coyne, Michael. *The Crowded Prairie: American National Identity in the Hollywood Western.* London: I. B. Taurus, 1997.
Cuevas Gutiérrez, Tomasa. *Mujeres de la resistencia.* Barcelona: Ediciones Sirocco, 1985.
Cymet, David. *History Vs. Apologetics: The Holocaust, The Third Reich, and the Catholic Church.* New York: Lexington Books, 2010.
Davie, Michael. "The Life and Lies of Lillian Hellman." *Observer*, 26 October 1986, 64.
Debray, Régis. *Charles de Gaulle: Futurist of the Nation.* London: Verso, 1994.
Demetz, Peter. *Prague in Danger: The Years of Occupation, 1939–1945.* New York: Farrar, Straus and Giroux, 2008.
Des Jardins, Julie. *Women and the Historical Profession in America.* Chapel Hill: University of North Carolina Press, 2003.
Desilets, Sean. "The Rhetoric of Passion." *Camera Obscura* 53, no. 2 (2003): 57–91.
Dick, Bernard F. *Hellman in Hollywood.* Rutherford: Fairleigh Dickinson Press, 1982.
Dickstein, Morris. "The Last Film of the 1930s: Nothing Fails Like Success." In *Perspectives on* Citizen Kane, edited by Ronald Gottesman, 82–93. New York: G. K. Hall, 1996.
Dieter, Marga. *Aamie's War: Women and Children on the German Homefront.* Bloomington, IN: iUniverse, 2007.
Dinnerstein, Leonard. *America and the Survivors of the Holocaust.* New York: Columbia University Press, 1982.
———. *Anti-Semitism in America.* New York: Oxford, 1994.
Doniol-Valcroze, Daniel. "Un homme marche dans la trahison." *Cahiers du cinéma* 3, no. 16 (October 1952): 58–60.
Doherty, Thomas. *Projections of War: Hollywood, American Culture, and World War II.* New York: Columbia University Press, 1999.
Drummond, Phillip. *High Noon.* London: BFI, 1997.
Ehrlich, Linda. "*Behold a Pale Horse*: Zinnemann and the Spanish Civil War." In *The Films of Fred Zinnemann*, edited by Arthur Nolletti, Jr., 139–56. Albany: State University Press of New York, 1999.

Eldridge, David. *Hollywood's History Films*. London: I. B. Taurus, 2006.
Etheridge, Brian C. "In Search of Germans: Contested Germany in the Production of *The Search*." *Journal of Popular Film and TV* 34, no. 1 (April 2006): 34–45.
European Resistance Movements 1939–1945: First International Conference on the History of the Resistance Movements Held at Liege-Bruxelles-Breendonk, 14–17 September 1958. London: Pergamon, 1960.
Fay, Jennifer. *Theaters of Occupation: Hollywood and the Reeducation of Postwar Germany*. Minneapolis: University of Minnesota Press, 2008.
Fernández, Alberta. *Espanoles en la resistencia*. Bilbao: Zero, 1973.
Fernández, Valentina. *La resistencia interior en la España de Franco*. Madrid: Editorial Istmo, 1981.
Fischer, Conan. *The German Communists and the Rise of Nazism*. London: Palgrave, 1991.
Foster, Gwendolyn Audrey. "Women in *High Noon*: A Metanarrative of Difference." *Film Criticism* 18, no. 3; 19, no. 1 (spring-fall 1994): 72–81.
French, Philip. *Westerns*. London: Secker & Warburg, 1977.
Frenay, Henri. *Night Will End*. 1973. New York: McGraw-Hill, 1975.
Friedlander, Saul, ed. *Probing the Limits of Representations: Nazism and the Final Solution*. Cambridge: Harvard University Press, 1992.
Geist, Kenneth. *Pictures Will Talk: The Life and Film of Joseph L. Mankiewicz*. New York: Scribners, 1978.
Gemunden, Gerd. *Foreign Affairs: Billy Wilder's American Films*. Oxford: Berghahn Books, 2008.
———. "In the Ruins of Berlin: *A Foreign Affair*." In *German Postwar Films*, edited by Wilfried Wilms and William Rasch, 109–124. London: Palgrave Macmillan, 2008.
Giles, James R. *James Jones*. Boston: Twayne, 1981.
Gilmour, David. *The Transformation of Spain: From Franco to Constitutional Monarchy*. London: Quartet, 1985.
Girgus, Sam B. *Hollywood Renaissance: The Cinema of Democracy in the Era of Ford, Capra, and Kazan*. New York: Cambridge University Press, 1998.
Gluck, Sherna Berger. "What's So Special About Women? Women's Oral History." *Frontiers: A Journal of Women's Studies* 2, no. 2 (summer 1977): 3–17.
———. *From Parlor to Prison: Five American Suffragettes Talk About Their Lives*. New York: Vintage, 1976.
Goldhagen, Daniel Jonah. *A Moral Reckoning: The Role of the Catholic Church in the Holocaust and Its Unfinished Duty of Repair*. New York: Knopf, 2002.
Golsan, Richard J. *Vichy's Afterlife: History and Counterhistory in Postwar France*. Lincoln: University of Nebraska Press, 2000.
Gordon, Ann D., Mari Jo Buhle, and Nancy E. Schrom. "Women in American Society: A Historical Contribution." *Radical America* 5, no. 4 (1971): 3–36.
Gottesman, Ronald, ed. *Perspectives on Citizen Kane*. New York: G. K. Hall, 1996.

Graebner, William. *The Age of Doubt: American Thought and Culture in the 1940s*. New York: Waveland Press, 1991.
Granet, Marie. *Combat*. Paris: Presses Universitaires, 1957.
Griffith, Richard. *Fred Zinnemann*. New York: Museum of Modern Art, 1958.
Grossmann, Atina. *Jews, Germans, and Allies: Close Encounters in Occupied Germany*. Princeton: Princeton University Press, 2007.
Hake, Sabine. "Political Affects: Antifascism and the Second World War in Frank Beyer and Konrad Wolf." In *Screening War*, edited by Paul Cook and Marc Silberman, 102–22. Rochester, NY: Camden House, 2010.
Harlow, Barbara. *Resistance Literature*. New York: Methuen, 1987.
Harrison, Alexander, et al. *Le défi à de Gaulle: L'OAS et la contre-révolution en Algérie 1954–1962*. Paris: Harmattan, 2008.
Haskell, Molly. *From Reverence to Rape: The Treatment of Women in Movies*. 1977. Chicago: University of Chicago Press, 1987.
Haskell, Thomas. "Deterministic Implications of Intellectual History." In *New Directions in American Intellectual History*, edited by John Higham and Paul Conkin. Baltimore: Johns Hopkins University Press, 1979.
Hawes, Stephen, and Ralph White, eds. *Resistance in Europe: 1939–45*. Harmondsworth, Sussex: Penguin, 1976.
Hendler, Jane. *Best-Sellers and Their Film Adaptations in Postwar America*. New York: Peter Lang, 2001.
Higham, Charles. *Audrey*. New York: Macmillan, 1984.
Higonnet, Margaret, Jane Jenson, Sonya Michel, and Margaret Collins Weitz, eds. *Behind the Lines: Gender and the Two World Wars*. New Haven: Yale University Press, 1987.
Higson, Andrew, and Richard Maltby. *"Film Europe" and "Film America."* Exeter: University of Exeter Press, 1999.
Hoberman, J. *Bridge of Light: Yiddish Film Between Two Worlds*. 1991. Hanover, NH: Dartmouth College Press, 2010.
Hoffman, Peter. *The History of the German Resistance, 1933–1945*. McGill: Queen's University Press, 1996.
Hoffman, Stanley. *In Search of France*. Cambridge: Harvard University Press, 1963.
Horak, Jan-Christopher. "The Other Germany in Zinnemann's *The Seventh Cross* (1943)." In *German Film and Literature*, edited by Eric Rentschler, 117–131. London: Routledge, 1986.
Huddleston, Sisley. *France: The Tragic Years, 1939–1947*. New York: Devin Adair, 1955.
Isenberg, Sheila. *Her War*. London: Palgrave Macmillan, 2010.
Jacobowitz, Florence. "The Dietrich Westerns." In *Movie Book of the Western*, edited by Ian Cameron and Douglas Pye, 88–98. London: Studio Vista, 1996.
Jeffrey, Charlie. *Social Democracy in the Austrian Provinces, 1918–1934: Beyond Red Vienna*. London: Leicester University Press, 1996.

Jenkins, McKay. "Dramatizing *Member of the Wedding*." In *Twentieth Century American Fiction on Screen*, edited by R. Barton Palmer, 90–105. Cambridge: Cambridge University Press, 2007.
Johnson, Diane. *Dashiell Hammett: A Life*. New York: Random House, 1983.
Judson, Helen. *Edith Cavell*. New York: Macmillan, 1941.
Kael, Pauline. "Raising Kane." 1971. In *Raising Kane and Other Essays*, 159–266. London: Marion Boyars, 1996.
Kaes, Anton. *From Hitler to Heimat: The Return of History as Film*. Cambridge: Harvard University Press, 1989.
Kedward, H. R. *Occupied France: Collaboration and Resistance, 1940–1944*. London: Blackwell, 1985.
———. *Resistance in Vichy France*. Oxford: Oxford University Press, 1978.
———. *In Search of the Maquis. Rural Resistance in Southern France, 1942–1944*. Oxford University Press, 1993.
Kibelka, Ruth. *Wolfskinder. Grenzgänger an der Memel*. Berlin: Basisdruck, 2003.
Killeen, Dennis. "Review of Lewy: The Catholic Church and Nazi Germany." *Western Political Quarterly* 18, no. 2 (June 1965): 406–408.
Kimche, Jon, and David Kimche. *The Secret Roads: The "Illegal" Migration of a People—1938–1948*. New York: Farrar, Strauss and Cudahy, 1955.
Kitses, Jim. *Horizons West*. London: BFI, 2004.
———, and Gregg Rickman, eds. *The Western Reader*. New York: Limelight, 1998.
Klemperer, Klemens von. *German Resistance Against Hitler: The Search For Allies Abroad, 1938–45*. Oxford: Clarendon Press, 1994.
Knightley, Phillip. *The First Casualty: From the Crimea to the Falklands: The War Correspondent as Hero, Propagandist, and Mythmaker*. London: Book Club Edition, 1975.
Koepnick, Lutz. "Unsettling America: German Westerns and Modernity." *Modernism/modernity* 2, no. 3 (September 1995): 1–22.
Königseder, Angelika, and Juliane Wetzel. *Waiting for Hope: Jewish Displaced Persons in Post-World War II Germany*. Translated by John A. Broadwin. Evanston, IL: Northwestern University Press, 2001.
Koppes, Clayton R., and Gregory Black. *Hollywood Goes to War: How Politics, Profits and Propaganda Shaped World War II Movies*. New York: Free Press, 1987.
Kozloff, Sarah. *Invisible Storytellers: Voice-Over Narration in American Fiction Film*. Berkeley: University of California Press, 1988.
Krippner, James. *Paul Strand in Mexico*. New York: Aperture, 2010.
Kurek, Ewa. *Your Life is Worth Mine: How Polish Nuns Saved Hundreds of Jewish Lives in German-Occupied Poland, 1939–1945*. New York: Hippocrene Books, 1997.
Lagrou, Pieter. *The Legacy of Nazi Occupation: Patriotic Memory and National Recovery in Western Europe, 1945–1965*. Cambridge: Cambridge University Press, 2000.
———. "Belgium." In *Resistance in Western Europe*, edited by Bob Moore, 27–63. New York: Berg, 2000.

Landy, Marcia. "The Hollywood Western, the Movement-Image, and Making History." In *Hollywood and the American Historical Film*, edited by J. E. Smyth. London: Palgrave Macmillan, 2011.

Langlois, Walter. "Anarchism, Action, and Malraux." *Twentieth Century Literature* 24 (autumn 1978): 272–89.

Lawrence, Amy. *The Passion of Montgomery Clift.* Berkeley: University of California Press, 2010.

Lehrman, Hal. "Austria: Way-Station of Exodus—Pages From a Correspondent's Notebook." *Commentary* 2, no. 6 (December 1946): 565–72.

Leiserowitz, Ruth. *Von Ostpreußen nach Kyritz—Wolfskinder auf dem Weg nach Brandenburg.* Potsdam: Brandenburgische Landeszentrale für Politische Bildung, 2003.

Les femmes dans la Résistance. Actes du colloque tenu à l'initiative de l'Union des Femmes Françaises, Paris, 22 et 23 novembre, 1975. Paris: Rocher, 1977.

Lewy, Guenter. *The Catholic Church and Nazi Germany.* New York: McGraw-Hill, 1964.

MacMaster, Neil. *Spanish Fighters: An Oral History of the Civil War and Exile.* New York: St. Martin's Press, 1990.

MacShane, Frank. *Into Eternity: The Life of James Jones, American Writer.* Boston: Houghton Mifflin, 1985.

Maerten, Fabrice. "Les femmes dans la résistance pendant la seconde guerre mondiale: Vers une plus grande part de responsabilités." In *Femmes des années 80: Un siècle de condition féminine en belgique (1889–1989)*, edited by Luc Courtois, Jean Rirotte, and Françoise Rosart, 165–75. Louvaine-la Neuve: Academia, 1989.

Maerten, Fabrice, Franz Selleslagh, and Mark Van den Wijngaert, eds. *Entre la peste et le choléra: Vie et attitude des catholique belges sous l'occupation.* Gerpinne, Belgium: Editions Quorum/Ceges/Arca, 1999.

Mangini, Shirley. *Memories of Resistance: Women's Voices From the Spanish Civil War.* New Haven: Yale University Press, 1995.

Malvern, Sue. "'For King and Country': Frampton's *Edith Cavell* (1915–1920) and the Writing of Gender in Memorials to the Great War." In *Sculpture and Pursuit of the Modern Ideal in Britain, 1880–1930*, edited by David Getsy. Aldershot: Ashgate, 2004.

Marcus, Alan. "Uncovering an Auteur: Fred Zinnemann." *Film History* 12, no. 1 (August 2000): 49–56.

Marrus, Michael. *The Unwanted: European Refugees in the Twentieth Century.* Oxford: Oxford University Press, 1985.

McCracken, Samuel. "*Julia* and Other Fictions By Lillian Hellman," *Commentary*, June 1984, 35–43.

McDonough, Frank. *Sophie Scholl, The Real Story of the Woman Who Defied Hitler.* London: The History Press, 2009.

Mefret, Jean-Pax. *Jusqu'au bout de l'Algérie francaise: Bastien-Thiry.* Paris: Pygmalion, 2007.

Michel, Henri. *Bibliographie critique de la Résistance.* Paris: Institut Pedagogique National, 1964.
Michman, Don, ed. *Belgium and the Holocaust: Jews Belgians Germans.* 1998. Jerusalem: Yad Vashem, 2000.
Milza, Pierre. *Fascisme francais passé et present.* Paris: Flammarion, 1987.
Molden, Fritz. *Fires in the Night: Sacrifices and Significance of the Austrian Resistance.* New York: Westview Press, 1989.
Moore, Bob, ed. *Resistance in Western Europe.* New York: Berg, 2000.
Montherlant, Henry de. *Textes sous une occupation, 1940–1944.* Paris: Gallimard, 1953.
Mullaney, Maria Marmo. *Revolutionary Women: Gender and the Socialist Revolutionary Role.* New York: Praeger, 1983.
Mulvey, Laura. "Visual Pleasure and Narrative Cinema." *Screen* 16, no. 3 (1975): 6–18.
———. "Afterthoughts on 'Visual Pleasure and Narrative Cinema,' Inspired by *Duel in the Sun.*" *Framework*, nos. 15/16/17 (summer 1981): 12–15.
Murphy, William T. *Robert Flaherty: A Guide to References and Resources.* Boston: G. K. Hall & Co., 1978.
Nash, Gerald. *World War II and the West: Reshaping the Economy.* Lincoln: University of Nebraska Press, 1990.
Navasky, Victor. *Naming Names.* New York: Viking, 1980.
Nicosia, Frances, and Lawrence D. Stokes, eds. *Germans Against Nazism: Nonconformity, Opposition and Resistance in the Third Reich.* Oxford: Oxford University Press, 1990.
Nogueres, Henri. *Histoire de la Résistance en France.* Paris: R. Laffont, 1967.
Nolletti, Arthur J., Jr., ed. *The Films of Fred Zinnemann: Critical Perspectives.* Albany: State University Press of New York, 1999.
Nolletti, Arthur J., Jr. "Spirituality and Style in *The Nun's Story.*" In *The Films of Fred Zinnemann,* edited by Nolletti, 119–38. Albany: State University Press of New York, 1999.
Nolte, Ernst. *Three Faces of Fascism: Action francaise, Italian Fascism, and National Socialism.* London: Weidenfeld & Nicholson, 1965.
Novick, Peter. *That Noble Dream: The "Objectivity Question" and the American Historical Profession.* Cambridge: Cambridge University Press, 1988.
Nowell-Smith, Geoffrey, and Steven Ricci, eds. *Hollywood and Europe: Economics, Culture, National Identity, 1945–95.* London: BFI, 1998.
Ostyn, Genevieve. "Pour qui sonne le glas: L'Espagne: non; Les Etats-Unis: oui." *Revue belge du cinéma,* no. 17 (autumn 1986): 43.
Paxton, Robert O. *Parades and Politics at Vichy: The French Officer Corps under Marshal Petain.* Princeton: Princeton University Press, 1966.
———. *Vichy France: Old Guard and New Order, 1940–1944.* New York: Alfred Knopf, 1972.
Payne, Robert. *The Civil War in Spain 1936–1939.* New York: Putnam, 1962.

Payne, Stanley. *Falange: A History of Spanish Fascism*. Stanford: Stanford University Press, 1961.
———. *History of Fascism*. Madison: University of Wisconsin Press, 1995.
Penaud, Guy. *André Malraux et la Resistance*. Paris: Faniac, 1986.
Perks, Robert, and Alistair Thomson, eds. *The Oral History Reader*. London: Routledge, 1998.
Phelps, Michael. *The Catholic Church and the Holocaust, 1930–1965*. Bloomington: Indiana University Press, 2001.
Phillips, Gene D. *Exiles in Hollywood: Major European Film Directors in America*. Bethlehem, PA: Lehigh University Press, 1998.
Polan, Dana. *Power and Paranoia: History, Narrative and the American Cinema, 1940–1950*. New York: Columbia University Press, 1986.
Pollack, Griselda, and Max Silverman, eds. *Concentrationary Cinema: Aesthetics as Political Resistance in Alain Resnais's "Night and Fog."* Oxford: Berghahn, 2012.
Pons Prades, Eduardo. *Guerillas españolas: 1936–1960*. Barcelona: Planeta, 1977.
———. *Republicanos españoles en la Segunda Guerra Mundial*. Madrid: La Esfera de los Libros, 2003.
Preston, Paul, ed. *Spain in Crisis: The Evolution and Decline of the Franco Regime*. Hassocks, Sussex: The Harvester Press, Ltd., 1976.
———. "The Anti-Francoist Opposition: The Long March to Unity." In *Spain in Crisis*, edited by Paul Preston, 126–82. Hassocks, Sussex: The Harvester Press, Ltd., 1976.
———, ed. *Revolution and War in Spain, 1931–1939*. London: Methuen, 1984.
———. "War of Words: The Spanish Civil War and the Historians." In *Revolution and War in Spain, 1931–1939*, edited by Paul Preston, 1–13. London: Methuen, 1984.
———. *The Politics of Revenge: Fascism and the Military in Twentieth-Century Spain*. London: Unwin Hyman, 1990.
Priestner, Andy. *The Complete Secret Army*. London: Classic TV, 2006.
Prince, Stephen. "Historical Perspective and the Realist Aesthetic in *High Noon* (1952)." In *The Films of Fred Zinnemann: Critical Perspectives*, edited by Arthur J. Nolletti, 79–92. Albany: State University Press of New York, 1999.
———. "'Do You Understand?': History and Memory in *Julia*." In *The Films of Fred Zinnemann: Critical Perspectives*, edited by Arthur J. Nolletti, 187–97. Albany: State University Press of New York, 1999.
Proctor, Tammy. "'Patriotism is Not Enough': Women, Citizenship, and the First World War." *Journal of Women's History* 17, no. 2 (summer 2005): 169–76.
Proudfoot, Malcolm J. *European Refugees: 1939–1952—A Study in Forced Population Movement*. Evanston, IL: Northwestern University Press, 1956.
Quart, Leonard. "There Were Good Germans: *The Seventh Cross*." In *The Films of Fred Zinnemann: Critical Perspectives*, edited by Arthur J. Nolletti, 69–78. Albany: State University Press of New York, 1999.
Quivy, Vincent. *Les Soldats perdus: Des anciens de L'OAS racontent*. Paris: Seuil, 2003.

Ramon, Jean-Bernard. *L'OAS et ses appuis internationaix: Alliés, influences et manipulations extérieures*. Paris: Atelier Folfer, 2009.

Rapf, Joanna E. "Myth, Ideology, and Feminism in *High Noon*." *Journal of Popular Culture* 23, no. 4 (spring 1990): 75–80.

Riley, Glenda, and Richard W. Etulain, eds. *By Grit and Grace: Eleven Women Who Shaped the American West*. Golden, CO: Fulcram, 1997.

Robé, Chris. "The Good Fight: The Spanish Civil War and US Left Film Criticism." *Framework: The Journal of Cinema and Media* 51, no. 1 (spring 2010): 79–107.

Rollyson, Carl. *Lillian Hellman: Her Legend and Her Legacy*. New York: St. Martin's Press, 1988.

Rose, Frank. *The Agency: William Morris and the Hidden History of Show Business*. New York: Harperbusiness, 1996.

Rosenberg, Emily. *A Date Which Will Live: Pearl Harbor in American Memory*. Durham, NC: Duke University Press, 2003.

Rosenhaft, Eve. *Beating the Fascists? The German Communists and Political Violence*. Cambridge: Cambridge University Press, 1983.

Rosenstone, Robert. "Inventing Historical Truth on the Silver Screen." *Cineaste*, 2004, 29–33.

Rossiter, Margaret L. *Women in the Resistance*. New York: Praeger, 1986.

Rowe, Newton. *Samoa Under the Sailing Gods*. London: Putnam, 1930.

Sampsell-Willmann, Kate, and Alan Trachtenberg. *Lewis Hine as Social Critic*. Jackson: University Press of Mississippi, 2009.

Sarris, Andrew. *The American Cinema: Directors and Directions, 1929–1968*. New York: E. P. Dutton, 1968.

Schneider, Tassilo. "Finding a New Heimat in the Wild West: Karl May and the German Western in the 1960s." In *Back in the Saddle Again*, edited by Roberta Pearson and Ed Buscombe, 141–59. London: BFI, 1998.

Schwartz, Stephen. "The Paradoxes of and Recovery of Historical Memory." *Film History* 20, no. 4 (December 2008): 501–507.

Sekula, Alan. "Dismantling Modernism, Reinventing Documentary: Notes on the Politics of Representation." In *Photography/Politics: One*, edited by T. Dennet and J. Spence. London: Photography Workshop, 1979.

Seldes, Gilbert. *The Movies Come From America*. New York: Scribners, 1937.

Shandley, Robert. *Rubble Films: German Cinema in the Shadow of the Third Reich*. Philadelphia: Temple University Press, 2001.

Shiber, Etta. *Paris Underground*. New York: Scribners, 1943.

Silberman, Marc. "What's New? Allegorical Representations of Renewal in DEFA's Youth Films, 1946–1949." In *German Postwar Films*, edited by Wilifried Wilms and William Rasch, 93–108. London: Palgrave Macmillan, 2008.

Sinyard, Neil. *Fred Zinnemann, Films of Character and Conscience*. Jefferson, NC: McFarland & Co., 2003.

Skinner, James M. "*December 7*: Filmic Myth Masquerading as Historical Fact." *Journal of Military History* 55, no. 4 (1991): 507–16.
Sklar, Robert. *Movie-Made America*. 1975. New York: Vintage, 1994.
———. *City Boys: Cagney, Bogart, Garfield*. Princeton: Princeton University Press, 1992.
———. "Historical Films: Scofflaws and the Historical Cop." *Reviews in American History* 25, no. 2 (June 1997): 346–50.
Sklar, Robert, and Charles Musser, eds. *Resisting Images: Essays on Cinema and History*. Philadelphia: Temple University Press, 1990.
Slotkin, Richard. *Gunfighter Nation: The Myth of the Frontier in Twentieth-Century America*. Norman: University of Oklahoma Press, 1992.
Smith, Henry Nash. *Virgin Land: The American West as Symbol and Myth*. Cambridge: Harvard University Press, 1950.
Smith, Sidonie. *Subjectivity, Identity, and the Body: Women's Autobiographical Practices in the Twentieth Century*. Bloomington: Indiana University Press, 1993.
Smyth, J. E. *Edna Ferber's Hollywood*. Austin: University of Texas Press, 2009.
———. "Fred Zinnemann's *Search* (1945–1948): Reconstructing the Voices of Europe's Children." *Film History* 23, no. 1 (winter 2011): 75–92.
———. "James Jones, Columbia Pictures, and the Historical Confrontations of *From Here to Eternity*." In *Why We Fought: Hollywood's Wars*, edited by Peter Rollins and John E. O'Connor. Lexington: University Press of Kentucky, 2008.
———. "*Julia*'s Resistant History: Women's Historical Films in Hollywood and the Legacy of *Citizen Kane*." In *The Blackwell Companion to the Historical Film*, edited by Robert Rosenstone and Constantin Parvelescu, 91–109. Boston: Wiley-Blackwell, 2013.
———. "'The Long Road of Women's Memory': Fred Zinnemann and *Julia* (1977)." In *Hollywood and the American Historical Film*, edited by J. E. Smyth, 76–101. London: Palgrave, 2011.
———. *Reconstructing American Historical Cinema from Cimarron to Citizen Kane*. Lexington: University Press of Kentucky, 2006.
Soriano, Antonio. *Exodos: historia oral del exilio republicano en Francia*. Barcelona: Crítica, 1989.
Soury, Robert. *French Fascism: The First Wave, 1924–1933*. New Haven: Yale University Press, 1986.
———. *French Fascism: The Second Wave, 1933–1939*. New Haven: Yale University Press, 1999.
Southworth, Herbert R. *El mito de la cruzada de Franco*. París: Ruedi Ibérica, 1963.
Sova, Dawn. *Forbidden Films*. New York: Checkmark Books, 2001.
Spoto, Donald. *Stanley Kramer*. New York: Putnam, 1978.
Staiger, Janet. "Hybrid or Inbred: The Purity Hypothesis and Hollywood Genre History." *Film Criticism* 22, no. 1 (fall 1997): 5–20.
Stehlík, Eduard. *Lidice: The Story of a Czech Village*. Translated by Petr Kurfürst. Prague: Kejrová, 2004.

Stephan, Alexander. "Ein Exilroman als Bestseller." In *Exitforschung: Ein Internationales Jahrbuch* 3 (1985): 239–47.
Sternhell, Zeev. *Neither Right Nor Left: Fascist Ideology in France*. Berkeley: University of California Press, 1986.
Stone, Dan, ed. *The Historiography of the Holocaust*. New York: Palgrave Macmillan, 2004.
Stott, William. *Documentary Expression and Thirties America*. New York: Oxford University Press, 1973.
Strobl, Ingrid. *Partisanas: Women in the Armed Resistance to Fascism*. Edinburgh: AK Press, 2008.
Suid, Lawrence. *Guts and Glory: Great American War Movies*. Reading, MA: Addison-Wesley, 1978.
Tagg, John. *The Burden of Representation: Essays on Photographies and Histories*. London: Macmillan, 1988.
Tellez, Antonio. *Sabaté: Guerilla Extraordinaire*. London: Davis-Poynter, 1974.
Thomas, Gareth. *The Novel of the Spanish Civil War*. Cambridge: Cambridge University Press, 1990.
Thomas, Hugh. *The Spanish Civil War*. New York: Harper & Row, 1961.
Thompson, Paul. *The Voice of the Past: Oral History*. 1978. Oxford: Oxford University Press, 2000.
Thomsett, Michael. *The German Opposition to Hitler: The Resistance, the Underground, Assassination Plots 1938–45*. Jefferson, NC: McFarland & Co., 1997.
Tussell, Javier. *Spain: From Dictatorship to Democracy*. Malden, MA: Wiley-Blackwell, 2010.
Vincendeau, Ginette. *Jean-Pierre Melville: An American in Paris*. London: BFI, 2003.
Vistel, Alban. *Héritage spirituel de la Résistance*. Lyons: Lug, 1955.
Vromen, Suzanne. *Hidden Children of the Holocaust. Belgian Nuns and Their Daring Rescue of Young Jews from the Nazis*. Oxford: Oxford University Press, 2008.
Waldman, Diane. "At last I can tell it to someone!": Feminine Point of View and Subjectivity in the Gothic Romance Films of the 1940s." *Cinema Journal* 23, no. 2 (1984): 29–40.
Warshow, Robert. "Movie Chronicle: The Westerner." In *The Immediate Experience*, 135–54. New York: Athenaeum, 1970.
Weiner, Justus Reid. "Lillian Hellman: The Fiction of Autobiography." *Gender Issues* 21, no. 1 (2003): 78–83.
Weitz, Margaret Collins. *Sisters in the Resistance*. New York: John Wiley, 1995.
Welles, Benjamin. *Spain: The Gentle Anarchy*. London: The Pall Mall Press, 1965.
White, Hayden. *Metahistory*. Baltimore: Johns Hopkins University Press, 1973.
———. *The Content of the Form*. Baltimore: Johns Hopkins University Press, 1990.
———. "Historical Emplotment and the Problem of Truth." In *Probing the Limits of Representations: Nazism and the 'Final Solution,'* edited by Saul Friedlander, 37–53. Cambridge: Harvard University Press, 1992.

White, Richard. *It's Your Misfortune and None of My Own: A History of the American West*. Norman: University of Oklahoma Press, 1991.
Whitfield, Stephen J. *The Cultures of the Cold War.* 1991. Baltimore: Johns Hopkins University Press, 1996.
Wieviorka, Olivier. "France." In *Resistance in Western Europe*, edited by Bob Moore, 125–55. New York: Berg, 2000.
Wiley, Bell Irvin. *The Life of Johnny Reb, Common Soldier of the Confederacy.* Garden City, NY: Doubleday, 1943.
———. *The Life of Billy Yank, Common Soldier of the Union.* Indianapolis: Bobbs-Merrill, 1952.
Willett, Ralph, ed. *The Americanization of Germany, 1945–1949.* London: Routledge, 1989.
Williams, Anthony. "Resistance and Opposition Amongst Germans." In *Resistance in Europe: 1939-1945*, edited by Stephen Hawes and Ralph White, 135–69. Harmondsworth: Penguin Books, 1976.
Wilms, Wilfried, and William Rasch, eds. *German Postwar Films: Life and Love in the Ruins.* London: Palgrave Macmillan, 2008.
Wilson, Colin. *The Outsider.* London: Victor Gollancz, 1956.
Wright, Will. *Six-Guns and Society.* Berkeley: University of California Press, 1970.
Wyman, Mark. *DPs: Europe's Displaced Persons, 1945–1951.* 1989. Ithaca: Cornell University Press, 1998.
Zahra, Tara. *Kidnapped Souls: National Indifference and the Battle for Children in the Bohemian Lands, 1900–1948.* Ithaca: Cornell University Press, 2008.
———. *The Lost Children.* Cambridge: Harvard University Press, 2011.
Ziemke, Earl F. *The U.S. Army in the Occupation of Germany, 1944–1946.* Washington: U.S. Army Center of Military History, 1975.
Zinnemann, Tim. *As I See It: A Tribute to Fred Zinnemann.* Edited by Walter Murch. Highland Films Production, 1997.

INDEX

Above Suspicion (1943), 37
Academy Awards, 4, 13, 22, 27, 47, 62, 88, 115, 212
Academy of Motion Picture Arts and Sciences, 22, 115, 235
Act of Violence (1949), 10, 19, 95, 124, 132, 151, 201, 242n40
Action Service, 50–52
adaptation, 12, 14, 19, 22, 28, 47, 96–97, 127–28, 132, 144, 149, 150, 152, 154, 163, 164, 176, 185, 200, 213, 220, 240n17
Addams, Jane, 201, 214, 235
Adler, Buddy, 127–29, 131–32, 136, 138–39, 141, 145, 262n14
African Queen, The (1951), 173
Against the Wind (1950), 206, 212
Aldgate, Anthony, 178
All About Eve (1950), 220
All Quiet on the Western Front (1930), 25
All This and Heaven Too (1940), 164, 219
All Through the Night (1942), 37
American Cowboy, The (1952), 112
Anderson, Robert, 158, 160–62, 165–68, 171, 174
Angel Wore Red, The (1960), 271n7
Angeli, Pier, 149
Angelotti, Marietto, 190
Annie Get Your Gun (1950), 150
Annie Hall (1977), 212, 231
Anschluss, 206, 208
anti-communism, 45–46, 97, 100, 116, 126, 193–94, 202, 250n32
anti-fascism, 10–13, 17–19, 22, 27–30, 33, 38–40, 48, 164, 177, 180–81, 185, 190, 195, 198, 202, 206, 208–10, 214–16, 217, 235, 240n17, 245n50
anti-Semitism, 48, 61, 65, 120, 126–27, 208
Armée des ombres, L' (1969), 19, 212
Aron, Robert, 154
Around the World in 80 Days (1956), 89
Arthur, Jean, 92, 138
Aubrac, Lucie, 154
Aubrey, James, 12
audiences, 5, 13, 29, 44, 54, 62, 74, 85–87, 97–98, 110, 112–13, 119, 131, 147, 150, 161, 172, 187, 199–200, 231–33, 237; and women, 111, 141, 150, 231–33
Auschwitz, 9, 57, 59–60, 75, 79–80, 87–88, 106–7, 170
auteur theory, 5–6, 13, 96, 98–100, 235, 240n8

Bad and the Beautiful, The (1952), 115
Badal, Jean, 176, 189, 194, 271n8
Badel, Alan, 53
Bader, Douglas, 156
Badlands (1973), 229
Balázs, Béla, 92
Bankhead, Talullah, 208
Barnes, Howard, 38
Barry, Iris, 16
Barthes, Roland, 174
Bastien-Thiry, Lt. Col. Jean-Marie, 49, 54
Battle for Algiers, The (1966), 42–43, 53
Battleground (1949), 145
Bazin, André, 96–97, 109
Beck, Beatrix, 164

[305]

Behold a Pale Horse (1964), 12, 16–17, 22, 55, 175–201, 225–26, 231, 271n7
Bell, J. Raymond, 129–30
Bell, Mike, 196
Belmondo, Jean-Paul, 164
Ben Hur (1925), 89
Benjy (1951), 16, 91, 213
Bergman, Ingrid, 62, 183
Berlin Correspondent (1942), 37
Berlin Express (1948), 63, 89, 92
Berman, Pandro S., 27–30, 34, 36, 38–39, 243n12
Berna, Emil, 4, 84
Bertolucci, Bernardo, 219
Bessie, Alva, 39
Best Years of Our Lives, The (1946), 84
Bierstadt, Albert, 104
Big Country, The (1958), 99
Bingham, Dennis, 151, 214
biography, 22–23, 150, 153, 155, 161, 172, 183, 210, 222, 224, 234, 276n8
biopics, 27, 29, 41, 151, 152, 156–57, 213–14, 223, 233, 265n6, 266n8; and women, 151–52, 156, 214, 233
Birth of a Nation, The (1915), 25
Bitzer, Billy, 25
Black Book/Zwartboek (2006), 19, 234
Black Legion (1937), 28, 126
blacklist, 98, 123, 185, 202, 211–12, 245n50, 256n16
Blanke, Henry, 160–61, 170
Blessed Is the Match (2009), 234
Blockade! (1938), 182, 243n11
Bogart, Humphrey, 28, 183
Bolt, Robert, 12, 41, 194, 200, 240n17, 242n41
Bonney, Thérèse, 61, 64, 68, 73, 251n51
Bonnie and Clyde (1967), 54
Borgnine, Ernest, 139–40
Borkowski, Leopold, 83
Bourke-White, Margaret, 64
box office, 54, 89, 97, 113, 172, 199

Brady, Mathew, 103–4
Brando, Marlon, 10, 27, 41, 95, 173, 204, 254n113
Brason, John, 281n109
Bresson, Robert, 152–53, 163, 166, 169, 171
Brick, Al, 130
Britton, Tony, 53
Brook, Vincent, 10
Brothers, Caroline, 178
Buckmaster, Maurice, 157
Buscombe, Edward, 98, 109
Buttinger, Joseph, 215

Camus, Albert, 57, 65
Canaris: Master Spy (1954), 19
Canaris, Admiral Wilhelm, 19
Canby, Vincent, 233
Capa, Robert, 178–79
Capra, Frank, 98, 235
Cardiff, Jack, 173
Cartier-Bresson, Henri, 52
Carve Her Name with Pride (1958), 152, 156–57, 206, 234
Casablanca (1942), 17, 28, 34, 37, 141, 155, 183
Catholic Church, 12, 16, 32, 150–54, 158–66, 168, 170–74, 184–87, 191, 194–95, 266n15, 266–67n22; and collaboration with Hitler, 150–54; and Spanish Civil War, 186, 195
Cau, John, 41
Cavell, Edith, 152, 155–56
Cawelti, John, 98, 109
Cayla-Legrand, Adrien, 49
censorship, 22, 40–41, 46, 85, 115, 129–32, 138–39, 158, 182–83, 187, 196–200, 237, 264n60, 265n85
Chaplin, Charles, 3, 36, 114–15, 260n70
Chavez, Carlos, 26
Chertok, Jack, 14, 27
Chetniks! The Fighting Guerillas (1943), 36

children, and Holocaust, 59–62, 65–67, 69–93
Children's Hour, The (1935), 204, 223, 226–27, 229–30
Chinatown (1974), 220
Chinese Revolution (1927), 40–47
Churchill, Winston, 47, 247n91
cinematography, 22, 96, 103–4, 121, 146, 171–72, 189, 219–20, 256n15, 270n85, 279n71
Citizen Kane (1941), 213–14, 220, 223, 229, 233
Clark, Suzanne, 116–17
Clarke, Charles, 176
Clift, Montgomery, 72, 75, 84, 86–89, 91, 93, 95, 124, 132–33, 137, 140, 161, 173, 204, 254n113
close-ups, 6, 22, 42, 76, 79, 91, 109, 120–21, 139, 157, 169, 170, 174, 196, 226–27, 258n40
Cohn, Harry, 127, 129, 130–31, 138, 141–42, 262n14, 264n60
Cold War, 97, 99, 100–101, 114, 116–17, 120, 125, 129, 154, 177, 202, 207, 240n17
collaboration, wartime, 10, 19, 28, 54, 153–54, 164, 166, 186, 195; and filmmaking, 5, 20, 23, 84, 86, 202, 219
Columbia Pictures, 47, 123–25, 127, 129–30, 133, 136, 140–41, 143, 147, 175–76, 182, 185, 190–92, 196–99, 206, 256n15
communist party, Austria, 217; and Belgium, 18; and China, 12, 41, 44; and France, 18, 154, 164; and Germany (KPD), 30, 32, 39; and Spain, 179–80; and US, 202, 217
Confessions of a Nazi Spy (1939), 28, 155
Confidential Agent (1945), 271n7
Conformist, The (1974), 219

Cooper, Gary, 6, 62, 96, 101, 105, 111, 116–21, 149, 188, 194, 255n5
Cooper, Norman, 195
Corey, Wendell, 84, 89
Costello, Matthew, 116
Courtenay, Tom, 41
Coyne, Michael, 100
Crawford, Joan, 220
Cronyn, Hume, 33–34
Crosby, Floyd, 14, 25, 27, 97–98, 103–4, 106, 109, 111, 119, 123–24, 136, 219, 256n15, 258n40, 260n84
Cross of Lorraine, The (1943), 37
Crowther, Bosley, 38, 90–91, 99, 102, 115, 259n51
Cukor, George, 27
Cusack, Cyril, 6
Custen, George, 214
Custer, George Armstrong, 12, 130, 134, 261n89
Czechoslovakia, 59–60, 65, 81–82, 85, 88, 251n39, 253n90

Dachau, 30, 153
Daniels, William, 176
Dantine, Helmut, 28
Dark Angel, The (1935), 26
David, Joanna, 50
Davis, Bette, 164, 220
Day of the Jackal, The (1971), 47, 50, 52
Day of the Jackal, The (1973), 47–55
Days of Glory (1944), 190
De Gaulle, Charles, 6, 11, 13, 19–20, 40, 43, 47–52, 54–55, 154, 191, 247n83
De Sica, Vittorio, 63, 78, 92
Deathmills, The/Die Todesmühlen (1945), 62
Debray, Régis, 48
December 7th (1943), 131, 265n85
decolonization, 16, 92, 255n137
Delerue, Georges, 228–29
Deleuze, Gilles, 109, 258n48

DeMille, Cecil B., 120, 257n23, 256n16, 261n88
Denham, Maurice, 53
Derode, Julien, 51, 53, 226
Des Jardins, Julie, 110, 210
Desirée (1954), 220
Desperate Journey (1942), 37
Deutsch, David, 47
Deutsch, Helen, 28, 33–35, 243n14
Devigny, André, 152, 164
Diary of Anne Frank, The (1959), 159
Dick, Bernard, 208–9
Dickinson, Thorold, 91–92
Dietrich, Marlene, 99, 138
Dillinger (1973), 213, 229
Directors' Guild, 13, 90, 123
displaced persons (DP), 39, 60, 64–66, 68–69, 71, 74–77, 81, 83, 86–89, 91–92, 150, 177, 189
Dobtcheff, Vernon, 51
Dodsworth (1935), 26
Doll, Dora, 19, 234
Dorn, Col. Frank, 130, 136
Double Indemnity (1944), 29
Dr. Jekyll and Mr. Hyde (1941), 32
Dr. Zhivago (1965), 40–41, 45
Dragon Seed (1944), 28, 36
Dreyer, Carl Theodor, 153, 169–72, 269–70n78
Drummund, Phillip, 97–98, 109, 114
Duel in the Sun (1946), 113
Dunne, Irene, 220
Dunnock, Mildred, 162, 184
Durrant, Tim, 114, 260n70
Duvivier, Julien, 67

Edge of Darkness (1943), 155
Edge of the World (1937), 185
editing, 22, 26, 55, 62, 95, 100–102, 133, 146, 169, 219, 229–30, 247n93, 248n108, 258n36, 280n90
Eisenstein, Sergei, 14, 26, 41, 44, 109

Engels, Frederich, 175, 217
Erice, Victor, 32, 182
Escape (1940), 155
Europe, postwar reconstruction of, 63, 71, 81, 87, 92
European Common Market, 47

Falconetti, Renée, 153, 169–70, 174
fascism, German, 28–29, 32–33, 37–38, 136, 228; and American, 12, 17, 22, 98, 120, 126–27, 137–38, 232, 262n15; and Austrian, 202, 207, 227; and French, 202, 223, 247n87; and Spanish, 184, 194, 199
Faye, Léon, 210
Fede, Ruth S., 59
Ferber, Edna, 110, 113, 152, 266n14
Feyder, Paul, 187
55 Days at Peking (1963), 45
Figueroa, Manuel, 171, 270n85
film noir, 10, 29, 99, 164, 242n40
Finch, Peter, 12, 46, 173, 255n137
First Circle, The, 12
First World War, 128, 146, 155
Five Days One Summer (1982), 22–23, 281n109
Flaherty, David, 14
Flaherty, Robert, 13–16, 26–27, 67, 121, 235
flashbacks, 80, 85–86, 128, 157, 223
Fonda, Henry, 182, 213
Fonda, Jane, 6, 23, 201, 202, 211–13, 220, 222, 224–26, 231, 234, 279n66
For Whom the Bell Tolls (1941), 183, 273n39
For Whom the Bell Tolls (1943), 176, 188
Forbidden Passage (1940), 58
Ford, John, 3, 98–99, 102, 104, 109–10, 112, 115, 120, 145, 213, 239n3, 257n23
Foreign Affair, A (1948), 63, 68, 89, 92, 138

Foreman, Carl, 7, 23, 95–103, 105, 107, 109, 111–16, 120, 123, 136, 188, 192, 214, 259n55
Forsyth, Frederick, 25, 47–50, 52, 248n95
Foster, Gwendolyn Audrey, 111
Four Days in Naples (1962), 42
Fourcade, Marie-Madeleine, 154, 204–7, 210, 223, 233, 251n44
Fox, Edward, 6, 11, 48, 50–52, 55
Francis, Jan, 160
Franco, ese hombre (1964), 197
Franco, General Francisco, 12, 17, 22, 40, 48, 126, 136, 176–77, 179, 180–82, 184–86, 189, 192–93, 194–97, 199, 271n7
Frankenheimer, John, 192, 242n41
Frankenstein (1931), 32
Franklin, Sidney, 26
Frankovich, Mike, 175, 190, 196, 200
French, Philip, 98–99
Freund, Karl, 33–34
From Here to Eternity (1951) 124–32, 134–36, 144
From Here to Eternity (1953), 4–5, 10, 12, 14, 16, 22–23, 43, 115, 123–48, 150, 152, 175, 185, 187, 196, 204
Funny Face (1957), 89

Gabin, Jean, 52
Gandhi, Mahatma, 12, 41, 201, 246n59
Garbo, Greta, 27, 174, 220
Gardiner, Muriel, 204–8, 214, 215–16, 233, 276n8, 278n59
Gardner, Ava, 260–61n87, 271n7
Garfield, John, 72, 76
Gatti, Armand, 40
Gellhorn, Martha, 210
genre, 5–6, 27–29, 39, 93, 96–99, 109–10, 112, 120, 127, 141, 145, 147, 150, 152, 164, 214, 216, 220–21, 235, 256n8, 257n20
genre cleansing, 109–10

Georges-Picot, Olga, 51
Germany Year Zero/Germania anno zero (1948), 63, 67, 74, 92
Gestapo, 59, 109, 157, 202, 252n44
Giant (1952), 110
Giant (1956), 152, 266n14
Gigi (1958), 89
Gilbert, Lewis, 156–58, 166
Gilliat, Sidney, 156
Glover, Julian, 217
Gluck, Sherna Berger, 231
Go-Between, The (1971), 50
Godfather, The (1972), 229
Golden Boy (1939), 83
Goldwyn, Sam, 25–26
Gollancz, Victor, 64
Gone with the Wind (1939), 127, 149, 219
Good Earth, The (1937), 45
Goodbye, Mr. Chips (1939), 89
Goodbye Girl, The (1977), 231
Gorgeous Hussy, The (1936), 220
Grapes of Wrath, The (1940), 213
graylisting, 119, 212
Great Depression, 124, 128, 134–35, 145
Great Lie, The (1941), 220
Great Man's Lady, The (1942), 219
Grey, Zane, 100
Grierson, John, 14
Grossman, Atina, 64
Grosz, Jichak, 83
Guernsey, Otis, 105, 115
Guns of Navarone, The (1961), 21, 188, 192, 206, 259n55, 274n65

Habets, Marie Louise, 150, 153, 159–61, 167, 174, 207, 268n40
Hall, Virginia, 154, 204, 233
Hammerstein, Oscar, II, 25, 99, 235
Hammett, Dashiell, 26–27, 39, 211, 224–26
Harrison, Earl, 64–65, 68
Haskell, Molly, 112, 233–34

Haskell, Thomas, 210
Hasso, Signe, 35
Hatful of Rain, A (1957), 8, 151, 171
Hawaii (1966), 175
Hawks, Howard, 5–6, 96, 98–99, 109–10, 113–14, 116, 120, 240n9, 259n65, 261n88
Heflin, Van, 10, 19, 27
Heidi (1952), 90
Heidi und Peter (1953), 90
Hellman, Lillian, 6–7, 21, 26, 179, 201–20, 222–30, 232–33; and political activism, 211
Hemingway, Ernest, 17, 23, 39, 127, 176, 179, 183–84, 187–88, 235, 241n22, 243n12, 273n39, 279n73
Henreid, Paul, 34
Henry V (1945), 62
Hepburn, Audrey, 16, 19, 36, 153, 159–61, 163–64, 168–70, 173–74, 190, 194, 204, 240n17, 269n78
Hepburn, Katharine, 28, 126, 155, 243n12
Hernandez, Silvio, 26
Herrick, Margaret, 88
High Noon (1952), 95–121; and Cold War, 115–21; and film criticism, 96, 99–100, 102, 109–10; and women, 109–13
Hiller, Wendy, 200, 204
Hine, Lewis, 61, 178
Hiroshima, Mon Amour (1959), 45, 219
historical films, 9, 22, 29, 74, 150, 152, 158, 163, 220–22, 229, 266n8; and the Resistance (see *Behold a Pale Horse*; *Julia*; *Nun's Story, The*; *Seventh Cross, The*)
historiography, women, 112, 154, 184, 202–10, 221, 231, 235
historiography of the Resistance, 17–19, 154, 184, 203, 207, 209, 221, 231
Hitchcock, Alfred, 3, 29, 221, 239n3
Hitler, Adolf, 11, 18, 33, 35, 37, 65, 67, 177, 193, 208, 213, 229

Hitler's Madman (1943), 37
Hoffman, Stanley, 154
Hogan, Michael, 155
Holbrook, Hal, 211
Holocaust, 7, 9, 15, 23, 59–60, 67, 75–76, 80, 82, 84, 93, 120, 159, 166, 168, 184, 194, 209, 231
Hostages (1943), 37
House Un-American Activities Committee (HUAC), 97, 100–101, 115, 120, 129, 202
Huddleston, Sisley, 154
Hulme, Kathryn, 22, 60–61, 64, 149–53, 159–62, 164, 166–67, 173, 207
Humoresque (1946), 83
Hunt, Marsha, 27, 36, 243n9
Hurt, John, 200
Huston, John, 3, 72, 173, 237, 239n3

I Know Where I'm Going! (1945), 185
I Remember Mama (1948), 220
Ingham, Barrie, 51
International Refugee Organization (IRO), 60, 68, 150
Intolerance (1916), 25
Israel, 59, 91, 212
It Happened One Night (1934), 98
Itami, Juzo, 45
Ivens, Joris, 179

Jacobi, Derek, 52
Jahoda, Maria, 215
Jandl, Ivan, 75–76, 82, 86, 88
Jarrico, Paul, 84–86
Jeanne Eagles (1957), 150
Jenkins, Jackie, 63
Jenkins, Valerie, 233
Joan of Paris (1942), 28, 36–37, 141, 155
Jones, James, 123–35, 138–39, 141, 144–45, 147, 153
Jones, Jennifer, 113, 260–61n87
Jongh, Andrée de (Dédé), 154, 159

Julia (1977), 6–7, 9, 11, 13, 18–19, 22, 44, 80, 151, 154, 162, 201–37, 240n17, 279n66
July 20th/Der 20. Juli (1955), 19
Jurado, Katy, 111

Kapo (1961), 170
Karloff, Boris, 32
Kedward, H. R., 209, 211
Kael, Pauline, 233–34
Kai-Shek, Chiang, 40–41, 43
Keeper of the Flame, The (1943), 28, 126
Kelly, Grace, 17, 111, 119
Kennan, George, 116
Kennedy, John F., 6, 54
Kerr, Deborah, 143
Kid Glove Killer (1942), 27
Killing a Mouse on Sunday (1961), 175–76, 185, 196
Kitty Foyle (1940), 149, 219, 229
Knight, Arthur, 214
Knightley, Philip, 178
Koestler, Arthur, 177
Korean War, 116, 130, 151, 177
Kramer, Stanley, 23, 95, 100–102, 235, 258n36
Krippner, James, 26
Kruger, Otto, 107

Ladd, Alan, Jr., 214, 281n109
Lagrou, Pieter, 18, 207
Lamprecht, Gerhardt, 67
Lancaster, Burt, 21, 140, 192
Lang, Fritz, 36, 98–99
Last Chance, The (1945), 62
Last Secret, The (1978), 12, 201, 237, 281n109
Last Train From Madrid (1937), 182
Lastfogel, Abe, 15, 63, 69, 73, 161
Launder, Frank, 156
Laura (1944), 29

Lean, David, 41, 45, 231
Legion of Decency, 185
Leigh, Janet, 36, 204
Léon Morin, prêtre (1961), 19, 164
Letterier, François, 153, 164–65
Lewy, Guenter, 154
Libik, André, 176
Lidice, 59, 81–84
Life and Death of Colonel Blimp, The (1942), 185
Little Foxes, The (1941), 202
Little Mr. Jim (1946), 57, 63
Locke, Katherine, 35
Locket, The (1946), 29
Loew, Arthur, 3, 14, 63, 69, 86
Longest Day, The (1962), 232
Lonsdale, Michael, 51, 53, 196
Lord Jim (1965), 45
Loring, Jane, 34
Losey, Joseph, 50
Love Is a Many-Splendored Thing (1955), 41
Love Me or Leave Me (1955), 150, 214
Lowe, Florence, 73
Lumet, Sidney, 199
Lynen, Robert, 67, 251n44

Macardle, Dorothy, 60, 64, 80
Macbeth, 104, 113
MacLean, Alistair, 192
MacLeish, Archibald, 179
Macomber, William, 45
Macready, George, 35
Magini, Shirley, 184
Magnificent Doll (1945), 220
Mailer, Norman, 133
Malraux, André, 3, 12–13, 40, 42–46, 48, 53, 95
Man Escaped, A/Un condamné à mort s'est échappe (1958), 153, 171
Man for All Seasons, A (1966), 8, 12, 22, 41, 43, 47, 194, 200, 204, 211, 231, 233

Man in the Gray Flannel Suit, The (1956), 151
Mankiewicz, Herman, 213, 219, 223, 233, 278n51, 281n108
Mankiewicz, Joseph, 149, 256n16, 257n23
Mann, Anthony, 98
Mann, Thomas, 126
Mannix, Eddie, 57
Man's Fate (1933), 3, 12–13, 95
Man's Fate (1969), 40–47, 201, 204
maquisards, 18, 206
Martin, Jean, 50, 53
Marx, Karl, 217
Masaryk, Jan, 83, 87
Matthews, Herbert, 178
Mauthausen, 78, 153
May, Karl, 96, 100, 257n27
Mayer, Louis B., 63
McCarthy, Joseph, 101, 214
McCarthy, Mary, 210
McGrath, John, 41
McKenna, Virginia, 152, 157, 234
Melville, Jean-Pierre, 18–19, 152, 163–65
memory, 22, 29–30, 75, 79, 80, 82, 87, 125, 134, 202, 205–10, 215, 220, 222–23, 225–26, 233, 235
Memphis Belle, The (1944), 84
Men, The (1950), 10, 95, 124, 151, 171, 201, 204, 279n71
Metro-Goldwyn-Mayer Studios (MGM), 7, 10, 12–15, 22, 27–28, 30, 34, 38–41, 45–47, 57, 63, 69, 73, 86, 89, 90, 92, 95, 221, 235
military, US, 9–10, 12, 16, 64, 88–89, 93, 125–27, 129–30, 133, 136–37, 139–40, 142, 145–47, 177
Miller, J. P., 188–89
Mirisch, Walter, 175
Mitchell, Thomas, 116
Moana (1926), 67
Montseny, Frederica, 180, 184
Moore, Bob, 207

Moorehead, Agnes, 35
Morgan! (1966), 200
Mortal Storm, The (1940), 37
Mortensen, Elisabeth, 19, 234
Mourir à Madrid (1963), 189
Movimiento Libertario Español (MLE), 180
Mrs. Miniver (1942), 28, 149
Murch, Walter, 214, 218–19, 225, 227, 230
Murder, My Sweet (1944), 29
Murphy, Rosemary, 211
musical scores, 49, 54, 83, 95, 102, 139, 170–71, 229
Mussolini, Benito, 139, 213
My Brother Talks to Horses (1947), 57, 63
My Darling Clementine (1946), 112–13

Nagu, Imre, 176
Neagle, Anna, 152, 155, 157
Neave, Airey, 159
neorealism, 74
Night and Fog (1955), 54
Niven, David, 46
North Star, The (1943), 39
Novotna, Jarmila, 82, 84, 89
Now, Voyager (1942), 164
Nun's Story, The (1956), 149–51
Nun's Story, The (1959), 5–6, 12, 16, 19, 22, 36, 47, 60, 89, 91, 149–74, 184, 187, 194, 201, 206, 229, 240n17
Nuremberg Trials, 59, 65
Nurse Edith Cavell (1939), 152, 155

Odette (1950), 152, 156–57, 234
Odessa File, The (1974), 47
Okada, Eiji, 45
Oklahoma! (1955), 99, 171, 261n89
Old South, The (1940), 27
Once Upon a Honeymoon (1942), 37
One Against the World (1939), 221
Ophüls, Marcel, 54, 154
oral history, 221–22

Organisation de l'armée secrete (OAS), 47–52, 54, 247n86
Orwell, George, 177
Out of the Past (1947), 29
Outsider, The (1956), 214

Paisà (1946), 67
Pakula, Alan J., 199
Papas, Irene, 192, 206
Paris After Dark (1944), 36
Paris Underground (1945), 36, 155
Parker, Dorothy, 211
Passage to Marseille (1943), 28, 164
Pawnbroker, The (1964), 83, 229
Paxinou, Katina, 183
Paxton, Robert, 154
Pearl Harbor, 130–32, 134, 138, 140, 143, 145–47
Peck, Gregory, 21, 45, 55, 88, 99, 151, 176, 180, 189–92, 199
Peg of Old Drury (1935), 155
Penn, Arthur, 199
Pieck, Wilhelm, 39
Pitt, Ingrid, 206
Planer, Franz, 171–72
Poil de carotte (1932), 67
Polanski, Roman, 220
Pollack, Sydney, 211
Pontecorvo, Gillo, 53, 170
Ponti, Carlo, 40–41, 45
Popular Front, 52
popular history, 124, 154, 214
Porter, Eric, 50, 53
postmodernism, 209–10, 219, 277n31
postwar Europe, 22, 39–40, 52–55, 57–93, 153–54, 177, 180–85, 193–96
Powell, Michael, 185
Power and the Glory, The, 36
Praesens Films, 15, 61–62, 79, 87
Pressburger, Emeric, 175–76, 180–81, 185–80, 235
Preston, Paul, 180–81, 271n2

Private Lives of Elizabeth and Essex, The (1939), 220
Production Code Administration (PCA), 127, 129, 138
production research, 22, 42, 45, 52, 68–71, 74, 103, 160, 186–96, 216, 219, 232
Pudovkin, Vselovod, 14, 109

Quiet Man, The (1952), 115
Quinn, Anthony, 188–92, 197, 199
Quo Vadis (1951), 89

Radványi, Géza, 65, 78, 92
Ravensbrück, 153, 156, 159, 170
Rebecca (1940), 29, 149, 164
Red River (1948), 89
Red Shoes, The (1948), 185
Redes (*Nets/The Wave*, 1936), 26–27, 178
Redgrave, Vanessa, 6, 19, 36–39, 44, 151, 200–202, 204, 211–12, 215–17, 225–28, 240n17
Reed, Donna, 142–44, 204
relativism, 48, 75, 91, 126, 175, 209–10
Remarque, Erich Maria, 28
Resistance, 9–10, 17, 19, 21–23, 28, 34, 37, 55, 58–59, 65, 81, 88, 124, 136, 140–41, 151, 160, 162, 164, 166, 192–95, 198, 201, 206, 208–9, 222, 227, 229, 233, 241n22; Austrian, 205, 207, 231; Belgian, 16, 18, 150, 153–54, 158–59, 161, 173; Chinese communist, 40–42; French, 11, 13, 20, 47–54, 154, 206–7; German, 29–30, 32–33, 35, 38–39, 244n29, 245n45; Mexican, 26; Spanish, 12, 177–85, 187; women in, 36, 44, 152, 154–56, 165, 174, 203–4, 206, 211–12, 221, 232, 234, 259n55, 268n39
Resnais, Alain, 54, 219–20
Richter, Conrad, 28
Riis, Jacob, 61, 67, 171
Rio Bravo (1959), 113–14

Ritt, Martin, 199
Riva, Emmanuelle, 164
Roaring Twenties, The (1939), 29
Robards, Jason, 211, 224
Rodakiewicz, Henwar, 26
Rogers, Ginger, 220
Roman Holiday (1953), 89, 159
Rome, Open City (1945), 67
Roosevelt, Franklin Delano, 129
Roosevelt, Theodore, 97, 100, 110, 135
Rosenberg, Emily, 145
Rosenstone, Robert, 165
Ross, Kenneth, 49–50
Rossellini, Roberto, 63, 67, 92
Rossif, Frédéric, 189
Roth, Richard, 23, 211, 225, 235
Rourke, Mary, 212
Ruttenberg, Joseph, 25, 176
Ryan, Robert, 132

Sabaté, Francisco, 22, 175–76, 179–81, 187–88, 195, 199
Sabrina (1954), 159
Sandoz, Mari, 120
Sands of Iwo Jima, The (1949), 145
Sansome, Odette, 152, 156
Saratoga Trunk (1946), 219
Sargent, Alvin, 201, 211–19, 222–27, 279n69, 279n73
Sarris, Andrew, 5–6, 109, 114, 120, 217, 233
Scala, Gia, 192, 206
Schallert, Edwin, 125
Schell, Maximillian, 234, 279n66
Schickel, Richard, 199
Schnee, Charles, 115
Scholl, Sophie, 19
Schweitzer, Albert, 69
Schweizer, Richard, 15, 73–74, 78, 84–86, 252n73
Scofield, Paul, 12, 136, 194, 200, 235, 240n17, 242n41

Scorsese, Martin, 200
Search, The (1948), 4, 10–11, 14–16, 18, 36, 39, 57–93, 114–15, 121, 124, 150–51, 188, 201, 204, 225
Searching Wind, The (1946), 202
Second World War, 124, 127, 145–46, 156, 173, 192
Secret Army (1977–79), 160, 281n109
Seghers, Anna, 28–30, 34, 37–38, 128 256n16
Selznick, David O., 149
Seventh Cross, The (1944), 5–7, 10, 16, 18–19, 22, 28–40, 35–36, 38, 57, 63, 67, 109, 115, 120, 124, 126, 164, 201, 220, 240n17, 245n52
Sharif, Omar, 190, 195
Shaw, Robert, 194, 200
Shoeshine/Ragazzi (1946), 74, 78, 92
Signoret, Simone, 206, 212
Silence of the Sea/La silence de la Mer (1947), 18, 152, 163–64
Silke, James, 5–6
Sinatra, Frank, 133, 139–40, 263n43
Sisters, The (1938), 220
Sixty Glorious Years (1938), 155
Sklar, Robert, 183
Slocombe, Douglas, 218–19, 224–25
Slotkin, Richard, 116
Smith, Betty, 62
Snows of Kilamanjaro, The (1952), 188
So Ends Our Night (1941), 36–37
So Proudly We Hail (1943), 141
Soldier of Orange/Soldaat van Oranje (1977), 19
Somewhere in Berlin/Irgendwo in Berlin (1946), 67
Somewhere in Europe/Valahol Európában (1947), 65, 71, 78, 92
Song of Russia (1944), 39
Sophie Scholl (2005), 19
Sorel, Jean, 54
Sorrow and the Pity, The (1970), 54, 154

Southworth, Herbert, 182
Spanish Civil War, 9, 16, 22, 175–200, 231, 243n11
Spanish Earth, The (1937), 179, 182
Spirit of the Beehive/El espíritu de la colmena (1973), 32, 182
Stalag 17 (1954), 137–38
Stalin, Joseph, 9, 126, 207–8, 214, 281n109
Star Is Born, A (1954), 150
Stavisky (1974), 219–20
Steiger, Rod, 83, 99, 173, 204
Stephan, Alexander, 30
Stern, Seymour, 91
Stevens, George, 159
Stoppa, Paolo, 190
Story of Dr. Carver, The (1938), 27
Story of GI Joe, The (1945), 141
Strand, Paul, 26, 178, 256n16
Strasberg, Susan, 170
Streep, Meryl, 177, 217
Sun Also Rises, The (1957), 260–61n87, 281n109
Sundowners, The (1960), 175, 264n70
Sunset Boulevard (1950), 29, 150
Surtees, Robert, 34, 260n70
Suyin, Han (Elizabeth Comber), 41–46
Szabo, Violette, 152, 156–58, 234

Tabu (1931), 14
Tagg, John, 178
Tandy, Jessica, 33–35
Taradash, Daniel, 129, 131–32, 134, 136, 139–42, 144, 146–47, 262n14
Tea and Sympathy (1956), 158
Teresa (1951), 36, 39, 124, 149, 201, 204
Terrorists, The (1964–65), 255
Thacher, Russell, 41
Thälmann, Ernst, 32
That Mothers Might Live (1938), 27
These Three (1936), 202

They Gave Him a Gun (1937), 36
They Were Expendable (1945), 232
They Won't Forget (1937), 28
Thomas, Gareth, 177
Thomas, Hugh, 182
Thompson, Dorothy, 38
Thompson, J. Lee, 192
Thompson, Paul, 165
Three Coins in the Fountain (1953), 89
Three Comrades (1938), 28
Three Women (1977), 231
Thunderbolt! (1947), 84
Tiomkin, Dimitri, 95, 102
To Kill a Mockingbird (1962), 190
To the Shores of Tripoli (1942), 130
Toland, Gregg, 25, 131, 145, 219, 224
Too Much, Too Soon (1958), 150–51
Torgler, Ernst, 32
Torrent, Ana, 32
torture, 18, 28–30, 35, 59, 75, 126, 154, 157, 179
Tourneur, Jacques, 63, 92, 190
Tracy, Spencer, 19, 28–37, 39, 57, 126, 164, 173, 234, 240n17, 243n12
Train, The (1964), 21, 192
Tree Grows in Brooklyn, A (1945), 62
Trilling, Steve, 170–72
Troniak, John, 82
Trumbo, Dalton, 39
Turner, Frederick Jackson, 97, 109–10, 135
Twentieth Century-Fox Studios, 130, 171, 211, 214, 260n87
Two Thousand Women (1944), 156

Ulbricht, Walter, 39
United Artists, 7–8, 11, 51, 102, 105, 108, 111, 281n110
United Nations, 60, 89–90, 93, 99, 231
United Nations Film Board, 91–92
United Nations International Children's Emergency Fund (UNICEF), 60, 174

United Nations Relief and Rehabilitation Administration (UNRRA), 11, 58–60, 64, 68, 71, 73–75, 77–87, 90–91, 93, 114, 150–51, 250n20
Unmarried Woman, An (1978), 231
Until They Sail (1957), 158
Ure, Mary, 206

Valkyrie (2004), 19
Van Cleef, Lee, 104
Variety, 39, 54, 73, 173, 197
Veidt, Conrad, 28
Vercors (Paul Bruller), 164
Victoria the Great (1937), 155
Viertel, Berthold, 14, 25, 64, 114
Viertel, Peter, 23, 63–68, 72–74, 88, 188, 235
Viertel, Salka, 14, 25, 27
Vietnam War, 193, 212
Village, The (1953), 90
Vincendeau, Ginette, 18, 154
Viva Villa! (1934), 27
Viva Zapata! (1952), 27
voice-over, 22, 29, 31, 34, 54, 74–75, 80, 128, 157–58, 163–64, 189, 220–21, 279n73
von Fritsch, Günther, 25–26
von Stauffenberg, Klaus, 19
Vroman, Suzanne, 153

Wald, Jerry, 123, 149
Wanger, Walter, 183
War and Peace (1956), 159
war genre, 28, 124, 141, 145, 176, 177, 232
Warner, Jack, 152, 169–71
Warner Bros. Studios, 28, 74, 126, 145, 152, 155, 162, 171–72, 183
Waxman, Franz, 23, 170–71, 235
Way in the Wilderness, A (1940), 221
Wayne, John, 96, 113–16, 232, 259n65
Wechsler, David, 74, 84

Wechsler, Lazar, 15, 23, 61–68, 72–74, 84–86, 90, 92, 252n73
Weitz, Margaret Collins, 18, 29, 221
Welles, Orson, 3, 200, 213, 219, 223, 239n3, 278n51
Wellman, William, 36
Wells, William, 73–74, 114
West, Samuel, 53
Westerns, 54, 95–121, 124, 141, 150, 199, 261n89
Whale, James, 32
White, Hayden, 209, 219
White Shadows in the South Seas (1928), 13–14
Whitfield, Stephen J., 99–100, 125
Wife Takes a Flier, The (1942), 37
Wilcox, Herbert, 152, 155, 157, 166
Wilder, Billy, 3, 62–63, 68, 88–89, 92, 137–38, 237
Wilson, Colin, 214
Winsten, Archer, 91, 142
Wister, Owen, 110
Wittek, Suzanne, 154
Woman Rebels, A (1937), 219
Women of the Shadows (2008), 234
women's films, 18, 36, 110, 112, 141, 149–52, 158, 164, 203, 220–21, 232, 279n75
women's history, 18, 22, 110, 112, 155, 165, 184, 202–3, 205, 207, 209–10, 219, 221, 223, 231–34
Wood, Sam, 176
Woolf, John, 47
World Moves On, The (1934), 146
Wyler, Margaret "Tally," 84
Wyler, William, 3, 26, 84, 98–99, 237, 257n20
Wyman, Mark, 60

Yankee Doodle Dandy (1942), 29
Young, Robert, 202
Young Lions, The (1958), 89, 201, 254n113
Young Mr. Lincoln (1939), 128, 213

Zanuck, Darryl F., 151, 213
Zapata, Emiliano, 12, 27, 201
Zinnemann, Anna Feiwel, 9
Zinnemann, Fred: and attitudes toward America, 74, 98, 232; and attitudes toward Germany, 37–38, 73–74; and censorship, 115, 129–39, 185; and difficulties with the studios, 14–15, 45–47, 57–58; early career, 25–27; and editing notes, 55, 280n90; and film criticism, 4–6; and film style, 5, 10, 13, 79–81, 31–32, 43, 103–4, 132–33, 140, 146, 170–72, 190–91, 213, 219, 225, 244n30; and personality, 10, 57, 73–74, 124, 170, 188; and relationships with actors, 7, 36–37, 86, 88, 159, 174, 217; and script annotations, 22, 32, 43, 112, 135–38, 142, 244n37, 255n137; and sketches, 31, 34, 201, 227, 244n30; and unfinished projects, 12, 40–47, 161, 201, 237, 261n89
Zinnemann, George, 9–10, 58, 123, 251n53
Zinnemann, Oskar, 9
Zinnemann, Renée, 47, 86, 176
Zinnemann, Tim, 63, 86, 102
Zunser, Jesse, 115, 147

www.ingramcontent.com/pod-product-compliance
Lightning Source LLC
Chambersburg PA
CBHW030607230426
43661CB00053B/1876